W9-ATQ-211

UNDERSTANDING
the Business
of Library
Acquisitions
SECOND EDITION

Karen A. Schmidt
Editor

AMERICAN LIBRARY ASSOCIATION
Chicago and London 1999

Cover and text design by Lesiak Design

Composition in Century Schoolbook and Univers Condensed using QuarkXPress by The Clarinda Company

Printed on 50-pound Windsor White Offset, a pH-neutral stock, and bound in 10-point coated cover stock by McNaughton & Gunn

The paper used in this publication meets the minimum requirements of American National Standard for Information Sciences—Permanence of Paper for Printed Library Materials, ANSI Z39.48-1992.∞

Library of Congress Cataloging-in-Publication Data

Understanding the business of library acquisitions / Karen A. Schmidt, editor. — 2nd ed.
   p. cm.
  Includes bibliographical references and index.
  ISBN 0-8389-0741-5
  1. Acquisitions (Libraries)—United States. I. Schmidt, Karen A.
Z689.5.U6U53 1998
025.2—dc21   98-41701

Printed in the United States of America.

03 02 01 00 99   5 4 3 2 1

CONTENTS

INTRODUCTION

The decade of the 1990s has been an exciting and challenging time for the acquisitions librarian. We have seen budgets drastically reduced and our creativity and good business sense sorely tested to find ways to stretch our library's material budget. We have absorbed electronic products, licensing, and new players and producers of material who have not always been knowledgeable about the library world. We have taken on integrated automated systems that have turned some of us into quasi-catalogers. Our work has been outsourced and our staff reduced or reengineered into new configurations that would be barely recognizable to an acquisitions librarian of just a few decades ago.

Through it all, some basic acquisitions principles and practices have endured. We are still the best and strongest connection between the not-for-profit and profit-making worlds. Our playing field is still replete with books and journals, and our fiscal responsibilities have not diminished. We are still managers of people, resources, and materials, and becoming daily a more and more important part of the library organization.

Since the publication of the first edition of this text, acquisitions has been challenged by and grown through the contributions of significant leaders in acquisitions; Joe Barker, Carol Pitts Diedrichs, Christian Boissannas, and Ron Ray are excellent examples of these pathfinders. They have critically examined the issues and forecast the future, establishing new ways of looking at the principles and processes that are intrinsically tied to acquisitions work. It is their work, as well as that of other insightful colleagues, that forms the chapters the reader finds here. The firm establishment of acquisitions as a known entity in libraries is due in large part to the consistent messages given by these individuals to the library profession as a whole.

This second edition of *Understanding the Business of Library Acquisitions* reflects these changes as well as the more permanent fixtures of our professional landscape. Many of the contributors to the first edition have returned to refine and refresh their work. One can see the stability and growth of acquisitions in areas so fundamental that a book on the topic would be considered to be incomplete without their inclusion: approval plans, gifts and exchanges, accounting principles, vendor relations, and serials. These chapters reflect the depth of the literature that has developed over time. Often we see many external factors that affect these areas but find that the inherent nature of the work itself remains solid.

This new edition also includes chapters on important issues that acquisitions librarians must face. These include licensing, personnel management, ethics, and the role of acquisitions in the library organization. Chapters have been recast to reflect changes in the marketplace or in the interaction of acquisitions with the profit sector. Issues related to serials acquisitions and administration have been highlighted in a separate new chapter. The discussion on personnel management adds dimension to a significant issue for most acquisitions librarians. Outsourcing as it affects acquisitions and related technical service and bibliographic areas is included as a new chapter as well.

The contributors have been asked to synthesize the literature in their area and to reach out to related fields of inquiry where appropriate. The writers were asked to consider the present and future and to focus on those principles of action that could most often be found in many types and sizes of libraries. Their assignments also included presenting the best practices found in libraries as they pertain to acquisitions librarianship.

The purpose of this book is to answer some deceptively easy questions that acquisitions librarians and other librarians or students of librarianship have about the process of obtaining material for their libraries. The nature of the advice given here is intended to stand the tests of time and place. As noted, some issues in acquisitions are quite standard and the principles and procedures for action routinely understood among practicing acquisitions librarians. This edition serves to highlight the many aspects of practice that make up acquisitions librarianship and to provide a common understanding of what is meant when librarians discuss the acquisition of materials. The reader will, it is hoped, come away from these essays with a sound appreciation of the myriad aspects of business and bibliography that are the common threads of all acquisitions librarians' work.

ACKNOWLEDGMENTS

I want to thank the wonderful contributors to this edition, all of whom are experts in their areas as well as good soldiers in sharing that knowledge with others. Each one has shown a terrific sense of collegiality and spirit in coming together to bring this volume to fruition. I have so much respect for each of them and have learned a great deal from our association and from the reading and editing of their manuscripts. Marlene Chamberlain of ALA Editions has been the most perfect of editors—present without being intrusive, and encouraging without being a nag.

In the years since the first edition of this book, my family has grown to include two beautiful and boisterous boys. Jacob and Jonas have brought me a deep happiness and enthusiasm for the day that I could not have predicted. My husband, John, steadfastly reminds me of all that I can do and be. I thank all three of them here for letting me find pockets of peace and quiet to finish my work with this book.

Karen A. Schmidt

1

Acquisitions, the Organization, and the Future

CAROL PITTS DIEDRICHS AND KAREN A. SCHMIDT

Acquisitions is the process of acquiring library materials. In many libraries a distinction is drawn between the selection or collection development process—the determination of what is needed, and acquisition—the securing of that material. In other organizations, the distinction between the two may be immaterial. Acquisitions includes *all* tasks related to obtaining *all* library materials. In the past, the type of material acquired was usually limited to books, serials, and occasional audiovisual material. Today, the scope of materials acquired has expanded whether one is acquiring a physical piece, a virtual document, or a disposable item that will be taken away by the patron and never added to a permanent collection (or, for that matter, may never exist in the library's control). A typical acquisitions process today might include books, serials, audio books, CD-ROMs, music CDs, access to an electronic publication on the Web, or document delivery of the full text of an article from the supplier directly into the hands of the requester.

A series of library-wide goals exists for the acquisitions process. Those engaged in delivery of this service must develop and maintain a knowledge of the publishing trade. This knowledge must now include the economics of publishing and scholarly communication, electronic publishing, and information technology. Acquisitions professionals must assist with the selection and collection development process, including the distribution of catalogs/flyers and the arrangement of tests for new electronic products. Functionally, acquisitions processes requests for items to be acquired for the collection, monitors the expenditure of collection development funds, receives and pays for material ordered, maintains all required records and produces reports regarding the expenditure of funds,

1

and pre-catalogs or copy catalogs material on receipt. Within the acquisitions department, the goals are to acquire material as quickly as possible; to maintain a high level of accuracy in all work procedures; to keep work processes simple (to achieve lowest possible unit cost); and to develop close, productive working relationships with vendors and other library units.

THE FUNCTIONS OF ACQUISITIONS

In 1989, Magrill and Corbin identified ten functions of acquisitions:

- obtaining information about materials
- initiating the purchasing process
- maintaining records for materials ordered
- receiving and checking materials
- authorizing payment for materials
- clearing order records
- claiming and cancelling orders
- handling materials that need special treatment
- dealing with special situations
- developing and analyzing performance statistics[1]

The later chapters in their book also cover specific aspects of these functions such as bibliographic searching, vendor-controlled order plans, gifts and exchanges, and acquisition of serials. These tasks certainly reflect many of the acquisitions librarian's daily activities, but one can see that new tasks are present as well. The acquisition of electronic products (including licensing), management of new outsourcing activities such as PromptCat or shelf-ready approval plans, acquisition of electronic items which have no physical manifestation, or copy cataloging performed at point of receipt are all contemporary components of many acquisitions departments. In an article focusing on the roles of professional librarians in technical services, Marion Reid and Walter High emphasize the activities which are clearly managerial: designing and evaluating workflow; determining format of order information files (including serials control); monitoring expenditures; evaluating vendor performance; and setting guidelines and resolving issues not covered by guidelines.[2]

Obtaining information about materials (bibliographic searching) is the first step in the acquisitions process. The first goal of bibliographic searching is to acquire the basic bibliographic data so that the correct piece is ordered. The process also includes identifying the estimated price and the possible source(s) of supply. This goal has been expanded in the recent past to include provision of information for controlling the piece in the library's online catalog. In some cases, this means providing a solid basic bibliographic description for public display and for control of the piece while it resides in a cataloging backlog so that patrons know what is on order. As libraries attempt to increase efficiency, this purpose of bibliographic searching has expanded to include the capture of a complete cataloging record at the point of order from bibliographic utilities such as OCLC or RLIN. As a result, on receipt the piece can be quickly compared to the cataloging record captured at point of order and the cataloging completed at the same time receipt is noted. The second goal is to determine if the library owns or has already ordered the item to prevent unwanted duplication.

These goals are easily achieved with traditional print material. They become more complex with the addition of out-of-print material, foreign language material (particularly from parts of the world with less sophisticated or underdeveloped publishing trades), and with new formats such as electronic products. The bibliographic searching process for electronic products may involve determining what constituencies of users will have access to the material, what type of hardware is needed to store or access the data, what licensing restrictions are imposed by the publisher, and whether the library can meet those terms. For disposable material purchases, the question of unwanted duplication may become irrelevant if the piece is being acquired and dispersed to the user and not retained by the library. Thus, for each type of material purchased, the purpose of bibliographic searching must be evaluated based on the *end result expected* and the particular library environment.

The order, receipt, and claiming process involves selecting an appropriate vendor, preparing and dispatching the order, encumbering the funds, maintaining records for the items on order, receiving the item, and invoicing. Today's library systems have integrated what once were discrete steps in the order process into a single seamless process. The selection of a vendor is rarely a title-by-title decision anymore. Overarching guidelines based on type of material, contracts for preprocessing of material by the vendor, and service are developed by acquisitions professionals. Actual vendor selection can then be delegated to the person completing the order information in the online system. A vendor code is keyed into the record, the order is composed and sent electronically, funds are encumbered by the system, and the online records are available via various meanings of searching such as purchase order number, author, title, or keyword. These online files show the status of the order and can be monitored to retrieve orders that should be claimed.

Upon receipt of material, the pieces are checked for damage, verified against the orders in the system to ensure that they are the items ordered, and, in some cases, checked against the invoice.

The invoice payment process, which is often done via receipt of an electronic invoice directly into the system, records the actual cost, thereby releasing the encumbrance and expending the actual cost. Either manually or through the system, authorizations to pay documents are created for submission to the parent institution.

Claiming and canceling processes are integral to the success of the acquisitions process. Of course, a high percentage of material ordered arrives within 90 days and requires no additional intervention from the library. However, the remaining percentage of orders, which varies based on the type of material being purchased, must be monitored to detect orders which have not arrived in a reasonable period of time. Again, automated systems provide various triggers to alert staff to review the outstanding orders. The claiming process involves reviewing orders which have been flagged as overdue, determining whether they should be claimed, and initiating claims or cancellations as appropriate. Automated systems provide easy mechanisms for reviewing the records and electronically (or on paper) issuing a claim to the supplier.

Acquisitions professionals need to exercise oversight in the guidelines for claiming.

When should the first claim be sent?

Does that time period vary based on the type of material (foreign or domestic) and the particular vendor?

What information needs to be included on the claim for it to be effective?

If the default claim formats in the system do not provide the appropriate information, what action should be taken?

When is some other course of action such as a phone call or a fax warranted?

Is additional information or a decision needed from the collection manager before proceeding?

When should claiming be abandoned and a cancellation issued?

Claim and cancellation information should be recorded in the online record for future information.

The allocation of the materials budget may be controlled by the library administration or the collection development area. However, day-to-day management and oversight of the budget usually falls to the acquisitions professional. Again, automated systems have dramatically improved the control and reporting capabilities available. The acquisitions librarian monitors the materials budget at a macro and a micro level. At the macro level, the budget is reviewed in categories of expenditures and encumbrances.

Is the approval budget under- or over-spent for this time of the year?

How do the expenditures on the serials budget compare to the expenditures for this time last year?

How does the actual inflation factor experienced on the serials budget compare to the projected increase added to the budget at the beginning of the year?

Is the library going to be able to meet institutional requirements for expenditure of funds or is some action required?

At the micro level, individual funds such as chemistry serials and physics approvals are reviewed.

Are any individual funds overexpended or overencumbered for this time in the year?

Are the individual approval budgets going to be adequate for the flow of material being received?

The acquisitions professional can also be instrumental in budget projections for the coming year, answering questions about current trends in pricing and expected changes in contract terms and discounts.

Additional duties include handling material that needs special treatment (serials, gifts, exchanges, approval plans, and electronic products), dealing with special problem situations such as negotiating credits and refunds, arranging for "rush" acquisitions and processing, and solving all kinds of problems. Much of this process is clerical in nature and performed by support staff.

Acquisitions professionals provide oversight and management of the vendor selection process, the implementation of the system and its performance, the evaluation of the system to determine if it meets the audit standards of the institution, the development and analysis of performance statistics (both of staff performance and vendors and suppliers), the exploration and implementation of new services such as electronic invoicing or electronic claiming, and policy determination.

ACQUISITIONS—VENDOR RELATIONS

Two additional responsibilities—liaisons with vendors and publishers, and personnel management—consume much of the acquisitions professional's time. Vendors are used primarily because they can save time and money for the library through the consolidation of orders and invoicing. Vendors are essential to most acquisitions operations. They provide fast, accurate service and are more adaptable to quirky, complicated procedures and delay (particularly for payment). Vendors are accustomed to providing periodic reports on the status of each outstanding order and they increasingly provide additional services such as cataloging/processing, approval plans, and book rental plans. They are also the main source of management information used to manage acquisitions budgets.

A vendor's service should be evaluated in three areas: the scope of material handled, specialized services designed to meet individual library needs, and customer service from the agent's staff. In addition, discounts and costs as well as automation services provided are essential determinants. In the vendor relationship, libraries have a responsibility to provide adequate bibliographic data, to place timely orders, to be reasonable about prices, to allow an adequate cancellation period, to make prompt payment, to have a reasonable returns policy, to maintain professional standards and operate ethically, and to keep paperwork to a minimum.

Vendor selection does not end with the selection of a vendor or the signing of an agreement. Vendor relationships are built on trust. It is important for each party to follow through on promises and to keep confidences even after the relationship has ended. Much damage can be done to a vendor's reputation through rumors. Rumors may be misinterpretation of the facts; they have on occasion been started by a competitor.

The terms of any agreement need to be evaluated on an ongoing basis.

Is the appropriate service charge actually reflected on each invoice?

Have the services contracted for been delivered in a timely fashion?

Do they function in the manner expected?

Is the library issuing payment under the terms negotiated?

Have the appropriate forms been supplied by the vendor?

Has the vendor representative been maintaining contact during the transition phase?

Problems should be identified and reported to the vendor promptly. There have been many reported cases of libraries withdrawing their business from a particular vendor for deficiencies that were never reported to the vendor for possible correction.

Today's vendor relationships have become more complex because of the addition of new players to the field. Acquisitions professionals are negotiating directly with producers of electronic products because many items are most effectively purchased directly at this time. These negotiations now involve much more than price. Licenses must be negotiated with the producer as well as the legal counsel in the institution. The access provided to the product is controlled by such licenses, and acquisitions librarians must be conversant with the telecommunications and hardware structures in their institutions. Products are often tested functionally on-site before purchase. The terms and criteria for such tests must be arranged and facilitated. Contracts for the purchase of material now include components for the purchase of services as well. The vendor who provides the best service for the acquisition of print material may be unable to provide the cataloging and processing services required. Additional library constituencies such as automation and cataloging must be consulted before final decisions can be made.

PERSONNEL AND STAFFING

The actual acquisitions process is a heavily clerical one usually performed by support staff. Traditional personnel management involves the selection, supervision, training, and evaluation of staff. Those functions still exist but the most pressing challenge for managing personnel in libraries today is the management and implementation of change. Acquisitions professionals have to respond to change initiatives from above as well as lead change efforts within their own departments. Processes must become more efficient than in the past, and most acquisitions departments are beset with the need to do more with less. Acquisitions professionals are expected to identify ways in which processes can be changed and streamlined and to implement those changes in their organization. Change is often met with resistance because people feel threatened with the loss of control, staff are concerned about their ability to be effective in the new culture or with the new process, and people fear an increase in workload. Managers are encouraged to empower their staff.

There is a common misconception that empowerment means giving power away. Empowerment is the creation of an environment in which employees at all levels feel that they have real influence over standards of quality, service, and business effectiveness within their areas of responsibility. Colleen Cook has summarized this issue well as it relates to acquisitions librarians:

> As a matter of fact, to function well, our sophisticated systems require substantive independent thinking for even the most elementary tasks. Automated acquisitions systems can function adequately only if employees are empowered to make skilled decisions at every point of entry. If managers attempt to micro manage, they will need to possess the wisdom of Solomon, the computing power of a Cray, and nerves of steel to succeed. We don't empower employees simply because we're nice guys; the simple fact is we must do it for survival.[3]

CHANGES AND THE FUTURE

One of the fundamental changes that has had the greatest impact on the acquisitions function in the 1990s is the incorporation of copy cataloging into the acquisitions receipt and/or approval process. As mentioned earlier, the capture of bibliographic information for the ordering process has been expanded to include priorities for capturing bibliographic data that can be used subsequently for cataloging, since the data needed for ordering are essentially the same data needed for cataloging. In the past, the data captured at point of order were discarded or ignored on receipt, and researching was done for the cataloging process. In today's acquisitions operations, the goals for the pre-order search have been expanded. Data captured at that point are downloaded into the online catalog and used for cataloging purposes on receipt. Some acquisitions processes also include the ownership marking, security stripping, labeling, and binding of materials in the same process rather than handing the material off to another area of the library. Firm order and approval vendors have expanded their services to include processing options.

Carol Pitts Diedrichs and Karen A. Schmidt

In another variation on this theme, the copy cataloging component is shifted to the vendor rather than the front end of the order process. This is particularly effective for approval processing where no initial order exists. Many now work with OCLC's PromptCat service to provide OCLC bibliographic records at the same time the book is provided. This service has been made particularly effective by the enhancement capabilities that have been extended to vendors allowing them to upgrade CIP records on-site when the book is first received in their warehouse.

The changing nature of publishing and the expansion of the market of electronic resources available to libraries have already begun to alter some components of acquisitions work and potentially will have a profound effect on how acquisitions work articulates with the rest of the library. Licensing for electronic products is more and more frequently being handled by the acquisitions professional, who has learned how to read, negotiate, and modify the boilerplate language of most licensing agreements. Working with the institution's legal staff and with public service librarians, the acquisitions librarian continues to serve as a key player in communicating between the marketplace and the library. This responsibility builds on the unique skills of experienced acquisitions librarians to work with producers and suppliers of information, to negotiate excellent terms, and to bring materials into the library setting for the users. It also catapults the acquisitions librarian and staff into a more public arena, where interaction with librarians who work most closely with the library clientele can spell out access and archiving issues that must be included in good licensing agreements.

As noted previously, acquisitions work is heavily affected by the introduction of integrated systems that lead acquisitions into other areas of library processes that have typically been the purview of other departments such as cataloging. Interlibrary loan is now more commonly articulated with acquisitions, for example, as many parallel functions and staffing patterns occur in both processes. The role of acquisitions has been expanded to include new options of this kind. Some functions have been refined to include new formats or expanded to include new routines. No one can be sure what the future holds in terms of the type of material to be acquired, but the functions of placing an order, being sure that the item is delivered, and paying for the item will continue to exist.

The issue of outsourcing has become a critical part of managing technical services in libraries, and acquisitions has not been ignored. It has often been pointed out in the literature that some components of acquisitions work have been outsourced for several years: approval plans and blanket orders, as well as heavy reliance on vendors and serial agents for large numbers of firm orders, serve as examples of acquisitions outsourcing in practice. These are practices with which both acquisitions professionals and the rest of the library organization are comfortable and would resist changing. Further outsourcing of acquisitions functions, such as vendor selection, serial claim initiation, or invoice payment, is far less likely to take place. These processes are tied to other business operations or to specific needs of the collection of a library which do not adapt readily to oversight from companies not related to the library or its parent institution. Outsourcing as it now exists for acquisitions is beneficial and a key component to the acquisitions librarian's ability to serve as a good steward of a library's fiscal and bibliographic resources.

The future of acquisitions work for many acquisitions librarians will at times seem quite uncertain in the next several years. The role of acquisitions in procuring material for ownership is no longer tightly defined. Libraries may find that they no longer need a traditionally structured acquisitions department, and the acquisitions librarian may find that he or she is facing some transitions in the definition of his or her role within the library. Nevertheless, the skills and knowledge that make up the work of acquisitions will continue to play a vital role in the mission of the library.

Acquisitions has struggled to gain recognition, to develop defined principles and standards, and to exert some influence over how librarianship grows. The work of acquisitions is reflected well in the literature; it enjoys a recognized structure within the American Library Association as well as within other professional organizations; and it is taught more frequently in library schools than was the case earlier in the century. With this basis, acquisitions professionals are better able to face the transformations that are emerging and impinging on acquisitions work and to continue to refine the aspects of acquisitions work that make it unique and invaluable parts of the profession of librarianship.

The fundamental aspects of acquisitions work—financial management, acquisition of material regardless of its disposition, negotiation of contracts, service-oriented activities, and personnel management, for example—continue to be critical to the fulfillment of the goals of libraries' work that reflects the very best principles of service and stewardship.

Notes

1. Rose Mary Magrill and John B. Corbin, *Acquisitions Management and Collection Development in Libraries,* 2nd ed. (Chicago: American Library Association, 1989), pp. 78–80.

2. Marion T. Reid and Walter M. High, "The Role of the Professional in Technical Services," *RTSD Newsletter* 11 (1986): 59, cited in Terry L. Allison and Marion T. Reid, "The Professionalization of Acquisitions and Collection Development," in *Recruiting, Educating, and Training Librarians for Collection Development,* ed. Peggy Johnson and Sheila S. Intner (Westport, Conn.: Greenwood, 1994), p. 22.

3. Colleen Cook, "After Acquisitions Automation: Managing the Human Element in a Large Library Context," *Library Administration & Management* 7 (Fall 1993): 221.

Bibliography

Atkinson, Ross. "The Acquisitions Librarian as Change Agent in the Transition to the Electronic Library." *Library Resources & Technical Services* 36 (January 1992): 7–20.

Eaglen, Audrey. *Buying Books: A How-to-Do-It Manual for Librarians.* New York: Neal-Schuman, 1989.

Hewitt, Joe A. "On the Nature of Acquisitions." *Library Resources & Technical Services* 33 (1989): 105–122.

Managing Serials. Ed. Marcia Tuttle. Greenwich, Conn.: JAI, 1996.

Miller, Heather Swan. *Managing Acquisitions and Vendor Relations: A How-to-Do-It Manual.* New York: Neal-Schuman, 1992.

Price Waterhouse Change Integration Team. *Better Change: Best Practices for Transforming Your Organization.* Burr Ridge, Ill.: Irwin, 1995, p. 95.

Reid, Marion T. "Acquisitions and Collection Development." In *Technical Services Management, 1965–1990: A Quarter Century of Change and a Look to the Future.* Ed. Linda C. Smith and Ruth C. Carter. New York: Haworth, 1996, pp. 57–75.

———. "Closing the Loop: How Did We Get Here and Where Are We Going?" *Library Resources & Technical Services* 39 (July 1995): 267–273.

Understanding the Business of Acquisitions. Ed. Karen A. Schmidt. Chicago: American Library Association, 1990.

2

The Business of Book Publishing

PATRICIA GLASS SCHUMAN AND CHARLES HARMON

These last few years of the twentieth century find both publishers and librarians immersed in an era of rapid change. Many old assumptions about the transcription, transmission, and archiving of knowledge are being called into question. The debate over copyright and other intellectual property issues in the digital age has exacerbated tensions between academics, librarians, and publishers. Librarians are wary of the repackaging of the same information with different titles; they look at the rising costs of books—and particularly of academic journals—and suspect price gouging. They wonder if publishers are exploiting the library market. Publishers see mass cancellation of journals, increased interlibrary loan, wholesale photocopying, and dwindling monograph sales. Some feel as if trusted customers have found ways of getting their products without paying for them. They view a new library philosophy of "access over ownership" as threatening to their very existence. Both groups view each other warily as new business arrangements like licensing are experimented with.

While publishers and librarians have each traditionally viewed their mission as "gatekeepers" of information and culture, publishers are actually the true frontline gatekeepers; they decide what to publish, when to publish, whom to publish for, and what to charge. Many publishing decisions have public policy, social, cultural, economic, educational, and political impact. Librarians are actually the "gateways." Librarians support a significant portion of publishers' output; they buy, organize, preserve, store and disseminate it; they raise awareness. Ideas are kept available, affordable, and accessible through libraries. How librarians perform these functions also has crucial impact on the social, cultural, economic, educational, and political fabric of society. That fabric is woven when writers, researchers, and creators draw on what libraries provide to create new information and ideas. Synergy between a healthy publishing industry and healthy libraries is essential for a democratic society.

Librarians work in more than 115,000 U.S. school, public, academic, and special libraries; publishers work in more than 20,000 private sector and nonprofit organizations (trade, professional, journal, electronic, association, textbook, university press, reference, mass market paperback publishers, etc.). Despite this diversity, there are some obvious commonalties of missions and self-interest that should mandate mutually supportive collaborations; clear and frequent communication should be a top priority. Unfortunately, neither communication nor collaboration is the current norm. Both professions are frequently unaware of the methodologies, economics, impacts, and policies of the other. This results in part from three factors: first, there are few formal education programs for those in the publishing industry. Second, few library education programs offer courses about the publishing industry. Third, libraries are somewhat of an invisible market for many publishers since a majority of libraries purchase books and journals through wholesalers rather than directly from publishers.

The historic development of children's book publishing, postal subsidies for books, anti-censorship campaigns, and the favorable recent Supreme Court decision about the Communications Decency Act (CDA) are examples of the benefits coalitions between librarians and publishers can bring. Nevertheless, relations between the library and publishing communities are often strained and sometimes nonexistent. Despite a frequent lack of recognition and understanding of their interdependency, publishers and librarians work in constant relation to each other. Their interaction transcends mere marketplace vendor/buyer transactions. For example, publishers have depended on librarians for the majority of sales for reference books, scholarly works, children's books, first novels, and poetry. Librarians have depended on publishers for a variety of steps in the scholarly communication chain from editorial review to prompt distribution of important research. Like all ecologies, though, this food chain has and must continue to evolve as external circumstances change. Librarians must learn to understand the publishing marketplace—and the essential roles they play in it.

This chapter will discuss book publishing as an industry, how the business of publishing is changing, and the effects of electronic publishing on the future of scholarly communications.

THE BOOK PUBLISHING INDUSTRY

It is important to remember that although publishing is often viewed as a somewhat monolithic industry, there are many different kinds of publishers. Although a handful of large conglomerates are responsible for the output easily viewed on bookstore shelves, tens of thousands of publishers—both private and nonprofit—also publish books and other materials. Some are in "business" to make a profit, others to communicate specific ideas and knowledge. The majority of publishers fall somewhere between these two extremes. In films, novels, and conversation, book publishing often is portrayed as a cultural enterprise. There is even a little bit of truth to this facade. Indeed, publishing—like librarianship—has always attracted well-educated, well-read people who are willing to work for fairly low salaries because of their love of the written word. For perhaps the first half of the 20th century or so, American book publishing was considered a "gentleman's" profession.

Publishing is both a cultural and commercial enterprise. In fact, the Latin roots of the word *publisher* mean "to make public." On the other hand, publishers are technically (according to the U.S. Department of Commerce's Standard Industrial Classification codes) in the "manufacturing" business. And manufacturing and selling a product, especially so many individual titles annually, are a costly and complicated process.

When the mergers and takeovers began in the late 1960s, publishing houses that had traditionally been as proud of their Nobel– and Pulitzer Prize–winning titles as they had of growths in their net profits became increasingly focused not only on the bottom line but also on growth. As publicly held conglomerates gobbled up smaller publishers, shareholders expected healthy profits, and also expanding ones. Nevertheless, the tension between culture and commerce in the industry is nothing new. As Coser et al. point out in *Books: The Culture and Commerce of Publishing,* "Book publishing in the past as in the present has operated under the pressure of the marketplace, the counting house, and the literary and intellectual currents of the day. The quest for profit and the demands of excellence have all too often refused to go hand in hand."[1]

Close to 600 mergers and acquisitions have been reported in the U.S. book publishing industry since the 1960s. A major source of the tension between the commercial and the cultural is what *New York Times* reporter Roger Cohen called the "era of the accountant-publisher."[2] More worrisome to some is that these publishers are multinational and threaten potential control of the media. Many own not only book publishers, but also film and record companies, newspapers, magazines, and radio and television stations. Ben Bagdikian has warned:

> Bookstores and libraries still offer miles of shelves stocked with individual volumes . . . but if this bright kaleidoscope suddenly disappeared and was replaced by the corporate colophon of the few who own this output, the collage would go gray with the few media multinationals that now command the field. . . . Neither Caesar, nor Hitler, Franklin Roosevelt, nor any Pope, has commanded as much power to shape the information on which so many people depend . . .[3]

To the library patron or the bookstore customer, who sees only the price of books and the numerous new titles on shelves and in catalogs, all publishers seem to be identical—and thriving—because their sole function seems to be distributing authors' words and images to the reader. Yet what this distribution function really entails is quite another story. Differences in types of publishers profoundly affect the library acquisitions process in ways ranging from selection avenues (the review media that cover different publishers) to economics (discount schedules of zero to 50 percent or more depending on the publisher and the purchaser). And, of course, the size and specialty of the publisher will affect marketing, distribution, and cost—all major concerns for the acquisitions librarian. The differences are closely tied to the actual publishing process.

There are, in fact, tremendous differences in types of book publishers. The most familiar publishing houses (e.g., Random House or Farrar Straus Giroux) are known as trade publishers. The primary consumer for trade publishers is the bookstore customer. Because print runs for trade publishers are often measured in the tens or even hundreds of thousands, the economics of their operations differ vastly from scholarly and reference publishers. Scholarly publishers, which include university presses like the University of Chicago Press, association publishers like ALA Editions (which published this book), and reference publishers like Gale typically have print runs that range from 1,000 to 15,000 copies. In addition to these dramatic differences in print run, there are other differences among these publishers as well, notably their editing and production costs. For example, scholarly reference works require intense editing by subject specialists. Medical books and art books frequently require high-resolution half-tones or full-color plates. These are in an entirely different class from the latest

Trade	27.3%
Mass Market Paperback	7.5%
Book Clubs	5.6%
Mail Order	2.7%
Religious	5.5%
Professional	19.8%
University Press	1.7%
Elhi	13.0%
College	12.5%
Standardized Tests	0.9%
Subscription Reference	3.4%

Figure 2-1 1997 Book Sales by Category as Projected by the Book Industry Study Group

Stephen King paperback. And scholarly publications, particularly proceedings, frequently have a very limited life span.

The Book Industry Study Group, one of the major collectors and distributors of publishing statistics, recognizes many types of books: adult trade, juvenile trade, mass market paperback, book club books, mail order publications, religious, professional, university press, education publishing, elhi (elementary and secondary school), and college. Most of these categories also have hardbound and paperback subcategories. The group projected publishers' net sales for all categories in 1997 at $21,131,300,000. The percentage sales for the types of books it tracks were projected as shown in figure 2-1.[4]

BOOK PRICING

Ironically, regardless of the type of publisher or the list price of the book, book publishing is not a high-profit industry. The average after-tax profit for most books is less than 10 percent. While publishing houses generally use a price formula that calculates the list price of a book at five to six times its printing and binding cost, these are only two of the many cost factors which must be considered.

Of particular interest to the acquisitions librarian is the place that the library market plays in the publisher's net profits.

Although the library market is an extremely important market, it is also a relatively small market. Books with a scholarly or library market often have only short print runs. Filling an order is a costly process and typically runs as high as 10 percent of the price of the book. Order fulfillment includes warehousing, packing, billing, shipping. Then customers take time to pay. Typically, libraries take anywhere from 90 to 120 days to pay a publisher—or a wholesaler. Bookstores take even longer. While libraries rarely return books, bookstores often return them after a year. The high cost of money today combined with the expected late payments actually can add another several dollars to the cost of the book. These costs are all in addition to production costs discussed later: the number of pages in a book, the number of copies printed, and the design and typography of the book. The type of binding used is a cost factor, but not really that significant. For example, a publisher will save only a few dollars per copy of a 300-page, 6-by-9 inch book by binding it in paperback—less than the cost of late payments. The publisher also has to consider overhead costs—office space, heat, light, and salaries. These can easily account for 30 percent of the list price. In some of the larger conglomerate houses, overhead is figured at 40 percent. A typical distribution of publishers' costs as a percentage of a book's list price is shown in figure 2-2, although the costs for any given title and publisher can be quite different.

Although best-sellers may show a net profit of up to 15 percent, many titles may show a net profit percentage in the single digits— or even a loss, substantially reducing the publisher's overall profit. With a very successful book, the costs in all areas will be reduced, and therefore the profit will be greater. However, with most titles, the costs are at the high end and the results unpredictable. This is why most trade publishers seek to enhance their bottom line with

Design, typesetting, and printing	20%
Damaged books and returns	5%-40%
Discounts	0%-60%
Royalties	10%-15%
Marketing	10%-15%
Fulfillment	10%
Overhead	25%-30%
Profit	0%-15%

Figure 2-2 Composition of a Typical Book's List Price

subsidiary rights sales for films and television—and, increasingly, for toys and other attractions.

One of the greatest cost factors for trade publishers is returns. In fact, the Book Industry Study Group called returns the "Issue of the Year" for 1996, pointing out that for the first time publishers were actually discussing how to deal with excessive returns, otherwise "a well-guarded secret of the publishing industry."[5] A library will not have a significant effect on a publisher's returns, but according to Open Book Publishing, which also tracks the book publishing business, the average independent bookstore returns about 20 percent of its books, and chains like Barnes & Noble return about 30 percent of their books.[6] And because the books frequently are too damaged or soiled to resell, they are either sold at great loss to remainder outlets, or they are pulped and recycled. Thus many publishers must plan on returns costing about half the cost of the production. These enormous costs, as well as the unpredictability of returns, have produced publisher responses ranging from speculating on the feasibility of a no-return policy to (what is more likely) efforts to obtain immediate information on the sell-through of titles. This information, if received in a timely fashion, would enable publishers to control the last print run of their books, which in many cases is equal to the number of books eventually returned.[7] Anything that helps the publisher maintain net revenue in the long run is a boon to librarians who are concerned about rising book prices.

THE STEPS IN PUBLISHING

The business of publishing involves a series of complicated steps— from the acquisition or development of a manuscript through the sale of the book to a customer. Publishing houses often have "personalities" and varying "missions," in addition to their incentive to earn a profit—or at least enough to keep the doors open and their lists growing. Obviously, certain publishers choose specific types of authors and disciplines; often they are well-known to the market they serve. The first step in the publishing process is the decision to publish. Formally or informally, publishers utilize some type of "decision tree" that is based on a set of criteria similar to those shown in figure 2-3.

This decision tree, which works equally well for fiction and nonfiction publications, also paves the way for future marketing efforts.

Is there a need for this work?

Does this manuscript fill that need?

Does it cover the subject?

Are there omissions?

What are the strong points?

Who is the major audience?

What is the competition?

Does this book differ significantly?

Are major changes necessary?

Is the author qualified?

Can we reach the market?

What are the costs?

Will this be profitable?

Figure 2-3 The Book Publisher's Decision Tree: "To Publish or Not to Publish?"

A decision to publish a given title is only the beginning of a long—and expensive—process. An understanding of this process will help the librarian understand some of the complexities of publishing: the costs, delays in publication, and what to expect should he or she consider becoming an author.

The responsibilities of the parties involved in the production of a book—the author and the publisher—are very consistent whether the title is a number 1 best-seller or a book intended for a very small market (like the book you're reading now). These responsibilities are typically detailed in a contract to publish, often called an "Agreement to Publish" or "Letter of Agreement." The standard clauses in most publishing contracts, as displayed in figure 2-4, are an excellent outline of the steps in this process.

The author's major responsibilities are, of course, developing the idea for the book, writing the manuscript, and delivering that manuscript to the publisher in an acceptable form. The contract will spell out the date the manuscript is due, its form, its size, the number of copies to be delivered to the publisher, and the author's responsibility for illustrations, indexing, and securing permission to quote previously published works. In addition, the contract will stipulate that this must be the author's own original work and that the author will have financial responsibility in case of a law-

Standard Publishing Contract Clauses

1. Manuscript
2. Grant
3. Warranty
4. Permissions
5. Publishing
6. Royalties

**Figure 2-4 Clauses Found in a Standard
Publishing Contract**

suit over the content. Finally, the author portion of the contract will include assignment of copyright ownership and the rights to publish, as well as setting the royalty rate (usually 10 percent, but depending on volume and publisher, this may be as high as 15 percent).

The publisher's role—and financial responsibility—usually involve the following: either accepting a proposal, finding the right author, or developing a topic or idea; evaluating the project and its potential market and revenues; producing the book (from editing to design, printing, and binding); marketing and selling the book (getting the book reviewed, advertising it, arranging for publicity, receiving orders, filling those orders, ensuring delivery, and collecting money); and finally, sharing a percentage of the collected money with the author. Most contracts say the publisher will publish the work within a "reasonable" time, or "at such time as [it] determines conditions are suitable," at the publisher's own expense, and in such style and at such price as it in its "sole judgment" shall consider "most appropriate" to promote its sale.

Clearly the publisher has a great deal of leeway in fulfilling these obligations. This does not mean that the author has no input; publishers are usually open to discussing these matters with the author. In the last analysis, however, where design, production, and marketing matters are concerned, the publisher makes the call. The publisher also has the entire financial risk from this point on.

Patricia Glass Schuman and Charles Harmon

What is this long, expensive process for which the publisher has main responsibility? In part this depends on the type of book—fiction, proceedings, scientific, textbook—and how the author has agreed to submit the text—camera-ready, in manuscript, or on disk. A project may require minimal editorial involvement for the publisher, such as proceedings that are submitted as clean, camera-ready copy and are printed as is, or very extensive editorial and production work, as in professional reference works. Most books follow a set of steps like those shown in figure 2-5.

Once the decision is made to publish the book, the publisher (usually represented by its acquisitions editor) and the author will negotiate a contract. Authors then write, usually with frequent consultation and feedback from an editor appointed by the publisher, often the acquisitions editor or a developmental editor.

Once the author finishes writing, the editor evaluates it. The manuscript is then copyedited. The copyeditor will correct grammar and syntax, check for adherence to the publisher's style, and in some cases suggest rewriting. The manuscript is then returned to the author for review and any rewriting. Once this is completed, design specifications such as type font and size, margins, indentations, arrangement of illustrations, placement of page numbers and chapter titles, and so forth are decided. Once all of these decisions have been made, the manuscript goes into production.

Acquisitions

Contract

Author/Editor Development

Copyediting

Typesetting

Proofreading

Indexing

Printing

Binding

Marketing/Sales

Fulfillment

Figure 2-5 Steps in the Publishing Process

Production involves two types of costs—fixed and variable. The fixed costs are design/composition/typesetting. Typesetting is an important factor in the cost and appearance of the book. This process changes as the technology changes; most authors now prepare their manuscripts on disk, and often publishers can work directly from the disk to create film. Scanning equipment even for full-color illustrations can produce high-resolution copy. Some publishers even use desktop publishing programs to set pages. The typesetter produces galleys or proofs, which are then proofread. The typesetter then produces another set of pages that are checked. When all corrections are made, the project is then ready to send out for printing.

Printing and binding are variable costs, depending on how many copies are printed. This is sometimes referred to as the "running cost."

The decision about the number of copies to print is one of the most important ones the publisher makes. Since there is a volume savings, it is tempting to print more books. For example, if 2,000 copies of a 200-page book cost $6,000 to print, 3,000 copies might cost only $7,200. Thus, theoretically the unit cost would be substantially lower (if all 3,000 sell) for the higher print run enabling the list price of the book to be reduced—and the profit margin to be higher. However, if only 2,000 of these copies eventually sell, the publisher has made a bad financial decision.

In recent years the cost of paper has been volatile, causing additional cost—and cash outlay—often before the first copy is sold. When the book is well into the production cycle, actual costs are examined and remaining costs are estimated. The actual list price and the size of the print run are often not finalized until this stage.

MARKETING

As displayed in figure 2-2, the final cost factors in producing and selling a book are marketing and fulfillment. Together they account for upwards of 30 percent of a book's total price composition; part of this cost stems from the fact that publishers have a large number of products that are sold to different customers, and different groups of customers are reached by different marketing methods. Marketing decisions are influenced by the nature of the audience, type of book, and distribution. Will it be widely sold through bookstores, or is distribution more specialized? The publisher will try to promote all titles, not just new books, while managing expenses. In the "heydays" of education funding, most large publishers had library marketing specialists. Now only a handful of publishers—mostly children's book publishers—do.

Marketing usually involves a mix of activities intended to reach potential buyers. These might involve a mix of a number of different activities. While publishers rarely advertise in the mass electronic media, they do place ads in appropriate magazines and periodicals.

Publicity (sometimes called author relations) might include book tours, story placement, news releases, media appearances, workshops, and so on. Book reviews can be extremely important, and many publishers send proofs for prepublication review as well as sending the actual books when published.

Direct mail of catalogs and flyers is an important sales tool for many publishers, although the cost here is becoming higher as postage rates rise. In the consumer sales area a 1 percent return is considered high. Professional publishers claim return rates of over 10 percent. Salespeople are frequently used by larger publishers to sell trade titles to bookstores and texts to educators, less frequently to libraries. The largest publishers have their own sales staffs; many smaller houses use outside sales representatives to whom they pay a commission. Telemarketing is becoming a more frequently used technique.

Special sales are increasingly important to publishers' bottom lines. Often these may be "rights" sales for film or television adaptations; they may be special editions, special promotions, toys based on characters, or premium offers. For scholarly, professional, and educational publishers, national or regional meetings of associations such as the American Library Association or the National Education Association are important. Because of both exhibit and travel costs, these meetings are expensive for publishers to attend, but they offer the publisher an opportunity to display books as well as to meet potential authors.

HOW THE BUSINESS OF PUBLISHING IS CHANGING

It is unlikely that anyone interested enough in library acquisitions to read this book is unaware of the tremendous changes that have occurred in publishing over the last ten years. Among the more apparent ones are simultaneous publication of popular works in paper, audio, or CD-ROM formats; increased serialization of important new works in major magazines like *Newsweek* and *Time* before hardcover publication; and the enormous influence of big chain bookstores like Barnes & Noble and Borders over what gets published and which new major books are promoted prior to publication as "major events." Also, the ambience of these super stores, which is very different from that of the independent bookstore, has an effect on sales. With fewer staff to guide the customer, it is harder than ever to sell the less popular titles—serious nonfiction, serious fiction, and literature in translation.[8] This, in turn, will affect some publishers' willingness to take the risk of publishing some of these titles. Fortunately, many of these titles will be taken

	Estimate of Growth over Previous Year		
Publishers' Net Dollar Sales	1994/93	95/94	96/95
Trade (total)	10.3	.4	1.2
Adult Trade (total)	11.2	−2.1	−2.1
Hardbound	9.8	−5.6	−4.4
Paperbound			
Juvenile Trade (total)	7.1	9.1	
Mass Market-rack size	2.4	7.7	2.3
Book Clubs	8.6	11.7	11.9
Mail Order Publications	−7.3	0.4	3.6
Religious (total)	5.1	5.9	6.5
Professional (total)	8.6	7.3	3.2
Hardbound	8.6	7.3	3.2
Paperbound	8.7	7.4	3.3
Business	9.6	10.3	7.8
Law	10.3	7.8	6.8
Medical	6.6	7.3	6.3
Technical, Scientific, & Other	7.4	4.9	−6.6
University Press (total)	11.2	4.3	2.8
Elhi (total)	−7.0	14.4	5.7
College (total)	1.7	6.8	6.9
Subscription Reference	6.5	4.6	5.3
All Books	4.9	5.8	4.0

Figure 2-6 Percentage of Change in Net Dollar Sales for 1993-1996 according to the Book Industry Study Group

up by scholarly or special interest publishers, such as association publishers, whose primary criterion is likely to be filling the information need. But these are then produced without the economies of scale that a more popular title would have.

As Michael Korda, editor in chief of Simon & Schuster put it, "I've been in publishing for nearly forty years, and in that time people have always behaved as if the sky were about to fall. The sky was about to fall because of television. The sky was about to fall because of discounting books. The sky was about to fall because of conglomerates. The sky was about to fall because of agents. The sky hasn't fallen."[9] Nonetheless, sometimes the publishers do feel as if the sky may be falling; change is so rapid that the current feeling among many publishers is one of urgency and vulnerability.

The most recent annual data from the Association of American Publishers show that both the amount spent and the number of adult trade hardcover books sold have declined for two years in a row, with hardcover sales falling almost 10 percent. The Association says that this is the first time in decades that there has been a sustained drop.[10] In 1995-1996 there was also a drop in sales of technical and scientific books, which were down 6.6 percent from the year before. And this comes at a time when publishing houses are scrutinizing the bottom line more than ever. Overall, in 1996 publishers did show a modest increase in sales (4 percent) as shown in figure 2-6, but most categories show slower growth than in previous years.[11]

Subcategories are shown for trade books and professional books, the two categories in which there were decreased sales in 1996. In both areas projections for 1997 showed growth: 2.6 percent for total adult trade books and 2.5 percent for professional books.[12]

THE LIBRARY MARKET

Although not broken out in the preceding figure, the library market for books—over four billion dollars—represents a little more than 10 percent of publishers' revenues overall. Nevertheless libraries can account for 50 to 90 percent of the sales of reference books, children's books, poetry, and nonfiction. *Publishers Weekly*'s John Baker notes that "more than 40 percent of specialized publishers responding to a joint ALA/AAP survey said they made the *majority* of their sales to libraries. But even the large general-interest publishers know that the library market is a dependable source of revenue from many books that might otherwise seem scarcely viable. Libraries also are an unexpectedly good market for backlist books."[13]

Libraries are not the market that can "make or break" potential best-sellers; they are instead steady and reliable customers. More than 50,000 books a year are published in the United States alone—over a million worldwide. Many are in print for less than one year. Less than 6,000 individual titles are reviewed each year. Libraries make available not only the most current titles and best-sellers, but books, journals, and other materials that are no longer available elsewhere. Few bookstores can afford to carry the large variety of titles that libraries can. With the average price of an adult hardcover book at over $20, paperbacks breaking the $6.95 barrier, and children's books hovering at around $16.95, few but the affluent can afford to buy great quantities of books; even fewer have space to store them. Through local libraries and interlibrary loan the public has access not only to current materials, but also to the thought, wisdom, and amusements of the ages in published form.

The fact is that libraries are a major market for poetry, children's books, reference books, scholarly books, and much new fiction and nonfiction. On average, most new trade books sell only about 4,000 to 7,000 copies. Reference and scholarly books sell even fewer. Best-sellers are rare.

Librarians traditionally have been quiet and steady customers. They do not generate the volume from which best-sellers are made; they are an essential base. But since most libraries order books through wholesalers, they are not particularly visible to publishers.

Nevertheless, librarians can be an important market force, one that can influence policy, economics, and law. They are an essential voice in the intellectual property debates and have a significant role in helping to ensure a healthy, independent publishing industry.

Rather than being passive, librarians must be active. It is essential that they get involved in the electronic debates, and it is equally essential that they understand the breadth and depth of the industry. Of the 6,000 books a year that are reviewed, most are books published by fewer than 200 publishers—the large publishers. One important category of publisher is often absent from the review media, standard bibliographic tools, and conference exhibits. These are often referred to as "alternative," "small," or "independent" publishers. While none of these labels is entirely satisfactory, "alternative" is probably the most appropriate because many of these publishers do indeed provide alternatives to the growing media-combines. All are independently owned, though, of course, not all small publishers can be considered alternative.

Many smaller publishers are often purposely set up to publish information with a particular point of view—political, cultural, or literary. By choice as well as by definition, their publications fall outside the mainstream of commercial publishing; often alternative publishers are also outside the mainstream of traditional distribution channels and the peripheral vision of most libraries. Sometimes they are even unaware of the potential for selling to libraries.

This situation is unfortunate, because alternative publishers are on the cutting edge of important literature and issues of our time. While publishers like Thompson and Elsevier gobble up larger publishers, smaller publishers do more than play a vital socio-political role; they also make an important cultural and literary contribution. And they are an essential part of the community of publishers that librarians must interact with.

TENSIONS BETWEEN LIBRARIANS
AND PUBLISHERS

Not since the federal government ruled in favor of the library community with respect to price-fixing of special library bindings for children's books have tensions about publisher conglomeratization, pricing, and new formats run so high. "The power of publishers to skew library spending threatens the entire system of scholarly communication," warn librarians Scott Bennett and Nina Matheson.[14]

Economic pressures and new technology are enabling librarians to turn to networks and electronic delivery systems, as well as to consider the question of bypassing publishers altogether. Librarians now talk about "access" to materials, rather than ownership. ARL reports that interlibrary loan is the fastest-growing library service. While twenty years ago scholarly publications could average a 2,000-copy sale to libraries, 500 copies is today's norm. The problem is a circular one as publishers with fewer and fewer sales require remaining buyers to bear the cost.

The late publisher Frederick Praeger stated the predicament aptly:

> Librarians, publishers and scholars are natural partners in the creation and dissemination of knowledge . . . the independent scholarly publisher . . . specializes in areas where the scholarly community needs fast, flexible, and enterprising support; highly specialized marketing; and a great variety of methods to produce scholarly materials in very small editions. Selecting, editing, designing,

proofreading, printing, binding, and marketing are essential steps in fulfilling this role. None of these steps can be skipped and all are expensive. Scholars need access to published materials in all their variety and the traditional role of the library has been to expand their access by purchasing published materials and organizing them for appropriate retrieval. Current events have disrupted this symbiotic relationship of scholars, publishers, and libraries. New technology makes it possible for scholars to gain distribution of their works while bypassing publishers. Libraries, confronted with rising costs and relatively decreasing revenue, have turned to networks and electronic delivery systems that often save time over the imperfect working of the market. These events threaten to disrupt publishing with its unique values and endanger the life of the book, which has served us in ways that can hardly be duplicated. . . . To deal constructively with the challenge, scholars, publishers, and librarians need to cultivate a consciousness of our dependence on each other.[15]

PHOTOCOPYING AND COPYRIGHT

The most visible schism between publishers and librarians appeared with the widespread use of photocopying technology in libraries. On one extreme, publishers viewed library photocopying as an infringement of copyright and disastrous to their revenues. On the other extreme, librarians considered access to information essential and much library photocopying to be fair use. Until 1972 a "gentlemen's agreement" formulated in 1935 had defined what constituted fair use of library copying of both copyrighted and noncopyrighted works. In 1972 the Williams and Wilkins Company filed suit against the National Institute of Health (NIH) and the National Library of Medicine (NLM) for copyright infringement. The court found that NIH and NLM had made photocopies of articles from scientific and technical journals at the request of scientists and scholars engaged in pure research activities with no commercial motivation. It ruled that such photocopies were "fair use." That decision delighted the library community; publishers remained convinced that librarians were engaging in wholesale unauthorized reproduction of copyrighted works—and that these practices had a negative effect on their revenues.

Some 25 years later the prospects of a digital future for publishing have multiplied these fears. Library document delivery services, cooperative resource sharing, cooperative collection development, and new electronic services are often viewed with alarm by publishers concerned about intellectual property rights in an electronic age. Librarians say that access is threatened by increasing monopoly control, rapidly rising monograph and serial prices, exorbitant fees for electronic information services and licenses, and privatization of public information.

Naturally the availability of the Internet has both publishers and librarians wondering what new developments are in store and whether they will be able to adapt with sufficient speed. Electronic ordering is no longer new, and Amazon.com, an electronic bookstore, has a worldwide clientele. In fact, 50 percent of their sales come from outside the United States.[16] Many publishers have Web sites to promote their titles, and although this has not yet paid off the Web is constantly changing.

But probably the biggest question is what will be the role of electronic publishing and how will it affect not only publishing and sales, but also literature? Electronic publishing is very fluid. This is a great asset for works that need frequent updating, as many of the online databases and reference sources do, but it also means that publishers, in their quest for the lion's share of the market, are constantly altering the product. Publishers may issue electronic documents that are no longer duplicates of the print product, and the libraries, with their limited budgets, must decide whether to buy print, electronic, or both. For the publisher, for whom format once meant design, size, and binding, there is now the question of print, electronic, CD-ROM, audio, interactive, all of the above, or none of the above. Answering this question is extremely difficult, because the size of the computer-literate market is constantly changing. How the information is best presented and used is probably the most important question, but not the only important factor by far. The hardware, the browsers, and the number of libraries that have computer equipment change constantly. A market analysis for an electronic reference work has nowhere near the longevity as the market analysis for a book—the electronic age has created a new set of expectations.

Many younger library patrons are interested only in electronic access, whether or not it is the easiest and the best way to get the information they need. Many patrons think that electronic sources are free, and librarians, who know there is a price attached, may be quite shocked at the size of the price tag. With the need to convert print products that would be more effectively used online, publishers have a new set of costs added to the existing production costs. Fortunately, they now are able to create text that is adaptable to many formats, but older print sources that are to be converted have to be rekeyed. And—most difficult of all—are the pricing questions: who the market is, how much it will bear, how to set licensing fees, who will reuse the information, how will they get paid. Despite the hype, few publishers are making money on individual electronic products for the general public or libraries.

Security is one of the biggest challenges, causing book publishers to be understandably reluctant to publish some texts electronically. The user can quickly download texts, at little or no cost, and distribute them electronically—the computer equivalent of photocopying. Academic reserve rooms are taking advantage of immediate, simultaneous delivery of as many electronic files as there are users. Many libraries have extensive services for remote users, including circulation, reference, photocopying requests. For many of these libraries, the availability of electronic publications would improve their services. Established procedures have been developed for securing permission to scan print copy and distribute it electronically. Academic photocopying services and commercial providers, such as Kinko's, can institute policies to require adherence to copyright law; there is no monitoring the Internet. The user can alter the text before distributing further, something that is not possible with print. And because no computer program is completely hacker-proof, there is even the risk that someone other than the publisher could alter the online text. To protect the publisher and the author, enhanced security measures, methods for assessing fees, reliable means for granting the right to use files, and attempts to fashion copyright law are all under investigation.

Although the demise of the book has often been predicted, it is unlikely that electronic publishing will replace traditional formats. Nonetheless, electronic publishing is already widespread and will no doubt become increasingly common.

Libraries may be an invisible market to larger publishing houses; nevertheless they have a significant role to play in helping to ensure a healthy publishing industry. Libraries are central institutions in the information arena. They are part of the marketplace of information and part of the underpinnings of the communications industry. Librarians and publishers must work together, synergistically, to keep the channels of access open.

Notes

1. Louis Coser et al., *Books: The Culture and Commerce of Publishing* (Chicago: University of Chicago, 1985).

2. Roger Cohen, "Hold the Drinks and the Shrimp," *New York Times,* July 29,1992.

3. Ben Bagdikian, "The Lords of the Global Village," *The Nation,* June 12, 1989, p. 805.

4. Book Industry Study Group, *Book Industry Trends 1997* (New York: Book Industry Study Group, 1997) pp. 2-1 to 2-6.

5. Ibid., p. 1-1.

6. Ken Auletta, "The Impossible Business," *The New Yorker,* October 6, 1997, p. 58.

7. Sandra K. Paul, "Book Production Industry Outlook," *Publishers Weekly,* June 1998, supp. p. S 3.

8. Auletta, "The Impossible Business," p. 59.

9. Ibid.

10. Ibid., p. 50.

11. Book Industry Study Group, p. 2-5.

12. Ibid., p. 2-6.

13. John Baker, "The Loyal Librarians," *Publishers Weekly,* June 12, 1987, p. 18.

14. Scott Bennett and Nina Matheson, "Scholarly Articles: Valuable Commodities for Universities," *Chronicle of Higher Education,* May 27, 1992, B1-B2.

15. F. A. Praeger, "Librarians, Publishers, and Scholars: Common Interests, Different Views. The View of an Independent Scholarly Publisher," *Library Quarterly* 54, no. 1 (1984): 21-29.

16. Auletta, "The Impossible Business," p. 62.

For Further Reading

MONOGRAPHS

Altbach, Philip G. and Edith S. Hosino. *International Book Publishing: An Encyclopedia.* New York: Garland, 1995.

Bagdikian, Ben. *The Media Monopoly.* Boston: Beacon Press, 1987.

Bielefield, Arlene and Lawrence Cheeseman. *Technology and Copyright Law.* New York: Neal-Schuman, 1996.

Bodian, Nat G. *The Book Marketing Handbook.* New Providence, N.J.: Bowker, 1980. Vol. 2, 1983.

Curtis, Richard. *Beyond the Bestseller: A Literary Agent Takes You inside the Book Business.* New York: New American Library, 1989.

Dessauer, John P. *Book Publishing: The Basic Introduction.* New York: Continuum, 1989.

Eaglen, Audrey. *Buying Books: A How-to-Do-It Manual for Librarians.* New York: Neal-Schuman, 1987.

Fulton, Len. *International Directory of Little Magazines and Small Presses.* Paradise, Calif.: Dustbooks. Annual.

———. *Small Press Record of Books in Print*. Paradise, Calif.: Dustbooks. Annual.

Horowitz, Irving. *Communicating Ideas: The Politics of Publishing in a Post-Industrial Society*. 2nd ed. New Brunswick, N.J.: Transaction, 1991.

Huenfeld, John. *The Huenfeld Guide to Book Publishing*. Rev. 5th ed. Bedford, Mass.: Mills Sanderson, 1993.

Machlup, Fritz. *Information through the Printed Word. The Dissemination of Scholarly, Scientific, and Intellectual Knowledge*. 4 vols. Westport, Conn.: Praeger, 1978-80.

Plotnik, Arthur. *The Elements of Editing: A Modern Guide for Editors and Journalists*. Old Tappan, N.J.: Macmillan, 1986.

Shatzkin, Leonard. *The Distribution of Books of Small Presses: A Study for the National Endowment for the Arts,* 1989.

Simon, Rita J. and James J. Fyfe. *Editors as Gate Keepers: Getting Published in the Social Sciences*. Lanham, Md.: Rowman & Littlefield, 1994.

Tebbel, John. *Between the Covers: The Rise and Transformation of Book Publishing in America*. New York: Oxford University Press, 1987.

PERIODICALS

Against the Grain. Charleston, S.C.: Against the Grain. 6 issues per year.

Book Industry Trends. New York: Book Industry Study Group. Annual.

Journal of Scholarly Publishing. North York, Ont.: University of Toronto. Quarterly.

LOGOS. North Bergen, N.J.: Whurr Publishers, Ltd. Quarterly.

Publishers Weekly. New York: Bowker. Weekly.

Publishing Research Quarterly. Bridgeport, Conn.: Transaction Publishers. Quarterly.

3

The Business of Scholarly Journal Publishing

GARY J. BROWN

Scholarly journal publishing is undergoing a profound transformation attributable in no small part to the budgetary stringency suffered by libraries, but more so to the technological advances of networked access, the standardization of electronic and printed text around HTML and SGML, and the widespread acceptance of the World Wide Web for access to pre-print and e-print servers in multiple disciplines. Accompanied by the decision of commercial, association, and university presses to place full electronic text of their print journals on the Web, these measures represent bold manifestations of innovative steps in search of new strategies for communicating, sharing, and selling scholarly information.[1]

Electronic journals have mushroomed into existence on the Web, changing the way in which publishers traditionally disseminate journals, readers access them, and libraries purchase them. In 1994 the ARL (Association of Research Libraries) survey listed 74 peer-reviewed electronic journals; one year later there were 142.[2] By 1997 approximately 1,500 peer-reviewed electronic journals in all disciplines appeared on the World Wide Web, reflecting the cumulative influence of numerous e-journal projects in the United States as well as the HEFC project in England, accompanied as well by the commitment of commercial publishers such as Academic Press, Blackwell Science, Elsevier, Kluwer, Springer-Verlag, and Thomson International. At the same time serial vendors and consortia were announcing third-party aggregation services to access and archive the burgeoning number of e-journals.[3]

THE JOURNAL IN SCHOLARLY
AND SCIENTIFIC COMMUNICATION

This chapter focuses on the changing nature and economics of scholarly and scientific journal publishing as it is transformed by the challenges of access to electronic text.[4] The role of the journal in communicating scholarly and scientific information, particularly in such disciplines as physics, mathematics, and the pure sciences, has been dramatically re-centered around researchers' primary need for direct and immediate scholarly communication. Stevan Harnad has stated the case boldly and succinctly: "I don't think any scholar or scientist would willingly collaborate in restricting access to his work. There is no longer any need to make that Faustian Bargain in the PostGutenberg galaxy where learned inquiry can at last be skywritten, free for one and all."[5]

Indeed, the journal article in the discipline of physics, now preceded by ready and immediate access to the electronic pre-print article, is the preferred medium of communication, continuing to maintain its position over the monograph, as studies as far back as the 1970s have corroborated.[6] Given an academic structure that rewards and grants tenure to faculty largely on the basis of published contributions to scholarship, and given the need for an established scholarly reputation to attract grants and research monies to an institution, the mandate to publish one's research is widely understood. The need for rapid dissemination of one's research now made possible by the advances of technology has influenced the creation of e-print servers. But where does this leave the print journal publisher?[7]

Obviously this presents new challenges to publishers who initially have not been an integral part of this pre- and post-print access scenario.[8] Perhaps the saving grace of publishers is their role of adding value to the process of scholarly communication. Publishers traditionally gather, select through peer review, and enhance the expression of ideas in publications of prestige and value, a fact recognized or underplayed in one way or another by Harnad and Odlyzko in their early announcements of the end of the print journal. It is interesting to note that we do not see the same e-print activity in the areas of medicine or chemistry as we see occurring in the disciplines of mathematics and physics. Could part of an explanation be the habits of researchers in those disciplines? Harnad points out that there is a safety net under the Ginsparg e-server "held in place by the 'Invisible Hand' of peer review, which is still being financed by the publishers whose paper journals are still the final resting place for virtually every e-print in [the Los Alamos server]."[9,10]

THE JOURNAL PUBLISHING PROCESS

Traditionally the publishing process has organized itself around the sequence of planning, producing, and disseminating. These activities are assigned to "editorial," "production," and "marketing," whether represented by entire divisions within large publishing houses or by one person in a very small operation. Publishers of both monographs and journals generally fall into the categories of university presses, commercial publishers, and learned societies or professional associations.[9,10]

In book publishing an editor (acquisitions, developmental, or copy editor) deals with the process of acquiring, preparing, and editing the manuscript for publication.[11] Levels of editorial involvement and responsibility vary depending upon the nature and perceived market for the book whether mass-market paperback, trade, scholarly, professional reference, medical, or textbook. In contrast, editorial responsibilities in journal publishing differ markedly, since the editors and the editorial board of a journal often are not members of the publishers' staff, but instead are affiliated with an academic, corporate or governmental institution where they conduct research and/or teach, and publish within their discipline. The relationship between author and editor, then, is often a relationship between colleagues. Large publishers, however, maintain an editorial staff to manage the editorial and production procedures.

Thus the process of acquiring manuscripts for publication and the decision to publish rests not with the publisher, but with academic or professional peers who anonymously referee submitted or requested material. (Of course, this varies when the item being considered for inclusion in the journal is a report, letter, or note of information.) As a result, many journal publishers traditionally do not incur the major costs of a salaried editorial staff to the extent that book publishers do, nor do journal publishers provide royalty payment to authors as is the practice with commercial publishers of monographs. In the case of many learned societies in the United States, page charges which are paid by the authors are assessed to help defray journal publication costs.

The traditional production process for a book or a journal essentially follows the same procedures: (1) Design decisions need to be made about what type font and size to use, whether illustrations or half-tone reproductions will be employed. (2) Specifications involving page size, paper quality, and weight need to be established. (3) Composition vendors are selected (if not handled in house or if the author does not supply an electronically formatted version of the manuscript). (4) Printing and binding require scheduling or vendor assignment if not part of a publisher's operation.

The journal, like the monograph, has fixed and variable production costs. Fixed costs include items such as composition, author corrections, plates and illustrations. Costs such as paper, printing, binding operations, and postage fees increase with the number of pages and copies printed.

The important distinction for the journal, however, involves its serial nature. Because of its frequency pattern and the successive repetition of these production procedures, both fixed and variable manufacturing costs are higher. Special issues and larger page counts made to accommodate the increasing number of accepted articles also contribute to the rise of costs and subscription prices.

The marketing efforts made to publicize, promote, and distribute a book vary widely according to the nature of the book in question (e.g., mass-market paperback versus a university press scholarly title). The author tours, television appearances, and radio talk show interviews used to promote a popular title obviously do not fit for a specialized monograph such as *Scholarly Publishing: The Electronic Frontier* (MIT Press, 1996) and much less for a scholarly or scientific journal such as *Brain Research* (Elsevier). The scholarly journal has to develop a much more conservative marketing plan which targets research libraries, academics, and specialists, relying principally upon traditional means of advertising: brochures, catalogs, direct mail, and recommendations among colleagues. In addition a prestigious editorial board with a widely recognized body of researchers and academics is a valuable "advertising asset" that will help a new journal on its way to success and ensure the continued subscription by libraries and individuals.

The e-journal has radically changed certain aspects of the journal publishing process while at the same time relying heavily on standard, traditional editorial, production, and marketing procedures. Publishers have experimented with different ways to integrate new procedures necessary for the conversion to electronic text. Peter Boyce has articulated the new skills learned in editing an electronic version of the *Astrophysical Journal Letters* in cooperation with the University of Chicago Press. He lists six steps and issues in the electronic publishing process rooted in traditional procedures but centered on the essential and critical process of database preparation, which involves the design and tagging of electronic text of SGML and PDF formats, the construction of access, and the provision for open links, and interoperability among platforms, systems, and software:

1. Author preparation—the first step in the publishing process
2. Peer review
3. Copy editing and typography
4. Database preparation—core electronic system to ensure access and interoperability
5. Production and Distribution
6. Archiving[12]

The experience of the development team in producing the *Electronic Astrophysical Journal Letters* (EApJL) exemplifies the reengineering of a print journal. A sampling of topics from their project notes and diary updates provides an inside view of the challenges presented: the question of how to render mathematical symbols on the screen, the use and integration of different text processor software (Word, TeX, Scientific Word, LaTeX), what authoring software tools to use, and the conversions to SGML for preparation in HTML and PDF formats. Also of concern are consideration of new Extensible Markup Language software (XML) for converting SGML documents to the Web, internal linking, thumbnail presentation of article text, selection of search engine software and compliance with Z39.50, citation service planning and linking procedures, the issues of "forward referencing," access and links to outside resources, construction of the "Urania Resource" with easy links among the entire body of astrophysical journal articles, references, citations, data and catalogs, and—last but not least—the decision to mount the complete archive of all back issues of EApJL.[13]

JOURNAL COSTS AND REVENUE

Like any organization, in order to continue operations journal publishers need to ensure that income exceeds expenses; commercial publishers cannot survive without profit, and where profit is lacking for society publishers and university presses some form of subsidies are sought.

By way of summary, the cost side of the balance sheet for a journal lists such expenses as editing (copyediting, proofreading, layout), production and manufacturing (typesetting, illustrations, printing, binding and paper, reprints), marketing (advertising, direct mail), and distribution (postage, delivery, subscription fulfillment). On the income side of the balance sheet, journal publishers rely on the following sources of revenue: subscriptions (member or institutional), page charges, advertising, back numbers, reprints, microform sales, and permission rights.[14]

Since the journal has production and manufacturing costs that cannot be lowered readily by the economies of scale normally associated with monographic publishing, it must look at other areas on the balance sheet to recoup expenses. The principal source of revenue for a journal is its subscription base, which publishers try to keep as broad as possible through different member and institutional rates. Nonprofit association and learned society publishers in the United States can rely upon page charges to authors to help defray the fixed and variable costs of publishing, but university presses and commercial publishers traditionally have not used this procedure.[15] Added sources of revenue such as advertising, reprint, etc., contribute less significantly to overall profitability. Since the frequency of a journal and the number of pages directly affect costs, publishers rely upon an important analytic tool referred to as the break-even analysis. It allows the calculation of the number of journal subscriptions needed to offset basic costs, and the number beyond that point to ensure profitability. Cost per page can thus be determined and average price per page set (and thus the overall price of the journal) in order to ensure needed revenues and projected profits.[16]

Annual cost and revenue statistics for journal publishing are not available readily because traditional publishing industry sources such as the annual *Industry Statistics Report* of the Association of American Publishers do not break out cost figures for periodical or journal publishing. Nevertheless, extensive studies of U.S. scientific and scholarly journal publishing by Machlup and King in the late 1970s can serve as an initial point of reference for understanding the economics of journal publishing. As an example, Machlup's survey of 137 journals (72 from learned societies, 25 from university presses, and 40 from commercial publishers) revealed that nearly 65 percent of publisher revenue was derived from subscription sales. University presses relied upon subscriptions for a full 79 percent of their revenue. The second largest source of revenue, 13.7 percent, came from advertising. Page charges levied by 22 society publications and two university journals provided 8.3 percent of total revenue. In actuality these 22 society publishers alone derived a full 13.2 percent of their revenue from page charges. The sale of

back issues, reprints, microform, permission fees, and miscellaneous sources provided cumulatively 13.5 percent of revenue.[17]

In the 1980s a study of six journals published by the American
Institute of Physics (AIP), a nonprofit society publisher, provided
both cost and income statistics.[18] On the revenue side they coincide
in many respects with Machlup's findings for journals studied in
1974. For the six AIP journals, subscriptions account for 61 percent
of revenue as opposed to 65 percent in the Machlup sample.
Voluntary page charges, however, contribute almost three times
more—33 percent compared to 13.2 percent in Machlup's study.
Table 3-1 shows expenses and income for *Applied Physics Letters,
Journal of Applied Physics, Journal of Chemical Physics, Journal of
Mathematical Physics, Physics of Fluids,* and *Review of Scientific
Instruments.* Publication expenses for the six AIP journals amount
to $5,026,000, leaving earnings of $1,174,000 from the total income
of $6,200,000. The overall margin of profitability for these journals
is thus calculated at 23 percent.

The cost of journals in the 1990s has continued to increase, and
although comprehensive data are unavailable, the most recent esti-
mation provided by the American Chemical Society, which publishes 26 journals, projects publishers' costs within the following
ranges: "An average journal has a circulation between 1,000 and
10,000 subscribers, small to minuscule by popular publishing standards, resulting in proportionately higher per-page publishing costs.
Editorial management, including peer review, represents about 10
percent of a journal's cost. Editorial mechanics adds another 30

Table 3-1. Summary of Expenses and Income for Six AIP Physics Journals

1982 Journal Expenses				1982 Journal Income		
	Amount	Percent			Amount	Percent
Editorial	$1,360,000	27%	Page Charges		$2,039,000	33%
Composition	1,378,000	28%	Subscriptions		3,835,000	61%
Illustrations	50,000	10%	Advertising		57,000	1%
Paper	525,000	1%	Microfilm Sales		67,000	1%
Printing and Binding	506,000	10%	Back Number Sales		29,000	1%
Mailing	468,000	9%	Reprint Sales		141,000	2%
Subs. Fulfillment	142,000	3%	Royalties		32,000	1%
Reprints	362,000	7%				
Misc.	235,000	5%				
Total Expenses	$5,026,000	100%	Total Income		$6,200,000	100%

percent. And finally, electronic production, including design, layout, and illustration represents an additional 30 percent."[19]

Andrew Odlyzko made the following estimate of explicit and implicit costs associated with the production of a typical article based on samples from mathematics and theoretical computer science journals:

1. Estimated median cost of publisher $4,000
2. Library costs other than purchase of journals
   and books $8,000
3. Editorial and refereeing costs $4,000
4. Costs of preparing a paper $20,000

Although these are rough approximations of the cost to produce an article, Odlyzko points out that most attention in the discussion of library or scholarly publishing "crises" has been paid to his estimate of publisher revenue at $4,000 per article. "Even the least expensive print publishers still operate at a cost of around $1,000 per article. Electronic publishing offers the possibility of going far below even that figure."[20] This is a point that is obviously debated by publishers and for which there remains some skepticism. Relying upon the experience of developing EApJL, Peter Boyce maintains that the wide speculation about cutting costs in half by producing a refereed journal in an electronic form was unfounded even taking into consideration the savings gained in printing and mailing costs. "We now know that the savings realized by the elimination of in-house keyboarding are just about offset by the additional cost of copyediting a manuscript online. Moreover, there is strong demand that journals continue to be produced in the old paper form as well as in the new electronic form. Preparing the electronic material for both paper and electronic delivery is a significant additional cost that makes electronic production a break-even proposition at best."[21] Boyce does posit a possible 25 percent savings once publishers have gained sufficient experience and more effective production tools and procedures become commonplace.

ELECTRONIC JOURNALS AND PRICING TRENDS

The 1980s and 1990s have witnessed a continuous increase in serials prices. Study after study and graph after graph have demonstrated what is now painfully obvious to all—the curve always goes up. Shrinking budgets and the need to cancel print subscriptions have led to the optimistic expectation that the electronic journal would provide relief from such budgetary suffocation. It remains to be seen, however, whether the electronic dissemination of scholarly information can effectively address the issues of rising prices and the needs of both the academy and publishing community. Scholars view the electronic journal and e-print servers from the perspective of researchers attempting to disseminate their ideas quickly to the widest body of interested readers. Publishers, on the other hand, scholarly as well as trade, are in search of the means of growing profits by exploring the alternatives of e-commerce while maintaining the market share of their paper-based products.

Some innovative pricing scenarios have evolved in the light of the accepted challenge to transform the dissemination of scholarly information. Drawing upon analogous pricing models in the telephone and cable service industry, some publishers, in cooperation with consortia and universities, have adopted a bundled subscription approach. Others have combined traditional pricing with "pure bundling" and "mixed bundling" options.[22] Three examples will suffice to exemplify such pricing strategies: the International Digital Electronic Access Library (IDEAL) of Academic Press, Elsevier and the PEAK project at the University of Michigan, and Blackwell Science Publishers.

In 1996 Academic Press launched IDEAL, converting all of its 175 journals to HTML and mounting them on the Web. The IDEAL approach to pricing best represents a "pure bundling" model, which only permits licensed access to the entire 175 electronic journals by library consortia—excluding individual subscriptions by an institution and the purchase of individual articles. The cost of the consortial license is calculated on the original base of all print journals subscribed to by members of the formed consortium, adding 10 percent for unlimited, full electronic access to all licensed AP journals. Faculty, staff, and students have access from the library or remotely for printing, downloading, creating course packs, or electronic reserves. Given this pure bundled model, advantages are provided to both buyer and seller, though not necessarily to every buyer or potential buyer. For those buyers to whom it presents a viable option, valuation depends upon use and access. For the seller, value is dependent upon elimination of market inefficiencies and extraction of return on all products in the bundle. In such a scenario "the more goods included in the bundle, the less likely it is that any given consumer's valuation will be very low or very high. Such a reduction in "buyer diversity" typically helps sellers extract higher profits while reducing the deadweight loss from non-zero prices. The benefits of bundling are greatest when the marginal cost of the goods is very low, and when the valuation for individual goods are of comparable magnitude."[23]

The PEAK project at the University of Michigan in cooperation with Elsevier, as described from the perspective of economists Jeffery MacKie-Mason and Juan Riveros, "concerns a controlled field experiment to investigate the effects of product bundling and pricing structure for electronic access to scholarly literature."[24] The benefit of this "experiment" presumably will help determine, by careful analysis and evaluation of user experience, the effectiveness of multiple pricing scenarios, the variations of bundled and unbundled electronic subscriptions—e.g., differently arranged subscription packages, purchase of individual articles, pay per access, etc.—and the benefit to both university and publisher. It is in this respect that they point out that "electronic access enables both publishers and libraries to engage in new product bundling and non-linear pricing schemes. The first will often involve unbundling of traditional journal components, and then rebundling in a greater variety of packages, some of them customized for customers, or customizable by them."[25]

Finally the development and pricing of e-journals edited by Blackwell Science provide an interesting mixture of unbundled strategies that reveal a different approach to testing the market, presenting the consumer with a variety of individual choices. Blackwell Science has chosen to mount the data for its e-journals on host partners, initiating their project in cooperation with UK Higher Education Institutions under a National Pilot Site License facilitated by Bath Information & Data Services (BID). Print and electronic versions are maintained with separate and combined pricing; a subscription solely to the e-journal reflects a lower price (10 percent) than the corresponding print subscription. Subscription to both the print and electronic versions reflects an approximate 30 percent increase to the base price of the print version. Personal subscriptions, where allowed, also reflect the same options and pricing ratios. There is also discussion about permitting the purchase of individual articles.

The different pricing scenarios in operation currently are, in effect, attempts by publishers in conjunction with their "partner" buyers to evolve a viable pricing policy that permits survival, growth, and the development of newly focused, added-value information services. The efficiencies that eventually are realized by new software tools and production procedures can help contain expenditures, but the ongoing costs of continuing to develop and provide paper and electronic "editions" are considered factors that will continue to keep prices high in scholarly publishing.

CONCLUSION

The challenges of scholarly publishing reflect an evolving, radical transformation of the information chain, the process through which we create, acquire, and use information. High costs, the branching out of knowledge and traditional disciplines, the digitization of information and its consequent alteration of the ways in which we access, acquire, store, and utilize this information—all are contributing factors that have altered the ways in which we read and write. We now find ourselves entering a new stage in the development of infrastructures for the creation of digital libraries and the elaboration of archival strategies for the maintenance of electronic information.

The scholarly print journal, if it survives as we know it, increasingly will fulfill a secondary role to that of immediate electronic access provided by the interchange of author-publishers who present their work in different stages of evolution on pre-print and post-print servers. The major issues of the past decades—the dissemination of scholarly information, access, resource sharing and costs—are prologue to the chapters we are finalizing through models of trial and error. How we will complete these new chapters depends in great part on how successfully we redefine our roles in creating, accessing, and disseminating scholarly information.

Notes

1. For an overview of information on electronic publishing, consult the comprehensive and regularly updated bibliography maintained by Charles W. Bailey Jr., *Scholarly Electronic Publishing Bibliography,* http://info.lib.uh.edu/sepb/sepb.html. E-print servers have appeared in many disciplines, principal among them physics, astronomy, economics, international relations, and political science. The first e-print servers appeared in high energy physics at Los Alamos and Stanford University. See P. Ginsparg's discussion of his e-print archives in "Winners and Losers in the Global Research Village," a presentation at the conference on Electronic Publishing in Science, held at UNESCO HQ, Paris, Feb. 19-23, 1996, http://xxx.lanl.gov/blurb/pg96unesco.html. For information on the SLAC/HEP (Stanford Linear Accelerator Center/High Energy Physics) databases, consult http://www-spires.slac.stanford.edu:80/FIND/spires.html. See the American Astronomical Society home page for information about Urania Resource at http:// www/aas.org/. The Economics Working Paper Archive can be consulted at http://econwpa.wustl.edu. Columbia University Press created Columbia International Affairs Online (CIAO), a database of papers-in-progress on international

relations: http://www.ciaonet.org/. The American Political Science Association in cooperation with Harvard University Library has launched "PROceeding: Political Research Online" for access to conference papers, http://pro.harvard.edu/.

2. The *ARL Directory of Electronic Journals, Newsletters and Academic Discussion Lists* can be consulted at http://arl.cni.org. For a listing of other directories see http://www.coalliance.org/other.html.

3. For a listing of electronic publishing and related projects in the United States and Europe see http://www-leland.stanford.edu/group/stepp/, and for an annotated directory of links to major electronic text projects consult http://frnak.mtsu.edu/ ~kmiddlet/libweb/electpub.html. The Higher Education Funding Councils of Great Britain (HEFC) funded a two-year project (1996-97) that provided Web access to the electronic journals of Academic Press, Blackwell Science, and The Institute of Physics for 180 universities and colleges of higher education in England, Scotland, Wales, and Northern Ireland. Serial vendors have loaded table of contents and abstract data with access to full text of e-journals (Blackwell's Electronic Journal Navigator, Swetsnet, Dawson's Information Quest), while other aggregators OCLC, ISI, Ovid Technologies, and EBSCO Host are storing text on their server. The question of archiving e-journals is being addressed by JSTOR, OCLC, CICnet, and the National Libraries of Canada and Australia. For a useful summary of these developments see George Machovec, "Electronic Journal Market Overview—1997," http://www.coalliance.org/reports/ejournal.htm and the excellent survey of activity in the first five years of this decade by Steve Hitchcock, Leslie Carr and Wendy Hall, "A Survey of STM Online Journals 1990-95: The Calm before the Storm" in the 6th edition of the *ARL Directory* (see note 2).

4. Our use of the term *journal* coincides with the traditional understanding of a scholarly journal of refereed articles; a type of literature Stevan Harnad refers to as "esoteric" or non-trade literature as distinguished from trade periodicals in which authors are paid for their work. See Harnad, "The PostGutenberg Galaxy: How to Get There from Here," *Times Higher Education Supplement,* May 12, 1995.

5. Stevan Harnad, "The Paper House of Cards (and Why It's Taking So Long to Collapse)," *Ariadne,* Issue 8, March 1997, http://www.ariadne.ac.uk/issue8harnad/.

6. Studies of scholarly publishing in the 1970s and early 1980s by King, Machlup, Fry, the National Science Foundation, and the National Endowment for the Humanities addressed major issues facing scholarly communication which now must be read in the light of the technological developments of the 1990s. See the following: Donald W. King, et al., *Scientific Journals in the United States: Their*

Production, Use, and Economics (Stoudsburg, Penn.: Hutchinson Ross Publishing Co., 1981); F. Machlup, et al., *Information through the Printed Word: The Dissemination of Scholarly, Scientific, and Intellectual Knowledge.* Vol. 1: *Book Publishing;* Vol. 2: *Journals;* Vol. 3: *Libraries;* Vol. 4: *Books, Journals, and Bibliographic Services* (New York: Praeger, 1978-80); Bernard M. Fry and Herbert S. White, *Publishers and Libraries: A Study of Scholarly and Research Journals* (Boston: Lexington Books, 1976); *Scholarly Communication: The Report of the National Enquiry* (Baltimore: Johns Hopkins University Press, 1979). For an analysis of British journal publishing see Alan Singleton, chapters 9-11, in Peter J. Curwen, *The UK Publishing Industry* (Oxford: Pergamon, 1981).

7. The early predictions of the demise of the paper journal have subsided with the realization that radical change is arriving later than originally perceived and with the fact that traditional publishers are forging a role for both print and e-journals. See Andrew M. Odlyzko, "Tragic Loss or Good Riddance? The Impending Demise of Traditional Scholarly Journals" (1994) and "The Slow Evolution of Electronic Publishing" (Preliminary Version, Sept. 10, 1997) http://www.research.att.com/~amo/. See also Stevan Harnad's articles from 1990 to 1997 at http://www.princeton.edu/~harnad/intpub.html. In their paper "Economics and Electronic Access to Scholarly Information," Jeffrey K. MacKie-Mason and Juan F. Riveros make a compelling argument for the value publishers add to authoring: "Publishing adds significant value to authoring. The digital revolution is changing sources and amounts of value added, but not eliminating it. The costs of some functions are decreasing rapidly, but other costs are not. Meanwhile, as new information services are developed, new opportunities for publishing value-added are also created." Section 2.1 Publishing Economics, delivered at Conference on Economics of Digital Information and Intellectual Property, January 23–25, 1997, http://ksgwww.harvard.edu/iip/econ/econ.html#Conference Papers.

8. In the development plans for the *Electronic Astrophysical Journal Letters* (see below) attention is given to coordinating and maintaining pre-print server capability in the community of researchers, representing an attempt of a society publisher to become an integral part of the pre-publication process. Presumably the pre-print server includes articles other than those destined for appearance in the *Electronic Astrophysical Journal Letters.*

9. Harnad, "The Paper House of Cards . . ." See also Harnad, "Implementing Peer Review on the Net: Scientific Quality Control in Scholarly Electronic Journals," in R. Peek and G. Newby, ed., *Scholarly Publishing: The Electronic Frontier* (Cambridge: MIT Press, 1996), 103-120, and the discussion between Harnad and Fytton Rowland in *Ariadne,* Issues 7 and 8, as well as between Harnad and

Steve Fuller, *Times Higher Education Supplement,* May 12, 1995. Harnad clearly sees a role for traditional publishers: "This new [electronic] medium would not necessarily mean the demise of established publishers. A mutually beneficial, cooperative solution can be found. If publishers recognize and accept the non-trade mode ushered in by electronic-only publication and reorganize their role accordingly, their role will still be important and will still yield a fair return for their contribution." In Harnad, "Electronic Scholarly Publication: Quo Vadis?" *Serials Review* 21, no. 1 (1995): 72.

10. See Colin Day, "Economics of Electronic Publishing," http://www. press.umich.edu/jep/works/colin,econ.html. "Gathering . . . Now it may be that in an electronic publishing world, the task of gathering will be eliminated. . . . Enhancement . . . Under this term I include everything that is done to the Author's work which changes it before it reaches the reader."

11. For discussions of monographic and journal editorial procedures see Elizabeth A. Geiser, ed., *The Business of Book Publishing: Papers by Practitioners* (Boulder: Westview Press, 1985) and Lewis I. Gidez, "Editorial Questions," in *Economics of Scientific Journals,* ed. Ad Hoc Committee on Economics of Publication (Bethesda, Md.: Council of Biology Editors, 1982).

12. In November 1993, the National Science Foundation awarded a grant for three years beginning in September 1994 to the American Astronomical Society for the development of the *Electronic ApJ Letters* project. The description of the project and its step-by-step development can be consulted at the AAS Web site http://www. aas.org. It allows an interesting insight into the development and cooperative efforts involved in the creation of an electronic journal presenting meeting agendas, project topics, liaison with digital library projects, and database developers. The description of the editorial process is taken from the paper by Peter B. Boyce, "A Successful Electronic Scholarly Journal from a Small Society," http://www.aas.org/~pboyce/ epubs/icus-art.html#ICSU.

13. See the AAS home page, "EApJL project TOC file," http://www.aas.org/ Epubs/webinfo/eapjl.htm.

14. An example of a balance sheet for the *Journal of Mathematical Physics* can be consulted in Robert H. Marks " 'Not for Profit' Doesn't Mean 'for Loss,' " *Proceedings of the Third Annual Meeting of the Society for Scholarly Publishing* (1981), p. 184. Marks describes the cost factors involved in publishing eighteen primary journals, three member society bulletins, and nineteen Russian translations for the American Institute of Physics.

15. For a discussion of the practice and history of assessing page charges see Marjorie Scal, "The Page Charge," *Scholarly Publishing* 3

(1971): 62-69 and A. F. Spilhaus Jr., "Page Charges," in *Economics of Scientific Journals,* ed. D. H. Michael Brown (Bethesda, Md.: Council of Biology Editors, 1982), pp. 21-27.

16. See Ben Russak, "The Economics of Journal Publishing," *Proceedings of the Third Annual Meeting of the Society for Scholarly Publishing* (1981), pp. 174-177, for a discussion and application of break-even analysis for a new journal.

17. Machlup, *Information,* vol. 2, 137, table 3.4.13. For a more complete discussion consult vol. 4, part 8, "Journal Publishing: Costs and Gross Margins." In King, et al., *Scientific Information,* see chapter 4, "Publishing Scientific and Technical Journals," and chapter 8, "Economics of the Scientific and Technical Journal System."

18. Rita Lerner, "The Professional Society in a Changing World," *Library Quarterly* 54 (1984): 36-47.

19. The American Chemical Society in "The Economics of the First Copy," http://pubs.acs.org/journals/wspp/econ.html.

20. See his discussions in "Tragic Loss or Good Riddance? . . ." [section 9.4] and "The Economics of Electronic Journals," http://www.re-search.att.com/~amo/doc/economics.journals.txt.

21. "Electronic Publishing of Scientific Journals," Peter B. Boyce and Heather Dalterio at http://www.aas.org/~epubs/pt-art.htm.

22. For a discussion of these pricing concepts see the following: J. Y. Bakos and Erick Brynjolfsson, "Bundling Information Goods: Pricing, Profits and Efficiency"; John Chung-I Chuang and Marvin Sirbu, "Network Delivery of Information Goods: Optimal Pricing of Articles and Subscriptions"; Jeff MacKie-Mason with Juan F. Riveros, "Economics and Electronic Access to Scholarly Information," papers delivered at the conference Internet Publishing and Beyond: Economics of Digital Information and Intellectual Property, http:-//ksgwww.harvard.edu//iip/econ/econ.html#Conference Papers.

23. Bakos and Brynjolfsson, "Bundling Information Goods."

24. MacKie-Mason, "Economics and Electronic Access."

25. Ibid.

4

Publishers, Vendors, Libraries: Troublesome Issues in the Triangle

AUDREY MELKIN

How do publishers look at the library market? How do they distinguish it from the bookstore market or the direct mail market? Publishers often feel that it is an invisible market. Are they right in this perception? And in what ways are they wrong? How does the publisher regard the bookseller-vendor-wholesaler, the oft-chosen conduit for the distribution of the publishers' products to the library?

These are some of the questions that librarians ask about publishers and that publishers wonder about themselves. Although the library market has been estimated to generate from one to three billion dollars, some 12 percent of the publishing market as a whole, there still remains an enormous gulf between the various players in this market and their understanding of each other's modes of operation.[1] Understanding the reasons why this gulf exists provides the basis for appreciating the difficulties the major players in this market have in interpreting each other's roles.

It is as difficult to speak about how *all* publishers view the library market as it is to speak about all types of libraries. Although some remarks may apply to all publishers selling to all libraries, the type of publisher being considered here most closely approximates a commercial scholarly and professional publisher. Naturally, therefore, marketing to academic libraries, larger public libraries, and special libraries will be emphasized.

Audrey Melkin

QUANTIFYING SALES TO LIBRARIES

In publishing, as in other businesses, what one can measure or quantify as the effect of one's efforts gets high visibility, prominence, and attention. When advertising can be directly related to an increase in sales at bookstores, when sales significantly exceed production costs, or when a direct mail brochure has a favorable cost to net sales ratio, a publisher can point to the effectiveness of his or her marketing techniques.

For many reasons, this quantifiable factor has been missing from the library market. Librarians respond to many different stimuli to purchase—from favorable reviews, to inclusion on a vendor's approval plan, to publishers' advertising, to faculty requests. Librarians also are likely to order materials through many different channels: directly from the publishers; through a varied number of booksellers, both wholesalers and retailers; and from subscription agents. Most publishing houses cannot easily determine which part of the business of these various channels actually represents library sales. This occurs because the method of sales reported in publishing houses is more accurate in reflecting the sales of particular titles. Sales to libraries are often reflected in several channels including wholesalers (which may include trade as well as library wholesalers); direct mail response orders; and institutional, industrial, and government categories.

Since publishers are aware that they cannot easily or authoritatively determine their sales to libraries, they are more likely to give their attention to other more quantifiable channels. Not too long ago, particularly in the 1960s and early 1970s, publishers had become accustomed to a boom market for library sales. There was a routine sales expectation that certain titles, mainly cloth-bound books, would *automatically* sell to libraries. These sales usually took place without any additional effort on the part of the publishers other than the usual advertising and marketing to their more identifiable channels and, of course, the usual advertising in the library media.

The economics of the educational market have changed in the last ten years or so. College textbook publishers have slowly but surely been waking up to that fact. To a great extent educational budget changes have been imposed upon the library market through decreased funding for school, public, and academic libraries. More recently, special and corporate libraries, which are so sensitive to the state of the nation's business health, have also felt the pinch.

The dynamics of the library world have changed as well. Librarians more readily question the assumptions that they suspect publishers hold about the library market, including the notions that the library market is invisible, that it is not price sensitive, and that it does not need to be specially targeted, unlike other markets. Publishers gradually are beginning to see the necessity of clarifying to themselves, and to the vendors and libraries with which they are inextricably connected, their perceptions of the library market. On the publishing side, many sales and marketing people are waking up to the fact that times have changed and that the library market is definitely inelastic and has more special needs and requirements, such as acid-free paper, full bibliographic information in all promotions, and the need to be recognized and treated as a major market. A growing number of programs, surveys, and forums for communication are taking place between the three critical players (publisher, vendor, library). While there may often be an element of acrimonious interchange between librarians and publishers, an increase in meaningful dialogue is occurring as well.

STRATEGIES FOR SELLING TO LIBRARIES

Although the library market has seemed invisible to many publishers for the reasons indicated, sales and marketing strategies have evolved over the years. Publishers are using distribution channels and promotions to achieve their sales targets and expectations in the library market.

Not all publishers have a library or educational sales force in place. The decision to go directly to the library market through a specialized sales force usually is based on the historical circumstances of a publisher, the types of titles published, and the size of the publishing house. With a large list of products from many divisions to sell, the economic justification for having a library sales force becomes more feasible. With this decision, of course, come other economic realities. To support such a sales force, a publisher will need to attract a large amount of direct orders from libraries, and the discount to libraries will need to be competitive with that offered by the library wholesaler. Likewise, some publishers will try to get a high percentage of library sales as direct business by mounting extensive and attractive direct mail or telemarketing operations. While many academic, public, and special libraries will buy only through vendors, a publisher's sales force can be effective in the many elementary and high school libraries, as well as in smaller public and special libraries. When a publisher's sales representative develops a special and close relationship with the librarians in his or her territory, this technique of selling can prove highly productive. When a direct mail piece or telephone sales call comes just at the right moment, that is, when the product offered and the price quoted are agreeable to the librarian, a sale can be made as well. Of course in other cases these sales initiatives will find themselves in the wastebasket or will be met with silence at the other end of the receiver.

Librarians as well as wholesalers have become concerned in recent years with the tendency of some publishers to sell "direct only" to the library market, thereby eliminating an element of choice otherwise available to librarians. For the vendors, of course, this is a loss of business, and their ability to provide service to the library community is diminished. Likewise, as Eaglen writes, librarians often are incensed to find that they are forced to purchase books directly from the publisher.[2] Eaglen also points out, "there are a growing number of major trade publishers who are severely restricting libraries' options to buy their books directly from them." The main issue appears to be one of denying choice to the consumer—in this instance the librarian. Such a situation is not often encountered in our consumer-oriented society. It is the assertion that publishers *know* the best way for libraries to receive their material that really irks librarians. In the case of best-sellers, for example, it is imperative that libraries be permitted to order directly from publishers if they are to be able to satisfy their patrons in a timely fashion. Additionally, if one regional distributor is given the responsibility to provide a publisher's book to a large market, there may be some abuse of service without any real method of checking or redress on the part of the library.

There is a middle ground between publishers who only sell directly to libraries (known as sole source publishers) and publishers who sell only through wholesalers. These are the publishers who for sound economic reasons prefer that their sales to the library market be primarily through the wholesalers, yet who routinely accept direct orders from libraries, although they do not encourage them. The discounts to libraries from these publishers are usually small or nonexistent in order to avoid competition with the publishers' primary customer, the wholesaler. Such publishers may continue to spend their advertising dollars to inform the library market of their particular products, but with the expectation that those products will be bought from the vendor. For these publishers the vendor often becomes an ally, a partner in reaching an ultimate end customer, the library patron. It may be that this middle-ground scenario is most conducive to the mutual benefit of all three players in the library market: the publisher, the vendor, and the librarian. Certainly the opportunity for communication and open dialogue among all three is greatest with this arrangement, and it has seen some encouragement among large publishers with the establishment of offices focused on the library market.[3]

Two channels of distribution and the incentive strategies that are likely to accompany each approach have been discussed: direct library sales and sales through the wholesaler. Direct library promotion is a constant in almost all publishing houses that aim to sell to libraries, however the sale is made. Although a wholesaler may be the prime channel of distribution, it is the publisher who is uniquely qualified and expected to publicize and promote the house's list. What varies from publishing house to publishing house is the specificity of this promotion. Is there a regular catalog of new titles mailed to libraries? Is there a mailing piece designed specifically for librarians? Are institutional ads (ads in the library media specifically designed to reach librarians) placed regularly? Attendance at major library meetings both as exhibitor and as participant in the committees and activities of library associations is another arm of library promotion. Although publishers often hear complaints about the surplus of mailing pieces librarians receive and how many are simply thrown away unread, hope springs eternal in the publisher's heart and library promotion managers continue to produce promotion pieces with no quantifiable way of knowing which piece will "clinch the sale." Since a survey has shown that second to reviews, librarians rely on the publishers' own promotional material in making their acquisition decisions, the in-house library mailing list continues to be greatly prized and utilized.[4]

DISTRIBUTION ALTERNATIVES

In contrasting libraries to bookstores as channels of distribution, librarians are often concerned that the publisher favors the bookstore. Public librarians, in particular, need to be treated and seen as a bookstore when it comes to marketing books to the ultimate consumer, the retail customer or library patron. Both the bookstore and the library share a goal of making materials as attractive as possible to their customers. Although the library has no sales target to attain, it does have to improve circulation figures in order to attract more revenues for library support. But the bookstore is perceived as receiving higher discounts and better terms, even though the return rate of unsold items is considerably higher. From the publisher's point of view the bookstore, even though it is a retailer, bears a great similarity to that other bookseller, the library wholesaler. Both are set up with a resale number for tax purposes, and both are in business to buy books and other materials and then resell them. The library, however, is the final place of sale. The materials have been bought to be presented to a third party, the library patron, but this is different from a buying and selling relationship. In this area it may be that the publisher can be educated by the library community to acknowledge that libraries and bookstores are more similar than dissimilar. A publisher can provide libraries with additional book jackets and promotional materials, and can keep the library community informed about promotion and publicity, just as the publisher always does vis-à-vis the bookstore.

Bookstores and wholesalers are resellers while libraries are not; thus a higher discount is justified for the bookstore and wholesaler. In addition to the resale issue, a bookstore qualifies as another class of customer for the publisher. While the Robinson-Patman Act specifically prohibits publishers from offering different discounts for the same product to the same class of customers, they are permitted to set a discount schedule that is based on the type of customer.[5] What goes into determining the cost of doing business with a given type of customer? Certainly purely economic factors such as the order quantities, the volume of sales, and turnover will affect the cost of doing business with a certain type of customer. In the case of many scholarly publications, for example, the number of copies that can be sold may be small. If a sizable discount were offered to the library (which may represent the primary customer for the title but which will only buy one copy), the book would probably be very expensive or so unprofitable that it would not be feasible to publish at all. Publishers also feel that in order to attract well-known and prestigious authors it is necessary for the books published by that house to have high visibility and, by definition, bookstore distribution. For university and smaller presses, especially, this may mean offering advantageous terms to bookstores in order to get shelf space.

Although the purchase of a publisher's title by a library may ultimately ensure a much greater distribution of that title to the general public, the bookstore buy is more visible, more easily tracked, and therefore receives a higher priority. Of course, if a book really sells well, there will be greater chance for multiple sales through bookstore distribution than through the libraries. For university presses, just as the offering of more advantageous discounts to bookstores is a relatively recent phenomenon, it may be that the next evolution will be the realization of the benefits of extending a similarly favorable discount to that other group of booksellers, the library wholesaler. Since university press titles are so heavily purchased by academic libraries and these libraries buy primarily through vendors, it may be that the university presses will see a similar advantage in supporting the services that the vendors do provide to their ultimate customer.

That university presses may have even closer ties to libraries, particularly academic libraries, was pointed out by Herbert S. Bailey Jr., director emeritus of Princeton University Press in a paper given at the fiftieth anniversary meeting of the American Association of University Presses in Tucson, Arizona, in June 1987.[6] He suggested that as the system of scholarly communication develops, the differences between a university library and a university publisher will become much less visible. For example, if network publishing among libraries becomes common practice, there will be serious repercussions for university press publishing. Perhaps university presses can be instrumental in the effort to save brittle books by selective reprinting or by doing on-demand editions on acid-free paper. As parts of the same university system and as providers of services in a large degree to the same market—students and scholars—the university library and press have a natural affinity that can become the basis for greater cooperation in the future. There are, however, issues that have to be worked out.

For the present, it is clear that certain practices of the university presses contribute to conflict between the two rather than harmony. Joyce Knauer, the owner-manager of the Tattered Cover Book Store in Denver, Colorado, reports that bookstores are finding that the university presses are undermining the market for the trade store through direct mail discounting.[7] While this policy represents a clear loss of sales for these bookstores that stock books for the academic community, it may also be an irritant for the librarian who is unable to take advantage of the discount since the library wholesaler has often not been offered the same or equivalent discount.

In fact, many of the larger commercial scholarly and professional publishers run large direct mail programs, but generally *without* offering a discount, thereby driving business into bookstores as well as to wholesalers. Even though increasingly it is the librarian who chooses and buys the scholarly book in academic libraries, the mailing of brochures to faculty by the publisher can serve to promote the use of the scholarly books already acquired by the library.

John Secor, president of Yankee Book Peddler, expressed the concerns of the library vendor on these matters.[8] Secor believes that without appropriate recognition of the vendor's services to the academic library community on the part of both publishers and librarians alike, this important link in the distribution network may be in serious trouble and could thereby jeopardize the orderly and efficient flow of information from scholar to practitioner. He also thinks that an increase in communication and dialogue in the publisher/vendor/library community, if constructive, can lead to creative solutions to problems faced by all three players.

The area of net pricing provides an interesting example of the importance of dialogue. The practice of setting a net price in lieu of discount for retailers and wholesalers primarily originated in some publishing houses as a response to challenges in the college textbook market. College bookstore managers wanted greater flexibility in setting prices, and publishers, hurt badly by the increasingly well-organized used book business, were ready to cooperate. The implications for the library market were often not fully considered within the publishing house and also not carefully explained to the wholesaler or librarian. Typically, a publisher charges the wholesaler and bookstore the net price and charges the library customer who buys directly from the publisher a higher-than-net suggested list price for the title. The publisher's library promotion department also must decide at what price to list the title in advertising and promotion materials. The publisher may feel that it is problematic to advertise the title at the publisher's suggested list price since there may be a vendor who has set a higher price. The vendor's customers might be incensed to see that the title could be bought for less directly from the publisher, which they can in any case easily find out by calling the publisher and asking for the price that the publisher would charge the library. The option of advertising without a price remains, but that seems undesirable since the library community needs price information even when it is only an approximation.

The better informed the librarian is about the net pricing structure—why it's been instituted, what it means for the vendor, and so on—the less likely it is for misunderstandings to arise. Studies such as the one presented by Marsh and Lockman can go a long way toward illuminating the issues involved.[9] In their study, they present the background and explanation of net prices and illustrate several net-priced titles as supplied by the publisher and by three separate vendors. They point out that librarians should be aware that it is a legitimate practice for wholesalers to mark up the margin on net books in order to cover their costs. They conclude that "there are no grounds for accusations of unfair practice if the dealer marks up the margin on these net-priced items."

Another factor in the eternal triangle of publisher, vendor, and librarian is the assumption that underlies the relationship between the publisher and the vendor, namely, that the vendor's role is only to fulfill demand and not to create it. In a sense, vendors and publishers agree on this issue, since vendors often articulate it as part of their business credo. In fact, given all the competing publishers whose materials they stock, it might prove unwise to attempt otherwise. Yet, understandable as the vendor's position may be, publishers may feel some resentment. They ask, "Why should I, the publisher, extend to you, the wholesaler, a discount to sell my product when you don't really attempt to aggressively sell it?" The argument follows that many publishers feel that they can do better by continuing their direct relationship with librarians by offering some added discount to them, but not as high as that given to the wholesaler. The difficulty here is that the vendor may be providing something in addition to direct selling, namely, service in the form of consolidated ordering, bibliographic information, and time savings in payment and in claiming. The publisher cannot provide such service. Only when all three parts of the publisher, library, vendor triangle are taken together can solutions to problems be found.

CHANGING RELATIONSHIPS
AND CHANGING TIMES

Library schools have not generally included curriculum in the acquisitions process; therefore, little has been presented to student librarians about the publishing process and its dynamics. Similarly, the publishing industry has been slow to create special departments or marketing and sales people specifically designed to focus on the library market. Where there should be a natural affinity there often seems to be none. Several publishers have for a long time recognized the importance of the library market to their publishing programs and have active library advisory boards as well as librarians on their staff. But, in general, publishers have hesitated to create such departments or specialties because they have not felt sufficiently knowledgeable about the discipline. And since library sales in many publishing houses are somewhat invisible, these publishers have not felt a great need to learn more about the library market. As noted earlier, this situation is changing.

Natural bonds exist between publisher and librarian: they are both interested in encouraging reading, fighting illiteracy, and opposing censorship. The issue of acid-free paper may be another potential rallying point, especially as more publishers discover that the costs of using such paper are not substantially greater. With the establishment of the Copyright Clearance Center, the historical disagreement over photocopying may be handled more harmoniously.

Likewise, there has been a historically close relationship between the publisher and the retail bookseller. There are often job exchanges between these two industries, and the fact that neither industry requires any formal specialized education may be a link. Both also have perceived themselves as businesses involved in marketing and selling as well as publishing. Perhaps with the growing emphasis on marketing library services and a growing sophistication as librarians are increasingly seen as business managers, more dialogue among the players will occur. However, more conscious efforts will have to be made since these historical groupings are so well entrenched.

Similarly, vendors seem to have evolved closer relationships with librarians than publishers have with vendors. Perhaps there is more understanding of the role of the librarian in the vendor's business, which regularly has librarians on staff. Since the publisher may be trying to sell to the library directly as well as through the wholesaler, there can be a built-in competition between the publisher and the wholesaler which is not so prevalent in the publisher-bookstore relationship.

The future seems to portend a closer relationship among the players, if only for purely business reasons. As publishers have realized the necessity to become market driven rather than product driven, all of the publisher's many markets are being scrutinized anew. Publishing executives are now beginning to ask themselves what their customers want, rather than to whom they can sell a given title. Librarians are particularly well equipped to tell publishers which subject areas and formats are most in demand.

The library has become a different institution from what it was years ago. With the advent of the information manager, the position of librarian has achieved greater prestige, whatever one's personal opinion of this trend may be. All types of libraries, including public, academic, and special, are being run by more sophisticated, quantifiable, business-oriented methods. The librarian's role and voice have changed. Librarians are asking more questions of both wholesalers and publishers. Wholesalers and publishers are being challenged to demystify the process of which they are a part. After the initial panicked reaction on the part of publishers and vendors passes, this request leads to a much richer exchange among all three.

Although there may be no utopian solutions to these problems, through varied efforts some workable partial solutions can be found. If the educating process continues among the players, and if each comes to better appreciate the business requirements of the other, some insights will likely result to the benefit of everyone involved. If greater understanding can be fostered among the publisher, the librarian, and the wholesaler, the real winner will be the end customer of them all, the reading public.

Notes

1. Book Industry Study Group, *Book Industry Trends 1997: Covering the Years 1991-2001* (New York: B.I.S.G., 1997), pp. 3-6 (1).

2. Audrey Eaglen, "Publishers' Sales Strategies: A Questionable Business," *School Library Journal* 34 (February 1988): 19-21.

3. See, for example, "McGraw Refocuses on Library Market," *Library Journal* 121 (June 15, 1996): 14; "HarperCollins Looks to Library Market," *Library Journal* 121 (June 15, 1996): 14; and Jim Milliott, "Libraries Opening Up Once Again," *Publishers Weekly* 242, May 29, 1995, pp. 58-60.

4. Hendrik Edelman and Karen Muller, "A New Look at the Library Market," *Publishers Weekly*, May 29, 1987, pp. 30-35.

5. 49 Stat. 1526 (1936), 15 U.S.C.A. 13.

6. Herbert S. Bailey Jr., "The Future of University Press Publishing," *Scholarly Publishing* 19 (January 1988): 63-69.

7. Joyce Knauer, "Scholarly Books in General Bookstores," *Scholarly Publishing* 19 (January 1988): 79-85.

8. John Secor, "A Growing Crisis of Business Ethics: The Gathering Storm Clouds," *Serials Librarian* 13 (October-November 1987): 67-90.

9. Corrie V. Marsh and Edward J. Lockman, "Net Book Pricing," *Library Acquisitions: Practice & Theory* 12 (1988): 169-176.

5

The Cost of Service: Understanding the Business of Vendors

SCOTT ALAN SMITH

WHY USE VENDORS IN THE FIRST PLACE?

A library can order directly from publishers—and, despite the collective best efforts of vendors to persuade librarians to the contrary, a few do. But the majority of libraries elect to utilize vendors for some fairly basic reasons—efficiency, economy, and to benefit from value-added services.

Let's look at what ordering directly really means. Every order must be dispatched to a separate address and, unlike most wholesalers, many publishers are not equipped to accept orders electronically. Try to telephone a publisher, and odds are you'll be greeted by one of those obnoxious automated switchboards. After you have navigated your way through the maze of choices, chances are also pretty good you'll end up leaving a voice-mail message which, if you're lucky, may get returned within a couple of days.

After you have placed your order, then what? If the book does not arrive promptly, you'll need to claim, but many publishers are not in the business of replying to claims. Even if the publisher does respond, how accurate is the information? If publishers were truly interested in serving individual libraries, and consequently had the kind of user-friendly, accuracy-oriented service vendors deliver, there would be little need for wholesalers. Vendors exist in part to buffer libraries from the error rate of publishers. This isn't to say that every publisher is inept or disinterested in quality service—some deliver consistent and top-notch service. But let's face it: it's more efficient for the publisher, as well, to consolidate distribution with wholesalers, rather than to deal with every customer directly.

When the book does arrive, you have an invoice to pay. Every payment transaction—every time you cut a check—is a cost. The fewer checks you issue, the lower your cost.

All of the above presumes a firm order. Approval privileges are not common with publishers, and even though most publishers who issue books in series can accommodate standing orders, their capabilities are limited. If you want a copy of a directory every other year, publishers will have difficulty arranging that.

What about book processing? Binding? Corresponding MARC records? When we start to discuss value-added services, shelf-ready options, and interface capabilities with local integrated library systems, publishers are not usually interested or able to engage in the conversation about these now basic services that vendors provide.

Let us say you want to establish a deposit account to prepay your purchases for the next fiscal year, thereby eliminating the need to process payment for each and every invoice. While you *might* find a few publishers willing to accept money on deposit, you'd have to prepay dozens, if not hundreds, of sources, instead of consolidating your business with a single vendor.

By using the services of a vendor, you also benefit from the company's expertise. Vendors deal with publishers daily and maintain records of title availability, price, and where and how to order. These data change daily too—books go out of print, distribution arrangements change, payment and return policies are revised—and all of this must be tracked. Because a vendor is serving hundreds or perhaps thousands of libraries, this information is more extensive and more current than similar files maintained by a single library.

There's also the issue of a discount. Some publishers extend discounts to wholesalers but not to individual institutions (or to individuals, for that matter; many publishers don't want to incur the cost of selling directly to the public). Most give higher discounts for multicopy orders. Although there are some publishers who will not sell through vendors, and others who promote direct sales (this is an odd characteristic of this industry; it's not common in most businesses for wholesalers to compete with their suppliers), most publishers give bookdealers better discounts than a library can obtain by ordering directly. By using a vendor you can obtain a better net price for the majority of the books you buy.

All of the above refers to book wholesalers, but the same advantages apply to periodicals agents—it is simply far more effective to order subscriptions through an agent than to order directly. Although the order and payment process is different (you order, or renew, your subscriptions once a year and typically pay one major renewal invoice with a few supplemental, reconciliation invoices, rather than the ongoing dispatch of orders and payment of invoices common with monographs), many of the value-added service and systems interface issues noted here with book purchasing are found with periodicals as well.

Having made the case for utilizing vendor services, let's next look at the question of how many vendors to use.

CONSOLIDATION: MAXIMIZING EFFICIENCIES AND DISCOUNTS

In the late 1970s, in the years following the demise of the Richard Abel Company, many acquisitions librarians adopted an approach summed up by the phrase "I don't want to put all my eggs into one basket." Regrettably, this view endures and is often invoked by someone who splits his or her library's book business among two, three, or more bookdealers but has all subscriptions consolidated with a single journal agent.

It is not necessarily a bad idea to place all of a library's subscriptions with one periodicals vendor. On the contrary, and in light of what I have just said about the virtues of dealing with vendors versus buying directly, I think it makes perfect sense to maximize the services of an agent. This argument holds just as well for books.

Consider the relative advantages and risks of using one vendor or many. With periodicals, you must prepay, based on publisher requirements. You get a renewal invoice several months before you'll actually begin to receive the product, and for a major research library this renewal will be for several hundred thousand dollars, or possibly a million plus dollars. Are you at risk? Probably not. Most major journal agents are large, financially secure companies. If you have any doubts, you can and should get Dun & Bradstreet reports on any vendor with which you do a significant amount of business. Almost every company doing business in the library market is privately held. If vendors were publicly traded companies, libraries could get 10K reports (annual reports required from all publicly traded companies by the Securities and Exchange Commission) on us, or check out our annual reports to shareholders.

What does this say? Well, for one thing, venture capitalists aren't attracted to the library market. The return is too limited. Also, library budgets have been shrinking for several years, even though the range of products to buy has been multiplying steadily. The simple book now competes not only with print journals but also with CD-ROMs, videos, full-text indexes, online resources, document-delivery services, to name a few. Hence books are not what one might call a growth market. Of all the domestic book dealers and journal agents in business in 1996, only three were large enough to be included in the Forbes list of 500 privately held companies, and, not surprisingly, all three are major suppliers to the public library market, as well as serving retail bookstores: Baker & Taylor, Ebsco, and Ingram.

Back to that basket with the eggs for a moment, and back, too, to the 1970s. The prevailing preference for using multiple vendors compelled many suppliers to define their service with some kind of specialization. Some dealers did so by limiting their service to certain kinds of publishers, e.g., university presses, or sci-tech publishers. After all, if you're unlikely to persuade a library to send you all of their orders, shouldn't you target the easiest and most profitable publishers in the mix? Vendors do not generally solicit orders from societies and associations, which offer little or no discount. Other vendors defined themselves through the kinds of services they offered—approval plans, standing orders, firm orders, out-of-print books, etc. Increasingly, though, the trend among academic libraries is one of consolidation. This trend is driven by three major factors: economy, technology, and staff resources.

As has been pointed out, library materials budgets are shrinking. With fewer books to buy, it's critical to get as much as you can for what money you have. But even in an era of tighter budgets, vendor selection should not be motivated solely by price. Service should still be ranked first. If you get the wrong book, or suffer unacceptably slow delivery times or fulfillment rates, you haven't gained much for an extra point or two in discount. Assuming service is acceptable (or, to put it another way, if the library's needs and the vendors' services match and complement one another), the library can negotiate a more favorable discount by agreeing to consolidate much of its business with a single vendor. Moreover, as an industry, vendors have tended to view each sales type as a separate category—again, approval plans, standing orders, firm orders, each priced separately—but consolidation compels us to consider the totality of what a library buys and to extend discounts as a package. A few companies can even support the consolidation of books *and* periodicals. Why do vendors do this? Two basic issues answer the question: economies of scale and predictability of volume.

Technology is also influencing the issue. Although most vendors can now receive electronic orders and provide machine-readable records in conjunction with books, the increasing demand for shelf-ready services makes it far more practical to consolidate as much business as possible with a single supplier.

There's also the issue of staffing. For many libraries, the simple fact is there are fewer people in technical services than there used to be. More often than not this has come about through attrition, but some libraries have cut staff or shifted positions completely away from technical services, and as more libraries restructure, reorganize, and reengineer, this process will likely continue and perhaps accelerate.

In practical terms this means a couple of things: when you had a bigger staff, using multiple vendors was less of an issue—perhaps you had two order clerks, and you decided to let each of them select a separate vendor so you could easily identify incoming shipments. With more staff as a buffer, maximizing efficiencies was less of an issue. But as fewer people are expected to handle comparable (or increased!) workload, it is essential to achieve the benefits consolidation provides. Moreover, such fundamental shifts in staffing and library resources may lead to a reevaluation of the nature and extent of vendor services to consider.

BACK TO BASICS: THE RIGHT BOOK IN THE RIGHT BOX

What *is* service? How do you measure it? What should you do about a situation in which you are not getting the service you think you should?

I will tell you how I define service: the right book in the right box, delivered in a timely fashion and sold at a competitive price. Add to that a competent and responsive customer service staff and the flexibility to accommodate special requirements, and we arrive at a pretty simple definition.

What is not so simple is what it takes to get that book into that box and to your library. Each vendor must develop and maintain a complex system of buying, warehousing, and shipping books, as well as training and retaining knowledgeable and dedicated people. Effective sales reps and marketing staff are required, as well as technical support, research and development specialists, finance and accounting departments, data processing divisions, and human resources managers.

Consider the process from the beginning. Most often a library starts using a vendor as a result of a visit to the library by the vendor's sales representative. Ideally, the representative has been able to make a convincing case for using his or her company's services. Ideally the vendor representative listens to your needs and wants, then describes how he or she can respond to them. He or she should know what the company can and cannot do and give you an honest assessment of how well your needs will be met, if indeed you do give this firm a try. The representative should come well prepared, both because it's not in the company's interest to waste your time, and because it's costing the company money for him or her to be there in the first place. The plane fare, car rental, hotel bills, and meals all add up.

Your order will likely either be printed as a purchase order and mailed to the vendor (perhaps in postage-paid envelopes supplied by the company, another cost) or transmitted electronically. If it's a printed order, the vendor will receive your mailed envelope and will route the order to the order entry department. These staff must do two things: follow instructions about how your order is to be handled and locate the correct title in the company's database. Do you use a purchase order number for each title? Is this number to be printed on status reports and invoices? Then this too must be captured in the vendor's online system—and entered correctly. Making sure that the correct edition of the correct title is ordered is crucial—anything entered incorrectly here will carry through as an error all the way in this process.

If you order electronically, odds are that most of the orders will be entered directly into the vendor's system. Not every order will match—some titles may be new to the vendor's files, or the ISBN or title doesn't match exactly. These details may require research before the order is added.

Electronic ordering presupposes the vendor has developed the capability for such ordering in the first place and supports the necessary data processing infrastructure to receive such orders. There's a cost to this, too.

The aforementioned also presupposes the creation and maintenance of a bibliographic database. This file will likely include information on publishers, e.g., does the publisher receive orders electronically? If not, to what address are orders sent?

If the vendor maintains an inventory (and not all do, despite claims to the contrary), this system will first check to see whether an unallocated copy is available. If so, the system will link your order to that book and initiate the process of picking and invoicing. If the vendor doesn't have stock on hand, an order to the publisher must be raised.

If the order is filled promptly, books are received and matched up with outstanding orders. If the order is not filled quickly, the vendor claims from the publisher. Some publishers respond quickly and accurately to claims, some do not. The vendor must also decide whether information furnished by publishers is correct or not. If the response to the order is "not yet published" (NYP), "out of stock" (OS), or "out of stock indefinitely" (OSI), the vendor will generate a status report and send it to the library. This is done to keep you up-to-date on the status of the order and to forestall your claim to the vendor.

The process of receiving shipments from publishers can be complex. Vendors order in advance of publication to obtain new books as close to their publication dates as possible. An initial order includes the number of copies needed to satisfy standing order customers (assuming the book is in a series); the number of copies needed to satisfy approval accounts; and the quantity the vendors' buyers have targeted for inventory. Additionally, orders received from libraries are added to the purchase order we dispatch to the publisher. The process of receiving is similar to order entry in that an error at receiving will carry through everything that follows.

Once books have been received, the system links them to outstanding orders. Books must be shelved in such a way that they can be readily located and retrieved. Staff then assemble all books for a given account, generate an invoice, pack the box, and ship the cartons to the customer.

If, indeed, something did go wrong along the way—the wrong book got in the right box, or the invoice was left out, or something was incorrect on the invoice—the library can call customer service.

CUSTOMER SERVICE: ARE YOU BEING SERVED?

If your vendor is good, the company has long ago recognized the important role played by the customer service staff. Hence, it has devoted the appropriate resources to hiring, training, and keeping personable, effective customer service representatives. There are several basic rules that define customer service:

Does the company assign a specific representative for your account?

Can you reach this person quickly and easily?

When you do reach him or her, does that person know what he or she is talking about?

Does the representative do what he or she says? Given the complex nature of vendors' systems described above, if the vendor representatives do not understand the system or can't describe its capabilities effectively, who will? What does high turnover of staff tell you about a firm?

Sales representatives depend on customer service people for a lot, too. A representative's principal in-house contacts are usually the customer service representatives who handle the territories that are covered. It takes a remarkable person to fill this kind of role. In essence, customer service is dealing with problems—all day, every day. Few customers of any business call to say "Things are great!" or "Everything is fine!", although it does happen, and it is pleasing when it does.

When the library makes a telephone call or sends an e-mail, does the company respond quickly and to your satisfaction? Ideally, yes—but again, to do so requires two things: the company must value your business enough to absorb the cost of having that easy access to customer service in the first place, and must make a commitment to accepting returns, issuing replacement invoices, or crediting the return postage for a misdirected shipment. All of this carries a cost for the vendor, and if it is truly customer-oriented it will do this as normal operating procedure. If, on the other hand, the company is simply conceding to current management-babble about "empowerment," "TQM," or "proactive engagement" but in the end doesn't adequately address the library's problem, it's time to go shopping for a new vendor.

BEYOND THE BASICS: SHELF-READY OR NOT?

One of the most profound changes affecting the academic library market today is the increasing demand for shelf-ready books. The outsourcing of many traditional technical services functions to vendors is both a practical necessity for a growing number of libraries and a logical extension of vendor services in the first place.

One can argue, for example, that approval plans are simply a way of outsourcing certain pre-selection functions. What is a new and radical idea to one market sector may be a long-established practice for another: school libraries have been outsourcing processing and cataloging for decades. But there is no disputing that the requirements of major academic libraries pose considerable challenges to those libraries and the vendors serving their needs when the subject of shelf-ready books comes up.

Let us look at what shelf-ready involves, and what it doesn't. Generally most ARL libraries evaluating the concept do so with a primary assumption that the process will address English-language material only, and very likely only current imprints at that. While it is possible to establish arrangements for the delivery of processed foreign-language books accompanied by corresponding files of machine-readable data, such arrangements are atypical. Budget constraints and increased reliance on approval plans tend to translate into a concentration on recent imprints; even the largest research libraries lack the resources to undertake sustained retrospective collection development projects, and acquisition of non-English titles by U.S. libraries has been in decline for several years. There are three areas in outsourcing where libraries and vendors interact closely: processing, machine-readable data, and vendor interface with the bibliographic utility.

Processing is perhaps the most prosaic function of the three. Much of the processing that a library used to do to books locally is now done by a vendor. The library gives the vendor very specific instructions about what to do, and the vendor follows through. Processing can include property-stamping books, inserting security targets, and attaching bar codes and spine labels.

Providing corresponding machine-readable records is the second area of outsourcing. These records can serve several purposes. For books shipped on approval (or, if the library is using a selection profile to deliver preprocessed books for the collection, books shipped as "keepers"), there will presumably be no record resident in the acquisitions module of the library's integrated library system, unlike the situation with a firm order. The ability to receive a vendor-supplied record eliminates the need to create or download one for order-level and processing functions.

The third area of outsourcing is the interface between the book vendor and the library's bibliographic utility. If the library has decided to contract the delivery of newly published books in shelf-ready form to a vendor, and has thereby established an agreement whereby it commits to "mark and park" at least some definable percentage of current acquisitions, then having the vendor provide data to update holdings information in the utility's database is a natural sequence to this process.

Vendors are still working to identify the pragmatic boundaries of this dimension of outsourcing. Because vendors handle books, there is an opportunity to perform certain logical steps that until recently were not assigned to vendors: if CIP-level records can be upgraded to full LC standards, other non-LC source records can also be upgraded to full LC standards (e.g., UK MARC). If vendors can perform original cataloging for books lacking any source record, they may also then be presumed to upgrade and enrich records with additional data elements, such as tables of contents and author-affiliation information.

Beyond this is the emerging realm of vendor-supported Web-based products and services. Increasingly the *lingua franca* of library-vendor interchange is assumed to be Z39.50, and most major bookdealers and serials agents have either introduced interactive Web-based serials, approval, or firm order products, or are in the process of developing them.

The combination of traditional book vendor services (the right book in the right box) and the delivery of processed books with machine-readable data and ancillary services is likely to redefine library-vendor relations in some very fundamental ways. For one thing, it challenges the traditional "I don't want all my eggs in one basket" philosophy; such arrangements inherently favor consolidation, as noted earlier. Also, the infrastructure needed to support these capabilities compels vendors to invest in new or expanded technical services operations. This both enhances the range of vendor offerings and influences fixed and variable costs. The good news is: vendors with sufficient capability and capacity will re-bundle traditional products and services in new and innovative ways. The bad news is: vendors who haven't reinvested profits wisely or who lack adequate capitalization are likely to go out of business.

THE DISMAL SCIENCE—
OR, LET'S DO THE NUMBERS

As a vendor, I suspect my experience has not been unusual. What drew me to the book trade was a love of books and a fascination with publishing; what in practice defines (at least in part) my professional life is a quiet but unrelenting obligation to the bottom line. Vendors are in business to make money. Most vendors seek to do so by achieving a balance between the obligation to treat employees and clients equitably on the one hand, and to turn an honest profit on the other. Thus we come to that dreaded bottom line—and it had best *be* dreaded, if one wants to stay in business. Bookselling is a low-margin business, and it's all too easy to drift over the line to nonprofit status without the attendant benefits.

There are three basic concepts at work here: cash flow, revenue stream, and gross margin. Cash flow simply means that vendors need money coming in on an ongoing basis to keep the business afloat. To do so, the company must offer libraries something compelling that makes it worthwhile to send in orders. At any given moment vendors have money tied up in inventory, in receivables, in fixed and variable costs, and possibly in interest or debt payments. Herein lies a major difference between the book and periodicals industries. The library pays the journal agents up front, so the journal agent knows (at least for the forthcoming year) what the customer base and ready cash will be. Book vendors guess at what libraries will do week to week for the year ahead, but it is an informed guess at best, unless the library has prepaid or established a deposit account.

Another way to look at cash flow is this: imagine that every library decides, for whatever reason, to stop sending Acme Library Service orders for the next few months. Instead, they'll order from Direct Express Fulfillment. Acme still has to pay employees, pay publishers, pay the electric bill, and keep the computers humming, even if no orders are coming in. If Acme has sufficient cash on hand, they'll weather this and still be in business. But if they do not, lack of money will lead to bankruptcy.

Cash flow can be viewed as a constant necessity; the revenue stream defines a longer-term strategic goal—to make money. It is all well and good to be able to have enough cash on hand to meet one's immediate financial obligations, but the primary reason people launch businesses in the first place is to earn a profit.

Companies achieve profits with capable management and through the development, marketing, and sustained delivery of competitive products and services. Sometimes businesses are able to dominate their industry sectors, enabling them to set pricing, outmaneuver competitors, and generally define the rules by which the game is played. This may result from innovative product development and the ability to reap the benefits of patents or other fruits of their research and development efforts. Or, dominant market share may result from genuinely good service. In any event, companies with such power can often protect their margins and thus sustain a satisfactory revenue stream. Examples of such companies can be found in the high tech arena: Intel and Microsoft.

In other industries no single company dominates. For example, in recent years there has been a move to upscale supermarkets, catering to people who are looking for greater selection of products and are willing to pay more to find it. Still, a grocery store is a grocery store, and although location and product niche may provide some differentiation, these businesses still compete largely on price. No single chain really controls the market, and each company must pay attention to the behavior of their competitors.

To academic libraries, book vendors still resemble Kroger's more than they do Hewlett-Packard. None possess something so unique that any can control the market, and all vendors are market-driven to the extent that they must pay attention to what services and discounts our competitors are offering. However, library material vendors represent an industry in transition. Technology is providing a medium whereby truly unique services *can* be developed and introduced to the market, and a greater degree of differentiation can be achieved. It is likely that we will see a substantial redefinition of vendors in the next few years.

Up to a point, profit is a choice: a company can elect to distribute profits to shareholders, or to reinvest in new products or services, or both. For publicly traded companies, dividends may be expected by shareholders, and management may be wary of facing unhappy investors at annual meetings if performance doesn't meet expectations. In the vendor industry, as noted above, virtually all companies are privately held, which means it is up to the owners to decide whether they want to take profits (if there are any to be had) or plow the money back into the business. An owner might decide to forego profits if she thinks maintaining more competitive discounts will pay off in the long run, for example, or a vendor might feel he has no choice but to keep all money invested in the shop just to stay afloat.

Even if a vendor cannot dominate its sector or provide a unique product, it can still succeed, if it manages its business well. Success is the basis for a short discussion of gross margins. Simply stated, gross margin is the difference between what the vendor pays for a book and what he sells it for. What is in between defines a lot about the long-term success or failure of a bookseller.

First of all, vendors must buy the books from publishers. They get a discount (see figure 5-1 for some representative discount schedules for different kinds of publishers) off list price. Vendors then sell to libraries at a (lower) discount. Then they factor in what it costs them to accomplish all this wizardry and subtract said costs from said gross margin.

Vendor discounts are also influenced by order quantity, i.e., the more copies ordered, the higher the discount received. Hence the

Scott Alan Smith

Type of publisher	Trade list	Non-trade
University press	30%-35%	10%-33%
Trade publisher	25%-40%	20%-32%
STM publisher	20%-35%	15%-32%
Reference publisher	5%-40%	0%-20%
Societies and associations	0%-10%	0%-5%

Figure 5-1 Common Discounts Available to Vendors

chart shown above can be refined by showing discount A for 1 to 24 copies, discount B for 25 to 99, discount C for 100+, and so on. It is not unusual for larger presses to have separate discount schedules for different categories or imprints. Their trade list carries one schedule, their reference list another, their professional list another still.

Let us look at two examples. In our first example the book is a trade novel with a list price of $19.95. The publisher gives a high discount, 48 percent, or $9.58 off the list. Hence our cost for this book is $10.37. The second example is a sci-tech title with a list price of $90.00. The publisher offers a 33 percent discount, so the vendor cost is $60.30.

What will the vendor sell these books for? The library will either have a sliding scale or a flat discount. For the purposes of this exercise, let us say the library has negotiated a flat 12 percent discount in return for a commitment to spend a certain amount with the vendor each year. The first book yields a gross margin of $7.19. That's the list price less 12 percent, representing what the vendor sells the book for, less the list price, less 48 percent—what was paid for the book. The second book yields a gross margin of $18.90. Again, this is the list price less library discount, less the list price, less 33 percent.

In between the cost of the book and what the vendor sells it for are a number of basic costs, which are divided into fixed and variable costs. Fixed costs are costs that are relatively constant regardless of the number of books handled: salaries and wages for full-time staff, warehouse maintenance or rental, data processing infrastructure, utilities, marketing. Variable costs include invoice stationery, shipping cartons and packing materials, and other expenses that increase or decrease in relation to the volume of business.

Some expenses must be incurred. For example, the vendor has to hire order entry clerks and people to pack and ship books. Other costs are sustained by choice: which library conventions to attend, where to advertise, how much to spend on direct mail or other marketing projects.

Once the vendor subtracts fixed and variable expenses from gross margin, it arrives at pre-tax profit (assuming there's something left). The vendor must pay taxes, and what is left over is available for distribution to owners or shareholders, or for reinvestment in the business.

Back to the examples: if the sum total of the vendor's fixed and variable costs works out to $7.00 a book, then whatever is earned beyond that is pre-tax profit. In the first example, there was a gross margin of $7.19. The sum of $7.19 less $7.00 leaves $0.19 as pre-tax profit.

The sci-tech book, on the other hand, earned $11.90. After the vendor subtracts fixed and variable expenses and pays taxes, it has left, on average, between $.50 and $1.25 per book as clear profit. This should also serve to illustrate the importance of order mix. In effect the latter example helps subsidize the cost of delivering the former.

Another way to look at this is as follows: out of every dollar libraries pay vendors, $.80 is the cost of the book. This is spent before the vendor even begins to look at anything else. Only twenty cents per dollar is left to cover expenses, pay taxes, and make some profit.

In an effort to ensure there *is* something left at the end of the process, vendors forecast, budget, and manage every stage of the company's financial life. If the company husbands these resources well and plans wisely, the company prospers. If it fails to take account of changes in the market or does not control costs effectively, it loses money and possibly goes out of business.

Typically the sales staff develops a forecast for the year ahead, predicting how much business will be done. Anticipated gains and losses are calculated for each sales territory, and the numbers are added up to provide a total. Each department develops a budget for the year ahead, taking into account routine expenses (salaries and wages, travel and entertainment, conventions) and any planned capital expenditures (new laptops for the sales force, for example). Management then considers all requests and makes decisions about where to allocate resources, and where to defer major expenses. How well these decisions are made has an enormous effect on the company's financial well-being.

Scott Alan Smith

BIDS, CONTRACTS, AND NEGOTIATIONS: RIGHTS AND RESPONSIBILITIES

Increasingly the relationship between materials vendors and their library customers is being defined by legal bids and contractual agreements. This marks a departure from the more informal nature that's characterized these relationships for several years, but it is not necessarily a bad thing. Having a well-documented process of vendor evaluation and selection provides more scientific rationale for vendor assignment, and may well serve to reaffirm long-standing library-vendor relationships that predate this trend.

For more and more libraries, state or municipal purchasing requirements mean this more formalized relationship is a fact of life. As long as the process is controlled by librarians and can benefit from their knowledge of the market and their informed sense of what features are of greater or lesser importance to the objectives of getting books and periodicals into the library in an efficient and cost-effective way, there is little cause to worry. If the process is under the direction of purchasing agents or university legal staff who may view books as products no different than desks or computers, there may be trouble for the vendor. Every book is a unique product (unlike, say, paper clips), and the skill and infrastructure needed to deliver the right book in the right box are not always immediately evident to non-library personnel.

Bids and contracts provide some very useful functions. A bid describes the library's needs in a formal and framed structure. The vendor responses describe their capabilities in a comparable format. Ideally there should be no ambiguity about the rights and responsibilities of all parties involved. As outsourcing and systems interfaces become more common, the products and services in question become more complex. Hence by having a formal structure in place for stating requirements and examining responses, a library is better able to define the scope of what's being bid in the first place. Consequently the evaluation and selection of a vendor or vendors can be done using comparable criteria. Ideally this ensures fair treatment of all participating vendors.

Regardless of whether your library bids for such services, a critical aspect of vendor-library relations is communication. If a library is not satisfied with its current supplier, it must tell the vendor about it. Vendors have toll-free numbers for many reasons, including giving libraries the opportunity to complain. Vendors should take complaints willingly (and ideally, politely), and try to correct the problem. If cartons are routinely being damaged in shipment, the vendor will very likely opt to ship using a different method.

As another example, a library may still print purchase orders and mail them to the vendor. If the library thinks the vendor's service is slow, the library needs to communicate this to the vendor, who should look at every step in the process and may discover a problem that can be readily resolved. The vendor may compare the date on the purchase order to the postmark on the envelope and discover a significant gap; the library may think its mail is being dispatched quickly from its parent organization, but may discover that packages sit around for a week or more. If a library has a problem, it needs to be vocal about it. Furnish examples. Vendors can respond much more effectively when they have a record of what did or did not happen with a given transaction. Give the vendor a fair chance to remedy the situation. If he does, the library is set. If he does not or cannot—and your expectations are realistic—then it might be time to shop for a new vendor.

It is important to acknowledge that libraries, as customers, are entitled to some basic rights and privileges—and so is the vendor. As a customer, the library has some obligations, too.

6

Vendor Selection: Service, Cost, and More Service!

MARY K. McLAREN

Vendors, publishers, patrons, librarians,
Paperbacks, hardbacks, software, cybrarians;
AVs, serials, access, delivery,
Make my work exciting, but shivery!

Reminiscent of old jump-rope jingles from my childhood, these terms tumble along in my consciousness, intertwining the activities that are so real in my life's work today.

Let us step back for a minute and take stock of acquisitions, the business we're in. What is it really about, and what is our everyday work really about? By definition, we are acquirers. Our common mission is to acquire, or provide the means for our clientele to acquire, the information they need or desire. Librarianship in general is a service role, and ours, as acquisitions librarians, is no different. We serve to provide for the needs of our own institution, our patrons or customers, and the scholarly community at large, both present and future.

What about the role of the library materials vendors? They are also cast in a service role, although with a profit mission underlying their work. Their goal is to successfully serve the needs of their customers—publishers, producers, and libraries alike—as well as their parent organizations. They, too, must provide for the needs of today while simultaneously planning and preparing for the needs of the future.

What do vendors and librarians have in common? To varying degrees, the library and the vendor are dependent upon each other. To varying degrees, each can help the other achieve its mission, its role. This is no easy job for either player, but through honest, open communication, mutual cooperation, and a shared service orientation, both players can achieve success. Service is the concept at the core of what we are each about, and service can appear in many forms.

BENEFITS OF VENDOR USE

Libraries partner with library suppliers in order to benefit from the vendors' technological, physical, and personnel resources, their pre-established connections with publishers and producers, and their expertise as buying agents. Ideally, these agents facilitate the procurement of materials, or access to materials, in a timely and cost-effective manner. Fiscal benefits to the library include both direct and indirect savings. Direct savings are realized by discounts offered on the cost of some materials, usually firm order, approval, or standing order monographs. Indirect savings appear in the form of reduced library staff time that is required to identify, verify, order, claim, and pay for materials. Compatibility between the vendor's and the library's technological resources can drastically improve a library's workflow procedures, thus reducing the amount of required in-house staff time. Fulfillment time savings are made possible by the functionality of the vendor's online database, the vendor's electronic communication capability with publishers, its personal arrangements and staff contacts with producers, its internal efficiencies, its warehousing capabilities, and its delivery mechanisms.

DEFINING AND COMMUNICATING NEEDS

First and foremost, it is essential for every organization and the departments that function therein to understand and agree upon the organization's basic role or mission. It is then up to the staff who work within these units to explore and define those needs which must be met in order for them to fulfill that role successfully. It follows then that both the role and the needs must be clearly articulated so that a common understanding can be shared by every person who works in, or who works with, that unit.

Institutional and departmental roles are not static. What may have been of prime importance at one time may be less so at another point in time. An example of this is the shift we have been experiencing over the past decade regarding the importance of predictive use vs. immediate use of our libraries' collections. The current phrases "just in case vs. just in time" capture the fundamental paradigm shift which has set our professional foundation rocking. Changing economic realities, institutional priorities, technological capabilities, and business management philosophies all bear directly on a library's priorities and needs.

It is important to understand that all libraries will not experience the same needs and priorities as all other libraries, even within a given time frame. What may be of high importance to one library may be of low importance to another. The importance of services offered by library materials vendors fall into this conundrum of variance. Based upon its own individual needs, each library must evaluate the wide array of services available and then decide which of these are required, which are desired, and at what cost.

It should also be kept in mind that the importance or value a library places on specific services will undoubtedly vary according to the circumstances of the time. The results of a research project undertaken in 1995 by the National Acquisitions Group in the United Kingdom illustrate how some libraries' perceived importance of specific vendor-supplied services changed when the libraries were faced with the probability that new or increased costs for these services might be introduced. The study listed and described services currently provided by library suppliers. These services were accompanied by vendor-supplied cost data that offered a basis for calculating estimations of the costs of replacing the services if they were no longer supplied in the present manner. Public library authorities, along with select academic and special libraries, were asked to rank the value they currently placed on each of these services and were also asked to rank their value if "radical change" occurred. The radical change referred to was the anticipated, and later actual, demise of the Net Book Agreement (NBA) and the related Library License. The collapse of the NBA introduced a basic shift in the library/library supplier relationship in that country. In the new environment, competitive pricing or discounting would be allowed, thus adding it to the service factors which, in the past, had primarily set library suppliers apart. The study pinpointed perceptions of what should be classified as "added value" and what should be "normal suppliers' costs" related to marketing their services. It offered preliminary forecasts of what library authorities will continue to require on a fully costed "buy back" basis and predicted potential growth in demand for additional services.[1] The prospect of balancing potential price discounts with potential charges for services forced these European libraries to examine and evaluate their priorities in a new light. So too will every library need to occasionally reexamine its own priorities in light of its own changing circumstances.

VENDOR IDENTIFICATION

How can a library learn about the services offered by various agents? A first step would be to consult general directories, such as *Literary Market Place, International Literary Market Place*, and *International Subscription Agents*, or specialized directories, such as *Book and Serial Vendors for Asia and the Pacific, Book and Serial Vendors for Africa and the Middle East* (the first two volumes in the ALCTS Foreign Book and Serials Vendors Directories series). Listings of general and specialized vendor identification guides can be found in Miller's *Managing Acquisitions and Vendor Relations*.[2] A guide to commercial document delivery vendors is included in Walters' article on document delivery vendor selection criteria.[3]

Participation in electronic discussion groups such as ACQNET and SERIALST, accessing the acquisitions and collection development Web site, ACQWEB, consultation with colleagues, and attendance at conference exhibits are other ways to learn about vendors. Logging into a vendor's Web site affords a convenient overview of that agency. Subsequent personal contact with the vendor will assure the most comprehensive and accurate information possible. It is through these initial and subsequent personal contacts that the crucial step of library/library supplier communication will commence.

INFORMATION GATHERING

Some institutions may be required by law to put their business with vendors who have been designated by state or institutional agreements as the result of bid contracts. Others may be limited to doing business with only those vendors who have been pre-approved by a governing body. Most others, however, enjoy the freedom to evaluate and choose from the full complement of available agencies.

As with any successful relationship, clear and honest communication is essential. The library must understand and state at the outset its needs, requirements, and expectations. The agent must likewise clearly state its capabilities and limitations, its costs, and options available for both its basic services and its supplementary added-value services.

Information gathering can proceed along either formal or informal processes. Formal procedures might include the issuance of governmental or institutional requests for proposals (RFPs) or self-designed RFP or RFP-like questionnaires. Regardless of the issuing body, a good document will involve a number of library staff in the process, from the design of the instrument through the collection and evaluation of the criteria. Examples of RFPs can be found in Wilkinson and Thorson's report on the University of New Mexico General Library's RFP process and in the Hirshon and Winters outsourcing guide.[4] The State University of New York at Stony Brook's "Vendor Service Expectations and Questions" document included in a 1997 ARL SPEC Kit clearly presents the library's expectations in tandem with its questions.[5]

Although RFP documents are sometimes confusing because of the inclusion of legal jargon and the time commitments required by both the issuer and the respondents, librarians and vendors generally agree that this method is a valuable tool to be used in vendor selection. Such a process sets the stage for fair competition, affording each agent an equal opportunity for consideration. Libraries stand to learn about previously unknown vendors and also about services of which they had been unaware, sometime even from vendors with whom they currently are doing business. Responsibility for the examination and comparison of the policies, procedures, terms, capabilities, and limitations presented in the responses should be shared by both the technical and professional library staff. Specific terms proposed in the responses can be accepted as submitted or they can be further negotiated, as appropriate.

Due to tight staffing levels, time constraints, limited business expectations, and other factors, libraries may opt to use more informal methods of inquiry. Vendor-supplied materials, personal conversations with company representatives, and written communication can all play a role in the development of an informal service agreement.

SELECTION CRITERIA

There are a number of published guidelines and articles available advising librarians of criteria to consider when deciding whether or not to employ the use of service agents. Exhaustive criteria can be found in the "how-to" manuals by Miller and Basch, pamphlets within the ALCTS Acquisitions Guidelines series, and other sources included in this article's bibliography. I would, however, like to offer this brief list of qualitative and quantitative components of vendor attributes for consideration during the selection process.

Fulfillment Ability

Specialization (subject, format, geographic origin, source, e.g., small presses, societies, government agencies); scope of formats able to supply (print, electronic, microform, AV, monographs, serials, periodicals, newspapers, licensed materials, in-print, out-of-print); scope of purchase plans (firm orders, standing orders, approval plans, subscriptions, memberships, back issues, document delivery, license agreements); primary library clientele (academic, research, special, school, public).

Customer Service

Knowledgeable staff; service-oriented staff; adequate number of staff; commitment to prompt problem resolution; designated account representative; sales representative; company produced newsletters; communication options (e-mail, WWW, FAX, toll-free telephone number, mail); customization options provided to meet the individual library's needs (order submission, invoice frequency and format, status reports, claims submission, cancellations, rush requests, shipment schedules); returns policies and procedures; responses to claims; delivery methods.

Pricing

Discount plan (flat fee, sliding scale, net, cost plus); discount terms; order mix requirements; service charge plan (flat fee, title by title, cap on charges, unbundled); service charge terms; postage, handling; payment terms (designated time, early payment credit, late payment fee); payment options (partial payments, instant credit memos); end-of-the-year allowances or exceptions; supplemental charges; foreign currency exchange; charges for optional services.[6]

Speed

Prompt placement of orders; timely renewals; adequate and knowledgeable staff; efficient procedures; ability to receive orders electronically; connectivity to publishers and producers; local inventory; geographic location; use of standard identifiers (ISBN, ISSN).

Management Issues

Financial condition of the company; ownership and control; service orientation; quality control procedures; management philosophy; business practices; experience; reputation; references; company persona; commitment to and participation in the library profession (work toward the development and adoption of standards, involvement in national/international projects, participation at library conferences, publication in professional literature).[7]

Automation

Availability of an automated system; ease of use; hardware/software required to use system; connectivity options (Internet, WWW, phone line); hours of operation; interfaces with library systems; interfaces with publishers' systems for transmission of order and dispatch information; interfaces with bibliographic utilities or electronic products (e.g., *Books in Print* products); variety of system features (online database, inventory status, order transmission, claims transmission, electronic funds transfer, secure transmissions, status reports transmission, message capability, payment data, dispatch data, management data, management reports); graphics, spreadsheet applications; use of and adherence to national and international standards (e.g., X12, EDIFACT); system use of non-proprietary code.

Special Services (Some offered at extra optional cost)

New products announcements; current awareness services (personalized electronic notification utilizing PUSH or PULL technologies, electronic listings); prepared bibliographies; customized management reports; printed catalogs; tables of contents; book reviews; provision of sample/missing copies; retrospective conversion records and assistance; assistance with subscription or standing order transfers; serials check-in; technical processing (providing local, LC, or bibliographical utility cataloging records); physical processing (prebinding, jacket covers, labels, security devices, barcodes, pockets, cards); shelf-ready options for partial or complete accounts.

COST/BENEFIT CONSIDERATIONS

As was stated earlier in the chapter, cost considerations are of considerable importance when deliberating the use and selection of vendors. Direct costs and cost savings as well as indirect costs and cost savings all need to be identified, calculated, and analyzed. Indirect costs and cost savings, however, are neither as apparent nor as straightforward as the direct costs.

Morris, Rebarcak, and Rowley report on a study of staff costs involved in monograph purchases at Iowa State University (ISU) between 1990 and 1995. Also including cataloging cost comparisons, they contend that the ISU time/cost study substantiates the benefits to the library of cost analysis. [8]

Hirshon and Winters provide a model spreadsheet which could be used to calculate both in-house and outsourced expenses for selected processing procedures.[9] Their spreadsheet includes indirect costs such as space, telephones, computer expenses, and supervision, which may sometimes be taken for granted or overlooked. Their model can be adapted to gather comparison data for any vendor-supplied service under consideration.

Reports from the 1993 NASIG Conference include results of two studies which compared direct costs realized by multiple libraries which used various vendors. The first study, conducted by Heather Miller at SUNY Albany, was designed to determine whether or not libraries pay different base prices for the same book in a monographic series. The results showed that the base price did vary and that different vendors charged different prices.[10] The second study, conducted by Michele Crump at the University of Florida, compared prices and service charges paid for periodical subscriptions included in the Aqueduct Benchmark study. Her findings concluded that, "librarians were making good choices and that vendors billed within the same range."[11]

Addressing direct costs, Barker suggests that librarians are not always aware of the true savings or expenditures which are realized by their financial terms. He advises the library to examine both its discounts and its service charges in cost/benefit models. His data plainly demonstrate the effects that various discount and service charge rates have on the University of California, Berkeley, library's monograph and serials accounts.[12]

WEIGHING THE VARIABLES

Once the library has gathered all the pertinent information, the next step, evaluation, begins. Assuming that all those who are to be involved in the evaluation process agree on the needs and priorities of the library, they must now come to an agreement on the importance of the criteria to be compared. Ray contends that vendor impact is increasingly broad-based and because of that, input and representation from all these bases need to be considered and incorporated into the process.[13] Participation should include staff from all units that will be impacted by the final decision. These might include cataloging, reference, and electronic support staff, in addition to the prescribed acquisitions and collection development staff. Faculty liaisons or the faculty at large may be invited to attend vendor presentations and to submit their recommendations.

Along with the input from the varying camps must come consensus on the importance or weight of each criterion. Whereas cost may be the prime consideration in the opinion of some, fulfillment or speed may be more important to others. Customer service conditions may be of the utmost importance to a staff which is seeing its numbers decline. The availability of management data will be important for some, while others will consider the availability and ease of use of a vendor's online database as their top priority.

The goals and values of the institution, in conjunction with the actual realities of the local situation, should be the final determinants of the assigned weights. Various weighting methodologies have been designed to meet specific needs; examples of such can be found in the writings of Davis, Bachmann-Derthick and Moran, and Anderson.[14]

Technical, professional, and administrative staff should all be included in the evaluative processes leading up to the formulation of the final recommendation. The ultimate decision will be made or approved by the person or unit that has been accorded that authority by the library.

CONSOLIDATION QUESTION

If a library decides that it is in its best interest to employ the services of a materials supplier, it must decide on the number of suppliers to contract with. Depending upon the variety and nature of the materials needed, several different suppliers may be required. However, if more than one vendor seems comparable for a given segment of business in terms of service, cost, and services offered, then the library must decide whether to consolidate its business with one vendor or to offer its business to more than one.

The debate over the advisability of consolidation is long-standing. Proponents extol the financial benefits realized by higher discounts/lower service charges which most vendors will offer in response to larger volumes of business. Libraries wishing to capitalize on this might increase their purchasing potential by bundling their approval plans, firm orders, and standing orders with a single vendor. Libraries within system organizations or consortia might consolidate orders from their branch or member libraries with one vendor.[15]

Another advantage of consolidation relates to the efficiencies made possible by use of the vendor's technology. Interfacing the library's system or resources with those of a vendor is not always a straightforward or an easy matter. Significant troubleshooting or programming time is sometimes required on the part of the library, the vendor, or both in order to achieve satisfactory communication. It would not be reasonable, therefore, for the library to require complicated or costly interfaces with a significant number of vendors.

Tied to the technical requirements of automation are related personnel issues. Staff training and internal workflow and processing procedures are influenced by the technology in use. Consideration must be given to the amount of time that would be required for staff to become proficient in the use of multiple vendor technologies and knowledgeable of the policies and procedures required by each. Standardization of staff training and consistent procedures are more easily achieved through the use of one or a limited number of vendors.

One further benefit of consolidation which should be mentioned is the value of management data supplied by the vendors to the libraries. The value of this data is most likely commensurate with the proportion of the budget or volume of library activity to which it applies.

The lingering arguments on the opposing side of the consolidation issue are those related to service concerns and vendor viability. Competition has been considered to be the "carrot," or that which keeps the vendor on its toes when dealing with the library. Some feel that the library's business will not be taken for granted if the vendor knows that other agencies also have their feet in the library's door. A false feeling of security may result from such a perception.

Other considerations favoring the distribution of business among multiple vendors include the distrust of "putting all your eggs in one basket." Concerns about vendor viability are valid, although they could be eased somewhat by the library's monitoring of the financial conditions of its business partners. The decision to distribute business beyond a single vendor also helps to keep a viable number of agents in operation. This serves the interest of not only the vendors but ultimately the library community, by assuring product development and competition through the continued presence of a mix of vendors within the marketplace.

Anderson cites monetary advantage, convenience, increased clout, and the ease of future vendor changes if desired as factors favoring consolidation. She counters the opposition's customer service concern with this concluding thought: "Along the lines of the old adage, 'The customer is always right,' it's also true that the larger the customer, the more right they are likely to be."[16]

THE FINAL STEPS

Once the library has reached a unified agreement on its service needs, requirements, and expectations; has gathered and evaluated vendor information; has established weighted values; and has reached a decision on the consolidation issue, it is ready to finalize the business agreement. This agreement can take many forms. Legal contracts, signed memoranda of agreement, standard form letters, or even personal letters or e-mail may suffice.

If a legal contract is to be issued, the terms may be mandated by the bid or RFP process. If this is not the case, then negotiation may enter into the picture. Two sources that may be helpful to librarians preparing for negotiation are the lessons published in *American Libraries* explaining the principles of negotiation and the recorded role play presented at the 1997 ALA Conference which depicts unsuccessful and successful negotiation sessions.[17]

Before beginning any negotiation procedures, the library representatives must understand the dynamics of the agency's business. They should be knowledgeable about the factors that influence the agency's costs, its revenues, and its profit objectives.[18] Basch and McQueen summarize that negotiation has two objectives: "to reach the best possible service and pricing agreement and to clarify service requirements and commitments."[19]

It is suggested here that knowledge of the services to be contracted, clearly articulated requirements and definitions of terms, realistic expectations, consideration of multiple viewpoints, honesty, and a commitment to meet the needs of all parties involved are essential to a successful negotiation. These same attributes are needed to promote and sustain the business relationship after the service has begun.

As the introductory jingle suggests, we have progressed from a loose cacophony of terms to the advent of a newly established business partnership. Though still somewhat of a jumble, and on some days quite "shivery," the components of acquisitions take on a more manageable face. It is through the combined efforts of library and vendor staff together, each striving to produce the best possible service, that we ultimately progress toward our respective goals.

Notes

1. National Acquisitions Group, *The Value to Libraries of Special Services Provided by Library Suppliers: Developing a Costing Model* (Leeds: National Acquisitions Group, 1996).

2. Heather Swan Miller, *Managing Acquisitions and Vendor Relations: A How-to-Do-It Manual* (New York: Neal-Schuman, 1992), pp. 171-174.

3. Sheila Walters, "Commercial Document Delivery: Vendor Selection Criteria," *Computers in Libraries* 14 (October 1994): 15.

4. Frances C. Wilkinson and Connie Capers Thorson, "The RFP Process: Rational, Educational, Necessary; or, There Ain't No Such Thing as a Free Lunch," *Library Acquisitions: Practice & Theory* 19 (1995): 251-268. Arnold Hirshon and Barbara Winters, *Outsourcing Library Technical Services: A How-to-Do-It Manual for Librarians* (New York: Neal-Schuman, 1996), pp. 59-133.

5. Susan Flood, comp., *Evolution and Status of Approval Plans,* SPEC Kit 221 (Washington, D.C.: Association of Research Libraries, Office of Management Services, 1997), pp. 29-46.

6. Joseph W. Barker, "Unbundling Serials Vendors' Service Charges: Are We Ready?" *Serials Review* 16, no. 2 (1990): 33-43.

7. Kathleen Born, "Strategies for Selecting Vendors and Evaluating Their Performance—from the Vendor's Perspective," *Journal of Library Administration* 16, no. 3 (1992): 115-116.

8. Dilys E. Morris, Pamela A. Rebarcak, and Gordon Rowley, "Monographs Acquisitions: Staffing Costs and the Impact of Automation," *Library Resources & Technical Services* 40 (1996): 301-318.

9. Hirshon and Winters, *Outsourcing Library Technical Services,* pp. 46-47.

10. Heather S. Miller and Michele J. Crump, "Vendor Choice: Does It Really Make a Difference?" *Serials Librarian* 24, no. 3/4 (1994): 223-224.

11. Ibid., 224-225.

12. Joseph W. Barker, "What's Your Money Worth? Materials Budgets and the Selection and Evaluation of Book and Serial Vendors," *Journal of Library Administration* 16, no. 3 (1992): 31-37.

13. Ron Ray, "Who Makes the Decision? Time to Take Selection of Primary Vendors out of Acquisitions and Serials Departments?" in *Issues in Collection Management: Librarians, Booksellers, and Publishers*, ed. Murray S. Martin (Greenwich, Conn.: JAI, 1995), p. 71.

14. Mary Byrd Davis, "Model for a Vendor Study in a Manual or Semi-Automated Acquisitions System," *Library Acquisitions: Practice & Theory* 3 (1979): 53-60; Jan Bachmann-Derthick and Barbara B. Moran, "Serial Agent Selection in ARL Libraries," in *Advances in Serials Management* 1, ed. Marcia Tuttle and Jean G. Cook (Greenwich, Conn.: JAI, 1986), pp. 26-27; Janet Alm Anderson, "Challenging the 'Good Buddies Factor' in Vendor Selection," in *Advances in Serials Management* 3, ed. by Jean G. Cook and Marcia Tuttle (Greenwich, Conn.: JAI, 1989), pp. 169-171.

15. Ray, "Who Makes the Decision?" p. 67.

16. Janet Alm Anderson, "Order Consolidation: One Step in Containing Serials Prices," in *Vendors and Library Acquisitions*, ed. Bill Katz (New York: Haworth, 1991), p. 99.

17. Judy McQueen and N. Bernard "Buzzy" Basch, "Negotiating with Subscription Agents," *American Libraries* 22 (1991): 532-534, 644-647; *Prepare, Negotiate, Evaluate, Succeed: The Many Sides of the Negotiation Table* (Chicago: American Library Association, 1997), 2 sound cassettes.

18. McQueen and Basch, "Negotiating," 532.

19. N. Bernard Basch and Judy McQueen, *Buying Serials: A How-to-Do-It Manual for Librarians* (New York: Neal-Schuman, 1990), p. 116.

Bibliography

ACQNET. Acquisitions Librarians Electronic Network. Boone, N.C.: Eleanor Cooke, no. 1 (1990-). To subscribe: send the following e-mail message to: listserv@lester.appstate.edu: sub acqnet-l [first name last name].

ACQWEB. Edited by Anna Belle Leiserson. http://www.library.vander-bilt.edu/law/acqs/acqs.html. Web site for Acquisitions and Collection Development Information.

Alessi, Dana L. "Vendor Selection, Vendor Collection, or Vendor Defection." *Journal of Library Administration* 16, no. 3 (1992): 117-130.

American Library Association. Association for Library Collections and Technical Services. *Statement of Standards and Principles of Acquisitions Practice*. Chicago: American Library Association, 1994.

————. Association for Library Collections and Technical Services. Acquisitions Guidelines Series. Chicago: American Library Association, 1973- .
no. 1. Guidelines for Handling Library Orders for In-print Monographic Publications; no. 2. Guidelines for Handling Library Orders for Serials and Periodicals; no. 3. Guidelines for Handling Library Orders for Microforms; no. 4. Guidelines for Handling Library Orders for In-print Monographic Publications (2nd ed.); no. 5. Guide to Performance Evaluation of Library Materials Vendors; no. 6. Statistics for Managing Library Acquisitions; no. 7. Guidelines for Handling Library Orders for Serials and Periodicals (rev. ed.); no. 8. Guide to Preservation in Acquisitions Processing; no. 9. Guide to Selecting and Acquiring CD-ROMs, Software and Other Electronic Publications; no. 10. Guide to the Performance of Serials Vendors.

Barber, David. "Electronic Commerce in Library Acquisitions with a Survey of Bookseller and Subscription Agency Services." *Library Technology Reports* 31 (1995): 491-614.

Bazirjian, Rosann, ed. *New Automation Technology for Acquisitions and Collection Development*. New York: Haworth, 1995.

Bonk, Sharon C. "Toward a Methodology of Evaluating Serials Vendors." *Library Acquisitions: Practice & Theory* 9 (1985): 51-60.

Dannelly, Gay N. "The 'E's of Vendor Selection: An Archetype for Selection, Evaluation, and Sustenance." In *Understanding the Business of Library Acquisitions*. Ed. Karen A. Schmidt. Chicago: American Library Association, 1990, pp. 105-121.

Foreign Book and Serial Vendors Directories Series. Chicago: Association for Library Collections & Technical Services, American Library Association, 1996- . Vol. 1. *Book and Serial Vendors for Asia and the Pacific*; Vol. 2. *Book and Serial Vendors for Africa and the Middle East*.

International Literary Market Place. New York: R. R. Bowker, 1971/72- .

Johnson, Peggy, ed. *Guide to Technical Services Resources*. Chicago: American Library Association, 1994.

Katz, Bill, ed. *Vendors and Library Acquisitions*. New York: Haworth, 1991.

Kuntz, Harry. "Serials Agents: Selection and Evaluation." *Serials Librarian* 2, no. 2 (1977): 139-150.

Literary Market Place: LMP. New York: R. R. Bowker, 1988- .

Reidelbach, John H. and Gary M. Shirk, "Selecting an Approval Plan Vendor: A Step-by-Step Process." *Library Acquisitions: Practice & Theory* 7 (1983): 115-125; Part 2, 8 (1984): 157-202; Part 3, 9 (1985): 177-260.

Rouse, William B. "Optimal Selection of Acquisition Sources." *Journal of the American Society for Information Science* 25 (1974): 227-231.

SERIALST. Serials in Libraries Discussion Forum, no. 1 (1990-). To subscribe: send the following e-mail message to listserv@uvmvm: subscribe serialst [first name last name].

The Vendor Study Group. Association for Higher Education of North Texas. "Vendor Evaluation: A Selected Annotated Bibliography, 1955-1987." *Library Acquisitions: Practice & Theory* 12 (1988): 17-28.

Wilkas, Lenore Rae, comp. *International Subscription Agents.* 6th ed. Chicago: American Library Association, 1994.

Willmering, Bill. "Using the RFP Process to Select a Serials Vendor: A Work in Progress." *Serials Librarian* 28, no. 3/4 (1996): 325-329.

7

Vendor Evaluation

KAREN E. CARGILLE

As the business of library acquisitions continues to be downsized and outsourced, the acquisitions manager has an increasingly important job to perform in monitoring the effectiveness of the businesses that provide items for our collections, the library material vendors. All of us monitor the effectiveness of our vendors informally as part of our day-to-day operations, but few of us systematically set aside time to study and analyze how our vendors are doing. Yet, vendors are the people whom we trust to assist us in developing our libraries and in supporting our basic organizational missions. If we are truly following the second principle of acquisitions practice, "In all acquisitions transactions, a librarian strives to obtain the maximum ultimate value for each dollar of expenditure," then it is incumbent on us as acquisitions managers to develop systematic methods to track vendor performance in our libraries.[1]

GETTING STARTED

Once the decision is made to embark on a systematic vendor evaluation, the process of actually planning the study may seem bewildering. This is the point to spend some time defining the reasons for the study. As discussed later, these reasons may include improved vendor-library communications, internal procedural changes, or changes and improvements in the way in which the vendor handles the library business. Once you have answered the question, "What do I hope to learn?" the actual design process can start.

There are many different approaches to designing vendor studies, but the best basic guide to designing vendor performance studies remains ALA's 1988 publication, *Guide to Performance Evaluation of Library Materials Vendors*. This succinct guide offers suggestions on ways to apply quantitative measures to vendor performance. Although the scope of the guide is limited to firm orders only, it provides a strong basis for designing vendor studies of all types. Additional guidance can be found by conducting a literature search or consulting some of the references cited at the end of this chapter. Taking time at the beginning to plan and to understand the options is important to the success of the study. Read and digest the information available before starting the design process.

A great deal of management information is easily available if you have an integrated library system and many different statistical packages are most likely available in your library. Meet with statistical support staff and elicit their help in devising a study that will have minimal impact on the workload of staff. Ideally the study can run on data that are supplied as a by-product of daily system transactions. If so, the study will also have minimal impact on what is being studied. Without this, the study can have an impact on the productivity of the department at exactly the same time that vendor performance is being measured. In extreme cases it is possible to have skewed results that can invalidate the conclusion.

At this time, consider whether this is to be an ongoing study to be repeated at regular intervals, or whether this is a one time study to provide a snapshot. If the former, it is important to plan for potential coding changes that can be made in the library's integrated library system to make your task potentially easier in the future. Additionally, the methodology needs to be flexible enough to allow for future changes in your integrated library system due to modifications introduced by updated versions. If evaluation is becoming a part of ongoing workflow, and if benchmarks are being set for the future as a result of the study, then present decisions can have a significant impact on future operations and should be carefully considered.

It is also important to remember the importance of shared decision making in the design of a vendor study. Make sure you understand the procedures currently in use by staff in Acquisitions. If staff will be asked to do anything differently during the course of the study, then it is essential to involve them in the discussions regarding design and development of the methodology to be used in the study from the very beginning. Staff buy-in is essential to a successful study.

THE STUDY

Vendor studies can vary from simple one-dimensional studies to complex analyses that collect data on a large number of variables. The factors to be analyzed are as varied as there are acquisitions departments. In the first edition of this book, Marion Reid offered a lengthy list of factors that could be used as a basis for designing vendor studies. This list can still be used as a starting point to help identify those factors that may be important to your own unique library setting. Most factors also have the advantage of being easily measured by manipulating data from an integrated library system, although some may need to be gathered manually. These include, but are not limited to, the following:

- list price
- discount
- effective discount (discount plus postage and service charge)
- average cost per volume
- number of titles ordered
- number of titles received
- number of days required for receipt
- number of days from order placement to shipment/report of cancellation of order
- amount of time between receipt of book and payment of invoice
- number of reports
- number of claims
- number of cancellations
- imprint dates of titles canceled by vendor
- number of titles not received, reported on, or canceled by vendor
- number and type of vendor-related problems
- information included on the invoice
- publisher category according to *Literary Market Place*
- bibliographic accuracy of approval slips

A vendor study does not require including all of these factors, but should include a broad enough perspective to study the factors most important to the library. Once the factors are identified, the next step is to determine how to capture the data from the integrated library system, and to determine what programs will need to be written to import these data into a spreadsheet or database program. Database programs generally allow much more flexibility in data analysis over spreadsheets.[2]

Once the mechanics of the data collection are resolved, the next step is to determine the term of the study. One of the choices is whether the study will run continuously or use sampling techniques. For example, the study may capture every order placed in a three-month period, or every order placed with a single vendor within a given time frame. In the case of sampling techniques, it might also take every fifth order, or every order placed on Monday, or orders placed in a one-week period once a quarter over a year. It is useful to consider the planned interval between studies. If a snapshot study is planned, it is important to determine a representative time frame for the sample. Often the simplest approach is to design a study that analyzes specific data that come off your integrated library system on a monthly, quarterly, or annual basis, thus making vendor evaluation an integral part of your operation. Decisions about technique can be made on the basis of the amount of staff time involved in collecting the data, the type of institution and annual calendar of library ordering activity, and the desired outcome.

KINDS OF STUDIES

Given the power of today's integrated library systems and the flexibility of spreadsheet and database programs, the kinds of studies that can be done are really a reflection of the knowledge base and creativity of the staff managing the study and the needs of the individual library. As we have seen above, vendor analysis studies can track such things as timeliness, discounts, added charges, responsiveness, quality of reports, etc. Additionally, studies can be used to track one vendor at a time or to compare the performance of a number of vendors. In designing a study that compares vendors it is important to try to compare similar factors or services. The performance of a specialized vendor cannot be meaningfully compared with that of a general vendor. It is also difficult to compare approval vendors unless both vendors are supplying the same kinds of materials to the same kinds of libraries.

Some of the most common studies undertaken are quantitative measures of specific vendors used by the library for the same kinds of materials. For example, compare all firm order vendors by country for timeliness, all serial vendors for numbers of claims, all approval plans for return rates, or all out-of-print vendors for fulfillment rates. Try to avoid falling into the trap of collecting information just because it is there. If the study continues to produce information that is no longer of interest to the organization, it is time to reexamine the assumptions that were used in the initial phase of designing the study and decide to make changes, or, perhaps, stop the study. Occasional reality checks can save the organization from performing unnecessary work.

WHY STUDY A VENDOR'S PERFORMANCE

Acquisitions librarians are stewards of the resources of the library and its parent organization. As stewards, acquisitions librarians are required both legally and professionally to safeguard the budgets over which they have control and to assure themselves that dollars are being spent wisely and efficiently. In the first edition of this book, Reid identified six basic reasons to undertake a vendor study, which continue to have validity in today's marketplace:

1. To facilitate communication with the vendor(s) involved. Perhaps one of the most important reasons to do a vendor study is to open up communication between the library and the vendor. Results from a study can act as a specific basis for a discussion of services and expectations. Once accurate, measurable, repeatable data are available to inform opinions, better decisions can be made regarding the service received from a vendor. The library is also able to clarify its role in the library/vendor partnership and to make changes that might improve service from the vendor's perspective. Without data, these decisions will be made on the basis of informal evaluation, speculation, and preconception.
2. To confirm or contradict the acquisitions staff's informal evaluation of the vendor(s) involved. It is reasonable to check one's intuitive judgments occasionally with fact. Some factors such as the number of unfilled orders are not easily tracked using informal measures. All of us make informal judgments regarding our vendors. However, before action can be taken to change a process, it is important to document clearly and accurately any problems that may exist in the library/vendor relationship.
3. To establish or alter procedures. The process of studying vendor performance can lead to a process of introspection that can result in an analysis of how well the acquisitions department performs. Possibly changes can be made in the acquisitions operation to improve the performance of the

vendor/library relationship as a part of the more open communication that can result during and after a vendor study. For example, the department may be claiming too soon, or performing unnecessary tasks that are more appropriately done by your vendor.

4. To determine when to use a vendor. Studies usually result in a better understanding of the strengths and weaknesses of various vendors. Thus acquisitions managers are able to make better choices for the needs of the library, and also to improve the performance of the vendors chosen.

5. To reduce the number of vendors used or to determine which vendor to use exclusively. Studies can show if some vendors clearly outperform others, leading the acquisitions manager to change the vendor mix.

6. To establish a benchmark for future studies. In doing a vendor performance study, the acquisitions librarian establishes a methodology for subsequent measurements of that vendor, and perhaps for other similar vendor studies.

All or some of these reasons may be appropriate. The significant issue is developing and sustaining vendor studies as an important part of the stewardship of acquisitions to the library and its community.

ETHICS

Once the decision is made to embark on a vendor study it is important to decide whether or not to inform your vendors that such a study is in progress. They will be interested in discussing the results with you, and they may be able to assist you with the process of data gathering. On the other hand, results may be skewed by informing a vendor who will then strive harder to give you excellent service during the time of the study. In either case, whether informed in advance or not, the results of the study must be shared with the vendor before they are shared more broadly. There are differences of opinion among acquisitions librarians regarding whether or not such data should be published. If it is published, usually the identity of the vendors is not revealed, although it is often possible to infer which vendors are being discussed. In this day of electronic access to integrated library systems and to departmental Web pages, vendor evaluation data are more easily available to the community of acquisitions librarians. What this will mean to vendors is not yet clear, but it does increase competitive pressures.

It is necessary in any published studies to realize that results cannot be generalized from one library to another. Collections are unique. Policies and procedures differ, producing a potentially wide variety of results from one location to another. Before choosing to publish results either traditionally or on a Web site, be sure to consider the ethics of sharing such information with the world, and discuss the matter with the vendors involved.

CONCLUSION

As the work of acquisitions departments continues to change due to the impact of shrinking budgets and the new electronic options that are becoming available, it is increasingly important for acquisitions managers to design and conduct studies that evaluate their vendors. In many cases vendors are performing functions formerly done within the library. If we, as acquisitions managers, are willing to trust our vendors with these tasks, it is essential that we continue to perform the important role of ensuring that our institutions get the maximum value for their acquisitions dollars. This can best be done by designing studies that take advantage of the power of our integrated library systems, as well as the software packages that are increasingly available to analyze the data.

Notes

1. Association for Library Collections and Technical Services, Publisher/ Vendor-Library Relations Committee, "Principles and Standards of Acquisitions Practice: Statement on Principles and Standards of Acquisitions Practice," June 27, 1994, Miami Beach, Fla.

2. John F. Archer, "Producing Statistics by Downloading Data from Innopac: A Talk Given at the Third Annual Innopac Users Group Meeting, April 22-25, 1995, Oakland, Calif." URL:http://gort.ucsd.edu/jarcher/stattlk.html

Bibliography

Alley, Brian. "What Ever Became of Vendor B?" *Library Acquisitions: Practice & Theory* 4 (1980): 185-186.

Association for Library Collections and Technical Services. Collection Management and Development Committee. *Guide to Performance*

Evaluation of Library Materials Vendors. Chicago: American Library Association, 1988.

———. Publisher/Vendor-Library Relations Committee. "Principles and Standards of Acquisitions Practice: Statement on Principles and Standards of Acquisitions Practice," June 27, 1994, Miami Beach, Fla.

Barker, Joseph W. "Vendor Studies Redux: Evaluating the Approval Plan Option from Within." *Library Acquisitions* 13 (1989): 133-141.

Baumann, Susan. "An Extended Application of Davis' 'Model for a Vendor Study.'" *Library Acquisitions*: *Practice & Theory* 8 (1984): 83-90.

———. "An Extended Application of Davis' 'Model for a Vendor Study'" *Library Acquisitions: Practice & Theory* 9 (1985): 317-329.

Bell, JoAnn and others. "Methodology for a Comparison of Book Jobber Performance." *Medical Library Association Bulletin* 70 (April 1982): 229-231.

Bonk, Sharon C. "Toward a Methodology of Evaluating Serials Vendors." *Library Acquisitions: Practice & Theory* 9 (1985): 51-60.

Bracken, James K. and John C. Calhoun. "Profiling Vendor Performance." *Library Resources & Technical Services* 28 (April-June 1984): 120-128.

Brown, Lynne C. Branch. "Vendor Evaluation." *Collection Management* 19 (1995): 47-56.

Brownson, Charles W. "A Method for Evaluating Vendor Performance." In *Vendors and Library Acquisitions.* Ed. Bill Katz. New York: Haworth, 1991, pp. 37-51.

Bullard, Scott R. "Where's Ralph Nader, Now That Acquisitions Librarians Need Him?" *Library Acquisitions: Practice and Theory* 3 (1979): 1-2.

Bustion, Marifran. "Serials Vendor Evaluation." *Serials Review* 21 (Winter 1995): 93-94.

Case, Beau David. "Seeking Your Approval: Your Approval Plan Vendor Evaluation." *Against the Grain* 7 (September 1995): 30.

Davis, Mary Byrd. "Model for a Vendor Study in a Manual or Semi-automated Acquisitions System." *Library Acquisitions: Practice & Theory* 3 (1979): 53-60.

Grant, Joan and Susan Perelmuter. "Vendor Performance Evaluation." *Journal of Academic Librarianship* 4 (November 1978): 366-367.

Green, Paul Robert. "The Performance of Subscription Agents: A Detailed Survey." *Serials Librarian* 8 (Winter 1983): 7-22.

Hanson, Jo Ann. "An Evaluation of Book Suppliers Used by the University of Denver Library." Master's thesis, University of Denver, 1977. ERIC no. ED 156-132.

Henshaw, Francis H. and William H. Kurth. "Dealer Rating System at LC." *Library Resources & Technical Services* 1 (Summer 1957): 131-136.

Hulbert, Linda Ann and David Stewart Curry. "Evaluation of an Approval Plan." *College & Research Libraries* 39 (November 1978): 485-491.

Ivins, October. "The Development of Criteria and Methodologies for Evaluating the Performance of Monograph and Serials Vendors." In *Advances in Serials Management* 2. Greenwich, Conn.: JAI, 1988, pp. 185-212.

Joseph, Rosamma. "Procurement of Foreign Periodicals Direct and through Agents: A Comparative Study Based on a Cost-Benefit Analysis." *Library Progress* 3 (June-December 1983): 37-42.

Kim, Ung Chon. "Purchasing Books from Publishers and Wholesalers." *Library Resources & Technical Services* 19 (Spring 1975): 133-147.

Landesman, Margaret and Christopher Gates. "Performance of American In-print Vendors: A Comparison at the University of Utah." *Library Acquisitions: Practice & Theory* 4 (1980): 187-192.

Lawson, Clinton D. "Where in Hell Are Those Books We Ordered? A Study of Speed of Service from Canadian Publishers." *Ontario Library Review* 55 (December 1971): 237-241.

Lee, Sul H. *Vendor Evaluation and Acquisitions Budgets.* New York: Haworth, 1992. Also in *Journal of Library Administration* 16, no. 3 (1992).

Leonhardt, Thomas W., comp. *Approval Plans in ARL Libraries.* OMS Systems and Procedures Exchange Center Kit 83. Washington, D.C.: Association of Research Libraries, 1982.

———. "Vendor Performance Studies." Unpublished text of a paper read at the ALA RTSD Conference-within-a-Conference on Research in Library Resources and Technical Services, Philadelphia, Penn., July 11, 1982.

Lincoln, Robert. "Vendors and Delivery." *Canadian Library Journal* 35 (February 1978): 51-55, 57.

Lindsey, Jonathan A. "Vendor Discounts to Libraries in a Consortium." *Library Acquisitions: Practice & Theory* 5 (1981): 147-152.

Lynden, Fred C. and Arthur Meyerfeld. "Library Out-of-Print Book Procurement: The Stanford University Experience." *Library Resources & Technical Services* 17 (Spring 1973): 216-224.

Miller, Heather S. *Managing Acquisitions and Vendor Relations.* How-to-Do-It Manuals for Libraries no. 23. New York: Neal-Schuman, 1992.

Miller, Ruth H. and Martha W. Niemeier. "Vendor Performance: A Study of Two Libraries." *Library Resources & Technical Services* 31 (January-March 1987): 60-68.

Mitchell, Betty J. "A Systematic Approach to Performance Evaluation of Out-of-Print Book Dealers: The San Fernando Valley State College Experience." *Library Resources & Technical Services* 15 (Spring 1971): 215-222.

Pickett, A. S. "An Experiment in Book Buying." *Library Journal* 84 (February 1, 1959): 371-372.

Reid, Marion T. "Evaluating the Work of a Vendor." In *Understanding the Business of Library Acquisitions.* Ed. Karen A. Schmidt. Chicago: American Library Association, 1990, pp. 123-135.

Reidelbach, John H. and Gary M. Shirk. "Selecting an Approval Plan Vendor. III: Academic Librarians' Evaluations of Eight United States Approval Plan Vendors." *Library Acquisitions: Practice & Theory* 9 (1985): 177-260.

Rouse, William B. "Optimal Selection of Acquisition Sources." *Journal of the American Society for Information Science* 25 (July-August 1974): 227-231.

Rouzer, Steven M. "A Firm Order Vendor Evaluation Using a Stratified Sample" *Library Acquisitions* 17 (Fall 1993): 269-277.

Scott, Peter. "The Library's Role in Vendor Performance Analysis." In *Conference on Acquisitions, Budgets, and Collections* (1st: 1990: St. Louis, Mo.). *Acquisitions 90.* Comp. and ed. David C. Genaway. Canfield, Ohio: Genaway & Associates, 1990, pp. 401-411.

Shafa, Zary Mostashari, Julie S. Alexander and Kristine L. Murphy. "Vendor Evaluation: A Selected Annotated Bibliography." *Library Acquisitions* 12 (1988): 17-28.

Stokley, Sandra Lu and Marion T. Reid. "A Study of Five Book Dealers Used by Louisiana State University." *Library Resources & Technical Services* 22 (Spring 1978): 117-125.

Sumler, Claudia, Kristine Barone and Art Goetz. "Getting Books Faster and Cheaper: A Jobber Acquisitions Study." *Public Libraries* 19 (Winter 1980): 103-105.

Thorton, S. A. and C. J. Bigger. "Periodicals, Prices and Policies." *ASLIB Proceedings* 37 (November-December 1985): 437-452.

Uden, Janet. "Financial Reporting and Vendor Performance: A Case Study." *Journal of Library Automation* 13 (September 1980): 185-195.

Veenstra, John and Lois Mai. "When Do You Use a Jobber?" *College & Research Libraries* 23 (November 1962): 522-524.

8

Selecting and Acquiring Materials from Abroad

THOMAS D. KILTON

Successful endeavors to systematically acquire library materials from a foreign region or country rest on a thorough knowledge of two processes: the routes leading to a timely identification of new titles; and the methods for obtaining those titles once they are identified and selected for acquisition. Such knowledge is, of course, necessary for any program to procure the books and journals from a defined world area, domestic or foreign, but in the case of foreign materials, particularly those from the so-called Third World areas, such knowledge is of particular importance. Library materials from abroad do not, however, always arrive at a library in response to previous identification and ordering. Blanket order as well as blanket exchange programs are routes of a different nature by which many titles not having been individually identified or requested by selectors are shipped en masse by foreign vendors or partner libraries in accordance with profiles prearranged between the receiving libraries and the foreign vendors and exchange partner libraries. A final category of foreign materials is that of gifts which may arrive solicited or unsolicited from either foreign or domestic organizations or private parties.

AREA STUDIES ASSOCIATIONS FOR LIBRARY SELECTORS

Although American libraries did indeed collect foreign materials throughout the nineteenth and early twentieth centuries, it was really not until after World War II that much stress was placed on acquiring books outside of the domain of what we have come to call Western Europe. As post-World War II university budgets rose and national grant funding opportunities of the early 1950s soared, funding could be found in most research libraries to allot an increasing percentage of budgets to the purchase of non-English language material.

Starting in the late 1950s and early 1960s the emergence of the concept of "area studies" stimulated bibliographers and selectors to systematically collect materials across many social science and humanities disciplines from large regions, such as Africa, Asia, Latin America, and Eastern Europe. This frequently resulted in the establishment of separate units within the larger research libraries to collect materials from these specific areas. Soon ambitious consortial arrangements among major libraries, most notably the Farmington Plan, sought to ensure that greater collecting intensity would be placed on areas of the Third World previously neglected.

These area studies initiatives placed considerable responsibilities on librarians suddenly charged with collecting systematically from specific world areas. This was particularly true in the case of large research collections. Whereas the inclusion of non-English materials in collecting parameters from many of these world areas formerly was not really taken seriously, now it was. In place of a social sciences selector occasionally picking a few "nice" Portuguese titles on secondary school education from a recent Brazilian book list, or a few illustrated Chinese art books for the quaint and perhaps obscure "Oriental" section of the bookstacks, a well-trained area language specialist was now charged with building up and maintaining a respectable collection of materials from one or more world areas. Significant medium-sized and small academic libraries also mounted successful efforts at collecting foreign materials at this time, although perhaps without establishing separate area units. Certainly not all of the larger research libraries went to that extent either. In those cases subject selectors responsible for disciplines such as history or literature; discipline selectors, such as those responsible for the humanities or social sciences; or language selectors, such as Romance language specialists, merely accelerated their accumulation of foreign language titles from the various world regions attracting scholarly attention by researchers and students alike.

To successfully discharge responsibility for collecting in such an area, a thorough knowledge of all aspects of collection development was mandated. The commercial as well as the scholarly book trade; the most cost-effective foreign vendors to facilitate purchase and distribution of materials to libraries; and the best book selection sources were among the more basic aspects of this work.

Soon librarians involved in foreign acquisitions formed groups to address these and other cogent issues, and in 1956 the first of these, SALALM (Seminar on the Acquisition of Latin American Library Materials) was formed. To this day SALALM has been a model forum for librarians to exchange current information about the Latin American book trade, major vendors, the pricing of materials, and bibliographic control of books and serials from this area of the world. The 1960s and 1970s saw the formation of similar groups (both independent groups such as SALALM, and groups within existing library associations, such as the American Library Association): SEES (Slavic and Eastern European Section of the Association of College and Research Libraries, American Library Association), AAASS (the American Association for the Advancement of Slavic Studies), the Council on East Asian Studies of the Association for Asian Studies, the Africana Librarians Council of the African Studies Association, SASS (the Society for the Advancement of Scandinavian Studies), and WESS (the Western European Specialists Section of the Association of College and Research Libraries, American Library Association). All of these library association groups continue to exist, and their functions have become even more valuable with the advent of new technologies, such as Web sites, which have enhanced even further their communications functions. Their list services and newsgroups enable librarians developing and maintaining collections to keep informed on an up-to-the-minute basis on book trade and vendor news, and participants can debate online the merits of expensive publications just out or advertised in announcements of forthcoming publications. The associations provide librarians with the opportunity to meet and participate in their annual or biannual meetings, and they sometimes even tend to form a sort of "union" or "front" of subject or area specialists vis-à-vis the publishers and vendors in the countries with which they routinely deal.

These and other similar area groups for librarians with common collection development assignments issue regular newsletters, both paper and online, in which valuable articles of common interest are published, new major sets and online publications are reviewed, and institutional news of participating libraries (new collections just acquired and perhaps named, new staff appointments, etc.) is disseminated. Examples include the *WESS Newsletter* (Western European Specialists Section of ACRL) and the *SALALM Newsletter*. Cooperation between these specialist librarians' groups and the major vendors of the countries or regions of their interest frequently results in the vendors attending librarians' meetings, presenting papers, and often sponsoring special programs at which notable librarians, booksellers, and bibliophiles deliver presentations or participate as panelists. The vendors also have traditionally been very generous in sponsoring various events of the associations through cash donations, and even in subsidizing research trips abroad for librarians. A notable case in point is the Martinus Nijhoff International West European Specialists Study Grant awarded by Martinus Nijhoff, a major vendor headquartered in The Hague. This award supports travel, lodging, and board for two weeks for a wide variety of research topics pertaining to the acquisition, organization, or use of library materials from or relating to Western Europe. The award was established by WESS in 1985 under the sponsorship of Nijhoff.

BIBLIOGRAPHIC RESOURCES FOR IDENTIFYING NEW PUBLICATIONS

Perhaps the most enticing aspect of acquisitions work is the positive feeling of "control" sensed by a selector when he or she knows that the best current methods for identifying new titles have been found and that they are being utilized on a regular basis. No single source for this knowledge fulfills collecting needs from any given area. For most regions or countries the basic tools are national bibliographies, commercial trade lists, books-in-print publications, publishers' advertisements in scholarly journals, advertisements and brochures most publishers are willing to send regularly to selectors upon request, notices in book trade journals (such as *Publishers Weekly* and its foreign equivalents), and bibliographic citation slips distributed to library selectors upon request by foreign or domestic vendors.

Throughout the 1996 calendar year and into 1997, countless World Wide Web sites emerged that supply information on newly published or forthcoming titles—services which clearly demonstrate the true wave of the future for materials selection via electronic access. These services include electronic bookstores listing both new and antiquarian materials, advertisements from the publishers' own home pages, and, very recently, lists of new books and journals which selectors can search by subject. Such selections by vendors are in most instances created by their own bibliographers through a scanning of the current issues of national bibliographies and publishers' announcements. A last category of identification sources for new titles is online catalogs of major research libraries in countries from which materials are being collected. By use of their interfaces permitting searches to be delimited to year of publication, selectors can spot new relevant titles which may still be available for purchase.

For a librarian beginning to collect from a given world area, the project of identifying these selection tools may be simple or complex. National bibliographies do not even exist for many Third World countries, and if available they are apt to lag so far behind in publication as to be unusable for the prompt procurement of current titles. Some published guides list the national bibliographies of less prominent Third World countries, the most useful being *Guide to Current National Bibliographies in the Third World* by G. E. Gorman and J. J. Mills.[1] This work lists and annotates national bibliographies covering the major regions of the world (Africa, Arab States, Asia, Caribbean, Latin America, and the Pacific). It also treats national bibliographies for seventy-four individual countries. R. R. Bowker is scheduled to issue an update to this work in 1999. The well-known guides to reference works, such as those by Balay and Walford, can also be of use for identifying national bibliographies of large as well as smaller countries. For instance, Balay's *Guide to Reference Books* (11th ed., 1996) lists the currently issued national bibliographies for many smaller countries, such as Barbados, Bermuda, the Dominican Republic, Jamaica, Puerto Rico, and Trinidad and Tobago. In the past, some area-specific guides have been issued in serial form, such as *Bibliographia Actual del Caribe/Current Caribbean Bibliography/Bibliographie Courante de la Caribe, 1951-1976*. Fortunately, national bibliographies from a few major countries of the world are now beginning to be available electronically, such as the *Deutsche National Bibliographie* which can be purchased on CD-ROM.

Beginning area selectors are often surprised to learn that books-in-print publications do not exist for certain countries, including some countries with high per-capita book production rates, such as the Scandinavian countries. For instance, although Denmark, Norway, Iceland, and Sweden have an established tradition for their excellent bibliographic publications and high rates of per-capita book production, none of these counties issues a books-in-print type publication. This contrasts dramatically with the fact that superb ones are produced for Britain, France, Germany, and Italy, and for many developing countries. Many of the vendors in the Scandinavian countries do, however, maintain select lists of current titles arranged by subject on their Web sites which inform selectors whether or not specific titles are still available and for what price.

VENDORS

The terminology used with reference to a commercial firm which acts as a supplier of books from publishers to libraries has over the years varied, the most commonly used labels being supplier, agent, jobber, dealer, or vendor. Increasingly the term vendor seems to be used, although a bookstore is also a vendor in the traditional sense. Examples of the more prominent vendors for Western European acquisitions are: Jean Touzot and Aux Amateurs de Livres (France), Martinus Nijhoff (Benelux), Otto Harrassowitz (Germany), Livres Étrangèrs (French supplier for former Soviet Union), Nardecchia and Cassalini (Italy), B. H. Blackwell (Great Britain), and Almquist and Wicksel, Munksgaard, and Tanum (Scandinavia). Some of these vendors have been in business for almost 100 years. These dealers have served to perform three important functions for libraries: (1) to provide a central point that will fill firm orders for title-by-title book and serial selection, ensure that the ordered materials are sent by their publishers to the libraries, and consolidate billing for materials from various publishers onto single invoices of a uniform nature; (2) to supply materials to libraries on blanket order programs tailored to profiles established by those libraries; and (3) to serve as information sources for selectors concerning miscellaneous acquisition questions including the willingness and ability to search for out-of-print or hard-to-obtain titles.

Foreign publishers, whether in countries with mature economies or developing countries, usually welcome vendors as intermediaries between themselves and library selectors, and generally they prefer not to have foreign libraries place orders for their publications directly with them. This helps to dispense with currency conversion problems at the sales end, since the vendors always allow their foreign customers to remit payment in their own currencies. It also allows the consolidation of invoicing furnished by the vendors to their library customers in which bills for multiple publishers are included on the same invoice which helps clarify billing data. Clearer invoicing naturally guarantees prompter payment to the publishers by libraries. Libraries, of course, benefit from these simpler payment transactions as well as from the discounts offered by the vendors, despite the service fees which the vendors must assess their library customers for their services.

The best way for a beginning selector to identify vendors who provide the best services for the lowest cost is to become active in professional library organizations at whose conferences the country vendors have representatives. The quality of services provided by the various vendors tends to be discussed among library selectors attending the conferences. Almost all of the library organizations that specialize in acquisitions work for specific countries administer electronic discussion groups and list services on which new services provided by the vendors, both print and electronic, are regularly discussed and critiqued. Because leading vendors are often members of these electronic discussion groups, it is more difficult for the participating librarians to make negative evaluations and perhaps catty comments about their services over these electronic discussion groups, but the presence of the vendors has the advantage of their publicizing new services to the memberships in a timely fashion and interacting with selectors with a common focus concerning many issues.

Following are examples of some leading electronic discussion groups which may be of value to area selectors. For Western Europe, several exist within the framework of WESS (Western European Studies Section of the Association of College and Research Libraries of the American Library Association): "German-E" for German studies <campbell@virginia.edu>; "ROMList" for Romance studies <jeffry.larson@yale.edu>; and "DISC-NORDLIB" for Scandinavian and Nordic area studies <disc-nordlib-request@mail.unet. umn.edu>. For Africana the chief discussion group is maintained by the Africana Librarians Council of the African Studies Association. Latin America is covered by "LALA-L" <lala-l@uga.cc.uga.edu> which is operated by librarians associated with SALALM (Seminar on the Acquisition of Latin American Library Materials). The Council on East Asian Libraries (Association for Asian Studies) supports the CEAL list service <eastlib@listserv.oit.unc.edu>. "Slavlibs," a discussion group for librarians concerned with Slavic and Eastern European studies, is not directly associated with SEES (Slavic and Eastern European Section of ACRL) or AAASS (American Association for the Advancement of Slavic Studies), but its contributing librarians are in most cases members of one or both of these groups. Its list service address is <slavlibs@library. berkeley.edu>.

In addition to the list services and discussion groups supported by these professional associations, each association maintains a home page on which useful information on acquisitions and vendor services is frequently included. A good example is WESSWeb (http:// www.lib.virginia.edu/wess/).

Thomas D. Kilton

THE NORTH AMERICAN "NATIONAL COLLECTION"

Over the past three decades the ability of North American libraries as a group to procure a satisfactorily high percentage of foreign monographs and serials of research value has been steadily diminishing. Consequently, copy exists in North America for many of these works. The term *national collection* has consequently come into use as a concept with regard to the ability or inability of American libraries to corporately acquire important foreign research materials. If no copy of a significant European imprint is held by any library throughout North America (i.e., in our "national collection"), access to it does not exist for all practical purposes, despite improved document delivery services for international library loan requests.

The problem is attributed to various factors: dwindling library budgets, curtailments in federal funding grants, hikes in the prices of foreign publications, currency ratios unfavorable to the dollar, increased publishing output in many areas, notably Western Europe and Latin America, and inflation in many countries. This is not a problem just of our times; it is one which has long been recognized, and for which action was taken as early as 1948 when the Association of Research Libraries (ARL) launched the Farmington Plan, a national effort on the part of thirty participating research libraries to cooperatively acquire foreign materials. This effort, funded by the federal government and conducted under the auspices of ARL, continued until 1972 at which time its federal funding was withdrawn. The method employed in many respects resembled those envisioned today by those advocating a revival of nationwide coordinated collecting programs. Participating libraries committed themselves individually to collect intensively from specifically assigned subjects and countries, and the program did achieve some of its goals in improving our national collection from the end of World War II until its demise. One of the aims was to ensure that at least one copy of each new foreign publication that might reasonably be expected to interest researchers in the United States would be acquired by at least one American library. This ambitious aim was, however, not fulfilled.

Following the demise of the Farmington Plan, concern for the national collection problem did not abate. It was dealt with in many journal articles and monographs of the 1970s and 1980s which advocated concerted national efforts to foster collaborative collection development and access through conspectus projects which would map out the strengths and weaknesses of individual library collections, thereby enabling participating libraries to cooperatively establish collecting responsibilities among themselves for various subjects and geographical regions of the world.

To address this concern, efforts such as the Research Libraries Group (RLG) Conspectus and the National Collections Inventory Project (NCIP) emerged for the purposes of establishing profiles of library collections and using this information to help determine which libraries would collect which materials. Within these programs "pcr's," or primary collection responsibilities, were voluntarily adopted by member libraries which agreed to collect as comprehensively as possible in specific subject areas for both domestic and foreign publications. This would assure the procurement for the "national collection" of not only the best books and journals from the best publishers, but even more importantly, the so called "grey literature"—those marginal, alternative, or out-of-scope items not selected in times of budget constraints by libraries trying to individually supply their users with the top-tier publications. The overall effort, however, was not to systematically ensure that one copy of each foreign publication of research value would be acquired by at least one American library, an original aim of the Farmington Plan, but rather more broadly to contribute to the enrichment of our national collections. Administered by ARL and funded by the Andrew W. Mellon Foundation, NCIP has died out due to a cessation of funding, and the RLG Conspectus, although still maintained, has not fully realized the collaborative collection development goals envisioned by its framers. Furthermore, its online version was recently terminated. All of the enthusiasm expressed by selectors during the 1980s, a period of great optimism for collaborative collection building on a national scale, has resulted in very little progress. In a 1992 assessment of the causes for the stagnation, Richard Hacken addressed the question, "Is resource sharing in limbo?" The answer is yes, and the reasons he cites pretty much boil down to the fact that in practice selectors rely more heavily on institutional self-interest than on an idealistic notion of national interaccessibility.

Challenging the fuzzy notion that selectors will willingly spend even a small proportion of their funds on items not of immediate benefit for them but rather for the common good, he convincingly concludes that a consortium serves its members best when each member acquires materials primarily according to local needs. Evidence suggests strongly that a major cause of the failure of the nationwide progams lay in the fact that in many cases the "pcr's" were adopted out of charitable motives on the parts of libraries rather than from a demand-driven need to collect in the chosen areas in support of local curricular or research needs.[2]

Over the last few years the national collection issue has nonetheless been yet again revived by groups, such as the Association for Research Libraries' Foreign Acquisitions Project, and area studies groups, such as the Seminar for the Acquisition of Latin American Library Materials (SALALM) and the Western European Specialists Section (WESS) of the Association for College and Research Libraries, American Library Association. Thanks to the ever-increasing percentage of catalog records for foreign materials having been acquired by North American libraries and entered into bibliographic utilities, such as OCLC and RLIN, statistical assessments concerning the inability of our libraries collectively to acquire materials from various areas of the world in sufficient number are now possible. Several of them with revealing results have been reported and published over the past few years. In 1996, for example, a landmark publication addressing the seriousness of the state of our national collection in its inability to adequately collect foreign publications was issued by the Association of Research Libraries (ARL). Authored by Jutta Reed-Scott, Senior Program Officer for Preservation and Collection Development at ARL, this study, entitled *Scholarship, Research Libraries, and Global Publishing,* documents the results of ARL's Foreign Acquisitions Project, a four-year study of trends in "global information resources" funded by the Andrew W. Mellon Foundation.[3]

The study recommends, as foremost cooperative action in the way of collaborative collection development projects, the digitization of journals and improved methods of document delivery. The project has included three pilot or "demonstration projects" set up by ARL in connection with the Association of American Universities. These projects are working toward final recommendations on North American collecting from three areas: (1) German politics and public life since 1945; (2) Japanese scientific and technical serials; and (3) Latin American serials. Although the ARL Foreign Acquisitions Project is now concluded, work of the three demonstration projects is continuing as part of the ARL Global Resources Program. Coordinated by Deborah Jakbus of Duke University, this program is continuing the work of the pilot projects of the ARL Foreign Acquisitions Program, but under the new names: Latin Americanist Research Resources Project, German Demonstration Project, and Japanese Scientific and Technical Information Project. Two additional world regions slated for demonstration projects are Africa and Southeast Asia. Selectors interested in the future progress of these projects can keep abreast by reading *ARL*, the bimonthly newsletter of the Association of Research Libraries, and by visiting the ARL World Wide Web site for its Global Resources Program at <http://arl.cni.org/collect/grp/>.

Although other projects examining ways of improving foreign collecting are making valuable contributions to solving the overall problem, the concerns for access to serials are far outweighing concerns for access to monographs, a very sore point with many selectors in the humanities and social sciences. Nationwide programs for digitization and document delivery are workable for providing users with access to journal articles. A user in South Carolina, for instance, can have a journal article faxed from the University of Oregon. But the same user might have to wait a week or more to receive a monograph from the West Coast via interlibrary loan, and copyrighted books in their traditional format are unlikely to be digitized *en masse*, at least in the near future. In order to ameliorate this crisis concerning foreign monographic literature, some sort of nationwide collaborative program for collecting needs to be established on a national basis. Such a program, if it is to achieve even modest results, will have to be one in which already existing regional consortia, such as the Research Triangle (North Carolina, North Carolina State, and Duke) or the Berkeley-Stanford Group share a role in the planing and assignment of collecting responsibilities to libraries.

It should be noted also that "as the world gets smaller," strategic alliances being forged between the North American and many foreign library communities to foster collaborative collecting are also on the drawing board. Proposals for such joint ventures are outlined in the "Strategic Plan for Improving Access to Global Information Resources in U.S. and Canadian Research Libraries," included in the appendix to *Research Libraries and Global Publishing*.[4] This strategic plan has as its goal the restoration of the range of significant foreign publications to the national collection, and a seamless web of interconnected, coordinated, and interdependent research collections that are accessible to geographically distributed users. The mechanism for all of this is an envisioned "North American digital library" with ultimate access to international networked collections.

Such visions may not be so far down the road of reality as far as serials are concerned, but for monographic publications digitization and access via computers, especially to foreign imprints, is still a way off. Fortunately, for the short term some progress is being made to induce cooperative collecting of foreign monographs. For instance, the Research and Planning Committee of WESS in cooperation with the vendor Otto Harrassowitz has recently proposed a unique solution to encourage libraries to buy grey literature as a means of rounding out the national collection. The plan is for Harrassowitz to periodically generate and distribute to library selectors lists of scholarly imprints from Germany, Austria, and Switzerland for which no orders have been received from North American libraries and for which no records can be found in OCLC or RLIN. Those libraries that are participating in the plan will then assume the responsibility of periodically ordering a predetermined number of titles from these lists. Details for subject parameters have yet to be worked out, but this is an innovative and promising solution to an old problem.

On another front, the Latin Americanist Research Resources Project, an endeavor sponsored jointly by the Association of American Universities, the Association of Research Libraries, and the Seminar on the Acquisition of Latin American Library Materials (SALALM) is promoting a program with an approach similar to that of the Farmington Plan. This project is discussed in the section on Latin America. Furthermore, the continued work of the various "demonstration projects" spawned by the ARL Foreign Acquisitions Project may be successful in identifying future efforts to help improve our national collection.

The following sections of this chapter address foreign acquisitions with respect to some major regions of the world. Currently popular methods for collecting materials from these regions are highlighted so as to offer beginning as well as more advanced selectors an overview of the art of materials procurement from these regions.

WESTERN EUROPE

For North American scholarly libraries, the concept of foreign acquisitions has historically been obtaining books and serials from Europe. James Campbell, an expert on European publishing, has noted, "Western Europe has traditionally been the second most important acquisitions area for North American libraries, and for scholarly libraries it was probably even more important than the United States well into this century."[5] Of course, since this statement was made in 1989, the dividing line between Eastern and Western Europe no longer strictly follows the boundaries of the old "Iron Curtain." Nonetheless the concept still obtains, and for most purposes means those Western European countries whose languages exclude the Slavic and Finno-Ugric families. Certainly at most universities the demands for materials from Western Europe exceed the demands for materials from other parts of the non-English speaking world with the exception of Latin America. And the fact remains that book production per country in Western Europe by far exceeds that of regions of the other continents, with the exception of China.

In the effort to acquire materials across many disciplines, American research libraries approach acquisitions from Western Europe in much the same way as domestic publications, with the exception that rather than being sent directly to publishers, most orders for European serials and monographs are placed with European vendors who are willing to transact their business with acquisition units in English and who are willing to consolidate bills from a number of publishers onto a single invoice. When libraries place orders directly with separate publishers in a foreign country, invoices from those separate publishers are received in diverse formats and often in the language of the publications ordered, a major source of confusion and error for the staffs of acquisition processing units. Subject-based blanket orders are usually maintained with separate vendors located in each of the respective countries, and exchanges for serials and certain monographic series are maintained with a variety of libraries, research institutes, and learned societies that do not market their publications commercially.

The task of identifying and acquiring Western European materials is in general much easier than the efforts necessary to identify and acquire them successfully from Eastern Europe, Asia, Latin America, or Africa. In almost all cases the national bibliographies for the Western European countries are arranged according to a logical and easy-to-use subject classification, and they are issued regularly. Some, such as the *Deutsche National Bibliographie*, are available online or on CD-ROM for a subscription fee. Since many of these include "forthcoming books" editions, having direct access to such up-to-the-minute information is a superb way for a selector not only to have the assurance of truly being "on top" of important new titles, but also to be able to place orders for them before their print runs are exhausted. Books-in-print sources are excellent for countries such as France, Germany, Italy and Spain, but, as previously noted, for others, such as the Scandinavian and Low Countries, they are not produced at all. Book-trade journals, such as the German *Börsenblatt für den deutschen Buchhandel*, provide selectors with relevant annotations for new books, book reviews, and articles on trends in the publishing and book distribution industries. Online resources, many Web-based, are being developed at an amazing speed, so that OPACs (online public access catalogs) of university and national libraries, books-in-print publications (e.g., the German *Verzeichnis lieferbarer Bücher* <http://www.buchhandel.de/>), offerings of commercial bookstores, and catalogs of academic publishing houses, are all available over a computer to North American selectors. *Verzeichnis lieferbarer Bücher* is unique in being the only books-in-print source for a major country (the third largest producer of books) which is available on the Web at no charge. An additional fairly recent development which is of use for selectors is the catalog entries for new monographs entered by the vendors Cassalini (Italy) and Puvill (Spain) into OCLC. Other Western European vendors, such as Iberbook, are also reported to be in the process of initiating such cataloging programs.

The major vendors for Western Europe, all of which maintain North American offices for their representatives, maintain Web sites and e-mail and fax accounts for their customers. Price quotations for urgently needed monographs or serials from Western Europe can be obtained on the spot, rush orders can be placed, and miscellaneous acquisitions information, such as status reports on outstanding orders, can be supplied efficiently and promptly. And in some instances innovative services outshine those in the United States. Otto Harrassowitz (Wiesbaden, Germany), for instance, now provides a versatile Web site containing selections of the most recent imprints of Germany, Austria, and Switzerland. This site perhaps best demonstrates the ability selectors of the near future will have in identifying recently published monographs by a subject search and subsequently delimiting the search by date of publication, price, and other factors. In the "New Monographs" section of the Harrassowitz Web site <http://www.harrassowitz.de> one can, for example, ask to see citations to all monographs on philosophy published in German-speaking Europe from November 1, 1996, through April 1, 1997, and costing less than 200 German marks. A "New Serials" section is also available at this site. Aux Amateurs du Livres, a major vendor for France, is planning to mount a similar materials selection database.

As part of the 1992 Foreign Acquisitions Project of the Association of Research Libraries (ARL), a study conducted in 1994 by members of the Western European Specialists Section (WESS) of the Association of College and Research Libraries was undertaken to ascertain the approximate percentage of high-quality research monographs from Europe in the area of political science which are not owned by a single North American library. National bibliographies from 1990 were examined from France, Italy, Sweden, Belgium, Iceland, and Catalonia. The following percentages of imprints listed in these bibliographies were determined not to appear in either OCLC or RLIN: French (15); Italian (30);

Swedish (55); Catalan (19); Icelandic (75); and Belgian (57). Results of this survey were published in an eye-opening article of July 1994, entitled "Western European Political Science: An Acquisition Study," by Barbara Walden, Charles Fineman, William S. Monroe, and Mary Jane Parrine.[6] This has been the most extensive study reported to date on inadequate book procurement from a specific area of the world on the part of the "North American collection."

Two things need to be accomplished to ameliorate this problem: (1) collaborative consortial programs designed for monographs will have to be launched; and (2) funding for Western European materials within individual libraries will have to be increased. In large research libraries with departmental library units for various humanities and social science libraries, this funding often erodes because the funding for European blanket order programs is apt to be centrally administered as a "general" fund, as opposed to area studies (African, Asian, Latin American, Slavic, etc.) in which cases the selectors in those areas are apt to have discretion over their own area studies blanket orders. When general library funding dwindles due to inflation factors or budget crises, the general funds are usually the first ones to be raided, and library administrators frequently presume that these cuts will produce the fewest objections from faculty members and library selectors. This is indeed ironic, since of all foreign publications it is precisely those from Western Europe which receive the greatest use by humanists and social scientists. Economic, political, and historical factors affect this, in addition to the fact that foreign language expertise of faculty and students is usually based on a knowledge of one or more Western European languages.

In Western Europe, the political upheavals of the early 1990s had the greatest impact on Germany. All North American selectors of German materials whose work precedes the 1989 fall of the German Democratic Republic (East Germany) have witnessed dramatic changes in dealing with publishers in what is now called the "new German states." Buchexport Leipzig (located in Leipzig) was the central book distribution center; it exerted a rigid, centralized control over all export shipments of books and serials no less rigid than that of the Soviet Union's Mezhdunarodnia Kniga described further on in this chapter. During the Communist era, almost all North American research libraries took advantage of the excellent service provided by the Western vendor Otto Harrassowitz in Wiesbaden, West Germany, for firm purchase orders as well as blanket orders for East German imprints. Ironically, Buchexport Leipzig had been formed out of the former Harrassowitz Export Department in Leipzig after this venerable company was expropriated by the East at the end of the Second World War. Because of Harrassowitz's good responsiveness to its customers' orders for East German books and journals during the Cold War period, most Western libraries were able to place firm orders with Harrassowitz for individual East German titles despite their short print runs, rather than having to claim them on their blanket orders. Claiming was more difficult for library record keeping; ironically it was the procedure that selectors from other Communist countries had to use during the same Cold War period.

Almost a decade after the fall of East Germany, the business of procuring materials from the Eastern German publishers has become virtually the same as obtaining them from their Western German counterparts. During the Communist era, exchanges between U.S. and East German libraries flourished in the same way as they did between U.S. and Soviet libraries, and some of these exchanges with the Eastern German libraries are being maintained. There are, however, far fewer of them since the Eastern German research institutes as well as the libraries are no longer receiving the government subsidies that enabled them to produce prodigious quantities of scholarly research.

The only forum for library selectors for Western Europe is the Western European Specialists Section of the Association of College and Research Libraries, American Library Association. Since 1974 WESS has been a very active group with a wide representation of selectors, catalogers, and reference librarians for all of the Western European languages. Attending both the ALA annual and midwinter conferences, WESS continues to sponsor programs concerning collection development from the various countries of Europe in addition to discussion groups that meet at each conference to exchange views on current topics of interest: the Germanists Discussion Group, the Romance Languages Discussion Group, and the Scandinavian Languages Discussion Group. The WESS home page can be visited at <http://www.lib.virginia.edu/wess/>.

SLAVIC AND EASTERN EUROPE

Over the past decade no area of the world has precipitated greater changes for foreign acquisition procedures than have the former Communist regions of Central and Eastern Europe. What in particular characterized trading with these countries prior to the 1991-92 political upheavals was rigid, centralized book distribution. As a case in point, for the entire Soviet Union a government book distribution agency in Moscow, Mezhdunarodnia Kniga (the

International Book), censored and facilitated all monograph and serial exports as well as imports. Other Eastern Bloc countries likewise maintained such centralized distribution (as, for example,
Buchexport Leipzig for East Germany and Ars Polnica for Poland).

For Western libraries the primary book procurement methods
were blanket orders set up with various Western vendors and exchanges established with Eastern European research libraries.
Viktor Kamkin in Washington, D.C., and Livres Étrangèrs in Paris
are examples of Western vendors who successfully provided subject-
based blanket orders to a large number of U.S. academic libraries
for their Eastern bloc publications. Once these libraries established
blanket order subject profiles with their vendors, they were assured
of receiving book shipments that the vendors routinely obtained
from the central distribution centers. Instead of placing firm orders
for specific titles with their vendors, libraries usually requested desired titles on the blanket orders. This was the most efficient
method for procuring specific desired titles. Problems in remitting
payment to Eastern Bloc booksellers in countries whose currencies
were non-convertible in the West made dealing directly with them
next to impossible. Furthermore, the notoriously short print runs of
most publications usually meant that by the time a Western library
became aware of a title's existence and placed a firm order for it,
the work would already be out of print with its publisher, but might
still be obtainable from a vendor's stock.

The second most preferred acquisition method for obtaining serials as well as monographs was exchanges between Western libraries and their Eastern European counterparts. American research libraries collecting from Third World countries, or from
regions in which political or economic factors have made standard
purchase orders with vendors or booksellers difficult to fill, have
traditionally chosen to maintain exchanges with libraries in those
countries. Furthermore, exchanges have proven to be a particularly
good way to acquire elusive and noncommercial publications not
listed in national bibliographies and not customarily marketed and
distributed for export. Examples include non-book-trade titles issued by museums, government organizations, archives, scientific
research institutes, published conference proceedings, and serials
as well as monographs from remote provincial regions.

Exchanges have been successful primarily for large libraries
with either a sufficient number of duplicate copies of books and serials from their home institutions to offer or with the ability to purchase a sufficient number of monographs or serial subscriptions to
offer their partners, this latter method commonly referred to as

"bartered exchanges." For a bartered exchange, a library requests its domestic vendor to ship selected materials to a foreign exchange partner, whereupon the requesting library is billed by the vendor. Serial exchanges are normally maintained between partner libraries on a quid-pro-quo basis, and record keeping is pretty much straightforward. Programs between libraries for the exchange of large number of monographs, to the contrary, are labor intensive, requiring staff to identify and process publications, to claim items requested but not received, and to correspond with partners concerning materials received but considered to be out of scope in relation to the established exchange profiles.

Throughout the Soviet as well as the post-Soviet periods, monographic exchanges with Eastern European libraries have been of two varieties. Either bulk shipments of books whose contents presumably match the profiles established by exchange partner libraries are sent automatically, a process known as "blanket exchanges," or lists of titles, "offered lists," are mailed to exchange partners for title-by-title selection. In either case, libraries maintaining exchanges with one another need to take the time to analyze their exchanges for cost effectiveness and to see if they are balanced to the benefit of both partners. For offered lists, the generally preferred type of monograph exchange, the attempt has usually been to balance the exchanges, either on a title-for-title basis or on a value-for-value or "priced exchange" basis. During the Soviet era most American research libraries maintained title-for-title exchanges, but many selectors now claim that this was to their detriment with respect to balance. Paper, binding, and the general composition of the Eastern European publications were generally of very inferior quality, and they were cheaper to publish than were their North American counterparts, Also, unlike their North American exchange partners, with the exception of the Library of Congress, the Eastern bloc libraries had at their disposal enormous supplies of duplicate monographs and serials received gratis from publishers. Depository obligations imposed by the central Communist authorities on these publishers mandated that they ship large numbers of duplicates to their domestic libraries for use as exchange barter, and these duplicates did provide Western libraries with valuable publications often not obtainable through purchase routes. But because the balance of these exchanges was so often seen by Western libraries to be in favor of their partners, they often viewed themselves as subsidizing these Eastern European partners in the same way that the Eastern European governments did.[7]

POST 1991

The demise of the Communist regimes throughout Eastern Europe in 1990-91 and after brought with it the demise of the centralized distribution agencies. With the emergence of the many now independent states in the former Communist countries, the process of obtaining materials from these regions, whether through individual purchase orders, blanket orders, or exchanges, has become increasingly arduous. In the case of the former Yugoslavia, for instance, the loss since 1991 of central suppliers covering the entire region of the Western Balkans has made the acquisitions process very difficult as the former Yugoslav federal republics have been replaced by the independent states of Bosnia and Herzegovina, Croatia, Macedonia, Slovenia, and Yugoslavia (Serbia and Montenegro). In order to acquire needed books and journals from these countries and regions, selectors still need to employ the services of the vendors, and in some cases they use the same Western vendors which they used in the Communist era. But because the vendors now can no longer count on the former export monopolies to obtain centrally all of the materials desired by their clients, they have the enormous task of obtaining materials from the new independent republics whose booktrades and distribution systems are in total disarray. The transition from a state-controlled to a market economy has created a very chaotic situation as the older state publishers have either folded or become privatized. Countless mergers of publishing houses have occurred, and a plethora of new independent publishers has emerged.

The splintering of former super-states into small, new, and independent ones coupled with this reconstituted publishing scene has meant that libraries today need to deal with more vendors and exchange partners if they wish to maintain former levels of collecting from these areas of the world. Michael Biggins, in a 1994 article summarizing the horrendous problems in procuring materials from the countries of Southeastern Europe composing the former Yugoslavia notes: "The loss of centralized suppliers covering the entire region of the Western Balkans has made the acquisitions process cumbersome, if not impossible, on both sides of the Atlantic. The two or three central vendors of pre-1991 Yugoslavia, located in Zagreb and Belgrade, offered comprehensive coverage for the more than 11,000 monographs and 1,700 serials published in Yugoslavia each year, regardless of the republic of provenance. Now it is rare for a supplier to offer materials published outside the borders of a single republic."[8]

As the centralized control over book distribution disappeared overnight, so did the government subsidies to academic institutions and publishers which underwrote so much of the former scholarly output from the socialist countries. The lack of this support has resulted in a substantial reduction in the number of scholarly titles produced throughout Central and Eastern Europe and available on blanket orders or on exchange, and this, despite the fact that the number of new publishers emerging in the privatization process has increased. Typically, for most of these countries, scholarly research and publication are significantly down, while the production of popular mass-market literature of all sorts is up.

Perhaps the single factor which makes the identification of new titles of research value more difficult for Western libraries is the fact that so many of these new publishers as well as older ones are now attempting to act as their own distributors. According to Karen Rondestvedt, in one of the first assessments of the post-Soviet publishing scene, many of the Russian publishers now resent having to pay distributors as middlemen getting rich on their materials. In addition, she mentions that scholarly institutes, academic departments, and self-publishing researchers are also jumping on the bandwagon of self-distribution.[9] This emerging trend makes the identification of these materials practically impossible for library selectors, since the titles do not get listed in the national bibliographies, and since these various and sundry "publishers" are unsophisticated with respect to correct marketing techniques. Rondestvedt notes: "Many publishers in this group are not very sophisticated about the book and serials trade—domestic or foreign. They are likely to make little or no effort to market their material. . . . Such publishers are often not averse to dealing with vendors, but the burden is on the vendor to discover them. If a vendor does not discover them, of course their publications do not appear on the vendor's lists. If a publication does not appear on a vendor's list, many Western librarians will not find out about it, and it will therefore not be available for researchers at their libraries."[10] Because of this chaotic situation, most Russian and East European selectors recommend book-buying trips by Western library selectors to these countries in order to acquaint themselves directly with publishers' staffs and representatives as well as those of archives, learned societies, and other organizations whose publications are not listed and distributed commercially through vendors.

Exchanges of serials and monographs are still maintained between American and Eastern European libraries much as they were during the Soviet era. However, these exchanges need to be evaluated critically for their benefits to Western libraries. Disagreement exists among selectors responsible for American collections as to the continued value of these exchanges, at least those involving huge numbers of titles. A number of factors weigh against continuing them. On a title-for-title basis, Western libraries are still at a tremendous disadvantage in maintaining exchanges, and therefore many increasingly prefer "priced exchanges" as a means of ensuring a more equitable balance.

This seems to be the crux of the issue in dealing with Third World countries in general—their publications are of a lower intrinsic value due to the cheap materials (inferior bindings, acidic paper, for example). Tatjana Lorkovic and Eric Johnson state in a recent article, "In a priced (or value-for-value) exchange, each partner is responsible for assessing the fair-market value of their books. Partners in the former Soviet Union have always disliked this system, as it means that they have had to send two to five Soviet books in return for every one American book they received on exchange."[11] While the Western libraries have traditionally had to pay full market prices plus full postage costs for all of the books they send as barter, their Eastern European counterparts have generally supplied exchange desiderata from stockpiles of duplicates, or, if they paid to purchase the books, they paid lower prices than did their Western counterparts. At least under Communism the central government subventions prevailed, and libraries were able to send huge shipments of materials to their Western partners. Unfortunately, such subventions have largely disappeared, so that most of the former Soviet-bloc countries have far fewer scholarly publications to offer. The rate of materials now supplied to the West has drastically dwindled, in some cases by more than 50 percent.[12] Furthermore, many of the new commercial vendors in the former Eastern bloc states can now supply titles at rates lower than those paid for Western partners to balance exchanges. This fact, coupled with the difficulty in managing exchanges and calculating to assure they are balanced, plus the labor intensiveness required to service them in a time when many libraries are trying to reduce their staffs, has for many Western libraries called into question the very idea of continuing their existence. Margaret Olsen argues that, although exchanges will likely continue, they must be analyzed for their cost effectiveness, and such presumed cost effectiveness is not always supported by objective evidence.[13]

According to a 1997 assessment of the state of exchange programs between the United States and its East European partners, most American research libraries still exchanging "offered lists" with their partners are going the route of "priced" exchanges.[14] Current consensus among Slavic selectors seems to be that at least to some degree exchanges need to be maintained with Eastern European libraries, especially in view of the fact that such a large number of important titles for scholarly research still remain beyond the grasp of the commercial vendors, and this despite the improvements in the service these vendors are offering. As Olsen aptly asserts, the true value of an exchange cannot be stated in economic terms, and exchanges are most valuable when used as supplemental sources that supply items not available from vendors. She concludes by saying: "Western librarians would do well to cut back on exchanges and concentrate on purchase acquisitions wherever possible to avoid the expense of purchasing Western publications for their East European partners, but there is no reason to rule them out altogether."[15] One caveat regarding exclusion categories which Western partners need to convey to their Eastern European partners, and which would seemingly pertain to blanket exchanges, is expressed by Michael Biggins. In addition to traditional exclusion categories, such as technical manuals, textbooks, trivial literature, and how-to-do-it manuals, certain new types of publications currently enjoying wide readership in the "liberated" countries of Eastern Europe should also be considered for exclusion. In particular he cites reprints of long-suppressed nationalist works, of which American libraries may find they already hold serviceable first editions, and translations of foreign authors into Slavic languages.[16]

In summary, the following generalizations concerning current trends in acquiring materials from the former Communist areas of Eastern Europe can be made: (1) purchase orders may now be placed with a variety of vendors in these countries, including publishers and bookstores, without having to deal with the central distribution centers of the Soviet era via Western vendors; (2) despite the dramatic increase in the number of publishers in all of the countries of Eastern Europe, scholarly titles are on the decrease with popular mass-market works on the increase; (3) more vendors within the new states have to be dealt with for regional and provincial publications since central distributors responsible for vast geographical regions no longer exist; (4) library-to-library exchanges, both blanket exchanges as well as "offered list" exchanges, will likely continue to be maintained by research libraries, although to a lesser extent than they were during the Soviet era when more titles were available for shipment to Western libraries.

LATIN AMERICA

The impetus to collect materials from various regions has frequently surged suddenly in the wake of specific major events occurring in those regions. This has particularly affected U.S. library selectors since the Second World War. For instance, amid fallow periods of indifference in collecting from such areas as the Soviet Union and Latin America have emerged events such as Sputnik (1957) and the Castro revolution (1959) and the sudden thawing of relations between the United States and the People's Republic of China following the Nixon visit of 1972. Such events ultimately propelled the acquisition of materials from these areas to become "demand-driven" by virtue of scientific, political, historical, and literary interests by authors and scholars worldwide. Because the states of publishing, distribution, and bibliographic control for these areas were typically disorganized and chaotic, associations of librarians with common interests in getting a handle on systematic collection building were normally formed as soon as the need to seriously procure books and journals from these regions became apparent. Although the first U.S. forum established for libraries to collaboratively deal with Latin American collection building was created in 1956 (SALALM, or the Seminar on Acquisition of Latin American Library Materials), it was throughout the 1960s that acquisition programs for Latin American materials burgeoned and that relations between North American librarians and South American vendors and publishers were forged.

A 1980 article by Carl Deal, "Collecting Foreign Materials from Latin America," has served for almost two decades as a definitive, "state of the art" assessment of book procurement from the countries of South America and the Caribbean.[17] Numerous other articles, including the valuable proceedings of the SALALM conferences, have appeared since then on various aspects of collection building from these regions, but none has summarized all aspects of Latin American acquisitions so cogently. The Deal article is now very out of date, and in the almost two decades since its appearance significant improvements in the Latin American book trade, bibliographical control, and library-vendor relations have occurred. However, it should be noted that many of the problems for selectors described throughout Deal's article continue to prevail.

Historically, library-bookseller relations with Latin America have been typified by several conditions for most of this century. In the first place, only some of the countries have had high literacy and book production rates. Among these are Argentina, Brazil, Colombia, and Mexico. By contrast, for the remainder of Latin

America the book publication, distribution, and bibliographic control has generally been less developed. National libraries have been sparse, and therefore any sort of national record for the book production of many countries has been lacking. Bibliographic control in the form of national bibliographies has often been abysmal, with many of the existing ones being issued so irregularly as to be useless for routine book selection purposes. Reliable bookstores and vendors have been in short supply. Print runs have been extremely short, and well-organized book information sources, such as book-trade magazines and publishers' catalogs, have in many instances not existed. Many works across all disciplines have often been issued privately at the expense of their authors rather than by commercial publishers cognizant of copyright laws and depository requirements. Consequently these titles have received scant publicity through the book-trade media or national bibliographies.

As the end of this century approaches, Argentina, Brazil, Colombia, and Mexico still lead in terms of publishing output and bibliographic control. And although many of the characteristics outlined in the preceding paragraph still obtain, the ability of Latin American libraries to collect, record, and preserve their national heritages has generally improved, and the ability on the part of the Latin American vendors to procure and supply needed materials from minor publishers and obscure sources has surged. More national bibliographies are being issued, and new book trade and book review journals have appeared.

A significant feature of most Latin American vendors of today is that they also serve as bookstores in the cities and towns of their headquarters. Fernando Garcia Cambeiro in Argentina; Editoria Inca in Bogota which covers Colombia, Bolivia, Ecuador, and Venezuela; MACH in Mexico; and Susan Bach in Brazil, are notable examples. So vital to selectors are the vendors for Latin America that many large directories of vendors have appeared over the years, a notable one being Howard Karno's *Directory of Vendors of Latin American Library Materials* (4th rev. ed., 1993). Also improved is the general quality of binding and paper from all of these countries. Only ten years ago flimsy bindings and high acid content paper typified a large percentage of their publications, a fact which frequently raised the eyebrows of selectors. Today, however, the physical composition of most Latin American works is on par, if not superior to that of their U.S. and Canadian counterparts, and certainly superior to that of books and journals currently received from Eastern Europe. Book publishing output from all of these countries has risen steadily if not drastically in recent years.

Because much of Latin America remains impoverished with low literacy rates, and because even the best authors in such regions frequently do not have established publishing houses which they can approach for the printing and distribution of their works, a large amount of publishing is still done at the expense of the author and in extremely limited editions which are not widely publicized. Sleuthing on the part of vendors is thus necessary to identify and snatch these and other obscure but often high-quality items, and the most efficient way for North American libraries to procure these materials is through blanket orders established with Latin American vendors.

From 1960 to 1972 a massive program called LACAP (Latin American Cooperative Acquisitions Program) existed in which the Latin American-based vendors selected multiple copies of books which were shipped to the U.S. jobber Stechert-Hafner for distribution to about forty participating U.S. libraries. Since the demise of this endeavor, most of those libraries plus additional ones maintain blanket orders which they individually negotiate with a variety of Latin American dealers—a program commonly referred to as LABO (Latin American Blanket Order).

Most Latin American publishers prefer not to receive orders directly from libraries, so most selectors desiring specific titles simply request them from their dealers on blanket order rather than placing firm orders for them, either directly or with vendors. This procedure of requesting specific titles on a blanket order rather than submitting separate purchase orders for them is also common to acquisitions from Eastern Europe. Placing firm purchase orders directly with publishers for individual monographs is viable for countries with up-to-date national bibliographies and substantial print-runs, such as those of Western Europe. However, this is not viable for most Latin American imprints, since many titles from short print runs are apt to be out of stock at their publishers by the time a firm purchase order is placed. These same titles may, however, still be available in the stocks of bookstores and also with vendors who supply blanket orders. Academic and research institutes, on the other hand, prefer to receive orders directly from libraries and generally prefer not to deal with the library vendors. For Latin Americanist librarians this means having to take the time to correspond with a large number of organizations in order to receive their publications as gifts, on exchange, or through direct purchase.

Trips by library selectors to visit bookstores and academic institutions which issue publications are also necessary, especially for large collecting programs. In the case of Latin America the establishment of personal contacts with publishers and booksellers is very important. Although the blanket orders through vendors are essential, they cannot be relied on to catch every important title matching a blanket order profile. And since many titles do not get entered into the national bibliographies, not to speak of controversial titles in areas under heavy government censorship, the responsible selector will want to maintain as many personal contacts with the dealers and publishers as possible. Nelly Gonzalez and Walter Brem convey a vivid flavor of such trips in their 1985 article "Innocents Abroad: The Acquisitions Trip for Academic Librarians."[18]

Purchase standing orders for serials can normally be placed with vendors, and many serials can be received directly on exchange with Latin American university libraries. But many social science monographs and serials are not marketed commercially and tend to be issued by special research institutes or as departmental publications of the universities. To identify and to select these materials, a selector must exert a good deal of individual initiative, particularly when requests for significant numbers of titles in specific disciplines, such as labor relations, political science, sociology, and city planning are to be filled. For example, a selector who identifies a research institute issuing a number of relevant publications can frequently obtain them gratis simply by contacting the institute directors and requesting them. One selector at a large research library documents repeated success in composing sincere but flattering letters praising the quality of the publications, and stating that since her library is likewise state-supported, it lacks the funds to acquire needed materials and would appreciate receiving as many free imprints as possible. Similar successful results have been obtained by libraries which have requested publications from government research institutes, although increasingly these organizations are assessing fees for their publications, consciously basing their policy on that of the U.S. Government Publications Office.

Throughout 1996 and 1997 several European vendors began inputting catalog records into the OCLC Online Union Catalog for currently published titles, an action which, although hailed by selectors, has received mixed reviews from U.S. catalogers due to the inconsistencies with US MARC format and established LC subject headings. Cassalini (Italy), and Puvill (Spain) are examples of prominent vendors of European materials that are contributing records to OCLC. Latin American books are also included in the titles cataloged and input into OCLC by Puvill, and in the February 27, 1997, *SALALM Newsletter* it was reported that Iberbook International is also participating in this program.[19] Library book selectors can, of course, benefit from the prompt availability of these records for newly released titles, since by conducting OCLC keyword as well as subject searches delimited by date they can quickly identify relevant new titles for ordering.

It is a well-established fact that the best printed catalogs of Latin American publications are those issued by publishers, such as G. K. Hall in the United States, starting in the 1960s as a response to the collecting interests of North American libraries. Today, such catalogs as those of the Latin American collections of the Hispanic Society of America, the University of Texas Library, the University of Florida Library, and the Ibero-Amerikanisches Institut, Berlin, are considered to constitute the most thorough documentation of recorded knowledge for all of Latin America—a documentation which some maintain exceeds that of any single Latin American library. These resources continue to be valuable tools for retrospective collection development. However, inroads in retrospective conversion are now providing easier access to many of the titles of these collections through the online catalogs of their respective holding institutions, many of which can be searched remotely over the Internet.

Librarians with selection responsibilities for Latin America have been the most energetic group among foreign language area selectors in attempting to get a national cooperative collection development project under way, and to stress monographic acquisitions in the process. The original Latin American "Demonstration Project" of the ARL Foreign Acquisitions Project has evolved into the Latin Americanist Research Resources Project, an endeavor sponsored jointly by the Association of American Universities (AAU), the Association of Research Libraries (ARL), and the Seminar on the Acquisition of Latin American Library Materials (SALALM). Dan Hazan, Librarian for Latin America, Spain, and Portugal at Harvard University, outlined the approach taken in a recent article published in *ARL*, the newsletter of the Association of Research Libraries. As of 1997 the project, consisting of thirty-five member institutions,

> calls for each participating library to re-direct seven percent of its monographic allocation for materials from Latin America toward a specific, pre-arranged collecting area. Acquisitions can focus on a country, a group of countries, a subject area, or a subject area from a particular country. Libraries received their collecting assignments by first listing (in priority order) no more than three areas upon which they might focus. These choices were posted to the group as a whole,

along with the amount that each library will spend on its proposed target area. A process of voluntary, participant-driven fine-tuning ensued. Early results indicate that each library has been able to retain a high-priority assignment within a minimally duplicative collecting grid.[20]

The maintenance of core collections by the various libraries is encouraged. But in the process of selecting materials they are also urged to collect items likely to receive only occasional use so as to ensure the receipt of the "marginal" or "grey" materials so frequently missing from the North American collections of all foreign materials. It is precisely this sense of obligation to procure second tier titles which differentiates this work from so many collaborative efforts and which lends the aspect of cooperative collection development to the project in a real sense. Commitments are also made by the participants to improve coverage of serials through an evolving system of distributed subscription assignments, a table of contents database, and a mechanism for expedited interlibrary loan. The term *cooperative, distributed acquisition program* has been adopted to capsulize its efforts toward monographic as well as serial collaborative collection development for Latin American studies within the United States. The program includes efforts to render interlibrary loan cheaper and more effective, and it encourages regional (i.e., the various existing consortia) specialization as well as participation by individual libraries nationwide.

It should be noted that the project's stated goal is not, however, to promise comprehensive acquisitions, but rather to improve Latin American coverage. This goal of trying to simply improve the coverage of foreign literature in United States collections was that of both the RLG Conspectus as well as the North American Collections Inventory Project, described earlier in this chapter. Any thoughts of ever procuring exhaustive coverage of foreign publications on our continent are totally unrealistic. Nonetheless, Latin Americanists should be duly proud of being in the lead in attempting to systematically implement the recommendations of the ARL Foreign Acquisitions Project for area studies.

The Latin American Microform Project (LAMP) of the Center for Research Libraries (CRL) is another project of major import for improving the acquisition of materials from Latin America. Collections and sets of hard-to-obtain publications, documents of learned societies, serials, newspapers, certain government documents, and miscellaneous items elusive to the commercial booktrade are filmed, stored at CRL, and available through interlibrary loan to all subscribers to the project.

AFRICA

The continent of Africa is likely to be more challenging for an area selector than any other region of the world due to its geographical vastness, its multi-ethnic composition, its diverse language families, and the low level of organization of the book trade in most of its regions. Despite the diversity of the continent, in American research libraries of all sizes materials selection for Africa is often conducted by a single selector, although there is a wide variety of types of such selectors. A common approach is to have a Black Studies librarian position responsible for collecting African, Caribbean, and African-American publications. In other instances an Africana bibliographer, or the humanities or social sciences librarian responsible for this and other large areas of the globe has collecting responsibilities for the African continent. Some institutions provide a selector for collecting from Northern Africa and another for the sub-Saharan regions. If selection in a library is assigned strictly along language lines, the French specialist may select for Francophone Africa, the Portuguese expert for Lusophone Africa.

Although some African books-in-print publications and national bibliographies exist for the more literate areas with the highest per capita book production rates, these frequently lag too far behind in publication to be of use for title-by-title book selection purposes. Some vendors offer blanket order and approval plans, and they are truly indispensable in enabling libraries to obtain African materials in a timely fashion. But direct personal contacts on the part of selectors with African publishers and bookstores are essential where comprehensive collecting is a goal. Book buying trips and visits to African vendors and bookstores where long-lasting personal contacts can be established are more than worth the time and money expended. Such contacts can lead to the systematic procurement of materials otherwise not identifiable through national bibliographies and publishers' announcements in a continent in which so many countries are beset with very primitive bibliographic control and systems of book distribution. It is chiefly for this reason that trips by selectors to foreign booksellers and vendors are even more essential for African selectors than they are for selectors for other developing areas. A second reason for traveling abroad to improve acquisitions with developing countries is to attend bookfairs in the various countries. The Zimbabwe International Bookfair, the largest in Africa, is held every August. Many selectors recommend attending this bookfair as an excellent method to become acquainted with emerging booksellers and vendors, not to speak of established and new publishers and their latest titles.

Selectors can also become involved with the so-called field representatives to the various countries who scout around for current relevant imprints, such as those employed by the Library of Congress's
Nairobi Office. Since 1968 this agency has issued a bi-monthly bibliography, *Accessions List: Eastern and Southern Africa*. In this excellent selection resource the titles cited have all been selected by the
Nairobi Office field bibliographers. Materials included in these lists
can be supplied by the Office to North American libraries either on
blanket order or on an approval plan. An additional valuable selection tool is the quarterly *African Book Publishing Record,* which updates the sporadically issued *African Books in Print. African
Research and Documentation* is a British journal which publishes
excellent articles on Africana collections and library concerns.
African Book World and Press Directory is a useful guide to African
publishers and booksellers, very similar in its arrangement and
scope to *International Literary Market Place. Africa Bibliography*,
which has been published annually since 1984 by Edinburgh
University Press, contains a main body of separate listings of all of
countries on the African continent plus surrounding islands with
their respective publications. Concluding each issue is a single comprehensive subject index for the entries contained in the body.

Libraries with strong collections of African materials exist not
only on the African continent, but also in such countries as Great
Britain, France, and the United States. Publications in the many
indigenous languages of Africa are well represented in a few of
these libraries, although to a far lesser extent due to the paucity of
materials traditionally published in some languages. Publishing is
on the increase for a number of the indigenous languages, particularly Swahili and Zulu. The library at Northwestern University
houses the largest collection of materials in vernacular African languages in North America. The curator of these collections, David
Easterbrook, estimates that they contain approximately 10,500
volumes.

Alfred Kagan's article "Sources for African Language Materials
from the Countries of Anglophone Africa" presents a concise and
up-to-date guide to current reference sources, blanket order and approval plan dealers, bookshops and publishers, and printed as well
as online catalogs pertaining to Africana acquisitions work.[21] One
very interesting observation of Kagan concerns the role of exchanges in acquiring materials from Africa. He notes: "Exchange
agreements are also potentially very useful, but please be fore-
warned that libraries in rich countries will likely end up sending
more than they receive. Those of us with adequate collection development budgets in hard currencies should not mind helping out

African libraries that are suffering from the African "book famine."[22] This article also contains a listing of the major national bibliographies of Africa with notes on the latest issues reported. These bibliographies cover Kenya, Lesotho, Malawi, Nigeria, Sierra Leone, South Africa, Swaziland, Tanzania, Uganda, Zambia, and Zimbabwe. Other African countries' national bibliographies, some of which have ceased or been suspended, are represented in Yvette Scheven's *Bibliographies for African Studies 1970-1986.*[23] This work has since been updated by *Bibliographies for African Studies, 1987-1993.*[24] Kagan also cites the names of several blanket order/approval plan dealers, all of which supply books in African languages, and he lists what he considers to be the best dealers for the Anglophone countries of Southern Africa.

Previously, professional library groups as well as consortia have attempted to collaboratively collect materials from Africa, particularly for university dissertations and newspapers. For instance, the Africana Librarians Council of the African Studies Association, the chief North American organization for Africana librarians, launched a project some years ago for cooperative collecting along the role of the old Farmington Plan by which individual libraries would assume responsibilities to collect intensely from certain countries, particularly with respect to monographs. Unfortunately this project lasted only a few years. The most effective North American cooperative project to date for African materials is the Cooperative Africana Microform Project (CAMP) based at the Center for Research Libraries (CRL). Begun in 1963, this project is a joint effort by research libraries throughout the world together with CRL to promote the preservation of publications and archives from the nearly fifty nations of sub-Saharan Africa and to make these materials available to researchers in microform housed at CRL. Member libraries purchase or film research materials from Africa in cooperation with each other.

Multi-volume printed catalogs of the Africana collections in the United States have been available by publishers, such as G. K. Hall, Boston, for a number of years for institutions such as Indiana University, Boston University, the University of Rhodesia, and the University of London. But for current and future Africana selectors, the online catalogs of these and other libraries with substantial African imprints are of even greater value. The telnet addresses for these online catalogs, together with instructions for logging into them, are provided in the article by Alfred Kagan.[25]

Electronic resources available free on a subscription basis from African libraries are really only starting to emerge, but South Africa and Zimbabwe have made great inroads with online public access catalogs. In addition, databases for union lists of periodicals, subject indexes to periodical literature, and dissertations are being produced in CD-ROM format in a number of countries. These resources can all be of assistance to Africana selectors, but since so few countries in Africa are producing them, the work of selectors to acquire African titles will still require a good amount of resourcefulness and the will to travel to the countries on field trips for a long time to come.

Since its founding in 1957 the Africana Librarians Council has meet twice yearly, once during the annual meeting of the African Studies Association, and once at the institution of a member library. It has provided an excellent forum for discussion among librarians involved in the collection development of African materials. The group has contributed much time and effort to the work of the Cooperative African Microfilm Project (CAMP).

EAST ASIA

In contrast to Africa, Eastern Europe, and Latin America, sweeping statements and generalizations concerning acquisitions trends and methods cannot be made with regard to East Asia (China including Hong Kong, Taiwan, Japan, North Korea, and South Korea) as well as Southeast Asia (Vietnam, Laos, Cambodia, Thailand, Burma, Malaysia, Singapore, Brunei, the Philippines, and Indonesia). It is, however, important to realize that in some of these countries the state of book distribution and bibliographic control is very advanced, while in others it is extremely undeveloped. Owing both to political rapprochements between the United States and the countries of Asia still under Communism, as well as to the escalating economic prominence of the Asian countries and those of the Pacific Rim in international markets, research on all of these countries, particularly among social scientists, has been on the increase for over two decades. Such scholarly attention has consequently necessitated an aggressive acquisition of materials from this region for economists, political scientists, and historians. However, despite the enormity of the entire Eastern and Southeastern Asia territory, most large and medium-size American research libraries that collect vernacular and Western language materials from these areas focus primarily on China and Japan.

A significant factor affecting collection development of East Asian collections is the fact that in almost all university and other research libraries, even those which collect heavily in East Asian materials, the vernacular collections of East Asian materials stand relatively isolated from the rest of the collections, even from materials in English or other Western languages that relate by subject to East Asian materials. This is due to the fact that very few researchers in fields such as history, sociology, political science, or even comparative literature are sufficiently fluent in any of the East Asian languages to be able to conduct research using the vernacular scholarly publications of the East Asian countries. In the more advanced of these countries, particularly Japan, much of the research is issued in English, but, of course, most publications are issued in the vernacular languages in these countries also. Many of these publications are highly relevant to the interests of scholars in many fields, but, at least in American libraries, they can be consulted by very few scholars who have not specialized in the cultures and languages of the countries of the publications. As a consequence, the typical East Asian collections of segregated vernacular materials generally have a small clientele when compared with clientele of other area study collections, even Slavic. As shown in a 1993 article addressing the unfortunate isolation of many East Asian collections, this fact sometimes calls into question the cost effectiveness of East Asian collection development.[26] This said, the obvious importance that all of Asia will have in the next century suggests that collection building in Asian vernacular languages should be promoted, albeit based on perceived use and needs, and that generalist social scientists and comparative literature scholars seriously interested in Asia should make greater efforts to learn the Asian languages in their particular areas of interest. If these changes would occur, materials selection for Asia as an area study could be conducted on a broader basis as a means of coordinating the needs of both generalists in the social sciences and humanities with those of Asian studies specialists who are conversant with one or more Asian languages.

China, Hong Kong, and Taiwan

For a sizable developing area, China is unique in that the types of blanket order and approval plan arrangements favored for acquisitions from regions such as Latin America and Africa have not generally been regarded as effective by selectors of Chinese materials. Selectors are apt to criticize the quality of the blanket order shipments received and the fact that they are often out of scope with the profiles as established with their vendors. This fact notwithstanding, three prominent vendors in China (China International Book Trading Corporation, China National Publications Import and Export Corporation, and China National Publishing Industry Trading Corporation) do have a good reputation for supplying American libraries with blanket orders. In any case, it seems to be the consensus of East Asian librarians that title-by-title selection from book lists of current imprints prepared by Chinese as well as Western vendors and distributed to selectors constitutes the most effective method for becoming alerted to newly issued titles. Since Chinese vendors frequently distribute annotated lists of new imprints, these vendors are sometimes preferred by selectors over American vendors, and the services of the Chinese vendors are generally reputed to be as cost-effective and reliable as are services rendered by the American vendors. Firm orders resulting from monograph and serial selections from these vendor lists can almost always be placed directly with the vendors having supplied them. Online lists of selected recent imprints arranged by subject are also becoming available on Internet sites maintained by vendors in Taiwan and Hong Kong for materials from all parts of China. Selectors are increasingly perusing these lists in order to identify, order, and receive quality publications in a timely fashion. The section of this chapter on Western Europe cites a model for such service recently initiated on the Web by the German vendor Otto Harrassowitz for German-language imprints.

An additional reason for preferring vendor book lists is the fact that the national bibliography for China, *Quanguo Xinshumu*, is generally several years behind in publishing, and lists of forthcoming titles issued by Chinese vendors tend to be unreliable since an appreciable number of books announced for future publication ultimately do not appear. Furthermore, *Quanguo Xinshumu* is said to cover only about half of the titles published nationwide. This fact can be attributed to some degree to a relaxing of centralized authority in the People's Republic. Whereas prior to the early 1980s the one hundred or so publishers were all state enterprises, the five hundred publishing houses today include many that are collectively owned, and many private ones have also emerged, particularly in the provinces. A major reason for the poor coverage of *Quanguo Xinshumu* is that many of these new publishers fail to comply with their obligations to send copies of their works to the Editions Library in Beijing, the authority responsible for the compilation of *Quanguo Xinshumu*.[27] Although the National Library of China in Beijing serves as a national book collecting center for all of China, it does not function as a copyright office, and it consequently does not have a record of all new Chinese publications, a strange fact in a country with communications operations so highly centralized. Exchanges, a favorite acquisition route for both monographs and serials among many area selectors collecting from other world areas, have not proven particularly viable for obtaining publications from the People's Republic, although they have been effective for obtaining materials from Taiwan. The problem is due to the imbalance reported by many Western libraries in not receiving quality or quantity in return for the journals they have subscribed to as barter for shipment to their Chinese library exchange partners.

Since the birth of the People's Republic of China in 1949, there has existed a single book distribution agency, Hsin Hua, identical in function to Mezhdunarodnia Kniga for the former Soviet Union. Located in Beijing, Hsin Hua (New China Bookstore) has also maintained bookstores in cities throughout China. Until very recently all orders for materials from publishers throughout the Chinese mainland had to be routed through Hsin Hua, but within the past few years some Chinese publishers have been allowed to distribute and export books themselves. Consequently, foreign selectors can now receive book lists and catalogs directly from a multiplicity of distributors, bookstores, and vendors, and may deal with them without having to go through Hsin Hua. A notable factor affecting acquisitions from China since the 1970s is the fact that American libraries may now send U.S. dollars to Chinese vendors and booksellers, whereas previously all orders for published materials had to be routed through vendors in Hong Kong or other sites outside of the People's Republic in order for remittance in dollars to occur.

As in the case of Africa and Latin America, selectors of Asian materials, particularly Chinese, find book buying trips to bookstores, vendors, and book fairs to be of tremendous value in keeping up with trends in the book trade and for making personal contacts with the vendors and book dealers. Cooperative acquisitions work for Chinese materials by American libraries has still not occurred on the national level, but significant work in the area of cooperative acquisitions is being done on the two coasts of the United States: by the East Coast Consortium (Columbia, Cornell, Harvard, New York Public Library, Princeton, and Yale), and by the UC-Berkeley/ Stanford libraries and by the University of California Statewide East Asia Library System.

The acquisition of materials from China has constituted a major component of the ARL Foreign Acquisitions Project, whose July 1994 "Report on Chinese Materials" reports findings of a study to assess the strengths and weaknesses of North American collections in this area, and which recommends specific actions toward the goal of organized cooperative resource sharing. These recommendations include:

1. the designation of the Library of Congress as a national center of last resort for the collection of scientific Chinese-language materials;
2. an increased number of Chinese records in OCLC and RLIN to reflect better the holdings of libraries;
3. an increase in field acquisition trips by Chinese studies librarians;
4. the creation of an electronic bulletin board to report decisions of major purchases;
5. the mounting of union lists of newspapers and yearbooks;
6. a systematic procedure for assuring that every essential serial listed in *A Guide to the Core Journals of China* (published by Beijing University Press in 1992) is subscribed to by at least one North American library; and
7. the designation of specific libraries as centers to concentrate on specific types of publications.[28]

Library organizations to promote better nationwide collecting of Asian materials have been effective to date. The Council on East Asian Libraries (CEAL), under the aegis of the Association for Asian Studies, is a faculty-librarians' forum created for the discussion of East Asian library issues and problems of common concern. CEAL publishes a quarterly *Journal* (formerly *Bulletin*) in which library-vendor relations, current publishing trends, and other matters of concern to selectors are discussed in articles and reports of meetings. CEAL also maintains a useful Web site which, in addition to providing useful reference material on China, Japan, and Korea, offers information on the various CEAL committees on dealing with these countries. This site can be visited at <http://darkwing. uoregon.edu/~felsing/ceal/welcome.html>. In addition, the Asian, African, and Middle Eastern Section (AAMES) of the Association of College and Research Libraries, American Library Association, serves as a forum for general discussions of collection development, reference, and cataloging at the annual and midwinter ALA conferences.

Since the development of character codes capable of accommodating Chinese characters, many full-text databases have emerged in Taiwan, Hong Kong, and mainland China. A boon to selectors, libraries on both sides of the Pacific are currently developing online catalogs to include Chinese language records, such as that of the University of California, San Diego.

Japan

Japan has long had one of the best-organized book trades in the world and certainly the best in East Asia. Its thriving economy and educational system over many decades have been the principal factor. Japanese vernacular as well as English-language materials have received attention by scholars and selectors chiefly due to economic and political factors. After World War II there was interest in the Japanese imperial war machine of the 1930s and 1940s. Following this wave of attention the Japanese economic miracle of the 1960s stimulated research by historians, political scientists, sociologists, and economists. Then came a third wave of intense interest in Japan in the 1980s due to the heated trade conflicts between Japan and the West, in particular the United States.

In most research libraries with active programs to acquire Japanese materials, firm orders placed with Japanese vendors tend to be favored over blanket order programs. Most libraries also maintain standing orders for monographic series with the same vendors which they use for their monographic orders and journal subscriptions. In addition to general vendors supplying materials in all subjects to libraries, there are also many vendors with specific subject specialties, and it is not uncommon for an American library to use many of these subject-specific vendors, each of which supplies books and serials in its respective subject. Exchanges for both serials and monographs are also commonly maintained between American libraries and their Japanese partners, and monographic series are often exchanged with research institutes.

Japan, like the Netherlands, is a country which issues a relatively large number of publications in English. In many American academic libraries these publications suffice for most scholarly purposes. However, in research libraries with an emphasis on Japanese studies there is a need to collect Japanese language materials, and to this end there sometimes are two Japanese bibliographer positions—one for a selector to collect in the vernacular, and one for another selector responsible for English language materials from Japan, China, and North and South Korea.

CEAL is the chief professional group in North America for librarians dealing with Japanese materials. A second important organization in which these librarians participate is the European Association of Japanese Resources Specialists.

Not only are Japanese books plentiful in Japan, but Chinese and Korean books are also available there. Tokyo is one of the few cities in the world where North Korean publications can be found. Nippon Hanbai and Tokyo Hanbai are the two major vendors.

Japan Publication Trading Company and Isseido remain two of the best book exporting stores in the world.

Identifying and selecting materials from South Korea are similar to the case of Japan. Acquisitions from North Korea, on the other hand, present problems, particular for selectors from the United States. Limited exchanges can be arranged with the national library in Pyongyang, but these exchanges do not have a high success rate. One North Korean dealer, Korea Publication Export and Import Corporation, has attained some prominence, but the most effective route for purchasing North Korean publications has been through bookstores in Seoul, South Korea, Tokyo, or Hong Kong. It is almost impossible for an American librarian to obtain a North Korean visa to go there to buy books.[29]

SOUTH AND WEST ASIA

Of all of the developing countries, the countries constituting South and West Asia remain unique in that the Library of Congress serves as the chief acquisitions route for major U.S. research libraries collecting their materials. Accession lists are sent by the Library of Congress to libraries participating in its "South-Asia-LC" and "West-Asia-LC" programs, and selectors make monographic selections from these lists which are returned to LC for procurement and distribution to the selecting libraries. (Although such countries as Syria, Jordan, Israel, Lebanon, Turkey, Saudia Arabia, Iran, and Iraq are commonly referred to as the "Middle East," as a geographical designation for libraries they are frequently referred to as "West Asia," and this designation is also applied to the Saharan countries of Africa: Egypt, Libya, Algeria, and Morocco.) Selectors may participate in these programs for specific countries whose publications they express a desire to collect on a regular basis. For instance, a given library may declare it wishes to receive materials only from Sri Lanka, Bangladesh, Pakistan, Nepal, and Iran under the South Asia-LC program; and from Syria, Lebanon, and Egypt under the West Asia-LC program. Most libraries also place their subscriptions to serials with the LC offices for these programs.

Of the publications from the South Asian countries, approximately 50 percent are in English, with the remainder being in the vernacular of the respective countries. For the Arabic-speaking countries of West Asia, only about 15 percent are in English. All 38 of the libraries participating in the South Asia-LC Program receive about 50 percent of their publications from India free, since the Public Law 480 Program pays for 50 percent of the total number of titles received on the program. This PL-480 Program represents a huge initiative by the U.S. federal government since 1962 toward the objective of federally supported worldwide coverage of publications from developing areas. Under this program, foreign currencies from the sale of our surplus agricultural commodities have been used to buy and distribute to U.S. libraries current books and periodicals. For most of its life, the program comprised publications from seven countries (Ceylon, India, Indonesia, Nepal, Pakistan, Syria, and Yugoslavia). India was the last remaining country in the group and its program ceased in October 1998. After that time all of the publications from India acquired through the South Asia-LC Program will have to be purchased completely by the various participating libraries. Bookstores in these countries also serve as acquisition sources, particularly for smaller North American libraries not participating in the Library of Congress programs.

Because of nonexistent relations with Iran and Iraq, the LC programs do not include these two important countries, and thus the U.S. libraries wishing to obtain their publications have to rely on bookstores in neighboring countries such as Pakistan to purchase desired publications.

The chief professional organization for selectors of South Asian materials is the Committee on South Asian Libraries and Documentation (CONSALD). Convening for annual meetings, members of CONSALD are all participants in the South Asia-LC Program, and they publish an annual journal, *South Asia Libraries Notes and Queries*.

REMOTE ACCESS
TO FOREIGN MONOGRAPHS—A SOLUTION
TO THE "NATIONAL COLLECTION" PROBLEM?

Pertinent to access vs. ownership issues is the current raging debate over the future of the scholarly monograph in its present print form. Forecasters of a future "paperless society" have frequently been challenged on their predictions that the book in its traditional hardcopy form will be completely replaced by electronic versions. Although most scholars and librarians have hailed the electronic indexes and full-text version of journals as positive developments, few have regarded the digitized monograph as an imminent fact of life. Furthermore, the idea that huge numbers of domestic as well as foreign journals are available online is a gross exaggeration, yet one accepted by too many top-level university administrators.[30] And it is often asserted that administrators are currently under-funding their libraries not only because of this myth, but also from the misapprehension that the digitized titles are available at no or little cost.

Recently a lively debate has been raging over the future of the scholarly monograph in print format, particulary with regard to U.S. university press monographs which are said by some univer-sity press administrators to be undersold because of their cost to li-braries and also because of a perceived declining quality of many of them in the eyes of some scholars and library selectors. One pro-posed solution is that they be issued in electronic versions. The problem here, though, is that the production of electronic books is not inexpensive, untenured faculty are reluctant to publish their work in them, and it is unclear whether or not scholars and stu-dents are willing to read whole books online, at least on the desk-top computer in its present state of development. These issues were debated at a September 1997 conference convened by the American Council of Learned Societies, the Association of American University Presses, and the Association of Research Libraries. The consensus from the conference, entitled "The Specialized Scholarly Monograph in Crisis," was that the monograph is indeed in danger, but that it is too early to tell whether electronic publishing will cut the costs and help the marketing of monographs.[31]

Obviously the issue of the inadequacies of the "North American Collection" would diminish if our libraries could have immediate online full-text retrieval of the world's published books. But cer-tainly in view of the slow progress under way toward digitizing just U.S. university press publications, not to speak of publications from commercial presses or foreign publishers, this cannot possibly be entertained as a short-term fix. Immediate solutions to foster shared collecting of foreign imprints in paper format by our li-braries should be found and implemented.

CONCLUSION

Over the past fifty years the basic methods used for selecting and acquiring foreign materials have really changed very little. Firm orders, blanket orders, exchanges, and gifts have all played im-portant roles as routes to building up a national collection of for-eign materials. What in particular has changed the nature of this work in very recent years has been the advent of technology in its provision of remote access to the titles of works contained in collections, its facilitation of communications between selectors and vendors via e-mail and listing services, and its multiplicity of uses via the World Wide Web, many of which have been discussed in this chapter. This technology has, of course, had an impact on all forms of acquisition work, domestic or foreign, but its most dramatic effect has been on foreign acquisitions. A second factor is the political changes stemming from the fall of Communism in Eastern Europe. Both political and economic factors resulting from these shifts have significantly altered the way U.S. libraries obtain materials from the countries of that region.

Any serious effort to successfully acquire materials from abroad remains a challenge, but it is a rewarding one for selectors who are able to acquire these materials to a degree commensurate with their aspirations. As technology is more widely utilized, both at home and abroad, this work may well become less arduous for future selectors. In any case, questions of foremost importance include how, and to what degree, remote access to foreign materials via digitized texts will strengthen our national collection in the long term; and how our national collection can be improved in its holdings of foreign materials in traditional print format in the short term.

Notes

1. G. E. Gorman and J. J. Mills, *Guide to Curent National Bibliographies in the Third World* (Munich and New York: K. G. Saur, 1987).

2. Richard Hacken, "The RLG Conoco Study and Its Aftermath: Is Resource Sharing in Limbo?" *Journal of Academic Librarianship* 18 (1992): 22.

3. Jutta Reed-Scott, *Scholarship, Research Libraries, and Global Publishing: The Result of a Study Funded by the Andrew W. Mellon Foundation* (Washington, D.C.: Association of Research Libraries, 1996).

4. Ibid., pp. 143-144.

5. James Campbell, "Publishing and Export Bookselling in Western Europe," *Understanding the Business of Library Acquisitions,* ed. Karen A. Schmidt (Chicago: American Library Association, 1990), p. 59.

6. Barbara Walden, Charles Fineman, William S. Monroe, et al., "Western European Political Science: An Acquisition Study," *College & Research Libraries* 55 (1994): 286-295.

7. Margaret Olsen, "The More Things Change, the More They Stay the Same: East-West Exchanges 1960-1993," *Library Resources & Technical Services* 39 (1995): 7.

8. Michael Biggins, "Acquisitions from Yugoslavia's Successor States," *Library Resources & Technical Services* 38 (1994): 54.

9. Karen Rondestvedt, "Acquisitions Problems from Poland and Russia: Update on Causes and Potential Solutions," *Library Resources & Technical Services* 37 (1993): 215.

10. Ibid., p. 215.

11. Tatjana Lorkovic and Eric A. Johnson, "Serial and Book Exchanges with the Former Soviet Union," *Serials Librarian* 31, no. 4 (1997): 65.

12. Olsen, "The More Things Change," p. 7.

13. Ibid., p. 13.

14. Lorkovic and Johnson, "Serial and Book Exchanges," p. 7.

15. Olsen, "The More Things Change," p. 20.

16. Biggins, "Acquisitions," p. 54.

17. Carl Deal, "Collecting Foreign Materials from Latin America," *Collection Development in Libraries: A Treatise* (Greenwich, Conn.: JAI, 1980), pp. 219-239.

18. Nelly Gonzalez and Walter Brem Jr., "Innocents Abroad: The Acquisitions Trip for Academic Librarians," *The Central American Connection: Library Resources and Access. Seminar on the Acquisition of Latin American Library Materials XXVIII. Papers of the Twenty-Eighth Annual Meeting of the Seminar on the Acquisition of Latin American Library Materials* (SALALM Secretariat, 1985), pp. 151-154.

19. *SALALM Newsletter* 24 (1997): 81.

20. Dan Hazan, "The Latin Americanist Research Resources Project: A New Direction for Monographic Cooperation?" *ARL: A Bimonthly Newsletter of Research Library Issues and Actions* 191 (1997): 1-6.

21. Alfred Kagan, "Sources for African Language Materials from the Countries of Anglophone Africa," *Collection Building* 15 (1996): 17-21.

22. Ibid., p. 17.

23. Yvette Scheven, ed., *Bibliographies for African Studies 1970-1986* (London, New York: Hans Zell, 1988).

24. Yvette Scheven, ed., *Bibliographies for African Studies 1987-1993* (London, New York: Hans Zell, 1994).

25. Kagan, "Sources," pp. 20-21.

26. Diane E. Perushek, "A Branch Apart: East Asian Collections in a Research Library Context," *Committee on East Asian Libraries Bulletin* 101 (1993): 9.

27. Eugene W. Wu, "Special Report. ARL Foreign Acquisitions Project. Report on Chinese Materials," *Committee on East Asian Libraries Bulletin* 104 (1994): 111.

28. Ibid., pp. 117-118.

29. Krol K. Lo, "East Asia," *Selection of Library Materials for Area Studies, Part I.: Asia, Iberia, the Caribbean, and Latin America, Eastern Europe and the Soviet Union, and the South Pacific* (Chicago and London: American Library Association, 1990), p. 26.

30. William Miller, past president of the Association for College and Research Libraries estimated that as of August 1997, out of perhaps 150,000 journals available to scholars worldwide, fewer than 4,000 are currently available in electronic format. William Miller, "Troubling Myths about On-Line Information," *Chronicle of Higher Education,* August 1, 1997, A44.

31. Karen Winkler, "Scholars, Publishers, and Librarians Confer on Crisis Afflicting Monograph," *Academe Today. Chronicle of Higher Education,* September 15, 1997 (http://chronicle.com/che-data/ news . . . dailarch.dir/9709.dir/97091503.htm).

Bibliography

Farrell, David and Jutta Reed-Scott. "The North American Collections Inventory Project: Implications for the Future of Coordinated Management of Research Collections." *Library Resources & Technical Services* 33 (1989): 15-28.

Ferguson, Anthony W., Joan Grant, and Joel S. Rutstein. "The RLG Conspectus: Its Uses and Benefits." *College & Research Libraries* 49 (1988): 197-206.

Kilton, Thomas D. "Information Access with the Former East Germany: Book Procurement and Other Information Access Issues before and af-ter Reunification." *Library Resources & Technical Services* 37 (1994): 415-421.

Olsen, Margaret. "The End of the Cold War and Its Effects on Slavic and East European Collections in the West." *International Information & Library Review* 27 (1995): 89-112.

Winkler, Karen. "Academic Presses Look to the Internet to Save Scholarly Monographs." *Chronicle of Higher Education* (September 12, 1997): A18-20.

Zak, Peter. "Should Exchange Be the Main Source of Foreign Acquisitions in Polish Research Libraries." *Libraries in Europe's Post-Communist Countries: Their International Context.* International Librarians' Conference, Krakow-Przegorzaly, August 3-5, 1995. Krakow: Polskie Towarzystwo Bibliologiczne, 1996, pp. 184-187.

9

Approval Plans: Library-Vendor Partnerships for Acquisitions and Collection Development

JOAN GRANT

Approval plans as a means of acquiring books were first introduced in the early 1960s. Since that time they have been the subject of a series of four conferences and many presentations at professional meetings and discussion groups. Library literature is replete with both articles and monographs that discuss the history of approval plans, argue for and against their use, list the advantages and disadvantages of subject- or publisher-based plans, describe the experiences of specific libraries, and suggest models for selecting, establishing, and evaluating approval plans. A 1997 survey on the use of approval plans in research libraries shows that their well-established place as a collection development and acquisitions tool remains strong. Ninety-three percent of the respondents to ARL SPEC Kit no. 221, "Evolution and Status of Approval Plans," reported using plans. Earlier surveys showed 85 percent responding affirmatively in 1982 and 94 percent in 1988. Current trends revealed in this study included an increasing role for the Head of Collection Development as the administrator of the plan (17 percent in 1982 vs. 71 percent in 1997) and a more diverse list of benefits cited by users including "the freeing of selectors to focus on the elusive, while relying on approval to collect material from mainstream publishers; greater price discounts; staff time savings; review with book-in-hand; timely receipt of current imprints; and consolidated ordering."[1]

Librarians who are considering or are already involved with such an approval plan are fortunate to be working at a time when so much documentation exists. They are also in the happy position of being able to draw upon the now quite sophisticated experience of their colleagues at other institutions and the vendors who offer approval plan services. A good starting point for a review of the literature is Rossi's 1987 "Library Approval Plans: A Selected, Annotated Bibliography." Rossi's detailed annotations on 77 books, book chapters, and articles cover the period 1957 to 1986.

While it is wise to glean as much as possible from the experience of others via the literature and personal contacts, it is essential that every library consider the advisability of establishing an approval plan and the evaluation of an ongoing plan within the context of its own situation. Local staffing, organization, budget, collection development practices, not to mention politics and personalities, are all important factors that will have an impact on the success or failure of an approval plan. Similar variables should be borne in mind when selecting or evaluating vendors. There are a number of competent vendors who have successful approval plan programs. Choosing the right vendor for a specific plan, however, will have much to do with how well that vendor's plan meshes with the library's local needs.

The librarian who wishes to explore approval plans should embark upon a research project designed to gather information in three areas.

1. The business of approval plans: What are the general principles behind the operation of approval plans? What is it that a plan can and cannot do? What can reasonably be asked of a vendor?
2. Library's requirements:What are the library's acquisitions and collection development goals and objectives? How will an approval plan enhance the library's ability to reach its goals?
3. Vendor selection and evaluation: What services are offered by the vendors? How well do the vendors' services meet the library's requirements?

There is a natural progression in these steps. Knowing what services can be expected from the marketplace and what the libary needs greatly facilitates decisions about specific plans.

DEFINITION OF APPROVAL PLANS

An approval plan is a contractual arrangement between a library and a vendor. The vendor uses a "profile" based on a combination of subjects and publishers to determine the library's collecting interests. It agrees to make regular (usually weekly) shipments of current imprints that match the profile from the output of the publishers it works with. The books are shipped on approval, that is, the library reviews the books on receipt and reserves the right to return any that it deems unsuitable. There are many variations on this admittedly general definition:

1. Breadth of subject coverage: Plans may be broad enough to cover all the humanities, sciences and social sciences or limited to a single subject (art), or a special aspect of a subject (avant-garde poetry), or a type of material (music scores).

2. Selection slips: Most plans offer some combination of automatic shipment of books and provision of selection slips to be reviewed by the library staff. Slips may be preferred in subject areas where the library wishes to be very selective. Some plans, in fact, consist exclusively of slips in which case the vendor may restrict the library's return privileges. Vendors will assist with retrospective selection projects by using their approval databases to supply backruns of slips in areas the library wishes to strengthen.

3. Publisher-based plans: Plans with vendors can be publisher-rather than subject-based. For instance, some plans are limited to university presses; subject plans, such as some in the sciences, may be limited to an agreed upon list of key publishers. A number of publishers offer approval plans of their own. They have subject profiles and supply their books directly to the library.

4. Foreign imprints: Approval plans are not limited to vendors in the United States. Varieties of book and slip plans are available with vendors worldwide including coverage for Britain, France, Germany, Italy, Greece, the Netherlands, Spain, Latin America, and the Middle East.

5. Bibliographic, cataloging, and processing services: Vendors have developed technological enhancements to approval plan services such as interactive access to the vendor's database; cataloging services including upgraded CIP records and an interface with OCLC's PromptCat service; and processing services that result in fully shelf-ready books.

VIEW FROM THE VENDORS' SIDE

Approval plans represent a means of doing business that is very attractive to vendors. Successful plans develop into long-term relationships between the library and the vendor; sales are predictable and dependable. A library can change its vendor for firm orders relatively quickly and easily. In fact, it is not unusual for staff changes in an acquisitions department to lead to a sudden loss of firm order business to another vendor, one that the new acquisitions librarian is accustomed to using. Changing approval vendors is a far more complicated matter, involving as it does both acquisitions and selection staff in the operation of a complex project. Fine-tuning the profile and developing effective library-vendor communication concerning the plan require time and careful, hard work. All of this combined with the inevitable inadvertent gaps and duplication that occur with new plans make capricious vendor changes quite rare.

Not only can approval vendors depend upon a certain volume of sales, they also can predict the nature of those sales. The subjects and publishers to be covered are agreed upon in advance so the vendor can concentrate on providing full coverage in those areas. Responding to firm orders, on the other hand, may require that the vendor devotes a substantial amount of staff time to tracking down elusive small publishers, claiming and reporting out-of-print titles, for example. In addition, regular higher volume orders with publishers will in some cases allow the vendor to negotiate greater discounts. The discounts can be passed along to customers and eventually lead to an increase in the vendor's approval business.

The ways in which vendors identify publications, match them against the library profiles, and monitor their own performance vary from vendor to vendor.

1. Identification and acquisition: Scale is an important differentiating factor in the ways vendors identify and acquire books to be supplied on approval. The larger ones may have a staff of buyers who meet regularly with publishers' representatives. Other methods of identification include examination of pre-publication announcements, subscription to LC MARC tapes for CIP (Cataloging In Publication) information, and maintenance of blanket orders with publishers. Vendors will use some or all of these methods depending upon the size of their staff and the extensiveness of their publisher lists.
2. Subject analysis: Coding titles in order to match them with library subject profiles may occur at the point of identification or with the book in hand, or titles may be reviewed at both points with a greater refinement in coding done at the second step. Many vendors employ professional librarians and subject specialists with academic backgrounds to do both the selecting and profiling of titles.
3. Monitoring the plan: The variety of sources a vendor uses to monitor the coverage of the plan again depends on the size of the company and the scope of the plan. All vendors use

publishers' catalogs and customer claims for this purpose; many also use trade bibliographies and reviewing sources such as *Choice, Library Journal,* and the *New York Times,* professional journals and specialized bibliographies.

MAKING THE DECISION
TO HAVE AN APPROVAL PLAN

There are many reasons why a library might choose to initiate an approval plan. Theoretically the ideal plan would ensure that the library has the subject and publisher coverage it wishes at a lower cost and in the process not only saves on acquisitions and selection staff time but also gets the books on the shelves faster. While no plan will solve all of the library's selection and acquisition problems quite so felicitously, it will certainly have an impact on existing procedures, staff, budget, and selection practices. The decision to implement a plan should therefore be preceded by a self-study that examines the following factors and determines that an approval plan is suitable for the library.

Acceptance by Selectors

Responsibility for selection may be vested in one or in several librarians. In academic libraries it will rest primarily with the library or be shared to varying degrees with the teaching faculty. Regardless of the configuration of selection responsibility, for an approval plan to be appropriate and successful it is important that those involved understand and support the plan. They should view it as a reliable and effective tool, not an obstacle to be overcome. Logistics are an important consideration as well. Selectors must be able to review the shipments on a regular, usually weekly, basis. This has proven difficult for smaller academic libraries that depend on faculty members with their many other commitments as participants in selection decisions.

The time to assess selectors' attitudes toward approval plans is prior to the initiation of a plan. There will be many opportunities to involve a wide range of people in investigating the experiences of other libraries, interviewing vendors, writing the profile and devising new procedures for placing firm orders, and reviewing approval books. Deciding how far to cast the net in including people in these preliminary steps requires sensitivity to the dynamics of the local situation. In some libraries, for instance, it would be unthinkable to make such a decision without consulting the faculty. In others, as long as the library acquires the books that are needed, the faculty does not concern itself with the method of acquisition. Womack et al. describe a review process led by a committee composed of technical services and public services librarians because "Their different perspectives . . . complemented one another and increased their awareness of the varying concerns of technical services and public services staff."[2] At the very least those people who have primary responsibility for selection and who will be reviewing the books should be involved in the decision and be as knowledgeable as possible about the plan.

Budgeting

One of the first questions to be asked is whether or not the library can afford the plan it wants. There will be other demands on the budget for standing orders, foreign material, retrospective selection, and current imprints not covered by the plan. The cost of these commitments should first be assessed. The vendor can help with this determination by providing an estimate of the annual cost of the proposed plan. Local budgeting practices should also be analyzed. Political problems may arise if the budget for the plan must be drawn from funds previously set aside for another purpose such as selection by the faculty. Will expenditures for the plan be charged to a single fund or to book funds for the various subjets? It may be easier to do the former but the latter will provide potentially useful information about the way the collection is growing. The vendor's management reports can be helpful in this regard. If the detail they provide is sufficient for the library's local use they can be consulted to determine the amount spent by subject.

Acquisitions Procedures

An ongoing approval plan requires a complex set of procedures in order to keep it running smoothly. While not difficult to devise, the procedures will be different from those required for placing and receiving firm orders and should be carefully thought through before a plan is undertaken. Those involved in administering the plan should examine the new workflow and make certain that there are no staffing or procedural problems that might prevent the plan from reaching its full potential. Bazirjian points out the importance of careful attention to the processing workflow and making the best use of the available technology lest the approval plan introduce many exceptions causing it to be disruptive and very labor intensive for the acquisitions staff.[3] Examples of areas to be examined include support staff responsibility and procedures for sorting and searching the books received; record keeping for orders placed from selection slips; approval claims; invoices, credits, and returns; and ordering second copies and volumes previously published in a set or series. In addition, there needs to be regular communication between acquisitions and selection staff on matters ranging from notice of a late shipment to changes in personnel and procedures.

Selection Practices

In order for an approval plan to succeed, a library must first define its collection development policies and then communicate them clearly to the vendor via the profile. If a written collection development policy statement does not already exist, it may be that preparation for writing the profile will provide the impetus for discussing policy within the library. Regardless of the order of events, questions such as how interdisciplinary areas will be treated, which subjects are to be collected most intensively, general library policies on collecting types of material such as textbooks, and so forth should be clearly understood early on. The library should not, after all, expect the vendor to follow policies that are not uniformly understood and followed by the library's own selection staff.

Second, the selectors must be willing and able to switch from making choices based on publishers' catalogs, reviews and faculty recommendations to book-in-hand selections. This provides an opportunity for the selection staff to exercise independent judgment in evaluating the merits of a book and its suitability for the local collection. As interest in vendors' shelf-ready services grows and nonreturnable plans become more prevalent, selection strategies will focus on fine-tuning profiles and the judicious choice of publishers to minimize the rejection rate.

VENDOR SELECTION AND PROFILING

The selection process involves identifying vendors who offer the kind of plan the library is considering and investigating those vendors' services. Selecting the vendor to provide approval services is a detailed process that should be undertaken with care. The decision is one that will launch a long-term partnership between the library and the vendor, will very likely consume a significant portion of acquisition dollars, and will help shape the collection to meet local needs. Guidance for vendor selection is provided by Reidelbach and Shirk who, in 1983, described ten steps to be followed in the vendor selection process:

Vendor Selection Steps

1. Prepare a preliminary approval plan design.
2. Identify the vendors that offer the kind of plan or combination of plans required by the library.
3. Solicit information and summarize specific proposals from selected vendors.
4. Evaluate the information provided and determine the desirability of each proposal. Select the top-ranked vendors for on-site presentations.
5. Schedule vendor on-site presentations.
6. Solicit reactions from staff, faculty, and others attending the vendor presentations.
7. Gather reference information from other libraries currently utilizing the vendors under consideration.
8. Reevaluate all information amassed during the selection process.
9. Notify vendor participants of the results.
10. Schedule an appointment with the selected vendor to begin profiling of the plan.[4]

Many libraries, even those not required to do so by institutional or state procurement rules, choose to use the Request for Proposal (RFP) method as the means of notifying prospective vendors of their requirements and soliciting information from the vendors on their services and ability to meet those requirements. While time-consuming, the RFP process has many advantages. Writing a comprehensive listing for specifications requires the members of the library review team to carefully consider and reach consensus on a variety of acquisitions and collection development matters at a high level of detail. Most importantly, it ensures a level playing field for the vendors in that all will be responding to the same library-supplied information. In their 1995 article Wilkinson and Thorson give a detailed description of the RFP process followed at the University of New Mexico, including sample questions for the RFP.[5]

Less formal means of gathering information (that can be used alone or in conjunction with an RFP) include talking to colleagues at other libraries about their choices and experiences, interviewing vendors at conferences, scheduling on-site vendor presentations, and checking references by calling customers to whom the vendor provides comparable approval services. Some libraries choose to schedule the on-site presentation before the RFP is issued, while others do it after the responses are received. If the latter choice is made, the library can use the opportunity of the presentation to get clarification on points made in the proposal.

The following is a brief review of key factors to examine when choosing an approval plan vendor:

1. Profile—Is it structured in a way that is compatible with the library's organization of selection? Does it have an appropriate degree of detail? How quickly can changes be implemented? Is the return rate reasonable?
2. Selectivity and coverage—Does the vendor interpret the profile as expected? What sort of monitoring has the library done, and what were the results? Have gaps been noticeable? Is the number of claims reasonable?
3. Publishers—Is the list of publishers extensive enough? Is it suitable?
4. Cost—What discount is offered? Are shipping charges or service charges levied? Are prepayments accepted as a means of increasing the discount?
5. Slips—Do selection slips have accurate and complete bibliographic information? Are they coded by subject in a useful way?
6. Management reports—Are they useful? Easy to interpret? Issued in a timely way?
7. Staff—Do you have a good working relationship with the vendor? Are both the representative and the customer service staff responsive and helpful?
8. Timeliness—How soon after publication is the average book shipped?
9. Acquisitions procedures—Do shipments arrive on a regular schedule? Do returns, invoices, credits, statements, and claims move smoothly, or are there nagging problems? Is there an interface to prevent duplication with firm orders and standing orders?
10. Technology—Does the vendor make appropriate and innovative use of technology to provide bibliographic information and cataloging and processing services?

It is wise to look at all these factors when examining a plan rather than letting a single one, such as discount, determine the plan's fate. The importance of the various criteria will differ from library to library. Those engaged in selection and evaluation should think not only about how well the plan compares on each point but also how important each point is to the library.

Once the vendor has been selected, plans must be made for the vendor representative to conduct the all-important profiling session— an exercise that lays the groundwork for a communication pattern that will last the life of the plan. Other than the books themselves, the profile is the most visible and tangible evidence to the library of the way the vendor manages the plan. A profile consists of a subject thesaurus, a list of publishers and a set of non-subject parameters. The thesauri presently in use consist of either the LC classification outline or vendor-developed thesauri. The non-subject parameters allow the library to refine the plan beyond subjects by specifying treatment for academic levels, series, subsequent editions, reprints, price, format, language, and country of publication. Other non-subject decisions involve whether or not to take advantage of cost-saving vendor services to screen editions and supply the least expensive of the U.S. or British edition or to give preference to paperback editions when published simultaneously with cloth.

Ideally, the library will have given careful consideration to its collecting requirements and studied the vendor's profile in advance of the session. Nardini, writing in 1994, describes how the library and the vendor should prepare for the session and organize the profile writing meetings so that selection and acquisitions staff take advantage of this opportunity to get started on the right foot.[6] In developing the profile the library articulates what it expects from the plan in a careful and precise way. The vendor's representative in turn must ensure that the profile and the plan with all their potential and limitations have been understood. After the plan is in operation, the vendor will monitor the success of the profile by analyzing return rates and customer claims. Its representative should keep apprised of each customer's experience and work with the library to resolve any problems that become apparent.

A crucial profiling decision concerns the scope of the plan. Many libraries use large approval plans to cast a wide net bringing in a broad range of subjects from university presses, scholarly, commercial, small, and societal publishers. Their "selectors have, historically, valued the opportunity to review a universe of new titles significantly larger than their budgets can accommodate."[7] Yet Eldredge argues that "approval plan vendors work best with large, established publishers and are able to provide approval services at discounted prices because of the cost effectiveness generated by economies of scale."[8] Schmidt compares subject-based and publisher-based plans and observes that with mainstream publishers "true selection as an intellectual process occurs only once: when it is agreed that a press will be included in the plan."[9] Her conclusion is that publisher-based plans (plans where the subject parameters are applied to a core list of publishers) not only eliminate many of the ambiguities of interpreting subject-based profiles but allow specialists freedom from reviewing automatic acquisitions to concentrate on identifying material more difficult to collect. These are issues that are central to each library's philosophy of approval plan use and bear closer examination as more and more libraries look for efficiencies in acquisitions and collection development and turn to approval plans as a source for shelf-ready books.

AUXILIARY VENDOR SERVICES

The area of greatest change in approval plan services has been vendors' use of new technologies to enhance their product. The 1997 ARL survey showed that many libraries take advantage of interactive access to their vendor's database, vendor-supplied bibliographic records, and electronic invoicing.[10] The widespread use of the Web has prompted vendors to offer libraries "functional access to their databases with the ability to place, cancel, modify or check on orders."[11] Libraries can now consider doing away with paper notification forms and review forms and mark them for selection online. Outsourcing opportunities through approval plans are growing. They include OCLC's PromptCat service; upgraded CIP records and shelf-ready processing such as marking and the insertion of security devices. Of the 70 approval plan users who responded to the ARL survey, only eight were using PromptCat and five receiving shelf-ready books; but the use of these services is certain to grow and will undoubtedly cause libraries to rethink profiling decisions as they move toward nonreturnable shelf-ready plans.

IMPLICATIONS FOR COLLECTION DEVELOPMENT

A key attraction of approval plans is their promise to bring in to the library soon after publication books that would otherwise require time-consuming identification and selection by subject specialists. Opinion is divided on the degree to which approval books should be scrutinized on receipt. On the one hand, book-in-hand selection not only ensures the quality of additions to the collection, it also affords the selector firsthand knowledge of new literature in the field and the intellectual and physical quality of the output of publishers. On the other hand, a carefully crafted profile and a judicious selection of publishers can result in an approval plan with a low rejection rate. At a time when pressures on selectors' time are growing—to evaluate and select networked electronic resources, to manage serials cancellation projects, and to provide users with increasingly sophisticated support—taking full advantage of an approval plan's efficiencies by a less rigorous review of the shipments is compelling. The attraction of cost savings through outsourcing processing and the receipt of shelf-ready books is an added impetus to rethink the goals of an approval plan. Wittenberg describes a "three tiered" approach of "keepers, lookers and slips" for libraries moving from book-in-hand selection toward a nonreturnable plan.[12] During the transition period a portion of the plan is shipped fully processed and shelf-ready; another portion is reviewed by selectors with return privileges; and the third, those least likely to be accepted, are sent as notification slips. The distinctions are made by publisher, e.g. university presses in the "keepers" category. Or, subject specialists can create customized categories of publishers for each area of the profile.

Debate reigns about whether or not the widespread use of approval plans is creating collections that are so homogeneous that resource sharing with its dependence on specialization and unique holdings is stymied. Studies that appear in the literature are inconclusive. In 1985 Loup surveyed 28 ARL libraries that used Blackwell North America's approval plan to collect philosophy and political science. She found that "the libraries are receiving very similar collections through their B/NA approval plans," although they apparently did a significant amount of firm ordering as well with a relatively small portion of their expenditures devoted to the approval plan.[13] In the report of a follow-up survey to determine what kinds of selection activities were used to supplement approval plans, Loup concluded that the real danger to resource sharing stemmed from declining staff time and budget devoted to gift and exchange programs, acquisition of foreign language materials and non-trade publications, analysis of ILL statistics, retrospective selection, and other activities necessary to the development of unique research collections.

Other research, however, has found less evidence of collection overlap as the result of approval plans. St. Clair and Treadwell analyzed the approval selections supplied by four vendors (two major and two speciality) over a five-month period in response to a science and technology profile. They found that only 4 percent of the titles would have been supplied by all four vendors and concluded that "the diversity of titles that would have been supplied by different vendors using the same profile makes the selection of a vendor (and careful construction of a profile) even more serious."[14] Nardini,

Getchell and Cheever analyzed the books supplied on approval by a single vendor (Yankee Book Peddler) over a one-year period to two research libraries and two medium-sized libraries.[15] The results showed an overlap of 51 percent between the research libraries and 15 percent between the medium-sized libraries.[16] Not surprisingly, an analysis by publisher showed the greatest degree of overlap for university press titles. When the receipts of all four libraries were compared, only 6 percent of the titles were acquired in common.

Libraries' experiences over a period that spans more than 30 years have shown that approval plans are an effective collection development and acquisition tool. They have flourished because they have proven adaptable—their services changing as acquisitions and collection development issues have changed. Begun at a time when book budgets were generous, they served us well by ensuring that selectors could review a broad range of materials. Decades later tight budgets and escalating serial prices find libraries buying fewer monographs. Staff resources have been stretched, in some cases by cutbacks, and in virtually all libraries by the need to evaluate and select for collections resources that reflect the rich variety of formats and modes of access now available. Approval plans remain attractive in this environment. Profiles can be broad or specialized and with the help of management data they can be refined so that returns are minimized. Technological enhancements are a boon to the work of acquisitions and selection staff, with interactive access to vendor databases providing up to the minute information on plan activity and streamlining work routines.

While approval plans are not a panacea, well-managed ones can contribute to an effective collection development program. Through a careful process of defining local requirements and matching them with vendors' services, a library can use approval plans to ensure a steady flow of prescreened books—and enable selectors to reallocate some of their time to other collection development and service demands.

Notes

1. Association of Research Libraries, Office of Management Studies, Systems and Procedures Exchange Center, *Evolution and Status of Approval Plans,* SPEC Kit 221 (Washington, D.C.: ARL, 1997), p. 14.

2. Kay Womack, Agnes Adams, Judy L. Johnson and Katherine L. Walter, "An Approval Plan Vendor Review: The Organization and Process," *Library Acquisitions: Practice & Theory* 12 (1988): 366.

3. Rosann Bazirjian, "The Impact of Approval Plans on Acquisitions Operations and Work Flow," in *Approval Plans: Issues and Innovations,* ed. John H. Sandy (New York: Haworth, 1996), pp. 29-35.

4. John H. Reidelbach and Gary M. Shirk, "Selecting an Approval Plan Vendor: A Step-by-Step Process," *Library Acquisitions: Practice & Theory* 7 (1983): 116.

5. Frances C. Wilkinson and Connie Capers Thorson, "The RFP Process: Rational, Educational, Necessary, Or, There Ain't No Such Thing as a Free Lunch," *Library Acquisitions: Practice & Theory* 19 (1995): 251-268.

6. Robert F. Nardini, "The Approval Plan Profiling Session," *Library Acquisitions: Practice & Theory* 18 (1994): 289-295.

7. R. Charles Wittenberg, "'Reengineering' and the Approval Plan: New Process or New Perspective?" *Acquisitions Librarian* 16 (1966): 65.

8. Mary Eldredge, "Major Issues in Approval Plans: The Case for Active Management," in *Approval Plans: Issues and Innovations,* ed. John H. Sandy (New York: Haworth, 1966), p. 53.

9. Karen A. Schmidt, "Capturing the Mainstream: Publisher-Based and Subject-Based Approval Plans in Academic Libraries," *College & Research Libraries* 47 (1986): 366.

10. Association of Research Libraries, *Evolution and Status of Approval Plans.*

11. Daniel P. Halloran, "1996: A Bookseller's View of the Year," *Against the Grain,* February 1997, p. 27.

12. Wittenberg, "'Reengineering,'" p. 66.

13. Jean L. Loup, "Analysis of Approval Plans in ARL Libraries," in *Acquisitions, Budgets and Material Costs: Issues and Approaches,* ed. Sul H. Lee (New York: Haworth, 1988): 44.

14. Gloriana St. Clair and Jane Treadwell, "Science and Technology Approval Plans Compared," *Library Resources & Technical Services* 33 (1989): 387.

15. Robert F. Nardini, Charles M. Getchell Jr. and Thomas E. Cheever, "Approval Plan Overlap: A Study of Four Libraries," *Acquisitions Librarian* 16 (1966): 81.

16. Ibid., p. 90.

Bibliography

Loup, Jean L. and Helen Lloyd Snoke. "Analysis of Selection Activities to Supplement Approval Plans." *Library Resources & Technical Services* 35 (1991): 202-216.

Nardini, Robert F. "Approval Plans: Politics and Performance." *College & Research Libraries* 54 (1993): 417-425.

Rossi, Gary J. "Library Approval Plans: A Selected, Annotated Bibliography." *Library Acquisitions: Practice & Theory* 11 (1987): 3-34.

10

Acquiring Serials

JAMES R. MOUW

WHY SERIALS?

Why, in a book on the acquisition of library materials, do we offer
an entire chapter devoted to one specific type of library material—
serials? The short answer is because they behave differently as a
group and present particular challenges. The longer answer has
several facets:

> They are expensive, and a bad decision can cost a library
> hundreds or thousands of dollars.
>
> They account for a large percentage of library purchasing.
>
> They have a special vocabulary.
>
> They require special acquisition techniques, including records
> of volume receipts.
>
> They have a specialized vending community.

When we move beyond titles produced by the major publishers,
serials can become idiosyncratic and somewhat difficult to obtain.
Marcia Tuttle begins her monograph on serials management with
a quotation she attributes to "one serials librarian":

> Almost all books are published by sophisticated, experienced,
> well-defined professionals who understand their self-interest in as
> well as their customers' need for bibliographic consistency. Problems
> abound, but the standard is well-defined and usually adhered to. On
> the other hand, any knucklehead with a typewriter and access to an
> offset press can publish a serial.[1]

To this enumerated list can be added one other factor. Except in
very large libraries, serials are acquired by a general acquisitions

157

staff who, due largely to the relative percentages of new orders, deal mainly with monographs, and the staff members are often unfamiliar with serials acquisitions techniques. The topic is not often covered in any depth in library school programs, and indeed there is only one full-time library school faculty in the country who lists "serials" among her areas of expertise.[2]

Finally, we study serials because they are different. In an article in *Advances in Serials Management* Christian Boissannas eloquently argues that serials in actuality aren't all that different and that the establishment and continuation of separate serials departments have continued an artificial split of materials and workflows.[3] To a great extent he is right, and indeed the current trend is toward treating serials as one segment of overall material acquisition rather than treating them as a different animal. In a strange way this melding of duties makes this chapter all the more important since generalists are being called on increasingly to add serials to their roster of duties.

A few notes on the content of this chapter. It is impossible to cover all aspects of serials librarianship in a single chapter. Entire books can be, and have been, written on the topic. Several excellent ones are listed in the Resources section that concludes this chapter. The intent of this chapter is to give the reader an overview and a starting point, concentrating on general matters related to the serials publishing and vending communities while also talking about a few of the most important acquisitions techniques. It is not intended to be comprehensive, and for that reason several topics have been left out entirely, principally: cataloging, preservation and access, interlibrary loan and other forms of document delivery, and issues related to archiving. Licensing is also not part of this chapter, primarily since it is covered at length elsewhere in this book. I have avoided overuse of two phrases that could begin almost every sentence in this chapter. The first phrase is "unlike monographs . . ." or "like monographs. . . ." As this is a chapter on a specific topic within a book that is largely more general it should be obvious that the chapter on Serials will concentrate on the ways in which they behave differently. The second is "generally." It is the nature of serials that an exception can be found to every rule. For every well-behaved periodical we can find one that behaves oddly. For every annual that has come out routinely for decades we can find several examples that don't fit the mold. The reader should assume that every statement here is prefaced "Generally."

James R. Mouw

WHAT IS A SERIAL?

Before we can discuss how to purchase serials, we must explore what makes serials, how they are published, and the factors that influence their price. For the past several decades the principal definition of a serial has been that found in AACR2, which declares a serial to be:

> A publication in any medium issued in successive parts bearing numerical or chronological designations, and intended to be continued indefinitely. Serials include periodicals; newspapers; annuals (reports, yearbooks, etc.); the journals, memoirs, proceedings, transactions, etc., of societies; and numbered monographic series.[4]

As work begins on a successor to AACR2, some are beginning to question this definition, particularly as it pertains to the division between monograph and serial, and Jean Hirons and Crystal Graham have prepared a paper outlining proposed changes,[5] but for now this is the best definition we have. It lists several important characteristics that must be present for a publication to be a serial. These are:

It must be issued successively. Any work that is published at one time, even if published in many volumes, cannot be a serial.

It must bear some form of enumeration. To be a serial, a work must have a number or a chronology (copyright date doesn't count).

It must be intended to be published indefinitely. This has proven to be the hardest aspect to prove conclusively, since many times the first volume will be silent on the point. This has also caused many one-time publications that were *intended* to continue to be cataloged as serials when in actuality they ran out of steam after volume one. The intent to continue indefinitely becomes the primary distinction between multipart monographs and open-ended serials that are very similar in other respects. The monograph has a preplanned conclusion; the serial does not.

It can be in any medium. Unlike all other forms of publication, a serial is not limited to any one medium. A monograph is a printed book; sound recordings, microforms, and maps, for example, are monographs, sound recordings, microforms, and maps. Serials can be any of the above. In a recent presentation, Regina Reynolds talked of two of the more bizarre serials she has encountered. The US ISSN Center has in its possession a T-shirt that has been granted an ISSN—two T-shirts, actually, since it later underwent a title change, and the French ISSN Office has been asked to grant an ISSN to a newsletter that is printed on a bread wrapper.[6] People who work with serials come to see them everywhere.

By way of contrast, AACR2 defines a monograph simply as "a nonserial item, i.e., an item either complete in one part or complete, or intended to be completed, in a finite number of separate parts"[7]—in other words, everything that is not a serial.

As important as it is to understand the implications of the above definitions, it is also important to note that these are primarily bibliographic categories. Many libraries use the definitions to govern their acquisition treatment: a serial is ordered by the serials department and a monograph is ordered by the monographic acquisitions department. But many libraries do not, in recognition of the fact that many multipart monographs behave very much like a serial and can benefit from serial processing. To give but one example, a large encyclopedia, published over the course of several years, although bibliographically a monograph, can be ordered and received exactly like open-ended works.

THE TYPES OF SERIALS

The serial publication that most people automatically think of is the periodical, but in actuality serials come in many guises. The periodical has several distinguishing characteristics, several of which have a direct impact on library treatment. The most obvious is that they are issued in separate pieces that later combine to produce a complete volume. Libraries address this characteristic by maintaining a check-in system that allows them to receive individual issues as published, note issues that are lacking and need to be claimed, and eventually to note when a volume is complete and can be bound. In the not too distant past, libraries developed elaborate paper files (the most common of which was the kardex), that allowed them to track piece receipts, binding information, and bound holdings in a single file. Increasingly, these files have been moved online but they continue to serve the same function.

A second characteristic is that periodicals are paid in advance. A library or individual, whether ordering through an agent or directly with the publisher, will pay for a group of issues before they are published. This payment pattern, sometimes misunderstood by auditors, implies a level of trust that is inherent in the serial procurement process: libraries expend considerable sums of money, in some cases millions of dollars, with the assumption that issues will be delivered as published.

Periodicals also share physical characteristics that make them relatively easy to identify. They come in two or three basic shapes and tend to be soft-bound and "floppy" while in their unbound state. Libraries often segregate unbound issues of periodicals into a separate housing location, usually for reasons of security since these issues are easily mutilated or stolen. Another characteristic of periodicals is that they are almost always cataloged as a serial, only with no individual entries for individual pieces.

The easiest definition for the remaining serials is to call them "non-periodicals." The primary distinguishing characteristic of these materials is that they are invoiced as published. Common examples include annuals, numbered monographic series, and a wide variety of other publications that appear at regular or irregular intervals. These items are still recorded in the serial check-in file when received by the library, and they usually are accompanied by an invoice that needs to be processed for payment. Some serials in this category receive cataloging treatment only as a serial, usually when the individual volumes have no distinguishing characteristics as in the case of annual reports or review publications. Others are received as a serial and then cataloged individually either as a collected set (all bearing the same call number) or as separate monographs.

Finally, there is the category that has been called "near serials." These are publications that have some of the characteristics of serials but fail the definition on one or more points. They may be meant to continue indefinitely but have no enumeration or chronology; they may be numbered and published over time but have a preplanned conclusion. Many libraries treat these as serials for convenience.

Libraries have divided serials and non-serials into nice neat categories for their processing convenience. Publishers and vendors don't necessarily divide the world in the same fashion, and it is important to understand this when ordering titles. Just because we call something a periodical doesn't automatically mean that the publisher won't bill for each piece as it is published, or even that the publisher will accept a standing order at all. The line between "periodical" and "non-periodical" is a fine one, and definitions can get in the way at times. Libraries will likely have titles that they consider to be periodicals on order with standing order suppliers because the periodical vendor has said "this isn't a periodical; I can't handle it," and they may even have publications that are treated as serials but ordered as periodicals.

METHODS OF PURCHASE

There are two primary ways to obtain serials. Libraries can order through a vendor or they can place orders directly with the publisher. In recent years most libraries have purchased the majority of their titles from vendors. Periodicals (particularly domestic titles) are usually obtained from a specialized library agent located in the United States. A list of these agents is appended to the end of this chapter. These agents offer comprehensive title lists including most of the common foreign titles and claim to be able to supply all titles published, worldwide. Smaller libraries will typically order all of their titles through one of these agents. As collections grow in size and complexity, multiple vendors may be used, including non-U.S. dealers who specialize in titles from various parts of the world. These two options each have distinct advantages and disadvantages.

If you order all your titles from one dealer you can obtain comprehensive management reports that reflect your entire collection, and you can sometimes obtain advantageous service charges. You will be dealing with one vendor staff with one set of requirements. On the other hand, when locking yourself into one vendor you can lose track of general trends in the vending community and may find that some titles cannot be supplied by your sole-source dealer. Placing all your titles with a single supplier can also make your auditor nervous, especially when other options exist.

If you use multiple vendors you can take advantage of any special strengths that they might have, and if your list is divided geographically you can take advantage of country of origin sources with local knowledge. (Comprehensive dealers counter that they have sources located in all the major publishing centers of the world, achieving the same benefits.) This approach also has disadvantages. You will be dealing with several sets of personnel, and each vendor has its own personality, sets of requirements, forms to use, and databases to learn. You also lose comprehensive management reports from a single source. Most dealers now offer these reports in database format, and it is possible to merge reports from various sources into a single report, but that takes staff time and reports never seem to contain exactly the same data in exactly the same form.

The second choice is to order directly from the publisher. This can be more cost effective on the surface, since publishers will often bill libraries the same discounted price they charge the dealers and there is no vendor service charge to pay. To understand the actual cost of this approach, a library must add the staff time involved in performing all the tasks normally provided by their vendor, maintenance of the database information, and, particularly, comprehensive claiming and invoicing functions. It is more efficient to process one two-thousand line vendor invoice—especially if it is in electronic form—than it is to process two thousand individual publisher invoices. In addition, many publishers aren't equipped to handle customer service requests from individual libraries. While the mass-market publishers have thousands or millions of individual subscribers, individuals have different expectations than libraries. This is especially true with regard to completeness. Individual subscribers may not even notice a skipped issue, and if they do they are usually content to accept an extended subscription. Libraries expect completeness. Vendors understand that and will work on behalf of libraries, while publishers do not. The more scholarly publishers are used to working with vendors and have well-established procedures for doing so. They are not always equipped to deal with individual library subscriptions.

Non-periodical serials behave very differently from periodicals and are often ordered through a monographic dealer rather than from a subscription agent. Subscription agents are set up to bill in advance for materials that are shipped directly from the publisher to the library and are never touched by the agent. Serials ordered through a subscription agent are generally billed using the same terms granted to the entire account, even though serials frequently carry the same discount as other monographs. Many libraries have chosen to place serial orders on standing order with their monographic vendor. Serials ordered in this fashion are usually invoiced at a discounted price rather than with the service charge levied by serial vendors. To achieve even greater savings, some libraries are placing serial orders through an approval plan rather than as a traditional standing order. These titles act much more like monographs—they are invoiced as published and, when ordered through a dealer, are sent to the dealer's warehouse and then reshipped to libraries. Monographic dealers understand this type of material and subscription agents seem to have trouble with it. A seasoned acquisitions librarian is likely not to utilize a subscription agent for non-periodicals.

A purchased subscription is certainly not the only way to obtain serials, and although a lengthy discussion is beyond the scope of this chapter, libraries should remember the other options that exist. These include:

gift subscriptions   Many titles can be obtained as a gift upon request.

exchange programs   Although not as popular as they once were, exchange programs continue to be an excellent way to obtain materials from parts of the world where the publishing industry is not as organized and where titles are more difficult to obtain. In essence, a partner library collects items locally and then supplies them to your library in exchange for materials that you send them. The two main questions to consider are: Can they supply something you want? and Do you have a source of materials to send in exchange?

depository programs   These programs are an excellent, and sometimes the only reasonable, way to obtain a wide variety of publications issued by various government agencies.

VENDOR SELECTION AND EVALUATION

All of the major vendors doing business in the United States as well as most of the large foreign dealers offer a very similar set of services, and all of them deal with libraries in an ethical fashion. The choice of one dealer over another often hinges on other factors. When choosing to obtain titles from a dealer you are purchasing a set of services, and it is important that you are buying those services that you need and not paying for a large set of options that you will never exercise. As similar as they may seem on the surface, each serial vendor has a distinctly different personality. They deal with customers in a certain way, their records are kept in a certain fashion, and they have specific requirements and established ways of doing business. It is vital that you are comfortable with their way of doing business. None of the major vendors do business badly, just differently. Some major factors that should be investigated include:

service analysis   Does the vendor provide a set of services that you will utilize and are comfortable with? On the other hand, does the vendor provide a large number of services that you will pay for in your service charge but never use?

analysis of specializations   Is the vendor equipped to handle your type of title list? Does the vendor have other accounts that are similar to yours?

customer support   Are problems resolved quickly and professionally? Are you comfortable dealing with the customer support staff?

state of automation   Do they have the automated support you require?

flexibility   Can they accommodate customer requests for special products and reports or are you locked into one format?

state of their database   Are their records in order and current? Are they actively obtaining new information from publishers on a continual basis?

renewal processing   Are titles renewed in a reasonable fashion or are you missing issues because titles were not renewed promptly? Do you receive many supplemental invoices—an indication that new prices may not be entered promptly—or do your invoices generally reflect the current price? This can be problematic; as described in the section on the journal pricing season (below) the time between when publishers set prices and when libraries are invoiced can be very short, and it's always a race to the finish. Libraries will often be asked to choose between an early invoice containing a large percentage of old prices or a later invoice containing only final prices.

effectiveness of claiming   Do your claims have results? Are they acknowledged promptly?

accountability   Does the vendor do what they say they will do when they say they'll do it?

cost   Cost is certainly an important factor, but should only be examined after you have determined that the vendor can perform acceptably based on the other criteria listed above.

The information in some of these categories can easily be obtained by talking to potential vendors; other pieces of information can only be analyzed locally over time and with experience. Obviously, when considering a new vendor you have no local experience and by far the best way to find out about a dealer is to call references. Any vendor will supply you with a list of references upon request. Ask for a list of libraries that have similar collections, then call them and talk to them. Tuttle's book on serials management contains an extensive list of questions to ask references.[8]

THE ORDER PROCESS

For the purposes of this chapter, the ordering process begins after a title has been selected for inclusion in the collection. The order preparation begins with a bibliographic search of both the library catalog and external sources. This procedure serves several purposes:

1. to confirm the bibliographic information and to confirm that the title exists and is currently being published. Orders, particularly for serials, often begin their life with an incomplete or incorrect citation. The title may have changed since the citation was used to generate an order request or the source consulted by the selector may have been incorrect. A search of OCLC or RLIN will usually turn up a matching entry unless the citation is completely mangled, and these records are often the most complete in regards to the latest title of the work. These databases are often less current when it comes to publisher or current publication status, frequency, and so forth, since libraries tend to not keep this current in their local catalogs much less to contribute the information to the national databases. For current information regarding publication status Ulrich's or various vendor databases tend to be more accurate since they are continually updated.

2. to confirm price. Price can be an important consideration, especially in a serial purchase decision, since an expensive and frequently published title can raise expenses quickly. If the current price is radically different from the price quoted by the selector, the library should double-check before placing an order. Generally, the vendor databases contain the most current price.

3. to avoid duplication. Duplication of titles is something that most libraries wish to avoid, especially in the age of ever-increasing prices. Local catalogs must always be checked to confirm that the title desired is not already in the collection. This can best be done after the actual title has been determined through the database checks mentioned above. Non-periodical serials can often be problematic since individual volumes of a title may have been ordered and cataloged as individual monographs. These can often be found through a series search, but if the series statement wasn't traced there really is no hope other than to search by every individual title, a time-consuming step that is seldom performed. If individual monographs are located in the collection that information is usually noted on the order form and those volumes are rounded up and added to the serial record when the order begins.

4. to add the title into the catalog. In the age of the card catalog, temporary slips were added in the file to indicate that a title

was on order. In the online age, the preparation of an order record automatically adds entries into the catalog and this record will also serve as the basis of the eventual catalog record. Most libraries download a record from their utility at the pre-order stage, essentially providing complete, although not final, cataloging at the order point. This record then resides in the catalog until the first piece is received and the title receives its final cataloging treatment.

With the pre-order process complete, the actual order is prepared and this process is much like that for monographic purchases. The major differences are that the orders usually contain several additional pieces of information. The ISSN is included when known, since this helps the supplier identify the ordered title. Many serial titles are very similar, but the ISSN should uniquely identify the title wanted. The scope of the order is very important, since serials by their nature consist of multiple pieces. It is important to note if the order is for a single volume or range of volumes or if it is for a continuing order. These statements usually look like:

> v.1-10 only, or
>
> 1997 volume only, or
>
> v.2 and continue.

If the order is for both a back run and a current subscription it is wise to actually issue two purchase orders:

> v.1-10 only, and on a separate purchase order
>
> v.11 and continue on standing order.

Depending on order constraints, you may need to order from two different suppliers if your main vendor only supplies current subscriptions.

Sometimes you wish to ensure that you receive the most recently published volume. In that case it is easiest to say:

> latest edition only.

Vendors are usually fairly good about following library instructions, but publishers are not always as precise. Even when a vendor has accurately recorded your order there is no guarantee that the publisher will follow those instructions. Being as specific as possible helps—the use of the word "only" to indicate that you want only a specific volume is one good idea, but nothing you do can totally prevent the publisher from sending whatever they have around the office and then continuing to send you future volumes as they are published. This leads to a correspondence stream that can seem endless.

In addition to the ISSN, every major vendor uses a system of internal title numbers to uniquely identify titles. These numbers can be very specific, indicating a single or a multiple year subscription, a domestic or non-domestic price, a library or an individual subscription, and so on. This number is readily available in the vendors' databases. Whenever possible, include it with your order. This will help the vendor identify the exact title you want and will also enter the number in your system. This number will be helpful later during any claiming or reporting operations.

The order should indicate the account the order will draw on. Smaller libraries may have only a single account with their serial vendor. As collections grow in size it is often advantageous to have multiple accounts with the vendor, each account indicating a different ship-to address, billing parameters, reporting structures, and so on. If you are in this situation, your vendor needs to be informed.

It is helpful to supply all of the publisher information that you know, especially if the order is for a title not already in the vendor database. While vendor catalogs are quite extensive, they are in essence a compilation of every title ordered for a customer and are never complete. Vendors will gladly accept orders for titles not already in their database, but they will need to take them through the same research process you have just completed before they can order the titles on your behalf. Any information you can provide, especially current publisher (including address, if known) will speed the process and help avoid the supply of an incorrect title.

With this background work completed, the order can be transmitted to a supplier through a variety of avenues. In the past the most common way was by mailing a printed purchase order, or, in rare cases, a rush order was telephoned or sent via telefax. Many library systems now allow the electronic transfer of orders directly from the ILS to the vendors' databases, speeding the order and eliminating any transcription errors. A third method is to key the order directly into the vendor database, using their WWW interface.

There are three guiding principles that can be used when preparing orders to be sent to a publisher or vendor:

Be sure the order asks for what you want—as specifically as possible.

Be sure it will be clear to your vendor. If the "official" bibliographic title of a serial is not the one by which it is generally known, give the vendor *both* titles. If there are multiple publications with very similar titles let the vendor know through use of the ISSN, their title number, or other means exactly which title you desire to order.

Let the vendor know when you are uncertain. If your information is incomplete, if you haven't verified that a title exists, or if you are estimating the price, tell the vendor. It will only help them avoid trying to find a title that doesn't exist.

One final consideration is timing. How do you decide when a subscription should start? For non-periodicals it usually doesn't matter. The order will begin either with the exact volume you specified, or when the next volume is published if you haven't been specific on your order. Periodicals are another matter. Most publishers are only equipped to begin an order with a new volume. For many titles this means a January start date; other publications are on different schedules. If you know when a volume begins you can instruct your dealer to begin at that time. With some publishers if you miss a deadline you will need to wait until the following volume begins. For example, if a title has a January start date, any order placed through the late fall will guarantee a January start. Many times orders placed in January or February will still begin in January with the back issues being supplied on the order. Other publishers are less forgiving and orders placed after a volume begins will result in either an incomplete volume, or they will not begin to supply issues until the *following* January.

THE RECEIPT PROCESS

With any luck, the order that you placed will eventually begin to supply actual pieces. The receipt of the first piece should trigger several processes. The piece should be routed to someone in the ordering unit who will confirm that the title is actually the one ordered and will confirm that the correct starting volume was supplied. He or she will then mark the order as "received," preventing any further claiming from the order side. Subsequent claims will come from the serial check-in record. Online systems require that a prediction record be established, indicating to the system when individual pieces are expected. The best time to complete this record is with the first piece in hand since the information printed on the piece is almost always more complete and up-to-date than any information obtained from other sources. Finally, the piece will be routed to the cataloging unit for final cataloging.

At some point during the ordering and initial receipt process, any special post-receipt handling instructions will be noted on the receipt record. These instructions might include "bind on receipt," "catalog volumes separately," "do not mark," or specific routing instructions. It is important to have these instructions in a place where they will be noted by the check-in staff.

Once the title is finalized, normal receiving takes over, and unless something unusual happens, each piece is added to the central receipt file and then marked and distributed according to the instructions previously entered into the record. The check-in operation is a front line of defense in a serials operation. Since the people performing check-in are usually the first to see each piece, it is they who note most problems. These problems may include:

incorrect or incomplete title match   If the title in the serial record doesn't completely match the piece in hand you either have a title change or an incorrect title. This should stop the recording process until the issue can be resolved.

materials or invoices that are not from the correct source   In a perfect world every serial that arrives in a library would exactly match one that was ordered. In actuality this is not always the case. Publishers send materials to the wrong library, mail is misrouted, titles begin to appear from two suppliers at the same time—common problems during a transfer project. These occurrences will result in duplicate or otherwise unwanted pieces.

the entry is not found in the library system   This usually indicates one of two things: either the piece's title has changed—this can often be confirmed by reading the front matter of the issue—or the title is not the one ordered by the library. A title change will require changing your records. Materials not ordered will need to be returned (if substantial in number and you know why it was sent), discarded, or routed to selectors for retention decisions.

duplicate issues   This usually indicates that a publisher has entered your order twice, perhaps confusing a multiyear order with a multicopy order, but it may also indicate that two orders have overlapped slightly (typical during a transfer project). It may just be a one-time fluke. Make a note of it but otherwise ignore a single duplicate periodical issue, and research the title if duplicates continue to be received. Duplicate serial issues require more immediate resolution since a duplicate receipt can also involve a duplicate invoice.

materials out of the scope of your order Mistakes happen. An order may begin with the wrong volume, a title may not be canceled in a timely fashion resulting in additional unwanted pieces, or a publisher might treat a one-time order as a continuation. All of these conditions will result in unwanted pieces and the situation must be resolved to avoid the continued receipt of unwanted issues.

materials needing claiming If the library has missed an issue, this condition can often be spotted when the subsequent issue is received and a claim can be generated immediately.

While there are three general principles for placing orders, there is only one for recording, but it is important. The rule is: "A mis-recorded or mismarked piece will cause a ripple effect that can be enormous and take weeks if not months to fully resolve." A piece checked-in on the incorrect record causes two problems—you now show receipt of a title that you don't have, and you also have a piece of a title that hasn't been recorded on its record. One half of this problem will eventually result in a seeming duplicate receipt; the other half will cause a claim for a piece already in the collection. A piece that received the wrong call number will be lost in the collection. The list in endless. Correct recording is vital.

CLAIMING

The title that never needs to be claimed is a rare beast indeed. Eventually almost every title will come up on a claim list. Serial claims divide into two general categories.

The first is the gap claim. This type of claim results when an issue has not been received while subsequent issues have. In manual operations this was easy to notice since the lacking piece resulted in an empty space on the kardex. A gap is similarly easy to spot in an online operation, and in many systems the receipt of a later piece will automatically generate a claim for the gap.

The second type of claim is for a lapsed order. This condition exists when a title ceases to be received. This situation is harder to track down, especially in a manual operation, since there is no activity to call the title into question. The problems are easier to identify in an online system since systems have elapsed-date functions that will cause a list of all titles with no activity during a certain period to be generated. This list can be controlled by frequency, allowing titles to come up for review only after a reasonable time has elapsed. Lapses occur for a wide variety of reasons, and some research should occur before a claim is automatically generated. The title may have ceased, your vendor may have failed to renew your order, or the publisher may have failed to record the order. The two types of claims should generate different claim letters. The gap claim should generate a specific request, with a statement such as "we lack v.23 no.4." A lapse claim should be more general, such as "we have not received v.23 no.3 or any subsequent issues."

This claim should be sent to your vendor since they have your order records and you are paying them to claim on your behalf. Your claim should be as specific as possible and the inclusion of their title number and your order number will help them track down the title in question. Some systems will automatically supply payment information on your claim letter, giving your vendor their original invoice number as proof that the title was invoiced. Like orders, claims can take several forms. Many vendors supply claim forms that can be filled out and returned to them. This form is supplied for library convenience and needs to be used unless an alternative is preferred. Most library systems produce claim letters on request, and these can be either printed and mailed to the supplier or used to input the claims directly into the vendors database. Some systems use the X.12 standard to produce an electronic file that can be sent to the library's vendor.

There are several guidelines to use when determining what to claim and what not to claim:

Only claim titles that you have ordered. As simple as this sounds, the relationships between an order and a serial record can be complex and unless great care is used a canceled order may still be listed as "active" in the serial file, or a one-time order may be keyed as continuing in the check-in system.

Only claim titles that you have some reasonable assurance have been published. This is most often driven by past receipt history. If a title is published every year like clockwork and you haven't gotten one in eighteen months, a claim is warranted. On the other hand, highly irregular titles should be claimed with caution and the claim should be of the nature of "we haven't seen one of these in a long time."

Do not flood your dealer with claims. Unnecessary claims clog up the entire process and ultimately lead to higher prices for everyone. Let a month elapse between subsequent claims for the same title, allowing some time for the situation to be resolved. Do not claim a weekly the day after it was expected; give a little extra time.

Do not claim an item you lost after receipt. As tempting as this may seem, it is dishonest.

Be alert to claiming restrictions and respect them. If a publisher has a short claim period, note that in your record and set that title to allow a shorter period of time to elapse before a claim is generated.

Do not claim things that you throw away unless you have a pattern of non-receipt. If you only keep the current issues of a title, it is likely that the pieces will be nearing the end of their useful life before a claim is resolved. Let it go. Only claim these items if you note a continued problem of non-receipt.

A claim will generate one of several responses, and each of these responses should prompt suitable action. These include:

not yet published   This response will often be accompanied by an expected date, and this information should be used to adjust your check-in records precluding future claims until the new expected date has passed. Vendor databases increasingly contain detailed dispatch data, indicating quite specifically when issues have been or are to be released. If a library claims interactively with their vendor this information can be used to forestall the claim process completely until the expected date has passed.

too late to claim   If you have exceeded the claim period allowed by the publisher your only recourse will be to purchase the issue separately, either through the publisher or through a back issue dealer.

title not on file   This indicates that the dealer has no record of your order. This report should trigger a correspondence to sort out the problem.

out of print or supply exhausted   This indicates that even though your claim is valid, no more issues exist and so your claim cannot be fulfilled. The publisher will then often extend your subscription by an issue to make up the difference. This causes two problems: you will still need to fill in the missing issue from another source, and you also have an order that is out of cycle by one issue.

cannot locate publisher The vendor can no longer locate the publisher and has exhausted its avenues of research. If the title is important, the library will need to do more research. In many cases the ultimate result will be some indication that the publisher has gone out of existence and the title in question has either ceased or been picked up by another publisher. These situations can be complex to resolve, especially when titles have been paid in advance. Publishers that go out of existence without a trace are not generally known for the completeness of their records, and even if the title has been picked up by another publisher the subscriber list is unlikely be complete or accurate.

PERIODICAL INVOICING

Periodicals are invoiced in a fairly standard fashion, and this process is governed by factors that combine to form a somewhat complex matrix that has been called the "journal pricing season." I am indebted to Tina Feick of Blackwells for compiling much of this information for a presentation to my serials class at Dominican University.[9] The factors are:

the library budget cycle Most libraries operate on a fiscal year that begins in the summer or early fall. The amount of money a library will have to expend is sometimes, although not always, known some months prior to the beginning of the fiscal year. This budget is then divided and allocated to various types of library purchases. In the best situation a library will know how much it can expect on serials for the coming year as early as mid-spring. In the worst situation it may be October or November before budgets are set.

the publisher cycle Major STM publishers set their prices sometime between mid-June and mid-September. Agents in turn pay the publishers between late October and December for January start dates, trying to time the payment as tightly as possible to keep the money in the bank as long as possible.

the renewal cycle Agents send renewal lists to libraries during the summer months asking them to correct the list and annotate any cancellations. Libraries return these lists as early as June and as late as December. Agents then process the lists and send invoices to the libraries, as early as July and as late as December. Libraries then pay the vendor, optimally before January, but not always. A critical point here is that vendors pay the publishers in advance of receiving payment from libraries. It is often too late to cancel a title when invoiced since payment has already been made to the publisher based on the renewal list.

The various cycles combine to provide some interesting problems. Libraries are asked to fix their list for the coming year during the summer months. This is almost always before new prices are known and often before the library budget is known. This is one reason that serials are difficult to cancel. Libraries simply process the list for renewal and pay for it somehow, since they lack the information that lets them make more intelligent decisions. Secondly, the invoices that are sent even as late as October will not have a complete list of new prices since all the publisher prices will not have been set. This means that libraries are paying for titles when the final price is not yet known. Some interesting payment options are emerging that in some cases help alleviate these problems:

guaranteed price   Your agent will invoice you with a fixed price as early as the spring. This is a final bill and reflects not actual prices, since they are not known, but rather the vendor's estimate of what the price will be. This is usually a more expensive option since the dealer will try to set a price that will be at least as much as the final price, but it does offer the library a fixed price. By exercising this option a library can obtain a fixed price and make the proper budgetary decisions early in the budget cycle.

early payment   Libraries can prepay their subscriptions as quickly as funds become available and obtain a rebate based on the number of months by which the invoice is prepaid. This does not set any of the prices but it will stretch the library's dollar to some extent. It does not solve the other issues related to the journal pricing season, however.

fixed price payment   Libraries are only invoiced for titles that have had their price set. This allows the library to make final decisions with a firm price in hand but presents two major problems. The first is that this will result in many small invoices to process rather than the traditional single invoice with a final supplemental billing. The second is that by waiting to bill until the price is final the library will often find that the cancellation date has passed, meaning that a title has already been renewed on their behalf.

Resources

MAJOR VENDORS PROVIDING COMPREHENSIVE SERVICES TO U.S. LIBRARIES

All of these vendors provide a broad range of services including on-line catalogs, Web-based interfaces for order placement and claiming, electronic delivery of invoice and claiming information, comprehensive management reports, and a suite of other services. They all offer to supply both domestic and foreign titles, and they each have an extensive network of international offices.

Blackwell Information Services
New Jersey Service Center
   (specializing in Academic
   accounts)
P.O. Box 1257
901 Route 168
Blackwood, NJ 08012
800 458-3706
www.blackwell.com

New York Service Center
   (specializing in Business and
   Medical accounts)
22 Cortlandt Street
New York, NY 10007
800 221-3306
www.blackwell.com

Ebsco Subscription Services
P.O. Box 1943
Birmingham, AL 35201-1943
www.ebsco.com

Faxon (A Dawson Company)
15 Southwest Park
Westwood, MA 02090-1585
800 766-0039
www.faxon.com

Swets Subscription Service
440 Creamery Way
Suite A
Exton, PA 19341
800 447-9387
www.swets.nl

OTHER MAJOR VENDORS

Many other dealers supply titles to U.S. libraries. These range from dealers who specialize in certain types of materials to vendors who supply materials from certain geographic regions. Some offer comprehensive services and operate much like the major U.S. vendors; others are very small boutique-type companies and specialize in a very narrow range of materials. The American Library Association has compiled a directory of these suppliers. Rather than reprint an incomplete list here, the reader is referred to the existing directory: Lenore Rae Wilkas, *International Subscription Agents*, 6th ed. (Chicago: American Library Association, 1994).

RECOMMENDED MONOGRAPHS

Marcia Tuttle. *Managing Serials*. Greenwich, Conn., and London: JAI, 1996.

> This monograph, volume 35 of the Foundations in Library and Information Science series, is an excellent overview of the state of serials librarianship. Extraordinarily comprehensive, it has chapters ranging from "The Nature of Serials" to cataloging and public services to acquiring new materials. It covers, in much greater depth, many issues that are only touched upon in this chapter.

The International Serials Industry. Ed. Hazel Woodward and Stella Pilling. Brookfield, Vt.: Gower, 1993.

> This book provides excellent information on the serials publishing industry.

Andrew D. Osborn. *Serial Publications: Their Place and Treatment in Libraries*. 3rd ed. Chicago: American Library Association, 1980.

> Although now somewhat dated, this book remains an excellent source of information about the place of serials in libraries.

Serials and Reference Services. Ed. Robin Kinder and Bill Katz. New York: Haworth, 1990.

> A good source of information for those interested in the intersection of serials and reference services.

University Libraries and Scholarly Communication. Washington, D.C.: Association of Research Libraries for the Andrew W. Mellon Foundation, 1992.

> This book covers many issues related to scholarly communication and how they affect the ability of libraries to maintain access to that information.

RECOMMENDED MONOGRAPHIC SERIES

Two continuing series are dedicated to issues related to serial publications. Both are excellent sources of current information:

Proceedings of the North American Serials Interest Group, Inc. New York: Haworth, annual. The NASIG proceedings are also published in *Serials Librarian*.

Advances in Serials Management. Greenwich, Conn., and London: JAI, 1986– .

RECOMMENDED JOURNALS

Several journals are either dedicated to or routinely include articles related to serials. The following are especially recommended:

Library Acquisitions: Practice & Theory. New York: Elsevier Science.

Library Resources & Technical Services. Chicago: American Library Association.

Serials. The Journal of the United Kingdom Serials Group (UKSG). Witney, England: United Kingdom Serials Group.

Serials Librarian. New York: Haworth.

Serials Review. Greenwich, Conn., and London: JAI.

Notes

1. *Title Varies* 1 (1974): 29. As quoted in Marcia Tuttle, *Managing Serials* (Greenwich, Conn., and London: JAI, 1996), p. 1.
2. Association for Library and Information Science Education, *Directory of the Association for Libary and Information Science Education*, 27th ed. (Ann Arbor, Mich.: The Association, 1996).
3. Christian Boissannas, "But Serials Are Different!" in *Advances in Serials Management* 4 (Greenwich, Conn., and London: JAI, 1992), pp. 171-192.
4. *Anglo-American Cataloguing Rules*, 2nd ed. (Chicago: American Library Association; Ottawa: Canadian Library Association, 1978), p. 570.
5. Jean Hirons and Crystal Graham, *Issues Related to Seriality*. Paper presented at the International Conference on the Principles and Future Development of AACR, Toronto, Canada, October 23-25, 1997. URL: http://www.nlc-bnc.ca/jsc/r-serial.pdf.
6. Regina Reynolds, remarks made at Hamilton Park Conference Center, New Jersey, October 1997.
7. *Anglo-American Cataloguing Rules*, p. 568.
8. Tuttle, *Managing Serials*, pp. 124-128.
9. Tina Feick, presentation to Rosary College serials class, June 1994.

11

Out-of-Print and Antiquarian Markets

MARGARET LANDESMAN

The out-of-print market today is one of the book world's most exciting places. It is the last frontier for automation—being transformed from month to month as bookstores and dealers and librarians and collectors discover the possibilities of life on the Web—and, at the same time, a last frontier for holdouts who believe that life on the Web has absolutely nothing to offer book lovers and never will. But it is the very nicest sort of frontier, populated with interesting people, good stories, and the vast majority of all the books, maps, journals, and newspapers that have ever been published by anybody, anywhere.

Out-of-print buying is a frustrating field for librarians, despite the many ways in which automation has finally begun to make life easier. Though it is pleasant and rewarding to browse through catalogs choosing among tempting offerings, locating particular titles is still a problem and probably always will be. Many common and in-demand out-of-print books are now easy to locate, but requests for obscure, technical, and not-very-collectible titles remain difficult or impossible to fill. Out-of-print purchasing, whether catalog purchases or o.p. (out-of-print) searches, is labor intensive for acquisitions departments. It is hard on business offices, which do not understand why there is a rush about paying or why the library insists on leaving orders outstanding for years. Can they not just buy some other book? When the books do arrive, often looking like titles which could have been picked up at the local thrift store, it is hard to understand why such mundane objects should cost very much.

Out-of-print buying is not a major activity for most libraries. The reason is not lack of supply or demand, but that the budget does not seem to stretch to cover very many. The most important reason libraries do not buy as they did in the 1960s and early 1970s is undoubtedly the result of dried-up acquisitions budgets and the shift of available dollars from monographs to serials and electronic resources.[1] The volume of buying in-print books is down precipitously, and purchases of out-of-print ones, though numbers are less readily available, are probably down even more.

In addition, the growth of international bibliographic utilities and the resulting ease with which copies at other libraries can be located have lessened the reliance on ownership. Reprints and microfilms have provided alternatives that absorb some of the available funds that might be spent in this market. Improvements in interlibrary loan have probably increased the frequency with which libraries recommend it to patrons as the fastest route to an out-of-print title.

When libraries did a substantial amount of antiquarian buying, library staff naturally developed the expertise to work intelligently in this market. Larger research libraries even had staff who specialized in antiquarian buying. Today a library is much less likely to be able to afford someone who devotes enough time to the out-of-print market to develop expertise, and selectors are less likely to be knowledgeable about an area for which they lack funds and in which they are, therefore, relatively inexperienced. While special collections and rare book staff remain knowledgeable about the antiquarian market, especially with regard to catalog offerings, librarians with expertise in how to search for wanted titles are rare.[2]

Yet libraries need out-of-print books and must find ways to buy them in a timely and efficient fashion. While libraries have less money for retrospective purchases, the increasing speed with which books are going out-of-print means that even libraries with few retrospective interests need to enter the out-of-print market from time to time for current titles or replacements. And there will always be teaching and research needs for which an out-of-print book is required and interlibrary loan is not an option, such as when copies are needed for reserve.

The problem of buying on the out-of-print market is analogous to trying to purchase in-print books, but without wholesalers and without being able to order from the book's publishers. Add to this the stipulation that only a few copies of each book may exist and that publishers charge bookstores wildly differing prices from day to day, and one has a sense of the out-of-print market. In such a market, it is easy to find as many good books as the collection can afford. But, if a particular title is desired and no other will do, a certain amount of ingenuity and effort is required.

When purchasing an out-of-print book, the library is not only paying for the book, it is paying for its location—on the library shelf—and the time and effort it took both the library and the vendor to get it there. In short, the combined effort is higher for out-of-print books than for in-print books.

NATURE OF THE OUT-OF-PRINT MARKET

Out-of-print dealers are a different breed from in-print dealers. Except for those associated with large book shops and vendors, they are smaller, frequently one-person operations. And they are, almost without exception, book lovers.

The out-of-print market is a very fragmented one. Individual dealers are fiercely independent and proud of it. They maintain friendly support and advice networks with each other, but they do not see why librarians should consider it a virtue to do things in a uniform manner, all using the same system and the same terminology. They view the variety of ways in which the same book may be described by different dealers not as a cause for alarm, but as an opportunity to distinguish themselves from the competition through their superior descriptions. And, since libraries constitute a relatively small part of their business for most dealers, this seems unlikely to change.

Getting to know the subject is a necessity for out-of-print dealers in a way that it is not for in-print. They must choose from the mass of older published material that which is still desirable. To do this, they often research fields and, for rare books, individual titles extensively. One can complain of the quality of in-print titles purchased without hurting the dealer's feeling. The same is not true for out-of-print dealers!

Types of Dealers

Dealers may choose to describe themselves as antiquarian, old, out-of-print, used, or rare booksellers and are an extraordinarily varied lot, not subject to any very useful classification. Many dealers will fit into more than one of the following categories, but this list will give an idea of the varieties to be found.

Book scouts: Book scouts are people with a knack for spotting titles and remembering on which list they last saw them. They can walk into a store and pull books off a shelf with at least as great efficiency as a computer can match them. They search out desirable books and sell them to dealers or individual buyers. Some book scouts are more-or-less attached to a dealer or group of dealers; others are completely on their own. The scout's knowledge of sources for buying books and of the sorts of materials particular dealers are looking for makes it possible and even profitable to visit other stores and sales, purchasing stock to resell. The Web has made this easier to do. A scout can now can check want lists and query dealers by e-mail. One store notes that a lot of the packages arriving from scouts whose quotes have been accepted are post-marked Florida.[3] Scouting seems to make an excellent retirement occupation.

Neighborhood bookstores: There are many small shops run, part- or full-time, by book lovers willing to sacrifice their standard of living to be among books. They may be located in converted older houses or small storefronts, and they rely primarily on walk-ins and a clientele of loyal customers. They do not usually issue catalogs. They are part of the neighborhood cultural scene and may offer local alternative papers, announcements of pottery sales, and benefits for various causes (usually liberal), as well as books. A gratifying percentage have a resident cat. These stores expect customers to pay at the cash register when they buy the book. Given purchase orders, demands for multiple copies of invoices, and inquiries as to tax numbers, the owners tend to wonder if it's worth the effort—especially when they discover just how long it will be before the check arrives. Some, especially the newer ones, are enthusiastic about the online world. Others are not. There will always be out-of-print dealers—successful ones, even—who stick with fountain pens.

Specialized dealers: These are the people who have successfully transformed a passion into a livelihood—collectors who spend all day collecting. They are frequently authoritative scholars on the bibliography and history of publishing in their field. Though many have had a shop at one time, some have tired of the restrictions and expense and do much or all of their business by mail order—catalogs, quotes, visits to libraries. They will travel long distances to look at collections which interest them and call on their customers. Such dealers are most useful to libraries in supplying specialized wants and as a resource for patrons needing to purchase titles or get books appraised. A particular title will likely cost more once it has moved to a specialized dealer than if you had managed to spot it in a general used bookstore. Dealers know this too, and much of the movement of books among dealers is from general stocks into those of specialized dealers with a clientele that is knowledgeable and appreciative of these particular titles.

General out-of-print dealers: General out-of-print dealers have a large stock in varied areas and may have specialities as well. Some offer search services; some do not. Some issue catalogs; some do not. Many new dealers learn their field and get their start by spending some years developing expertise in such a store.

Mixed in-print/out-of-print dealers: As independent booksellers are hitting the ground right and left, overwhelmed by Barnes & Nobles, Borders, and MediaPlay incursions into their territory, mixed in-print/out-of-print stores are finding that out-of-print books can make a big difference. With their unruly nature and untidy habits, out-of-print titles are not very appealing to these stores and store personnel are unlikely to develop the knowledge base to help customers who want to find them.[4]

Web-only businesses: Web-based businesses clearly appeal to those thinking of entering the field, as well as to established dealers who would like to escape being tied down to the need for a live body in a particular place many hours a week, and who find the idea of not paying rent and utilities attractive. It is early to know whether or not entirely online businesses can successfully compete in the long run with the best of the antiquarian shops. It is clear, though, that they will never replace shops. You cannot handle the books and smell them and be among them on the Web. And the idea that most book purchasers would give up that experience seems most unlikely.

Academic library vendors: Major academic library book vendors here and abroad usually have associated out-of-print search services. These services do not maintain an inventory or offer catalogs. They are searching for titles their library customers want, either as a result of an order the library expected to be in-print or as an out-of-print search. You can, if you wish, have all out-of-print orders go immediately to the search service and authorize your vendor to ship automatically when found if the price is under an agreed-upon amount. Vendors usually ask that you give them exclusive rights to search for the titles for six months or a year, a most reasonable request.

Rare book dealers: Rare book dealers are mostly specialized, probably because it is not possible for one person to learn enough about a field to deal in the rare books for too many unrelated fields. Large out-of-print dealers often have rare book rooms, often very fine ones. Rare book specialization tends to be passed on from generation to generation with some dealers training a large part of the next generation of rare book dealers.

Libraries need to keep in mind when working with antiquarian dealers that even the largest are a different breed of animal from the large library wholesalers who sometimes seem not to notice overdue bills for months. Smaller dealers often really cannot afford to deal with libraries unless arrangements for prepayment can be made or, at the least, payment expedited. Even with the many dealers who sell a good volume to institutions and are painfully clear about the drawbacks of institutional purchasing, it is much appreciated if a library will make sure that those paying the bills understand that the seller may be counting on a check to pay the rent.

Dealers are useful to libraries in many ways beyond being responsible for adding certain books to library collections. Libraries can sell duplicates and other good but unneeded titles to out-of-print dealers, often at more advantageous prices than can be obtained otherwise. Some libraries choose to accept credit for future purchases rather than cash from a dealer with whom they deal regularly. This can be cumbersome administratively, but dealers are generally willing to pay more in credit than in cash. Many dealers will do appraisals for donors, although the library needs to be aware of all provisions of the current tax law. Sometimes dealers are responsible for referring potential donors to the library. It is well worth putting effort into building a good relationship with a dealer whose material is of serious interest to the library. When a dealer has choice items, he or she naturally is likely to offer them first to a reliable customer with known interests in the area.

Where Do Dealers Get Their Stock?

Librarians are always curious about where dealers get books. Dealers, perhaps somewhat suspicious of librarians' motives or perhaps just in the interests of professional mystique, may not be forthcoming on the matter and tend to murmur something vague about how much work it is finding the books.

The popular conception seems to be that dealers lurk. Just where this lurking takes place is unclear, but it seems to have a lot to do with attics. The reality is more prosaic. Dealers, especially new ones, frequent garage and estate sales and other used bookstores looking for salable titles. As they become more established, and if they have a shop, they are more likely to be offered books by individuals who want to sell them. Also, once they have an established stock, they can get more picky about which books they want to sell.

Established dealers have developed a network of contacts and may be offered individual titles and collections of books from many sources, including individuals, estates, and libraries. Many out-of-print books come from other dealers. Dealers often do not like to admit this because libraries resent paying the increases involved in moving books from one dealer to another. If a book could go directly from the retiring professor to the one library missing that particular title—preferably, of course, as a gift—efficiency would prevail. But, of course, acquisitions do not occur this way, and a book bought from another dealer costs just as much as it does from any other source. Dealers visit one another's shops, read one another's catalogs, and increasingly browse one another's stock online. A book that one dealer has at a very low price because of few or no likely customers may be one for which another dealer has several customers. The Web, again, is changing the patterns of what books a dealer will buy. A dealer in New Mexico told of a book on Hawaii that she would have passed up previously. Today, she knows that a Hawaiian dealer browsing the Web is likely to find it and snap it up for a store more commonly visited by Hawaiians than those in Albuquerque.[5] It is easier for dealers not only to reach a global audience of customers but also a global audience of other dealers. Librarians still don't like to browse generally for books on the Web—paper is much more pleasant—and collectors, unless highly focused on a narrow subject field, may or may not. But many dealers and book scouts find it a worthwhile investment of time.

Many dealers will search for books on the library's want list. Where do these books come from? Dealers use many of the same sources as libraries in finding wanted titles, but they are able to devote more energy and expertise to the search. They advertise, list on online search services, check other dealers' holdings, and use book scouts. Obviously, books that involve this extra labor will cost more than books supplied from stock. Searching is not a financially rewarding pursuit. Not all dealers are willing to do it; those who do search see it more as a service to their customers than as a main part of their business.

How Do Dealers Price Books?

How does a dealer establish a price and how does a library know prices are fair? This is a question that has always been—and will probably always remain—more difficult to answer in the out-of-print world. But it is not as difficult as it used to be. In the past, dealers relied on experience and memory for the pricing of ordinary out-of-print stock books. Research on individual titles, except for rare items, was not a feasible labor investment. Now, it is an easy matter to check online for offerings of the title in question or similar titles. This has made pricing more competitive, since customers check too.

Out-of-print books are one-of-a-kind objects that are greatly affected by their previous history. The book may have or lack a dust jacket. The library may or may not care about this. The book may or may not have been gently handled by previous owners. The library probably does care about this, especially if the previous owner did not treat books with kindness and consideration, unless, of course, the previous owner was the author or famous, in which case the graffiti constitute a desirable and possibly quite valuable addition. But, in general, condition, taken for granted in new books, is a concern in old ones. And now that the Internet makes it so easy and tempting to purchase from vendors the library has never heard of and knows nothing about, condition can be a substantial concern, as can the accuracy of the description. People offering books for sale may be knowledgeable, or they may not. One dealer ordering a first edition of a twentieth-century author from an unknown dealer over the Web found himself in the possession (temporary) of a book club edition. The seller was not clear about the difference.

Generally, dealers purchase for about 30 percent of what they expect to sell for. For very desirable books that they can expect to sell right away, they will often go higher, and for items they are only marginally interested in, lower. Sellers often are very interested in the dealer's taking all of the books they hope to sell rather than picking and choosing among them, and some of what any dealer buys is not really much wanted by the dealer.

For a dealer, the original purchase price may be the least important element in the selling price. Dealers buy more books than they sell, and the time between buying and selling is often years. Listing the books is a labor-intensive proposition and expensive if there is only one of each item to sell. Paper catalogs, with their production and postage costs and uncertain return rate, are very expensive indeed. In addition to what they pay for the books, dealers must add enough to cover these costs, pay the rent and taxes, and feed the children.

What Is a Book Worth to the Library?

Is a book worth the price? The first criterion, as always, is to judge the book against the rest of the collection, dollar for dollar, as one would any other proposed acquisition. Is the title worth what it costs in terms of the benefits it brings? Would the library buy it if it were a new book or information in another format? The library may want to know if the book is cheaper from another dealer, and it may now be easier to check this with the online search services. However, it is easy to invest more labor in checking than you save by finding a slightly cheaper book.[6]

Prices are a major source of disquiet for librarians. The wide range of prices for out-of-print materials leaves us feeling ill at ease. It is hard to know what a fair price is, and if the librarian is not familiar with the out-of-print market, prices tend to seem awfully high. Dealers, all too familiar with the economics of the trade, feel understandably disturbed at those who question their prices. While there are dealers whose prices are higher than others, librarians might note how few people have ever become rich selling old books.

Librarians and collectors, caught up in watching the ever-rising values of books in their collections as new copies come on the market, tend toward wishful thinking in terms of both buying and selling. When hoping to buy, we think in terms of what the title would cost should we just happen to encounter it at our local thrift store or used book dealers. When considering selling, we tend to recall the last advertised catalog price.

The best bet is to know the dealer. If the dealer is offering material at consistently reasonable prices, then buy. A few titles may be priced high and others low, but the library will come out about even in the end. What a book would have cost if the library had had the prescience to buy it new or if a selector had found a copy in the basement of the local used book store is not relevant. It is important to weigh the cost of staff time, however, and consider this when making decisions about out-of-print purchases.

It is a good idea, theoretically, to evaluate a dealer's timeliness and pricing periodically, but this is an area in which care should be taken. Do not look at the prices of individual titles. Every dealer is going to be off now and then, and the same book will cost one dealer more than another. Look at the average price in light of the sort of material you are getting. For most libraries, this is difficult because the number of titles bought from many dealers will not be enough for fair appraisal. In any case, this is likely to be in large part an intuitive judgment.

PRICE GUIDES

Three types of pricing guides are commonly used by dealers and libraries:

Guides based on dealer catalogs: These are compilations of the listings in dealer catalogs which have been collected by the person preparing the guide. The problem with using catalog-based price guides is that books listed in catalogs may or may not have sold. *Bookman's Price Index*, a Gale publication since 1964, collates the entries from catalogs issued by 200 antiquarian dealers in the United States, England, and Canada.

Guides based on auction prices: Auction prices, since they reflect the prices for which books actually sold, are among the more reliable. However, there are caveats here too. Run-of-the-mill used books are not usually sold at auction, and you are not likely to be able to find price information for such everyday books. Also, the buyer's premium paid when buying at auction is not included in the recorded price. By their nature, however, auction prices reflect demand for that book on that day; if an avid collector particularly wanted a title, it may have driven the price up. On the other hand, a very collectible title might have been sold for a lower price if the right buyer did not happen to be present. *American Book Prices Current*, issued annually since 1930, records prices realized at auctions in over forty auction houses in the United States, England, and Europe.

Guides produced by individual authors: Knowledgeable authors producing bibliographies of books by a given author or in a given field can often be useful. As they do not tend to appear in new editions every year as catalog and auction-based guides do, they are more useful for ascertaining relative desirability and availability of titles than for prices. These can be very good or very bad, depending on the author.

While print guides such as these are still useful to libraries and to larger bookstores, online searching is becoming increasingly attractive as an alternative. Checking through Interloc, Advanced Book Exchange (ABE), Bibliofind, Bowker's Books Out-of-Print (available free online), and other similar sources is rapidly replacing much of the use formerly made of print guides.[7]

How Do Libraries Find Dealers?

How does a library find dealers? In addition to the many subject and geographical guides available, more informal methods are often useful. Watch advertisements in professional publications and follow relevant discussion lists to see who is active in fields of interest to the library. Talk to other libraries of similar size and interests. Talk to patrons and faculty and to the dealers the library uses regularly.

While various printed guides to the out-of-print market in this and other countries still exist and are very convenient and helpful to have on one's shelf, it is difficult to beat the currency and availability of the many Web sources. The quality of these sites will, of course, vary with the conscientiousness of those producing them. An authoritative place to start is with the Web pages of the various professional organizations in the trade: the Antiquarian Booksellers Association of America (ABAA), the International League of Antiquarian Booksellers (ILAB), and affiliated groups in other countries.

Dealers are knowledgeable about other dealers and their specialties. They can be extremely helpful when a dealer with a particular location or specialty is needed. If money is involved—for example, when a dealer is needed to inspect a prospective purchase or to appraise specialized collections for the library—it is best to get a recommendation from someone the library knows and trusts.

EDUCATING ONESELF ABOUT THE TRADE

It is both rewarding and useful for librarians to get to know the antiquarian market. There are many ways of doing this. Online browsing is an easily accessible one. In addition to catalogs and search services, one can find a great deal of information about the out-of-print market and out-of-print booksellers. Major out-of-print dealers such as Powell's in Portland and Second City in Washington, D.C., have attached copies of printed publications and much other helpful material to their Web pages. Interloc has an excellent on-line newsletter, the Interloc News. A number of sites have book-seller profiles describing individual booksellers, how they got into the business, and what subjects and services they offer. A new digital periodical, *The Antiquarian Book Herald*, edited by David Meesters, is online under the sponsorship of NAN, the Netherlands Antiquarian Booksellers' Network.

There are also, of course, Web pages purporting to be authoritative sources which may or may not have good things to offer. Some, put up by enthusiasts, become dated and are not kept up. On others, the qualifications of the authors are not clear. It is perhaps best to be careful and use common sense in following links. The sponsorship of an organization known to the reader, or a link discovered from the Web page of a bookseller trusted by the library, is a good prerequisite to taking a site seriously.

Print publications, especially *AB Bookman's Weekly*, continue to be of major value. While *AB Bookman's Weekly* has decreased steadily in size over the last few years as fewer lists are submitted, the articles it publishes remain the best source of authoritative information on the antiquarian book trade. Jacob Chernofsky, the founder and editor, continues also to organize the Colorado Out-of-Print Book seminar each summer. This is a weeklong conference where librarians can hear talks by and meet many veteran book-sellers, as well as those new to the trade and other interested librarians.

There are also many antiquarian book fairs which are worth attending when possible. Lists can be found on the ABAA and other Web pages. At the American Library Association annual and mid-winter conferences, the Association for Library Collections and Technical Services Out-of-Print Discussion Group offers informative sessions.

The best way to learn about the book trade, however, remains taking every opportunity to visit used and rare bookstores and talk to the people who run them. The online guides make it easy when preparing for a trip to locate bookstores of interest, their addresses and their hours, and print them out to take along.

It also frequently falls to librarians, willing or unwilling, to educate patrons about the book market. Explaining to a patron or donor that old and leather-bound do not necessarily translate into "rare and valuable" can be hard on the librarian. A pamphlet prepared by the Rare Books and Manuscripts Section of the Association of College and Research Libraries of the American Library Association, *Your Old Books,* is a very useful tool and available on the Web.

Margaret Landesman

BOOKS ONLINE

Online out-of-print book services on the Web are being invented as we go along. They will change the nature of the market in many ways, although traditional used and rare book dealers will always exist. It is too soon to predict exactly which directions will prove to be lasting ones, but trying to foretell the future makes an excellent sport.

At this point, selling on the Web is proving very successful and is having a major impact on an increasing number of dealers. Buying, whether by dealers or by libraries, remains more problematic. It has always been easier to find attractive titles to purchase when perusing a listing of available books than to locate a particular wanted title, and this would appear to remain true online. Online searching has not yet shown that it can be a superior tool for locating wanted titles. Search services, such as Blackwell North America, and large out-of-print dealers, such as Sam Wellers in Salt Lake City, report that when they are trying to locate titles on their customers' want list, many more dealers still respond to printed lists than to online searches, and they feel the prices of the titles located from the printed lists are lower.

Many of the catalogs on the Internet are electronic versions of the print catalogs mailed to customers. However, dealers are beginning to take advantage of the way in which an online catalog can be used as an inventory of current offerings. As newer dealers begin to catalog on the Internet, a new species of online-only catalog is beginning to emerge. These dealers simply use the catalog concept to divide the stock they are entering into subject groups of a size the customer who wants to browse can manage.

There is yet another species of catalog emerging as a product of online services, the virtual catalog of a virtual collection that does not actually exist. Just as a librarian can create a bibliography from WorldCat, so a dealer can create a catalog of books on a particular topic offered for sale by many vendors by cutting and pasting together an anthology of listings. It would seem that such a practice might have its pitfalls.

Vendor Web pages: Some dealers, early adapters of technology or those with teenage kids, put up their own Web pages early on. Most larger dealers have done or likely will do this. Like large libraries, they have staffs that are large enough to contain someone good at this sort of thing, or the resources to hire someone especially to work on their online offerings. For smaller dealers, ABE, Interloc, and Bibliofind offer an easy and attractive alternative.

Want lists: Vendors, libraries, and individuals can post want lists on these systems. Sometimes there is a charge and sometimes not. Vendors browsing the want list may quote items to the would-be purchaser and, in some cases, the want lists are automatically matched against new stock as it is entered by member dealers.

E-mail for sale lists: There are discussion lists on most topics, and antiquarian books are no exception. AcqNet's postings regularly include discussions of out-of-print dealers and their fill rates, and ExLibris is useful to those interested in rare books. Bibliofind offers a number of lists to which anyone, a subscriber or not, can subscribe. Books under $100, for instance, daily contains offerings from dealers and queries asking for help with particular wanted items. This is a sort of "Nickel Want Ad" approach to selling books. And, amazingly, it seems to work. Libraries do not seem to yet be taking advantage of this ability to easily list titles for sale, but perhaps in the future they will.

Auctions: Online auctions seem to be a new game on the Internet. Whether or not they will prove useful rather than just gimmicks, it is too soon to say. Bibliofind offers the first of this sort of auction for used books.

BUYING ON THE OUT-OF-PRINT MARKET

Library book purchases, both for in-print and for out-of-print titles, can be divided into two modes. In the more common mode, the selector is in effect browsing through available titles to locate those which should be purchased for the collection. This can be a very systematic sort of activity—with the hope of covering all known titles in some category so that nothing appropriate and important to the collection is missed—or it can be a more serendipitous activity, looking in the best spots to see what one might find there.

In the other mode, a specific title is sought. A professor has requested a particular book. The library must research the title. Is it in print? Who publishes it or has it for sale? Is the citation accurate? Does this book actually exist?

The two situations have little in common. Generalized purchasing is easier in either case. One knows who to order from and what the price will be—it says so on the new book advertisement or in the catalog. In the other, research is required.

The biggest obstacle to out-of-print dealers taking full advantage of the possibilities of automation is that it has never been economically feasible for an out-of-print dealer to make any sort of title list of more than a fraction of available stock. It is not worth entering a book of which you have only one copy to sell when you reach a limited market for that title. However, when you can reach a global market, the economics change. It is still not economical to list every copy of every book, but many are worth the investment. Dealers seem to feel that a title which costs $15 or above and for which there are not too many other copies listed online is a good candidate. This figure was quoted to me both by a large established antiquarian dealer in San Francisco, Acorn Books, which now has 30,000 titles listed online and does an increasing share of its business by mail, and a small neighborhood store in Albuquerque, New Mexico, from a dealer who has only a few hundred books listed online.

The online antiquarian services emerging are networks that link dealers to each other and to customers directly. These services function in ways that are analogous in some ways to bibliographic utilities and in others to Integrated Library Systems. Like a bibliographic utility, the services allow every dealer and all the customers to see titles listed by all the participants, and the network puts the interested participants into direct contact with each other. Like an Integrated Library System, the service offers bookstores, if desired, the software and technical backup to run an online operation including a Web site, software to produce online and printed catalogs, and even accounting systems. How do they make their money? By fees charged the sellers. In all cases, searching is free to the buyer. A modest fee, usually monthly, covers the costs of the service providers.

In this country three online services are best known at this point—Interloc, Bibliofind, and ABE (the Advanced Book Exchange). Some dealers utilize one, some two, and a few use all three. They all offer the same basic services, but there are variations. Many other services come and go. There are analogous services in other countries; these are used as examples. Interloc, founded by Richard Weatherford who ran BookQuest for Faxon, is the oldest. Most services state a claim to be the world's largest or fastest growing or something of that nature. Interloc, it seems fair to say, is the one most dealers believe is the largest.

In addition, it should be noted that both the ABAA and ILAB have search capabilities that cover all the online catalogs of their members. Some larger bookstores, like Powells and Second Story, have their own online search systems which offer many of the same features.

Searching: Online services offer the ability for any comer to search the combined listings of all the dealers by author, title, key-word, and in the other usual ways. Search engines differ, and an individual user may prefer one over another. When a title is located, the viewer sees a list of the available copies. Clicking on the title will connect the viewer directly to the dealer. The purchaser can then enter a credit card number and submit the order over e-mail. Libraries usually choose other routes to send the order to the dealer.

To date, none of the online services has established a connection with an integrated library system so that purchase orders can be generated and transmitted online as they can with many in-print vendors. Nor do out-of-print dealers see the appeal of downloading descriptions from a central source such as *Books in Print* or OCLC. At this point, there is virtually no standardization of data elements used in the out-of-print market, which will make truly efficient interfaces almost impossible to achieve. Perhaps change in these areas will come about eventually. Or, it may be that universities, which are beginning to issue credit cards to be used for some purchases, will gain the ability to interface better with bookstore systems.

In theory, all books located in this way are known to be available and can be ordered from the dealer. In practice, this is not always true. A good many such orders remain unfilled and unacknowledged—either because the dealer has not updated the catalog or for a variety of other reasons. It is best not to notify a patron that a needed title has been found until its availability is confirmed by phone or e-mail.

Searching Amazon.com for an out-of-print book will often produce an offer to quote. Pick a title from Interloc or one of the other services and request a quote from Amazon in order to note the markup. Libraries will prefer to go direct, but Amazon.com is contributing to the success of dealers who through it can reach an audience previously inaccessible to them.

Matching: As a dealer or library enters inventory or want lists, those lists can be automatically matched with the lists of other dealers and customers and the resulting hit list used to contact likely purchasers. Such matching should eventually prove a god-send to libraries. However, at present, it would seem that the number of titles entered is still not large enough and does not include many of the scholarly and obscure and technical titles of interest to libraries. For a store needing twenty copies of a common title for a book club, the search and matching services work fine. But for an obscure title, you may be unlikely to find a match. A list of matches is likely to include many quotes for a few of the titles and no quotes for the remainder. And, as noted above, not all of the quotes will result in the successful location of a copy of the book.

Online catalogs: Some dealers never did—and still do not—issue catalogs or lists. For these dealers, especially, the transition to the Web is painful and expensive. For dealers who have always issued catalogs, the benefits of online listing became apparent fairly early as the word processor replaced the typewriter and the PC the word processor.

BUYING BY BROWSING

Catalogs: Catalog purchases make up the bulk of retrospective buying at most institutions. Special Collections and Acquisitions departments, faculty, and selectors are daily deluged with catalogs from out-of-print dealers. It is important to spend the time necessary to develop a system of handling catalogs and the orders resulting from them efficiently. To get catalogs to the right person quickly, ask to have selectors' names put directly on mailing lists. Make sure the person sorting mail can recognize out-of-print catalogs and knows to rush them.

There is an urgency to selecting items from catalogs and getting them through the bibliographic searching and ordering process since the items are one-of-a-kind and will be sold to the first person requesting them. Special Collections and Acquisitions must work together to devise a method of prompt attention to catalogs without seriously disrupting the workflow of orders for other areas of the collection. It is useful to phone the dealer, ascertain that the desired items are still available, and ask that they be reserved for the library. Dealers are usually willing to do this, but it can pose serious problems for them if the library is not prompt and conscientious about following up speedily.

Catalogs that have been inadvertently aged by those responsible for selection pose problems for acquisitions. Hours of searching may result in only a few books being added to the collection and in other more timely orders being unnecessarily delayed. It seems legitimate for Acquisitions to refuse to handle such orders at peak times or to request that the selector phone the dealer and find out what is still in stock before proceeding.

Browsing online catalogs does not seem to be a very popular activity as yet among library selectors. Utilizing paper catalogs that can be carried to meetings and worked on at home has obvious advantages to sitting at a terminal or printing out stacks of loose paper.

Quotes: Dealers will often quote items they believe may be of particular interest to a client library. It is courteous to respond promptly, whether one wants the item or not. It may be helpful to include the reasons for accepting or rejecting the quote, so that the dealer can adjust future quotes.

Be sure quotes do not bypass normal search procedures, or the library may end up buying duplicates. This can happen frequently if, for instance, the head of special collections and the head of collection development both act impulsively about ordering irresistible titles. It does not make either of them popular with the acquisitions staff.

Dealer visits: Some dealers like to visit libraries, bringing possible purchases and perhaps purchasing duplicates and unneeded titles from the library. Some libraries encourage this practice; others do not. There are advantages and disadvantages to such visits.

The main advantage is that looking at the material firsthand, especially when purchasing artists' books, maps, or similar materials, can be very helpful in making a decision. You can learn a lot about your field through seeing a lot of books, including those you cannot afford. And, especially, you can learn a lot from discussions with a knowledgeable dealer.

The disadvantage is that you are very frequently tempted to spend more than you had budgeted, or, less frequently, feel obligated to buy something from a poor lot to repay the dealer for all his or her trouble. These visits are also difficult for acquisitions staff. Searchers have to leave their normal workflow to check books on the spot and, especially in the case of rare and expensive material, your best trained searchers are needed to do this. Then the books have to be kept tucked safely away, but not forgotten, until the invoice arrives and they can be paid for and sent on. The nuisance level and error rate on such purchases can be pretty high.

Buying trips: Buying trips can range from selectors visiting local bookstores to selectors or faculty going off, cash in hand, to some distant place. Such trips tend to be labor-intensive for acquisitions personnel, but very worthwhile in the material they bring in.

The most frequent nasty side effect when buying away from home is unwanted duplication. This can be avoided by having the selector or faculty member select the books and ask the dealer to hold them while sending an invoice or list to the library. The library can cross off duplicates and return the invoice to the dealer, who ships and invoices in the usual way. The selector does not have to physically deal with the books and does not take personal responsibility for the money. The library avoids unwanted duplicates and does not have to work around normal payment procedures.

Occasionally, this procedure will not work and the selector needs to carry money and bring back the books. If the price of the materials is low enough to offset the duplicates and the extra paperwork, this approach can be useful.

When a library sends enthusiastic selectors to a bookstore with a sizable out-of-print stock, it is almost guaranteed that they will locate a dozen titles in the dollar bin for which the library would happily pay substantial amounts. By the time the library determines which of the titles are needed, it has in fact paid a substantial amount in staff time. Nevertheless, the value to the collection sometimes makes the time spent worthwhile, especially if it is possible to search the online catalog from the bookstore.

Going to library sales can also be an inexpensive way to acquire books. When one library sells its duplicates, another library can inexpensively replenish copies of worn-out books, though the same problems with searching apply.

Auctions: Only the largest libraries seem to buy regularly at auctions. The reason commonly given is the mysterious and intimidating nature of auctions, but it may have more to do with practicality. Most libraries are located a long way from the few cities having most of the auctions, and library travel budgets are seldom ample. Books sold at auction are frequently sold in groups, or lots, and auction catalogs often do not specify the titles of all the books in a given lot. This means the library may have to buy books it does not want to get those it does. If the library decides to enter an auction, the material being auctioned must be searched and a high and a low bid must be decided. A way of having the material inspected prior to the auction, bid for, paid for (cash usually is required), and picked up after the auction must be established. By far the most sensible thing is to ask a dealer trusted by the library to take care of the whole procedure for a commission. Dealers do not make a lot of money on such commissions, but are usually willing to undertake them for customers. Bibliofind has recently established an on-line antiquarian book auction, and it will be interesting to see how successful this is.

Collections: Collections are often offered to libraries both by dealers and by individuals. They pose difficulties for established libraries because the duplication rate is almost always unacceptably high. Collections from individuals also pose problems because the owner may not be disposed to wait the time required for institutional decision making and payment. For these reasons, libraries tend to buy only those collection they want quite badly. A good relationship with a dealer again may be helpful as a dealer may be willing to purchase a collection of interest and give the library first pick, or to agree beforehand to purchase all the duplicates from the library.

Searching for wanted titles: Libraries generally discourage selectors from searching for out-of-print titles unless they are very certain that they want a title, are willing to wait a long time for it to be found, and are not going to fuss if the price is fairly steep. Most libraries do not have staff assigned to specialize in the antiquarian market; it is very unlikely that a staff that also must cope with the problem of in-print acquisitions will be able to spend the necessary time to achieve outstanding results in the out-of-print market.

For this reason, it is a frequent practice when orders come back from vendors marked Out-of-Print or OSI, Out-of-Stock Indefinitely, (the same thing) to return them to the selectors, asking them to resubmit for an out-of-print search only if the title is a vital permanent addition to the collection. If a patron is actively in need of the title, he or she is generally referred to interlibrary loan as the fastest route.

In the past when such a report was received, it was well worth trying the publisher directly or reordering through another vendor who might happen to have a copy in stock. It was also worth a separate search through the various lists of reprint and on-demand publications. Whether or not this is still worth the trouble is debatable. Reprint publishers are now much more conscientious about listing in *Books in Print* so that a separate search is less likely to be successful; and while some search services do report calling publishers, the success rate is not particularly encouraging.

As with an out-of-print search, it is probably best to check first with the selector to ascertain how critical the title is to the collection.

As automation and consolidation continue to change the ways in which book publication works, innovative new ventures such as UMI's BookVault and Baker and Taylor's Replica may become viable alternatives for some titles. The UMI Books on Demand program covers 140,000 titles (somewhat pricey for systematic collection building, but worth it for an individual needed title), and Replica Books plans to make a limited number of newly out-of-print books available by obtaining the rights to suitable titles and offering them for sale at perhaps $5 over the publisher's price. A publisher's copy of the book will be cut at the spine and the pages scanned. Using this technology, it is expected that print runs of a hundred copies will be economically feasible.

It is sometimes possible to borrow a copy of a needed title from another library and photocopy and bind it, or, in some cases, to obtain such a copy from an owning library. In cases of urgent need, this is often the only sure and fast route to obtaining a copy for the library's collection, as opposed to borrowing a copy for an individual patron's use. But it is extremely labor-intensive and results in a less-than-satisfactory object (functional, but not aesthetically pleasing). The steps necessary to obtain copyright permission and a description of the whole process are outlined in a very thorough article, which has dated remarkably little, by Joseph Barker and his colleagues at Berkeley.[8]

There is no single answer to the question of how best to search for out-of-print books and no consensus on the question among librarians. Each library must determine the methods which best suit its needs. Most libraries use a mixture of approaches, depending on the type of material and the urgency with which it is needed.

There are two basic approaches to searching: the library does it, or the library asks someone else to do it. If the library chooses to do its own searching, it must decide whether to advertise first in print publications or to try the online services. A satisfactory response rate will probably require doing both. While this is very likely to be the route of choice for the largest libraries that do a lot of searching, other libraries may not find it worthwhile to invest the resources necessary to develop expertise. For a library that does most of its out-of-print buying through catalogs and only occasionally searches for particular titles, it is probably easier to rely on the search services of its in-print vendors in the United States and abroad, or to choose a large out-of-print dealer who is willing to handle library want lists. For specialized and technical titles, the library will probably have a dealer or two from whom it makes catalog purchases in the relevant subject on a regular basis. Asking them to find a copy of the needed title sometimes works. A number of articles have been published on the searching process, primarily in the journal *Library Acquisitions: Practice and Theory*. These and future similar studies will be helpful in keeping abreast of the progress of online searching efficiency.

There are any number of online services selling out-of-print books and any number of dealers offering to do out-of-print searches. The Web is replete with dealers offering "international searches," "computerized searches," and other services—each implying that it is somehow different from and superior to the others. It seems inherently unlikely that this is true; the methodology used by different dealers is much the same. What does differ is the network of contacts with book sources established by each dealer and the level of expertise as a bookperson each has to offer. Each library will need to examine currently available services to determine which ones it will use. And each library should probably expect that it will be desirable to keep abreast of new developments and to monitor how well present procedures are serving the library's needs.

Meanwhile, it seems safe to say that the paperless society poses no immediate threat to the future of antiquarian book selling. Indeed, it seems safe to say that it never will. If anything, the opposite may be true. The online world is providing a rapidly growing forum for the discussion of and dissemination of information about old books. Antiquarian sites, online newsletters, discussion groups, and e-mail lists seem to be germinating daily. Book collecting does not seem to be a habit in danger of dying out.

Nor do all purchasers hang on to their books indefinitely. At Powell's in Portland, 3,000 people come in every day with books to sell. Smaller bookstores see the same thing on a smaller scale. At garage sales, sellers turn excess "stuff" into cash and dealers arrive early—watching for the cars of other dealers—to forage for books. At libraries, gifts are accepted, some with enthusiasm and others with more mixed emotions.

All of these books are in need of new homes. Many of them will find them—and most of the new homes will not be in libraries. Libraries are a bit player in this market. However, it does seem possible that as more stock from more dealers is listed online, it will become steadily easier for libraries to locate the out-of-print titles they need.

Notes

1. See information on this subject on the Web page of the Association of Research Libraries, particularly the graph at http://192.100.21.90/newsltr/190/graph.html.

2. Douglas Duchin and Celia Scher Wagner, "Trials and Tribulations: Out-of-Print 101," *Library Acquisitions: Practice & Theory* 20 (1996): 341-350.

3. Reported by Joan Nye at Sam Weller's Zion Bookstore in Salt Lake City.

4. Powell's Books in Portland is probably the most innovative bookstore in this category and has an excellent Web site at www.powells.com.

5. A Novel Idea, in Albuquerque, N.M.

6. Patrick J. Brunet and Lee Shiflett, "Out-of-Print and Antiquarian Books: Guides for Reference Librarians," *RQ* 32 (Fall 1992): 85-101.

7. Brubaker, in an article published in the November 1996 *Biblio* and expanded in his Web site at http://members.aol.com/bookxpress/reviews/overview.nun, gives a very extensive list and descriptions of price guides.

8. Joseph W. Barker, Rebecca A. Rottman, and Marilyn Ng, "Organizing Out-of-Print and Replacement Acquisitions for Effectiveness, Efficiency, and the Future," *Library Acquisitions: Practice & Theory* 14 (1990): 137-163.

Bibliographic Sources

GUIDES TO DEALERS

AB Bookman's Yearbook. Clifton, N.J.: AB Bookman's Weekly, 1954- . Annual. Contains a list arranged geographically and by subject.

AcqWeb's Directory of Publishers and Vendors, Rare and Antiquarian Book Vendors at www.library.vanderbilt.edu. AcqWeb and all its parts are an extraordinarily valuable resource.

American Book Trade Directory. New Providence: R. R. Bowker, 1915- . Annual. Part 1, Retailers and Antiquarians in the United States and Canada, is an interspersed list of new and used book dealers, arranged geographically. Includes more information than many directories and is quite complete and authoritatively updated. No subject index, but a very useful source. Also includes a useful list of Wholesale Remainder Dealers.

Antiquarian Booksellers Association of America at www.clarknet:80/pub/. Directory lists members alphabetically, geographically, and by subject. The association is an authoritative source of information on the out-of-print and rare book trade.

Book Sales in America: Your Guide to Used Book Bargains. Hudson,
Mass.: BAYSYS Publishing, 1997. Available also at www.book-sales-in-
america.com.

Ethridge, James M. and Karen Ethridge, editors. *Antiquarian, Specialty,
and Used Book Sellers, 1997-98: A Subject Guide and Directory*. 2nd
ed. Detroit: Omnigraphics, 1997.

International League of Antiquarian Booksellers at www.clark.net/pub/
rmharris/ilab/english.html offers a directory of its members and links
to the national associations of other countries.

Robinson, Ruth Eleanor. *Buy Books Where, Sell Books Where: A Directory
of Out of Print Booksellers and Their Author-Subject Specialties, 1994-
1995*. 9th ed. Morgantown, W. Va.: Robinson Books, 1994.

*Sheppard's Book Dealers in North America: A Directory of Secondhand
and Antiquarian Books in the U.S.A. and Canada*. 13th ed. London:
Richard Joseph, 1996. The standard guide. New edition every few
years. Arranged geographically and indexed by subject. Sheppard
guides are also available for Great Britain, Europe, and India.

UMI BookVault: The UMI Books on Demand Database. [computer file]
Ann Arbor, Mich.: UMI, 1995. Lists 140,000 titles available. Details of
this program are at www.UMI.com under "Support Center" and "Books
on Demand."

PRICE GUIDES

American Book Prices Current. New York: Bancroft-Parkman, 1894/95- .
Annual. Cumulates with five-year indexes. Auction prices of books sold
in the United States and abroad.

*Book-Auction Records, a Priced and Annotated Annual Record of London
Book Auctions*. Kent, England: Wm. Dawson, 1902- . Annual.

Bookman's Price Index. Gale Research, 1964- . Annual. Based on dealers'
catalogs.

Book Prices Realized, a CD-ROM from Interloc, at www.interloc.com.

Brubaker, Robert. *A Review of Book Price and Reference Guides*.
http://members.aol.com/booksxpress/reviews/overview.nun expanded
from his article in *Biblio* magazine, November 1996. A very comprehensive list and description of price sources of many types.

Connolly, Joseph. *Modern First Editions: Their Value to Collectors*.
London: Orbis, 1993. An update of his 1977 *Collecting Modern First
Editions*.

Mandeville's Used Book Price Guide. Kenmore, Wash.: Price Guide
Publishers, 1998.

JOURNALS

AB Bookman's Weekly, 1948- . Weekly. Indexed in *Library Literature*,
it also frequently carries articles on dealers in specific cities and

specialties as well as articles on the nature and development of the antiquarian trade.

The Antiquarian Book Herald, at www.xs4all.nl/~artmed/herald.html.

The Library Bookseller: Books Wanted by College and University Libraries. West Orange, N.J.: Albert Saifer, 1949- . Biweekly.

E-MAIL LISTS AND DISCUSSION GROUPS

ABAA-announcements—A new list which will cover book fairs, public affairs announcements from nonprofit book-related organizations, and new online catalogs and Web sites. Send "subscribe abaa-announcements" to majordomo@angus.myster.com.

AcqNews, from AcqWeb. Frequently includes discussion of which book dealers are used by various libraries.

Bibliofind sponsors several lists including "Books under $100," "Books over $100," "Rare Books," "ModernFirsts" and "WTB" (Want to Buy) at www.bibliofind.com.

Exlibris, an Electronic News and Discussion Group for those interested in Rare Books and Special Collections at http://palimpset.stanford.edu/byform/mailing-lists/exlibris.

GENERALLY USEFUL TITLES

Carter, John. *ABC for Book Collectors*. 6th ed. Rev. by Nicolas Barker. London and New York: Granada, 1980. A classic for book collecting; other titles by Carter are also worth reading.

Gaskell, Philip. *A New Introduction to Bibliography*. Oxford: Clarendon; New York: Oxford University Press, 1972. Everything you might ever want to know in this field explained very clearly.

Miller, Heather S. *Managing Acquisitions and Vendor Relations*. New York: Neal-Schuman, 1992. A useful general text with a good chapter on out-of-print issues.

Peters, Jean, ed. *Book Collecting: A Modern Guide*. New York: R. R. Bowker, 1977.

Rees-Moggs, William. *How to Buy Rare Books*. Oxford: Phaidon, 1985.

Wingen, Peter Van. *Your Old Books*. Rare Books and Manuscripts Section, Association of College and Research Libraries. Chicago, ALA, 1994. Prepared for the RBMS Web site by members of the RBMS Electronic Information Technology Committee. www.princeton.edu/%/eferguson/yob.html.

WEB SITES CITED

Acorn Books, San Francisco at www.best.com/~acornbks/acorn.numf.

AcqWeb at www.library.vanderbilt.edu/faw/acqs.

Advanced Book Exchange (ABE) at www.abebooks.com.

Antiquarian Booksellers Association of America (ABAA) at www.clarknet:80/pub/.

Biblio at www.bibliomag.com.

Bibliofind at www.bibliofind.com.

Blackwells Book Service, Out of Print Books at www.blackwell.com/services/op.

Interloc at www.interloc.com.

International League of Antiquarian Booksellers (ILAB) at www.clarknet/pub/rmharris/ilab/english.html.

NAN, the Netherlands Antiquarian Booksellers' Network at www.antiqbook.nl.

A Novel Idea, Albuquerque at www.abebooks.com/home/novelidea.

Oasis Books, Albuquerque at www.abebooks.com/home/oasisbooks/.

Powell's Books, Portland at www.powells.com.

Second Story Books, Inc., Washington, D.C., at www.paltech.com.

12

Gifts and Exchanges

STEVEN CARRICO

This chapter will illustrate how gift and exchange programs in libraries have changed in the last few years. It will describe how the widespread use of computers in library gift and exchange areas is altering the methods of handling and processing materials, organizing records, compiling statistics, generating reports, and corresponding with donors and exchange partners. It will also review ways many libraries are using the Internet, list services, and e-mail to improve their gift and exchange operations. Finally, it will summarize the advantages and disadvantages of gift and exchange acquisitions, and identify trends that may influence the future of gifts and exchanges in libraries.

ORGANIZATION AND MANAGEMENT

The first edition of this book included the chapter "Gifts and Exchanges," written by Mae Clark. In her chapter, Clark, at the time the Gift and Exchange Librarian at the University of Florida Libraries, observed "the gift and exchange section of libraries has undergone many changes in policies and procedures in the past decade. Some of the most important changes have been caused by automation, the advent of collection development as a subdiscipline, and changing tax laws."[1] A decade has gone by, and Clark's observation is every bit as true today as it was then. Certain aspects of gifts and exchanges are still very similar to what they were twenty years ago. Most libraries continue to use gifts and exchanges as a means to acquire materials without direct purchase. Most libraries continue to accept gifts and use them to bolster their collections. Libraries with active exchange programs for the most part use locally produced publications as barter. While these fundamental aspects have not changed significantly, the organization and methods used by the libraries to administer gifts and exchanges are evolving rapidly.

Gift and exchange sections may be undergoing changes primarily because of the increased use and technical advances of automation, but another significant factor is the impact of vacillating budgets from one year to the next. In lean years when budgets are tight libraries must often defend their budgets and library operations, whether it is to a county board, library committee, or to the university administration. This justification extends to every department and to every area of library work, including gifts and exchanges. Now more than ever, libraries should improve the efficiency of their gift areas and the collecting scope and cost-effectiveness of their exchange programs.

GIFTS

From the founding of many of the earliest public and academic libraries in America, gifts have always played an important role in collection development. Gifts have become a recognized part of library operations, and it is safe to assume that as long as there are libraries there will be patrons and community members offering to donate gifts. While the libraries are the beneficiaries of gift materials, by default the entire mechanism of accepting gifts places obligations on libraries. Both the donors and their incoming gifts require staff attention, from the letters of acknowledgment to the cataloging of selected items. Despite their trouble, most libraries would be unwilling to stop accepting donations. This is in part because libraries want to foster positive public relations, but, more to the point, librarians and collection managers know gifts are crucial to collection development. Gift books can replace old shelf-worn items, or become a second or third copy of a highly circulated title. Sometimes rare and unique pieces are among the usual gifts, or a gift book comes along that matches a collection manager's out-of-print desiderata. If a gift contains many books in one subject area, it may present an opportunity for the subject specialist to build on that particular collection. At the same time, gift serials are beneficial to a library for filling in gaps and replacing deteriorated issues. It is when incoming gifts are added to the collection that they emerge as important to collection management and the library.

Gifts are a blessing in most cases, although frequently there are many problems associated with handling or disposing of them.

Dealing with unselected gifts and troublesome gift donors can be a nuisance for the library staff who routinely handle donations. For every gift item considered a valuable addition or replacement to a library collection, five or even ten or more donated items will be determined unsuitable for the collection. Large donations are time-consuming for library staff from the moment they arrive. In most libraries gift processing follows a similar path: the donated materials are organized and counted, the online catalog searched for holdings, then the appropriate collection managers review the gift. Lastly, a donor requires an itemized letter of acknowledgment or receipt from the library. All this requires a substantial amount of staff time and processing space—two commodities in short supply in many libraries. Gifts selected for the collection must be processed, cataloged, marked, and routed to the holdings location. Meanwhile, duplicates and unselected materials can pile up quickly and are problematic for many libraries, particularly large public or academic libraries that receive thousands of gift items each year. Staff must devote hours of their week to accomplish gift processing, including the disposal of unwanted items, if they are to stay on top of the never-ending gift flow.

It is because gifts demand so much processing time and storage space that the value of gifts to a library has come under question by many in the library community. For example, Dennis Dickinson challenges the notion that gift books are a boon to libraries. Dickinson writes, "Unsolicited gifts-in-kind, in fact, are not free, but represent a significant, continuing and expensive problem for almost all academic libraries. Such gifts occasionally do prove valuable, of course; but the vast majority is, at best, of only marginal utilization. They comprise materials that libraries do not want, cannot use, and that are encumbered by unacceptable conditions."[2] Dickinson points out that libraries always incur hidden costs with accepting and processing gifts, while disposing of unwanted items is a significant problem. He cites a survey that "over 70 percent of the librarians responding said that the problems of disposal outweighed the benefits received from gifts-in-kind, and that available options for disposal were costly, time-consuming, and labor-intensive."[3]

If Dickinson's viewpoint represents the extreme negative side of gifts in libraries, he certainly makes some valid points to consider. What can libraries do to improve the situation? Many of the obstacles Dickinson describes arise from the very point that libraries first accept a gift. Not long ago it was standard procedure for the majority of libraries to accept almost all gifts offered to them. Often, sight unseen and with few questions, library staff routinely accepted large quantities of assorted books, papers, reports, newsletters, records, magazines, and journals. This unorganized and unscreened method of gift collecting inevitably leads to the acquisition of large amounts of inappropriate, duplicate, and out-of-scope materials. Without a doubt, unscreened gifts will always cause more problems in the end. This all-too-common scenario of libraries dealing with unsolicited and unscreened gifts is only complete when the library holds a book sale and attempts to sell its stockpile of unwanted gifts back to the community. Obviously, if libraries want to avoid these pitfalls, they should employ more restrictive acceptance policies.

According to Benita Strnad, for a library to become more restrictive in gift acceptance, gift personnel have to abide by the library mission statement and collection development policies, and, if necessary, reserve the right to refuse materials.[4] Peggy Johnson also believes sticking to collection development guidelines is extremely important when accepting gifts, and adds "each potential (gift) addition should be evaluated according to relevance to program needs, scope of treatment, ability to fill gaps, quality of scholarship, currency of information, mutability of information, accessibility of information and language."[5] It certainly is evident that more academic libraries are establishing firmer gift acceptance policies. This is evident in survey results for the forthcoming update of the ARL Spec Kit, *The Gifts and Exchange Functions in ARL Libraries,* which shows that 22 of the surveyed libraries are either updating or instituting more restrictive acceptance policies. The responding librarians state that these are necessary changes and advocate the use of stronger collection management guidelines, although many admit they have a tough time saying "thanks but no thanks" to people offering gifts.[6]

A librarian having problems saying no to potential donors is nothing new. In 1988, Donald DeWitt drew up guidelines for gift acceptance and ways to say no to a gift offer. DeWitt concedes that his guidelines do not always work but emphasizes their importance. "Regrettably, none of the remedial measures that are available fully eradicate the lingering effects of a poor decision to accept gift materials that are of marginal utility. All consume staff time and frequently require difficult administrative decisions. While it is, indeed, sometimes difficult to say no to donors, control over accepting gift acquisitions is absolutely necessary and is a management issue that can affect the whole operation of a library."[7] In fact, adhering to sound gift and collection management policies could negate many of the problems associated with inappropriate gifts. And, like the anti-drug slogan, often it is simply a case of being able to "just say no."

THE IRS AND DONATIONS

In 1993, Congress passed the Revenue Reconciliation Bill. The bill contains three new requirements that affect libraries as not-for-profit organizations. Two of the three requirements deal with donee organizations furnishing goods or services in return for a gift donation (usually money), and do not directly influence gifts and exchanges in libraries. The third requirement does affect gifts and exchanges, as it now instructs donors to provide a written acknowledgment from the donee organization for any noncash donation in which they are claiming a deduction of $250 or more. This requirement pertains to any claim of $250 or more but not exceeding $4,999, since claims at or above $5,000 require formal appraisals from qualified, third-party appraisers. The requirement for all claims at or above $250 was lowered from the $500 originally set in the Tax Reform Act of 1984. The 1984 act forced many more donors to provide proof of their property donations, which in turn compelled libraries to rework many of their acceptance and acknowledgment policies. Clark noted five years later that the Tax Reform Act thoroughly affected libraries and their gift procedures in that it "placed new requirements and responsibilities on donors to substantiate charitable contributions."[8] However, the Revenue Reconciliation Bill of 1993 is only a minor adjustment to the 1984 act; as Lapsley and Blazek note "many libraries already send thank you letters to donors using computer systems with development software which efficiently generate such mailing. For them, this new requirement does not impose a difficult burden."[9] In other words, the mechanism and standard policies for gift acknowledgment are already in place in many libraries, so lowering the requirement for proving gift deductions to $250 is affecting libraries only marginally.

As before, the donee organization's receipt, or acknowledgment letter, must include three essential pieces of information:

1. The name of the charitable organization.
2. The date and location of the charitable contribution.
3. A reasonably detailed description of the property.

If the donor's total deduction for all noncash contributions for the year is over $500, the donor must file Form 8283 and attach the donee organization's acknowledgement letter of receipt. The donor is responsible for determining the fair market value of the gift; and, in accordance with IRS regulations, most libraries will not provide the donor with this information. Donors claiming a charitable contribution of property at or above $5,000 must retain a qualified appraiser who is responsible for determining the fair market value of the gift. Libraries must hold the gift for two years before disposing of the donation; if a library decides to dispose of the property before the two years have passed, Form 8282 must be filed, which will affect the donor's original deduction. Not surprisingly, most libraries refrain from taking this step since it means ultimately having to deal with IRS paperwork, not to mention an irate donor.

A Summary of the Advantages and Disadvantages of Gifts

POSITIVE POINTS OF GIFTS

1. Gifts can replace worn and missing items in a library.
2. Out-of-print desiderata often surface from gift donations.
3. Gifts can foster communication and goodwill in a library community.
4. Gifts may become heavily used or important research additions to a collection.
5. Some titles that are not available by purchase are available as gifts.
6. Worthwhile gift materials not selected for a library collection can be put in a book sale, sold to dealers, or given away to underfunded libraries and institutions.

NEGATIVE POINTS

1. Gifts require staff time and are costly to process.
2. Dealing with even well meaning gift donors is frequently an aggravation to staff.
3. Gifts take up precious space in a library.
4. Many collection managers give gifts a low priority, so they may sit on review shelves for a long time.
5. A large percentage of most gifts are not added to a collection, which creates disposal problems.
6. Overall, since most gift books added to a collection are older editions, they will be less frequently used by library patrons.

EXCHANGES

Exchanges and exchange programs in many ways are a legacy of the past. Most exchange programs in U.S. academic and public libraries began in the middle part of this century. There were good reasons for libraries to start up exchange programs. The major motivation for many libraries was the opportunity to acquire materials from other institutions that were available only through exchange. At the same time, U.S. libraries could extend, to a certain extent, a gesture of goodwill and cooperative sharing with poorer libraries and research institutions around the world. In the so-called golden age of libraries, when libraries had plenty of space, big budgets, and large staffs, collection policies were far more liberal than they are today. Libraries could afford to collect almost everything, and if certain items were only available on exchange, then exchange they would. By the end of the 1960s, most of the large academic libraries in this country were either exchanging various publications with other libraries on an irregular basis, or had exchange programs that included formalized agreements with their partner institutions.

Exchanges certainly have a unique place in the history of libraries. Exchange programs exist in varying sizes and structures in most academic libraries. They can be found anywhere in a library, from acquisitions to collection management to special collections. According to survey results for the update of the ARL Spec Kit, 37 percent of the responding academic libraries report that their gifts and exchanges are located in Acquisitions, 27 percent acknowledged that gifts and exchanges work out of Collection Management, and 24 percent of the libraries have some type of decentralized combination of the two.[10] In some libraries an exchange librarian and staff closely administer the exchange program, but many libraries, especially if exchanges are given a low priority, are cutting back or freezing the number of positions in the gift and exchange areas. This is evident in the ARL Spec Kit survey results, in which 38 percent of the responding libraries note that during the past ten years the number of staff handling gifts and exchanges has been reduced. Currently, 77 percent of the libraries deploy two or fewer staff to handle the gift and exchange programs.[11] The point underscored by this survey is clear; exchanges may be a legacy, but few libraries give their programs the resources of money and staff they enjoyed in years past. This turn of events shows a decline in the regard given exchanges and materials received on exchange; it also reveals that many library administrators and department heads believe that exchanges are wasteful and superfluous to the organization. Consequently, if exchanges are to survive and flourish, they must be important for collection development and demonstrate cost-effectiveness.

The simple and obvious fact is that in the library world of today *exchanges are business*. If a library wants to keep its exchange program economically sound, it is necessary to run it as a business. In years past, academic libraries with exchange programs often acquired materials published on their own campuses to use as barter. Campus departments and research centers could support the university library by offering free or discounted publications that were relatively inexpensive for them to print. They could *afford* to be generous. Now, this is not always the case. As the cost of publishing rose dramatically, many departments and research centers could no longer afford to give huge discounts or free publications to the library. It has become necessary for many libraries to absorb these increases and boost their exchange budgets to compensate for these higher publication costs. The fallout of this situation is that an increasing number of professionals in the library world now contend that exchange programs are too costly. To survive this dangerous opinion, exchanges can no longer operate as a quaint, inexpensive method of materials acquisition. Exchanges must become serious business.

Cost-Effectiveness

Exchange programs must achieve cost-effectiveness as they go about their business. If they are unsuccessful and become too costly, programs will face severe downsizing or complete elimination from libraries. One large academic library that has made large cuts to its exchange program is Ohio State University. According to Diedrichs and Davis, who spearheaded the project, the OSU Libraries elected to curtail their exchange program by "reviewing systematically each academic exchange agreement with the goal of eliminating serial exchanges through cancellation or conversion to regular subscription status."[12] This large project involved many departments in the library and on-campus publishers. Diedrichs and Davis believe this action was necessary because "like many academic libraries, OSU's exchange program was operating under the restrictions of a reduced staff and a severely limited source of free materials to exchange. The availability of funds to acquire these titles as paid subscriptions, however, provided the opportunity for a new approach."[13] By the end of the three-year project, the Ohio

State University Libraries canceled hundreds of exchanges that "proved fiscally beneficial for the OSU Libraries."[14] The decision to streamline exchanges not only resulted in considerable savings to their library materials budget, it also spared staff significant time from having to administer the program and process the exchanges. As is the case so often in the business world, time *is* money and money is the bottom line.

However, there is another side to the possible eradication of exchanges and exchange programs. Streamlining does not necessarily have to lead to the decimation or elimination of a program. The University of Florida Libraries conducted a comprehensive study of their exchange program, reviewing, among other things, its cost-effectiveness. They concluded, "virtually dollar for dollar, the University of Florida Library's exchange program was proven to be cost-effective."[15] To determine whether an exchange program needs downsizing or elimination, as was the case at Ohio State, or continues business as usual, as is the case at the University of Florida, libraries will have to carefully examine all facets of operating an exchange program. Exchange personnel must seek input from many areas of the library. Collection managers need to assess exchanges for their value to the various collections, while the administrators of the program must examine its structure and staff procedures. An examination of the exchange agreements for balance and the timeliness of the materials received on exchange must also take place.

After completely reviewing an exchange program and its administration, a library must answer the ultimate question: Is the exchange program worth the time and expense? The answer will depend on the size of the library and its exchange program, on the efficiency of the exchange operations, and on the collecting needs and mission of the library. Moreover, it will ultimately depend on the ability of the library to maintain the cost-effectiveness of its exchange program.

A Summary of the Advantages and Disadvantages of Exchanges

POSITIVE POINTS OF EXCHANGES

1. Exchanges between international libraries are an important intercultural activity and an important gesture of goodwill from one country's institution to another.
2. Exchanges are usually unaffected by subscription price increases.

3. Exchanges do not rely on currency conversion problems or international monetary fluctuations.
4. Certain titles are only available on exchange.
5. Many titles received through exchange programs would be expensive to acquire on subscription.
6. Some of the titles received on exchange are hard-to-find U.S. government and foreign university publications.
7. Exchange publications can be valuable additions to the collections of the library.
8. A small staff can administer an efficiently run automated exchange program.
9. Exchange programs offer a great opportunity to promote the library or research center and its parent university or organization.

NEGATIVE POINTS

1. Exchange programs can be extremely labor-intensive.
2. Exchange partners may send publications irregularly or not at all.
3. It is difficult to establish a reciprocal or cost-effective exchange agreement for journals with unlisted subscription costs.
4. Exchange programs often must purchase the journals and monographs they offer as barter to other institutions.
5. Exchange programs usually have hidden expenses, such as the cost of shipping barter materials.

AUTOMATION

In the business world, networked and personal computers have drastically changed how businesses operate everyday. Like the business world, the personal computer and automation have also dramatically influenced the work of gifts and exchanges. Much of the workflow of gifts and exchanges *is* business: there are order records to create, invoices for barter journal subscriptions to pay, files to manage, and stacks of correspondence to be handled. Fortunately, these functions are far easier and more efficiently performed through the advances of automation and the personal computer. The wide range of software available for business applications has been adapted for gifts and exchange, from spreadsheets to word processors and databases. As libraries stride into the Information Age, they are improving and speeding up their acquisitions functions through automation. Included in this advancement is more effective use of networked and personal computers to streamline many gift and exchange operations.

Personal Computers and Databases

Without a doubt, nothing has influenced the daily operations of gifts and exchanges as the advent of the personal computer. The automation of gifts and exchanges began over twenty years ago, but it has been within the past few years that personal computers have become such vital equipment for libraries. Increasingly, gift and exchange staff are incorporating personal computers into their daily activities; they are inputting their exchange agreements, macro letters, gift statistics, files, and all manner of documentation into the computer. By employing databases, word processors, spreadsheets, and other software, library staff are updating the speed and efficiency of tasks once performed manually. Most library staff would agree that the use of personal computers is changing gift and exchange work for the better.

Automated databases have been a tremendous benefit to gift and exchange programs in the past few years. The gift and exchange Spec Kit survey reveals that well over half of the responding academic libraries are using some type of automated database for their gift and exchange activities; of the 34 academic libraries that report the use of an automated database for gifts and exchange activities, 20 different software applications are being used by the respondents.[16] The diversity of the databases is extraordinary, but a few of the more popular ones are D-BASE, FoxPRO, FileMaker, Access, and PC-File. What they have in common is the ability to quickly store and retrieve great quantities of information. Loading the information from its primary source into the database, then creating the tables, indexes, and reports take a fair amount of time, but once the software is organized and programmed to perform the daily tasks of the exchange program, databases are a tremendous utility. Steve Johnson, librarian at Clemson University, is compiling research on how automation is revolutionizing gifts and exchanges. He makes several excellent points about the effect of personal computers and databases on gift and exchange work. "As would be expected, information can be sorted, something that would be mind-boggling with a manual system. In general, output capabilities include various printed reports (e.g., the number of copies of an item needed to send on exchange, monetary value of all items sent to an individual exchange partner), mailing labels, lists, and a variety of form letters."[17] The speed and ease of doing tasks in an automated environment have been a huge benefit for gift and exchange work, and as new technology is developed and improved, daily tasks in the gift and exchange areas will become that much faster and easier to perform.

Home Pages

It seems that every library—not to mention every library department, section, and unit—has a home page. The proliferation of home pages in libraries is staggering. The lure of the Web has also had its affect on the area of gifts and exchanges. The number of home pages dealing with gifts and exchanges is growing by leaps and bounds. Many of these pages offer information on gift and exchange programs, including the library's policies and procedures. These Web pages are accessible to library patrons and potential donors, whether dialing in from home or walking into the library and using a public terminal. Another group that is finding reason to access gift and exchange home pages is the library staff, who often have just as many questions about gift and exchange policies as do library donors. Gift and exchange home pages are an ideal way of providing information to staff in circulation, reference, and collection management; as a result, they have become valuable resources in and beyond the library.

A variety of gift and exchange home pages exists on the Web. While a few are basic text-only pages, most tend to be rather elaborate presentations deploying frames, graphics, and other Web innovations. The information available on gift and exchange pages is as diverse as their graphical style, although most of the pages focus on the gift policies and procedures of the various libraries. Almost all of the pages include sections detailing the mission of the library, the parameters of collection development, IRS and tax laws affecting gifts, book sales, gift acknowledgments, and bookplates. One advantage of the Web for gift programs is the way it lends itself to communicating this type of practical information. Donors and potential donors can click on the page and follow the steps of giving a gift. If they have a question they can either e-mail or phone the listed staff. The downside of home pages is that not everyone has the capability to tap into the Web, from either the home or office, but even this problem is vanishing as the number of Web users with personal computers increases each day.

Steven Carrico

Distribution Lists and E-Mail

E-mail is certainly changing communication patterns in libraries. No longer do we need to play "phone tag" with one another or spend valuable time running from one department or building to another looking for a colleague. E-mail allows us the luxury of typing out messages, reports, and other correspondence, and with a few quick keystrokes deposit it into one or many e-mail boxes. For staff working with gifts and exchanges, e-mail has become a valuable communication tool. For gift operations, e-mail is a great way to send collection managers information and questions concerning incoming donations. For exchange programs, e-mail is a fast and inexpensive method of contacting exchange partners all over the world. What we lose in human contact with e-mail, we more than make up in terms of speed, efficiency, and postal costs.

A distribution list is an online message service that automatically sends and receives e-mail postings to its subscribers. Using and subscribing to distribution lists are very simple and explain in part their increased popularity. Distribution lists are not the same as bulletin boards; bulletin boards are online sites where users can post messages, but that are not automatically delivered to subscribers. Although similar, the two types of message services are distinct, as anyone who has ever subscribed to a distribution list knows. These lists serve an extensive range of targeted online audiences, including those working with gifts and exchanges. In the gift and exchange community, distribution lists are fast becoming a highly used and appreciated mode of communication. Subscribers to these distribution lists discuss issues and topics affecting gifts and exchanges, pass along information, exchange items, or conduct research and surveys, all in an open forum setting. Distribution lists also offer libraries a new and effective means to dispose of their withdrawn and duplicate pieces, as library staff need only post title lists for their unselected items, which are then automatically sent to other subscribing institutions. If another subscriber finds useful items, which happens routinely, not only does the offering library rid itself of unwanted titles, the accepting library often fills in gaps and bolsters its own collections. The only loser in these cases is the recycling center.

Blackwell/Readmore's Backserv

In September 1994, Readmore began to offer a distribution list they called "Backserv." The project was developed by Amira Aaron and Marilyn Geller, who set it up as a type of "trading post" on the

Net. The idea was to create a distribution list on which libraries could post their lists of duplicate serials. Once posted, the title lists could be used by other libraries searching for items that would fill in gaps in their collections. At that point the interested library would contact the poster and arrange for shipping (standard practice was for the recipient library to pay postage costs). Readmore decided to offer this service entirely free, not only to help libraries build and improve their collections, but also to provide an attractive alternative to merely recycling or throwing out duplicate serials. This distribution list is particularly helpful to library staff who work in gifts and exchanges, since those areas routinely receive large amounts of duplicate and withdrawn materials.

Backserv offers the convenience of using e-mail to post and search lists of back issues and duplicates. The service caught on quickly and soon became a heavily used distribution list by library staff across the country. Marilyn Geller notes that "in its first month alone, Backserv had a subscriber base of about two hundred people and averaged about thirty messages a day."[18] In January 1995 Readmore expanded Backserv services by adding gopher access and a searchable database for messages going back eight weeks. In early 1995 Readmore offered Backserv on the Web and even included links to back issue serial dealers' catalogs. The service was extremely popular with medical and health science libraries, so eventually Readmore started a companion distribution list called "BackMed." Eventually, Readmore also removed their "unofficial limitation" of posting only serial titles on the distribution lists. According to Geller, "users were now able to post messages about materials in all formats and to subscribe to either or both lists depending upon their library's needs."[19] By the summer of 1997 Backserv had over six hundred subscribers, while BackMed had approximately five hundred fifty, and both generate up to one hundred messages a day. The popularity of Backserv and BackMed is still growing, and they have already become indispensable to scores of libraries, museums, and research centers.

BOOK SALES AND DEALERS

Almost every library donation contains books, journals, and other items that will go unselected. Whether individual pieces already exist in a library's holdings and the duplicates are unwanted, or the donated materials do not fit the library's collection parameters, after time unselected items are bound to accumulate and the library must make decisions about their disposition. Fortunately, there are a few viable alternatives for the library. A library can sell the pieces to collectors, back issue serial companies, out-of-print book dealers, or in a general book sale. Another alternative is for a library to donate the items to another institution that might be able to make use of them. Withdrawn titles are harder to sell, since dealers do not like to purchase and resell items marked with a library's ownership stamp. To make matters worse for the gift and exchange staff, many state and municipal institutions are prohibited from selling withdrawn state property, unless it is in an officially approved bidding sale or auction. Other libraries may not face these state restrictions but elect not to sell withdrawn materials in a general book sale, as it often angers book sale attendees to see library books sold for a few dollars. At this point, a library must attempt to donate its deselected materials to another library or collecting institution. Usually only a small percentage is successfully given away; and since there are fewer options for selling withdrawn materials, a large percentage of any library's deselected items is routinely tossed into the recycle bins.

Most libraries still hold public book sales that are usually extremely popular on a college campus or in the community. Friends of the Library groups organize many book sales but often library personnel—particularly gift and exchange staff—manage the events. Library book sales vary in size, presentation, and frequency. Some libraries hold one annual sale, others may hold two a year, and a few hold monthly sales. Libraries fortunate enough to have the space and resources designate certain areas for permanent book sale areas.

Book sales are beneficial to a library for a number of reasons: first, they generate money for the library; second, they are wonderful public relations vehicles, since they attract hundreds of book buyers and tend to receive attention in the local media; and third, book sales are necessary to relieve the surplus of unwanted gifts that take up valuable space in a library. Book sales may be lively events, but they are also the best way for a library to rid itself quickly of large amounts of duplicates and unwanted gifts.

In some libraries, selling the cream of their duplicate and unselected gifts to dealers is becoming commonplace. The reasoning is simple: dealers are willing to pay far more money for this material than most libraries could ever hope to make from their public book sales. Book dealers are always ready to buy out-of-print monographs and will often pay handsomely for rare pieces or sets. Back issue serial companies are often willing to purchase long runs of scholarly journals, particularly in the sciences, for many hundreds of dollars. Now that so many book dealers and bookshops have home pages on the Web, the process of selling monographs is much easier. Steve Johnson notes that

> several electronic sources for out-of-print (op) books have appeared recently on the World Wide Web. There tend to be two types: (1) electronic access to the inventory or catalog of a particular op dealer, or (2) an electronic marketplace where op titles can be advertised by sellers or buyers . . . our interest is "selling" duplicate books, not buying them. Buyers on the Internet have a definite advantage over sellers because they can search the databases and contact the sellers free of charge. On the other hand, a library listing books for sale, in all the cases I am aware of, must pay a combination of fees, including one or more of the following: annual membership, one-time start-up fee, monthly membership, or a per-book surcharge.[20]

Yet, even if the dealers or buyers have the edge over the sellers on the Web, the fact is that book dealers and buyers always have an edge over the seller. That is what sets fair market value. What the Web furnishes is a more expansive and competitive pool of potential buyers, providing the library better opportunity to sell its unselected stock at higher prices.

FUTURE TRENDS

Libraries have undergone enormous changes in the past few decades, and one of the areas most affected in many academic and large special libraries is gifts and exchanges. Although gifts and exchanges have a unique library history, libraries today must focus their attention toward the future of their programs. In an era of advanced automation and the World Wide Web, most gift and exchange sections have had to adapt their procedures to take advantage of the new information technology.

Gift and exchange programs must look at their operations as the business of gifts and exchanges; as with any good business operation, gift and exchange programs cannot remain static and be successful. Gift and exchange areas must anticipate the innovations of the future and adapt to ever-changing technologies, but difficult questions will arise involving exchanges in the future. How will programs offer exchange partners access to their locally produced electronic journals, or overcome such obstacles as copyright clearance, Web security, and production costs when exchanging digitized or online information? The ongoing challenge for gift and exchange programs will be to stay abreast of such technological developments, while carving out their own niche in information acquisitions.

To further tax gift and exchange sections, many large libraries have downsized their staffs in technical service divisions. Even in the best of times, many libraries placed a low priority on gift and exchange functions, routinely assigning gift and exchange tasks to a small number of staff incorporated into other units in technical services or collection management. The reality of the situation is that gifts and exchanges must be consequential for collection development and still maintain cost-effectiveness. As any other department or section in a business, gift and exchange programs must continually justify their existence to the organization. A precipitous but exciting road lies ahead for gifts and exchanges. The networked personal computer, new information technologies, and the untapped, unlimited resources of the Internet offer gifts and exchanges the forums to accomplish this mission.

Notes

1. Mae Clark, "Gifts and Exchanges," in *Understanding the Business of Library Acquisitions*, ed. Karen Schmidt (Chicago: American Library Association, 1990), p. 167.

2. Dennis Dickinson, "Free Books: Are They Worth What They Cost?" *Library Issues* 17, no. 5 (May 1997): 1.

3. Ibid., p. 2.

4. Benita Strnad, "How to Look a Gift Horse in the Mouth, or How to Tell People You Can't Use Their Old Junk in Your Library," *Collection Building* 14, no. 2 (1995): 29-30.

5. Peggy Johnson, "When to Look a Gift Horse in the Mouth," *Technicalities* 13, no. 6 (June 1993): 11.

6. Association of Research Libraries, *The Gifts and Exchange Function in ARL Libraries* (Washington, D.C.: ARL, 1997).

7. Donald DeWitt, "Unsolicited Marginal Gift Collections: Saying No or Coping with the Unwanted," *Library Acquisitions: Practice & Theory* 12 (1988): 361.

8. Clark, "Gifts," p. 175.

9. Andrea Lapsley and Jody Blazek, "Full Disclosure/Full Compliance," *The Bottom Line* 8, no. 3 (1995): 34.

10. *Gifts and Exchange Function.*

11. Ibid.

12. Carol Pitts Diedrichs and Trisha L. Davis, "Serials Exchange: Streamlining and Elimination," *Serials Review* 23, no. 1 (Spring 1997): Table of Contents abstract.

13. Ibid., p. 11.

14. Ibid., p. 21.

15. Steven B. Carrico, "The Cost-Effectiveness of Serial Exchanges at the University of Florida Library," *Serials Review* 23, no. 1 (Spring 1997): 30.

16. *Gifts and Exchange Function.*

17. Steve Johnson, e-mail from the author September 1997, excerpts from an upcoming article, "Automating Gifts and Exchanges: A Review of Current Trends," to be published in the *Acquisitions Librarian.*

18. Marilyn Geller, e-mail August 1997.

19. Ibid.

20. Steve Johnson, e-mail from the author.

Bibliography

GIFTS AND EXCHANGES: OVERVIEWS

Association of Research Libraries. *The Gifts and Exchange Function in ARL Libraries,* Spec Kit #28. Washington, D.C.: ARL, Office of Management Studies, 1976.

——. *The Gifts and Exchange Function in ARL Libraries,* Spec Kit #117. Washington, D.C.: ARL, Office of Management Studies, 1985.

Barker, Joseph W. "Gifts and Exchanges." In *Technical Services Today and Tomorrow.* Ed. Michael Gorman. Englewood, Colo.: Libraries Unlimited, 1990, pp. 23-37.

Kovacic, Mark. "Acquisition by Gift and Exchange." In *Acquisition of Foreign Materials for U.S. Libraries,* 2nd ed. Ed. Theodore Samore. Metuchen, N.J.: Scarecrow Press, 1982, pp. 37-51.

——. "Gifts and Exchanges in U.S. Academic Libraries." *Library Resources & Technical Services* 24, no. 2 (Spring 1980): 155-163.

Lane, Alfred H. "Acquisition by Exchange and Gift." In *Acquisition of Foreign Materials for U.S. Libraries.* Ed. Theodore Samore. Metuchen, N.J.: Scarecrow Press, 1973, pp. 46-53.

——. *Gifts and Exchange Manual.* Westport, Conn.: Greenwood, 1980.

Leonhardt, Thomas W. "The Gifts and Exchange Function in ARL Libraries: Now and Tomorrow." *Library Acquisitions: Practice & Theory* 21, no. 2 (Summer 1997): 141-149.

Magrill, Rose Mary and John Corbin. "Gifts and Exchanges." In *Acquisitions Management and Collection Development in Libraries,* 2nd ed. Chicago: American Library Association, 1989, pp. 216-234.

Reid, Marion. "The Gifts and Exchange Operations: Considerations for Review." *RTSD Newsletter* 10, no. 3 (1985): 21-24.

GIFTS: ACCEPTANCE POLICIES AND COLLECTION BUILDING

Buis, Ed. "Killing Us with Kindness or What to Do with Those Gifts." *Collection Building* 11, no. 2 (1991): 10-12.

Huston, Kathleen Raab. "How to Look a Gift Horse in the Mouth: Saying No to Donations." *Bottom Line* 3, no. 1 (1989): 14-17.

Johnson, Peggy. "Grace under Pressure: Relations with Library Donors." *Technicalities* 13, no. 8 (August 1993): 5-9.

Mielke, Linda. "Cost Finding: Why It Is Important," *Public Libraries* 29 (September/October 1990): 282-288.

Pearson, Richard C. and Alice Crockett. "Gifts to the Library, Boon or Bust: Does Your Library Have a Policy?" *Idaho Librarian* 46 (July 1994): 82.

EXCHANGES, EXCHANGE PROGRAMS, AND COST-EFFECTIVENESS

Barker, Joseph W. "A Case for Exchange: The Experience of the University of California, Berkeley." *Serials Review* 12, no. 1 (Spring 1986): 63-73.

Bluh, Pamela and Virginia C. Haines. "The Exchange of Publications: An Alternative to Acquisitions." *Serials Review* 5, no. 2 (April/June 1979): 103-108.

Deal, Carl. "International Exchanges in Academic Libraries: A Survey." *Library Acquisitions* 13, no. 3 (1989): 199-207.

McKinley, Margaret. "The Exchange Program at UCLA: 1932-1986." *Collection Development and Administration* 12, no. 1 (Spring 1986): 75-80.

Miller, Edward P. "International Library Exchanges." *Library Acquisitions: Practice & Theory* 11, no. 1 (1987): 85-89.

Olsen, Margaret S. "The More Things Change, the More They Stay the Same: East-West Exchanges 1960-1993." *Library Resources & Technical Services* 39, no. 1 (January 1995): 5-21.

Stevens, Jana K., Jade G. Kelley and Richard G. Irons. "Cost-Effectiveness of Soviet Serial Exchanges." *Library Resources & Technical Services* 26, no. 2 (April/June 1982): 151-155.

Stielstra, Julie. "Exchanges in Academic Libraries." In *Festschrift in Honor of Dr. Arnulfo D. Trejo.* Ed. Christopher F. Grippo. Tucson: University of Arizona Graduate Library School, 1984, pp. 229-236.

Yu, Priscilla C. "Cost Analysis: Domestic Serials Exchanges." *Serials Review* 8, no. 3 (Fall 1982): 79-82.

13

Non-print Trading

Y. PETER LIU

As a social institution, the library's most important contribution to society is the information and the services built upon it. Through its collection, services, and staff, the library is an essential information resource in the daily life of the community where it is located and which it serves. Although it is very difficult to predict precisely how society will change in the twenty-first century, the world is clearly moving into the Information Age where more and more information is available in non-print formats. Historically, it was the invention of the printing press that made it possible for the creation of the contemporary library, where human knowledge and records are collected systematically, professionally organized, and carefully preserved for storage, retrieval, and delivery.

Today, library collections exist in a variety of formats: print (books and serials), non-print (audiovisual materials, compact discs), and electronic materials. Millions of items in both print and non-print formats are provided daily by libraries to meet the user community's various informational needs. Among those items, books and periodicals are still and will continue to be the primary library collection formats for a long time, while non-print and electronic materials grow steadily. Since the 1990s, the theoretical and practical foundations of library non-print materials have been discussed in a number of books and scholarly publications authored by librarians and library non-print advocates. This chapter is not intended to repeat what has been written extensively in the previous edition; rather it aims to update and be a useful addition to what has changed or will be changing in non-print acquisitions and trade in the library world. This approach is based on the fact that there have been a number of well-written and comprehensive publications on non-print acquisition, especially in video format, by media librarians and information professionals since the first edition of this chapter. Over the past five years, the library non-print trading process has been undergoing significant changes as paper-based publishing continues to be supplemented, and in some cases supplanted, by the use of emerging computing and electronic technologies. As paperless publishing becomes more prevalent, issues related to selection, evaluation, acquisitions, access, and the economics of this non-traditional collection category challenge all parties involved in the library non-print trading policy and process, including users, filmmakers, producers, distributors, publishers, and librarians.

DEFINITIONAL EFFORTS: NON-PRINT MATERIALS

With the rapid technological advance of information storage, retrieval, and delivery, especially in relation to electronic desktop and multimedia publishing, the traditional boundary between books and non-books seems more indistinct. Creative writings and recordable history, originally published in print, may currently become readily available in multiple formats in books, microfilm, books-on-tape, video recordings, 16 mm films, CD-ROMs, digital videodiscs, or, more recently, full-text or full-content digital databases. The diversity of formats of one of the most popular publications, the Bible, serves as a good example in today's publishing market serving both consumers and libraries. In this sense, today's library users have much greater selection in various formats than ever before. This change also presents inevitable confusion in daily library acquisition practice, especially in non-traditional media collection development process. So what are library non-print materials?

Both the terms "non-print" and "non-book" are broadly used in libraries interchangeably, although each term may convey slightly different meanings and focuses, depending on the author's intent and actual circumstances. At first the term appears self-explanatory, but closer examination reveals that any definition attempting to describe the term more precisely proves to be difficult, because the term refers to complicated concepts and a multiple-layer reality, with overlapping subdivisions of many physical products. Library audiovisual and electronic collections can be generally considered to be windows of electronic and informational technologies on the global consumer market and publishing industry.

Unlike the book or printing world, the complexities and diversities of non-print materials seem to be unlimited. Furthermore, the subdivisions of non-print are constantly changing. Each year, new combinations of existing and evolving media products emerge. To make any classification attempt more difficult, few industrial standards are widely accepted. The evolution of consumer video formats serves to illustrate the point well. However, for the purpose of consistency, the library non-print collection discussions are brief. Library literature studies suggest there are at least three definitive approaches toward library non-print materials: simple formats, physical media, and actual library usage.

Defining library non-print materials by their simple format is the most popular method in libraries. One notable book, which addressed library collection management and user services in 1987, lists twenty-two subcategories in the library non-book collections.[1] This format-based approach listed the following under the name of the non-book family: art reproductions, audiotapes, films, filmstrips, flat pictures, posters, charts, study prints, holographs, machine-readable data files, maps, microforms, models, music scores, original art, overhead transparencies, pamphlets, phonograph records, photographs, programmed materials, realia, simulation materials, slides, videodiscs, and videotapes. It is obvious that some of the non-book formats are already out-of-date or obsolete. Some of them are no longer commercially available and are not actively used in most libraries. Needless to say, more recently emerging formats are not listed. It is interesting to note that some of the obsolete formats have presented challenges in terms of how to provide effective access and preservation. Evans employed a similar approach, but added a few new formats: CD, CD-ROM, and laser disc.

Technically, library non-print media should include three types of physical media: microforms, magnetic media, and optical media. Obvious defects of this definitive category are its exclusion of digital format and lack of details.

Microforms include microfiche, microfilm, and other film-based products. Microforms are difficult to classify by the book vs. non-book standard, because most microfilm and microfiche are special productions or copies of publications in print. Due to the fact that all microforms need equipment to provide access to AV materials, they are often under the acquisition and management of the library media department. Microforms have two advantages: stable medium and space savings. It is said that a microfiche may be usable for a period of 100 years. Many out-of-print items are often available on microform as a substitute.

Magnetic media and its technologies have been the primary "players" of today's library acquisition in non-print formats since the 1960s. Magnetic media has three major subcategories: data, video, and audio. Magnetic disks are the dominant computer data and storage forms, such as a library-server computer's hard disk, floppy disk, or magnetic tapes.

Optical media refers to any storage medium that uses lasers to read and write information. Optical media include laser disc, CD (audio CD or music CD), multimedia CD-ROM, DVD, or other new and emerging optical formats (Zip drives, for example). This category has shown great potential to supplement video, audio, graphics, and other multimedia components in existing library print collections. As desktop computers have become more powerful at affordable prices, more libraries have begun to acquire multimedia CD-ROM titles.

Multimedia data are indeed storage-intensive, especially the video data. For many years there have been few industrial format standards. With the Intel MMX (multimedia extension) chips, the Digital Versatile Disc or Digital Video Disc (DVD) finally becoming compatible with each other, consumer electronics, video, audio, graphics, and personal computers all now can share the same file formats and technical standards. This is designed to replace audio and information CDs, laser discs, and even videotapes. It is reported that each DVD can hold up to 17gb data. It is also backward compatible with CD-ROMs and music CDs. DVD presents a great opportunity to expand the library's multimedia resources, as it is compact and of high quality, although currently expensive. The price will definitely go down in the coming years, with mass production as the demands grow.

Charles Forrest uses the third definition for non-print format actual library usage, in the first edition of this book. According to Pemberton, non-print items are defined as library materials that require some form of equipment for access. This definition obviously abstracts the contrast between print and non-print. The former has minimal need of mechanical or electronic devices. For practical purpose, non-print materials are referred to as audiovisual and multimedia in today's libraries. Together with print and electronic materials, non-print media are an essential category in any library's collections and services.

DEVELOPMENT OF LIBRARY NON-PRINT SELECTION, ACQUISITION, AND COMPOSITION

Today there are few, if any, libraries which collect only print materials. No libraries, small or large, have the same collection and services. "A picture is worth a thousand words" is one of the most often quoted statements by media librarians. As the user community becomes more visually literate, and as their information needs become more complicated, the demand for more library non-print collections and services will certainly grow accordingly. The development of the computing and telecommunication technologies has had great impact on libraries in general and non-print materials in particular. According to Bill Gates, an information revolution has begun:

> The most fundamental difference we will see in future information is that almost all of it will be digital. Whole printed libraries are already beginning to be scanned and stored as electronic data on disks and CD-ROMs. Newspapers and magazines are now often completely composed in electronic form and printed on paper as a convenience for distribution. The electronic information is stored permanently— or for as long as anyone wants it—in computer databases: giant banks of journalistic data accessible through on-line services. Photographs, films and videos are all becoming converted into digital information. Every year, better methods are being devised to quantify information and distill it into quadrillions of atomistic packets of data. Once digital information is stored, anyone with access and a personal computer can instantaneously recall, compare, and refashion it.[2]

Unlike the print world, which has developed and established a funding base, an institutional infrastructure, and a core of professionals to perform daily library acquisition, non-print, as a newcomer, has yet to develop such an organizational structure, financial base, and commercial channels.

As the general public becomes more visually informed and the use of computer hardware and software becomes friendlier, library multimedia materials will also continue to grow. More libraries have started to acquire computer-based multimedia materials to expand and enrich traditional AV collections. The Libraries Council (ULC) survey showed that library paper-format collections were predicted to decrease from 86 percent of the acquisitions budget in 1990 to 69 percent by the year 2000.[3] It is clear that library collections are changing gradually from the traditional paper base to multiple-format resources. Historical statistics in the United States show that utilization of electronic media has grown steadily over the past two years (see table 13-1). As a result, since the early 1980s video as an analog format (as opposed to digital signals) has challenged every conceivable aspect of a library and information center's acquisition and trade: selection, ordering, access, copyright, budget, and delivery. This challenge has stimulated much thinking and discussion over the book vs. non-book issue in libraries.

Among all kinds of non-print materials, video (or "videorecordings") is the indisputable primary non-print format. In other words,

Table 13-1 Utilization of Television and VCRs in the US: 1970-1994

Item	Unit	1970	1980	1985	1988	1989	1990	1991	1992	1993	1994
Television	Millions	69	76	85	89	90	92	93	92	93	94
TVs in households	Percent	97.1	97.9	98.1	98.1	98.2	98.2	98.2	98.3	98.3	98.3
Average no. of sets per home	Number	1.4	1.7	1.8	1.9	2.1	2.1	2.1	2.2	2.2	2.3
VCRs	Millions	NA	1	18	51	58	63	67	69	72	74
VCRs in TV households	Percent	NA	1.1	2.8	58	64.6	68.6	71.9	75	77.1	79

NA: not available

Source: Statistical Abstract of the U.S. 1997

video recordings are the most popular non-print media in today's library AV collections. Since the first U-matic tape, known also as the ¾ inch tape, was introduced by Sony Corporation in 1971, followed by Betamax recorders, which became commercially available in 1975, great changes have taken place in library video recording collections and services. There has been a steady growth of videotape cassettes in VHS videocassette successfully marketed by Victor Company of Japan (JVC). The 1980s were the golden age for video collection growth. This growth resulted from the visual information demand in American families, according to the statistical report of the utilization of television and VCRs in the United States from 1970 to 1994.

A similar growth pattern was also observed globally. It was estimated that more than one-third of all world homes had television sets and VCRs in 1992.[4] The top 10 countries with most VCRs in 1993 are listed in table 13-2.

As the popularity of AV and consumer electronics has grown, non-print media usage has also developed steadily (table 13-3).

In contrast to the continuous non-print use expansion, AV material prices have decreased over the years (table 13-4). This trend certainly empowers libraries to build even stronger AV collections.

According to the most recent statistics reported by Bowker in 1997, non-print media in budget distribution among academic libraries are ranked as follows: microfilms (45 percent); computer materials (30 percent); and video recordings (15 percent) (see table 13-5 and figure 13-1).

Table 13-2 Top 10 Countries with Most VCRs

Country	Percentage of homes	No. Video households
1. US	81.4	78,125,000
2. Japan	78.0	32,224,000
3. Germany	58.5	21,221,000
4. Brazil	42.8	20,458,000
5. UK	77.0	16,771,000
6. France	65.3	14,142,000
7. Italy	44.0	9,879,000
8. Canada	70.3	7,810,000
9. Spain	55.1	6,543,000
10. Russia	13.5	6,515,000

Table 13-3 Media Usage in the US: 1989-1999

Hours Per Person	1989	1990	1991	1992	1993	1994	1995	1996	1997	1998	1999
Recorded Music	220	235	219	233	248	294	317	323	343	365	387
Home Video	39	42	43	46	49	52	53	54	56	57	58
Consumer Online/ Internet Services	Z	1	1	2	2	3	5	8	11	13	14

Z stands for less than an hour

Source: Statistical Abstract of the U.S. 1996. 1997-1999 are projected figures

Table 13-4 Academic Library Video Price Index
FY 1992-1995

1992 = 100 Fiscal Year	Video VHS Cassette	
	Price[1]	Index[2]
1992	$199.67	100.0
1993	112.92	56.6
1994	93.22	46.7
1995	84.19	42.2

1 Prices are for previous calendar year, e.g., current year prices are reported by FY 1994.

2 Cost per video

Source: The Bowker Annual of Library and Book Trade Information, 7th ed. New York: R. R. Bowker, 1997.

Table 13-5 Non-print Media in Budget
Distribution of Academic Libraries: 1992

Items	% Distribution
Microforms	45
Audio recordings	5
Video (TV) VHS recordings	15
Graphic image item use	5
Computer materials	30
Total	100

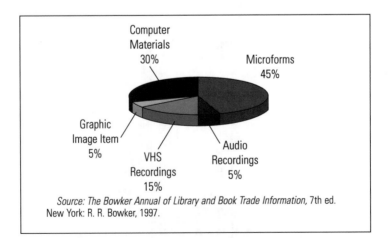

Source: The Bowker Annual of Library and Book Trade Information, 7th ed. New York: R. R. Bowker, 1997.

Figure 13-1 Non-print Media in Budget Distribution
of Academic Libraries: 1992

Y. Peter Liu

THE PRINT VS. NON-PRINT ISSUES
IN LIBRARIES AND DISCUSSIONS

Until now, library non-print collections and resources have primarily served a supplemental role. The print bias is integral to the daily practice of the library profession. It is fair to say that both print and non-print collections have their own strengths and weaknesses. In library daily services, they actually implement and support each other, not necessarily replace each other. Given the competitive nature of non-book vs. book for limited library resources, it is really up to the users to choose which format serves and best meets their informational needs. To this end, print and non-print information sources are both complementary and competitive. What, then, are the general differences between book format and non-book format? Understanding those differences should help acquisition and media librarians to make timely right and well-rounded decisions in the library's daily operation.

1. Access to media content demands use-enhanced tools such as players, viewers, and computers. So far, books are still the most simple and universal textual medium. The user can access printed contents so long as he or she is able to read. Audiovisual materials are different; they need additional hardware or equipment to access the information coded in analog, digital, and other formats. These contents are to a certain degree technology-based; enhanced tools add costly expense to library operations, whether mechanical, electronic, or personnel.

2. The bibliographic control mechanism is quite different. The majority of books carry Library of Congress cataloging information, which makes the technical process of internal handling of print materials much simpler and more economical. Cataloging AV is more time-consuming. Print-medium bibliographical information may or may not come with video or audiotape covers or labels. Even non-print items present unique access points or fields such as director, cast, format in VHS, Beta, laser disc, running times, rating, color, or black-and-white. These unique access fields must be preserved in order to build an effective textual indexing database.

3. Audiovisual materials are more expensive than books, in general. Although the cost of AV materials has declined over the years, most documentary and independently distributed videos are still expensive because of their limited distribution channels and potential audience (see table 13-4). Necessary equipment purchase and maintenance add additional stress to already stretched library operating budgets, which in turn have an impact on all the library acquisition resources.

4. There are special copyright constraints attached to audiovisual materials because audio- and videocassettes, and more recently computer software such as CD-ROMs, are much more easily duplicated. This aspect adds a heavy burden to the business of acquisition of library audiovisual materials. In most cases, librarians and publishers are friends, but copyright conflicts and interpretation tend to cause concerns and disputes. These constraints include public performance rights, fair use in educational settings, and off-air taping, to name a few.

5. Technically, AV materials are not a stable recording medium in comparison to printed materials. In addition, AV formats are constantly changing. For example, currently the consumer electronic markets are gearing toward digital high definition television for the next few years. Most digital TVs being introduced are wide-screen. As a result, many video manufacturers are now presenting a large portion of their films in the wide-screen version. The recently emerged DVD is not only a large storage device per se (it is reported that a DVD disk can hold 17 MB of data), it also denotes a trend toward a new and emerging video market. More and more libraries are likely to collect media in the newer and easier-to-use optical formats such as DVD, while other older formats, such as laser disc, may become obsolete in the foreseeable future. The next decade will see more digital and multimedia, especially visual resources, in light of the recent advent of the Internet, Internet II, and underlying computing and communication technologies and infrastructure improvement. The traditional model of library non-print collections in single, still, and analog formats (audio, slide, filmstrip, etc.) will be replaced with multimedia, dynamic, and digital libraries.

This brief book vs. non-book comparison can go on and on. The bottom line is that as library patrons become more sophisticated in their information needs, libraries should expand their collections beyond paper-based books and serials. Any comprehensive library collection and services should have well-balanced print and non-print materials based on the user-centered philosophy.

NON-PRINT SELECTION AND ACQUISITION AIDS AND TOOLS

It is generally agreed among acquisition media librarians that acquisition and use of library non-print materials is more time- and money-consuming than that of print materials. This proposition is supported by the lack of reference aids and tools specialized for non-print trading. In comparison to the process with books, acquiring AV materials is far from institutionalized and well organized. Commercial AV publishers or distributors are still small in number compared to print-based publishers. This difficulty is exemplified by the lack of "Books in Print" for AV materials. Consequently, it takes more time, training, and staff resources to locate and verify bibliographical information and commercial products.

Special considerations for library AV acquisitions also are reflected in the fact that those additional hardware and software facilities must be acquired in order to efficiently access AV collections. Facilities range from an obsolete CED (capacitance electronic disc system by RCA, released in the early 1980s) to the newly emerging DVD.

The dynamic nature of technologies in general and consumer home electronics, including the personal computer market in particular, is always keeping librarians, especially library administrator and decision makers, in constant check in terms of acquisition efficiency, format choice, equipment updating, user support, and staff training. For this purpose, comprehensive non-print selection and acquisition tools are essential. The following is a brief discussion of basic reference and selection aid resources, which can be used as a starting point in non-print trading.

Books

There have been many books published on non-print acquisition and collection development. They generally fall into two broad categories. Group one is a general text or hardcover book on library acquisition and collection development on philosophies, theories, policies, assessment, fiscal management, legal issues, and resource sharing. AV, multimedia, and electronic materials are usually addressed in the context of entire library collections and resources. Most of the authors are library science educators, library administrators, or collection development librarians.

The general principles of printed acquisitions can readily be applied to non-print collections. As librarians continue to stabilize and expand their non-print collections, a core list of books is clearly helpful to provide needed information in the library. This category can be used as a basic collection guide, which is a practical guideline, but most books lack details and in-depth discussion in the AV area.

The second category is a specialized monograph or collective edition on media or non-print collection developments. Most authors publishing in this medium have had personal experience in library media service or have acted professionally as advocates for the format. This group of publications often provides a theoretical framework and foundation.

Given the changing environment of non-print publications, the following annotated list includes only texts published in the 1990s. This brief bibliography by no means is a complete collection covering the non-print field, but rather a starting point toward a comprehensive research guide and resources. The attached annotations are intended to serve as no more than signposts to assist those finding their way toward intellectually rich texts in the field of media librarianship.

Directories, Indexes, and Ready Reference Tools

For an average library user, a few ready reference aids are probably adequate. For librarians, there are "core" bibliography utilities in both print and electronic formats, which serve as essential resources for verification, supply, and subject access in the selection process of decision making. Because video is the primary AV format used in most libraries, the following update lists more video resource and reference tools than other non-print materials. As costs of videotapes and CDs and other computer-based products have dropped considerably, more digital formats or electronic materials will be added to library resources. It is necessary to identify non-print as a special media category. Some of its unique fields are difficult to search. For example, today few libraries' automated systems, or online catalogs offer a comprehensive and effective search of media access points (actors, actresses, producers, and so forth). In addition, subject-based indexing and abstracting in print materials have always been challenging in non-print formats, especially in fictional movies, feature films, and graphic images. Recently, indexed movie guides and their CD-ROM versions became handy library acquisition tools, especially for public library and rental video stores, although users tend to need easy and quick guides by awards, MPAA ratings, and short summaries.

PERIODICALS AND REVIEWS

No matter how library collection formats change over time, the librarian's role to select, evaluate, and acquire information for general public use remains unchanged. To aid the selection process, many libraries have built a good collection of serials which provide timely and valuable information. Traditionally most of those periodicals carry reviews, abstracts, new releases, news, and evaluative items in print. Over the past decade the electronic version of some serials has become available online in full text. As a result, some recent reviews can be easily searched from a desktop computer. A good example is Video Librarian, which offers a cumulative index of every title reviewed between 1986 and 1996 on its Web site, and maintains reviews of current videos.[5] It is necessary to point out that only a few full-text online reviews are available. Many users still have to depend on the print periodicals to retrieve the full content of reviews. Movie video reviews can be divided into two groups: professional library reviews and general public reviews.[6]

Librarians and information professionals have contributed considerably to library non-print collection development. Their readers are likely to be public, school, and academic librarians. Personal reviews or previews of non-print titles are the option for many. Many distributors provide preview copies at no extra charge to qualified institutions and libraries. A request from a business or professional organization may be charged a moderate preview fee. In most cases return postage or shipping and insurance fees have to be considered.

The list included here is comprised of the most popular and broad-based periodicals and reviews currently commercially available. Many annotations are based on personal experience and colleagues' recommendations. When acquiring individual periodicals the inflation factor in the publishing business should be taken into consideration. The rate is around 10 percent or more annually on an individual title. If cost is the main concern, many new paper titles serve well as current media-collection review alternatives.

Rental Resources

Non-print rental is an option for many small libraries or for an individual user's special informational needs, such as research and scholarly purposes. Rental service is a unique component of library non-print acquisition and services. It is necessary to point out that many large libraries tend to purchase a media item rather than rent it, although many commercial distributors as well as educational institutions provide non-print rental services, especially in VHS videotape and 16mm formats. Due to the relatively high cost, some libraries offer commercial or fee-based rental services to their local users. Libraries and information centers that do not have a strong media collection may depend heavily on commercial or self-supporting rental services to meet the local user's needs in media formats.

However, rental service is a special function of the interlibrary-loan service for many libraries that cannot afford to build comprehensive non-print collections. Many rental service providers offer an option to purchase a rental item after use. In this way, rental services are also a process of review for purchase evaluation by end-users. In most cases, the purchase decision is made after the scheduled payday. The most popular formats that are commercially available are VHS video, 16mm films, laser disc, CD-ROMs and, most recently, DVD. Due to limitations of marketing and financial resources, many documentary and educational videos may not be as widely and easily available as the big-ticket Hollywood feature films on screen. For many out-of-print titles, the distribution rights licensed to individual distributors are expired, resulting in out-of-print status.

Needless to say, those out-of-print titles often make library acquisition even more difficult. For example, some out-of-print treasures listed on the National Film Registry are virtually impossible to locate through a current distributor. The supply-demand rule determines that film and video rental services are relatively expensive. Most feature films are almost always easily available from local commercial video stores, from national chains to a regional grocery supermarket, at an affordable price. Some research libraries offer educational and entertainment rental items in non-print formats. The best sources for renting educational videos often are the larger universities with strong humanity and social science programs, such as Iowa State University, Indiana University, University of Missouri, Penn State University, University of Minnesota, or Kent State University. However, most university provider rentals are, in fact, outside of the traditional academic library collections (with the exception of the recent re-organization at Penn State University, which has the largest film/video collection among ARL research libraries).

Given the history of 16mm films and the educational nature of most media collections, those rental services may be operated not by individual libraries but rather by other academic departments or colleges. Therefore, some of the rental collections show a lack of professional cataloging, with limited use of access mechanisms like library online catalogs. However, many of them provide extensive subject indexes and print catalogs. Recently, some services have made their catalogs accessible through the Internet and its World Wide Web.

It is not the intention of this chapter to argue whether the library should have played a stronger role in collecting 16mm films. Historically, as a primary information provider, libraries have been weak in collecting educational films or videos in comparison to other education support groups within the higher education domain. However, these collections have been an important supplemental resource, sometimes competitive, among large research libraries. This selective list of university media rental services reflects the growing need for expanding non-print collections library-wide. Some large, online rental databases can also be used as handy collection verification tools and bibliographic utilities.

Several reasons account for the existence of movie/video rental options in libraries. First, the cost per item for video is relatively high, compared with books. This characteristic is especially true for most documentary and educational video/film (see table 13-4). For example, the average price of a VHS cassette was $199.67 in 1992. Secondly, video usually covers a narrow subject or topic. The scope of its intellectual content is limited by viewing time of less than one hour. Thirdly, unlike books, video/film is usually distributed by a single distributor or producer. As a result, the sales volume for individual titles is considerably less than books. Media producers use few "jobbers" but instead market their products to major film/video rental collections.

Electronic Publications

With the emergence of the Internet and its World Wide Web, much non-print acquisition can be accomplished online. This development also means that users can now watch multimedia video on their own personal computers across the Internet. Over the past several years, electronic publication has changed library non-print trade practice considerably. This presents many opportunities and challenges for media collection development. With the electronic publishing industries growing at an unprecedented rate, every new non-print and electronic format or delivery mechanism needs to be evaluated by both librarians and information consumers. These new computer-based materials also come with noteworthy price tags. For end-users, there is, however, a training issue involved. With all these technical advances, electronic publication is and will continue to be a hotly debated issue. In using information technology for library acquisitions, such as online bibliographical tools, experienced technicians need to be hired, and computer systems need to be constantly upgraded. On a more positive side, electronic publication has enhanced and added a new dimension to today's non-print trading.

There are several desirable features an online electronic publication can offer that are not readily available from the printing world. An electronic database clearly has two major advantages over traditional publications media. The electronic environment allows both free text and Boolean searching. It takes only a few keystrokes to locate a movie review or an independent filmmaker from an online full-text database (such as OCLC FirstSearch, and Dialog AV Online). This task previously took more time and steps using traditional print sources. Another add-on value for electronic publication is its currency. Most print versions of library non-print catalogs and reviews, such as *Media Review Digest,* are not available until a year later. OCLC is considered to be the most popular electronic data source online in use by media librarians. It probably is the most widely used non-print reference source (www.oclc.org). As the access to electronic databases becomes more affordable and user friendly, more libraries will use electronic resources for selection, verification, and acquisition. The major concern for OCLC is the fact that its WorldCat is still a bibliographical control tool. This means that its records represent cataloging information which may not include timely data such as price or availability.

The growth of the Internet has resulted in many positive changes in library non-print trade. One of the popular forums for discussing and sharing AV acquisition information and experience is a distribution list service, an electronic discussion group on a specific topic and subject of interest. Users subscribe to an individual distribution list service through a standard procedure and comment format. Usually a subscriber posts a note or joins an ongoing discussion via electronic mail. Most postings should be considered public information with no editorial change or filtering. Anyone with Internet access or an e-mail account may ask a question, make a comment, call for help, or share information, but any postings should be directed to the right group on the right subject.

Although an electronic list service is designed to be a self-managed system, there are a few points of "netiquette":

1. Technical support questions or unsubscribed postings should be directed to the appropriate address (list owner), not the whole body of subscribers.
2. Make sure to be concise in the posting and to be polite. Subject line should be a summary or keyword in nature.

3. Only include previous postings in a response when needed to reduce net traffic or junk e-mail.
4. One has to be a subscriber to post to the members of a list.
5. Commercial use of the list is prohibited to preserve the ethical use of the Internet public domain.

Useful Non-Print Acquisition List Services

As electronic commerce becomes more of a reality, has the use of the list services for library acquisition practices also become more common? List service is an Internet mail program, available on many UNIX systems. It distributes copies of e-mail postings or messages to the subscribers of a mailing list. There are three wide audience list services currently on the Internet for non-print acquisition.

1. Videolib@library.berkeley.edu

   Listowner: Gary Handman, U.C. Berkeley Library

   This is a middle-value (50 messages posted weekdays) discussion group. The primary focus is on video collection, access, and use. Examples of postings are searching for a hard-to-find video/16mm film, library collection development policies and issues, and copyright questions. Most participants are librarians, non-print distributors, publishers, instructional specialists and teachers, or independent filmmakers.

2. VIDEONEWS@library.berkeley.edu

   Listowner: Gary Handman, U.C. Berkeley Library

   VIDEONEWS is an electronic forum for information about new video services, products, resources, and programs of interest to video librarians and archivists, educators, and others involved in the selection, acquisition, programming, and preservation of video materials.

   Most list services are open to all interested individuals. List submissions are unmediated. Both list services above are sponsored by the American Library Association Video Round Table.

3. MEDIA-L@BINGVMB. CC.BINGHAMTON.EDU

   Listowner: Jeffrey B. Banohue, Binghamton University, New York.

   Its full name is Media in Education. This electronic list server is another active media related discussion forum online. It covers subjects that interest educational media specialists, instructional support professionals, and librarians from school to academic libraries, especially in regard to instructional hardware and software, copyright issues, multimedia development, to name a few.

In short, electronic list services are a new non-print trade information resource on the Internet. They should be useful acquisition discussion forums, particularly to share some timely and hard-to-find non-print titles. Judged by any standards, the Net-based wisdom and information are prompt, current, and helpful, so long as the Internet user group follows the fundamental rules.

Media Resource Distributors

In general, the principles and process of acquiring non-print material are also applicable to the practice of library book and serial acquisitions. Due to their special formats and diversities, non-print trade with distributors tends to be a more time-consuming and sometimes confusing task.

For all practical purposes, there are three primary channels to order non-print materials: wholesalers, retailers, and single source distributors/producers.[7] A list of distributors and publishers is given here for reference purposes. This aid has two new add-on features. One is the inclusion of contact information on the Internet. The Internet fields collected in the annotation are: individual distributor or sales department e-mail address, and the Web site URLs. Other useful new data were generated by vendors' participation at annual American Library Association activities during the period of 1992-1997.

Wholesalers, such as Baker & Taylor, supply most widely distributed print and non-print materials. They offer a full range of AV and other multimedia materials at considerably lower or discount prices. Most wholesalers or "jobbers" also offer convenient electronic ordering, which cuts the order turnaround time substantially. This service is especially desirable for patrons (notably researchers) with short deadlines. Some of the wholesalers are already familiar to many electronic consumers. Many national retailer chains sell mainstream videos, music CDs, computer software, games, and multimedia CD-ROMs.

One difference between book and non-book acquisition is that many non-print titles are exclusively handled by single source distributors. It is not uncommon for many producers who are small business owners to market their own films/videos. As a result of their limited sales volume and low profit margin, most of the items carried by them are expensive. On the other hand, some producers who do not distribute their own products frequently contract individual film/video distribution rights exclusively to a single-source media distributor. This practice also results in high-price items and copyright constraints. Most of these distributors' collections are educational or non-theatrical in subject. Therefore, annual American Library Association conventions with their provision for exhibits provide a natural meeting place for librarians and representatives from the media publishing industry to communicate. Regular ALA conventions and film/video trade shows also serve as a special opportunity for independent film producers and videographers, since public, school, and academic libraries are the only places collecting most documentary and educational items produced for public view. Therefore, a distributor list by ALA activities is included here, compiled from 1992 to 1997 program reports. Major non-print business organizations cannot afford to miss this marketing opportunity.

In short, it is not a simple task to establish serious, comprehensive, well-balanced, and informative media resources in today's libraries. Electronic publication certainly helps librarians develop diverse non-print collections and facilitates the acquisition process. It also provides timely and searchable information, which may not be easily available in print collections, to use as selecting and acquisition tools.

SOURCES FOR NON-PRINT MATERIAL VERIFICATION OR SUPPLY

Books

Bruwelheide, Janis H. *The Copyright Primer for Librarians and Educators.* 2nd ed. Chicago, Washington, D.C.: American Library Association, National Education Association, 1995.

> Extensively updated from its first edition, the *Primer* can serve as a handy working guide to frequently asked questions about copyright (such as fair use, photocopy, off-air taping). It provides useful reference publications, landmark court decisions, and useful phone numbers.

Lenz, M. and M. Meacham. *Young Adult Literature and Non-print Materials: Resources for Selection.* Metuchen, N.J.: Scarecrow, 1994.

> This annotated bibliography includes more than six hundred books, periodicals, and non-book resources. It has a useful chapter, "Tools for Selection of Audiovisual Materials," covering audio, AV directories, computer software (very good), equipment, film, and video. It is a valuable selection tool for schools' and public libraries' young adult collections.

Mason-Robinson, Sally. *Developing and Managing Video Collections.* New York: Neal-Schuman, 1996.

> An excellent video collection development guide which can also be used as a textbook for media librarianship training. It provides many useful annotated lists related to building video collections in libraries, especially with respect to public and school library non-print selection and acquisition.

Pitman, Randy. *The Video Librarian's Guide to Collection Development and Management.* New York, Toronto: G. K. Hall, Maxwell Macmillan Canada, Maxwell Macmillan International, 1992.

> A well-written philosophical and practical guide for video collection development. Most articles were drawn from the author's previous publications.

Pitman, Randy and Elliot Swanson. *Video Movies: A Core Collection for Libraries.* Santa Barbara, Calif.: ABC-CLIO, 1990.

> A very useful collection development aid with a well-selected annotated list of five hundred movies on video that could constitute a "core" video/film library.

Scholtz, James C. *Video Acquisitions and Cataloging: A Handbook.* Westport, Conn.: Greenwood, 1995.

> This book is an excellent video collection development and organizational source. It was highly recommended by the American Library Association Video Round Table in 1996. This book also has a detailed industry chronology as well as information about copyright and acquisition in relation to video. This is a great value.

———. *Video Policies and Procedures for Libraries.* Santa Barbara, Calif.: ABC-CLIO, 1991.

A very useful collection on non-print administration and programs especially for public and school librarians.

Video Collection Development in Multi-type Libraries: A Handbook. Ed. Gary P. Handman. Westport, Conn.: Greenwood, 1994.

A useful and informative collection of essays on topics such as history, resources, issues, and policies of audiovisual collections in public, academic, and special libraries. Contributors are well-known library media professionals and scholars including Kristine Brancolini, Randy Pitman, and James Scholtz.

Video Collections and Multimedia in ARL Libraries: Changing Technologies. Ed. Kristine Brancolini. Washington, D.C.: Association of Research Libraries, Office of Management Services, 1997.

A useful overview of large academic libraries' audiovisual and multimedia collections and services in the United States and Canada. It includes 1993 and 1995 Association of Research Libraries (ARL) surveys to its members.

Directories

Audio Video Market Place. New York: R. R. Bowker, 1984- . Annual.

An informative and current directory listing audiovisual manufacturers and distributors. It can be useful for finding current information on the AV publishing industry and its contacts, events, organizations, and reference sources on film and television producers, periodicals, hardware, and software reviews.

Bowker's Complete Video Directory. New Providence, N.J.: R. R. Bowker, 1997. Irregular.

This is the "books in print" for videos, as well as a competitor to the *Video Source Book* (see below). It is a very useful catalog for home videos or feature films. The CD-ROM version, *Variety's Video Directory Plus* (updated quarterly), provides comprehensive search criteria such as title (encompasses subtitle, translated title, and series title); keyword within title; performer/director; other contributors (e.g., screenwriters); awards; keyword; manufacturer/distributor; producer; price; subject/genre; year produced; year released on video; language; MPAA rating; ISBN. It also supports truncation and Boolean logic methods and can be searched by items according to distributors, which is a very handy, cost-effective tool.

Video Source Book. Detroit, Mich.: Gale Research, 1997.
http://www.gale.com

> Known within the industry as the "bible," the most current
> version is the 19th edition, 1997/98. Two updating supple-
> ments are issued annually. A similar CD-ROM product by
> Gale's subdivision Visible Ink Press was unfortunately discon-
> tinued in 1996. The title was *VideoHound Multi-media.*

Ready References

Bergan, Ronald and Robyn Karney. *The Holt Foreign Film Guide.*
New York: Henry Holt, 1989.

Halliwell, Leslie. *Halliwell's Film and Video Guide.* 11th ed. New
York: Scribner, 1995.

Kael, Pauline, *5001 Nights at the Movies.* New York: Henry Holt,
1993.

Leonard Maltin's Movie and Video Guide. New York: Plume/
Penguin. Annual.

Maltin, Leonard, *Leonard Maltin's TV Movies and Video Guide.*
New York: New American Library, 1997.

Martin, Mick. *Video Movie Guide.* New York: Ballantine Books.
Annual.

Spencer, James R. *The Complete Guide to Special Interest Videos.*
1995-1996 ed. Scottsdale, Ariz.: James-Robert Pub., 1995.

*Texas Production Manual : A Source Book for the Motion Picture,
Television, and Video Industries.* Vol. 17 (1997 ed.). Austin, Tex.:
Texas Film Commission, Film, Music & Multimedia Division,
Office of the Governor, 1997.

Wiener, Tom. *The Book of Video Lists.* 5th ed. Kansas City, Mo.:
Andrews & McMeel, 1993.

Indexes

Audiocassette and CD Finder. Albuquerque: National Information
Center for Educational Media Services, 1986- . Irregular.

> A subject index for 29,000 educational audiotapes. It is also
> available on Dialog's AV Online or CD-ROM (File Number 46).
> Formerly known as *Audiocassette Finder: A Subject Guide to*

Literature Recorded on Audiocassettes (until 1992) and NICEM *Index to Educational Audio Tapes* (until 1986).

Index to AV Producers and Distributors. 10th ed. Medford, N.J.: National Information Center for Educational Media (for Plexus Publishing), 1997. Irregular.

Useful directory of non-print media equipment and materials companies and distributors.

Media Review Digest. Ann Arbor, Mich.: Pierian Press, 1974- . Annual.

This abstracting/indexing publication provides access to reviews of films, videos, filmstrips, audio, CD-ROM, and other non-print media. Using the general cataloging guidelines of Library of Congress subject headings, it has a video index, general subject index, alphabetical subject index, reviewer index, geographical index, index of film awards and prizes, as well as mediagraphies on educational and entertainment media. It contains 42,000 citations and cross-referenced entries indexed over 150 periodicals and services in 1997. There is also a producer and distributor directory. Formerly known as *Multi Media Reviews Index.*

New York Times Index. New York: New York Times, 1913- . Semimonthly.

First published in 1851, this abstracting/indexing publication provides detailed subject entries to all articles, news reports, and reviews in motion picture and other media materials. Timely full-text reviews are available through OCLC and other online resources. It is essential for any academic, public, and special libraries ready- and cross-reference collections.

Periodicals and Reviews

AudioVideo Review Digest: A Guide to Reviews of Audio and Video Materials Appearing in General and Specialized Periodicals. Detroit, Mich.: Gale Research, 1989- . Quarterly.

This is like a *Book Review Digest* for audio and video materials. It is especially useful for school and public libraries.

Billboard. New York: BPI Communications, 1894- . Weekly. http://www.billboard-online.com

This trade publication is a valuable resource tool for news and information in the music and home entertainment industries.

Booklist. Chicago: American Library Association. Bimonthly except July and August. http://www.ala.org/booklist/

> This is a librarian's leading choice for reviews of the latest audiovisual and other non-print or electronic media materials. More than 1,000 items are signed by reviewers and rated annually.

Choice. Middletown, Conn.: Association of College and Research Libraries, 1963- . Monthly. Also available on CD-ROM.

> This academic/scholarly publication each month includes one or more bibliographic essays, feature pieces, and reviews of 600 new academic titles.

Classic Images. Muscatine, Ia.: Muscatine Journal (Subsidiary of Lee Enterprises), 1962- . Monthly.

> This consumer newspaper contains articles on films (centering on the classics), personalities, and film history. It provides a good starting place for information. Former titles: *Classic Film-Video Images* until 1979, *Classic Film Collector* until 1978.

Fanfare. Tenafly, N.J.: Fanfare, 1977- . Bimonthly.

> This is the consumer publication for the "serious record collector" and for those serious librarians who need information for those not-so-serious patrons who need serious information regarding records and collecting.

Film Review Annual. Englewood, N.J.: Jerome S. Ozer, 1981- . Annual.

> This academic/scholarly publication compiles film reviews from selected newspapers, magazines, and scholarly journals.

Library Journal. New York: Cahners, 1876- . Bimonthly except in January, July, August, and December.

> This is one of those academic/scholarly publications that has successfully found a niche in the trade publications market. This publication covers news and events, book reviews, articles identifying trends, as well as magazine and audiovisual information.

Magill's Cinema Annual. Detroit, Mich.: Gale Research, 1982- . Annual.

> This consumer publication is an update to *Magill's Survey of Cinema,* containing reviews of films released during the pre-

vious calendar year, as well as interviews, major award winners, and obituaries.

Publishers Weekly. New York: Cahners. 1872- . Weekly.

This trade publication has found a place in the hearts of many public and academic libraries as a wonderful resource tool. It contains news and trends of interest to publishers, booksellers, and librarians. This publication also includes author interviews, advance book reviews, and a host of other information.

Rolling Stone. New York: Straight Arrow, 1967- . Biweekly. E-mail: rolling-stone@echonyc.com

This consumer publication covers many aspects of the pop and rock music industry and includes articles, interviews, and reviews. Features include topics on politics, movies, and fashion. This is an excellent reference to measure the current "pulse" of the "pop scene."

School Library Journal. New York: Cahners, 1954- . Monthly.

This trade publication is very useful for librarians serving children and young adults in either the public or school library.

Science Books and Films. Washington, D.C.: American Association for the Advancement of Science, 1965- . 9 issues/year. http://ehr. aaas.org/ehr

This bibliographic newsletter reviews print, film, and software materials in all sciences for all age levels. It is a good publication for librarians and educators.

Sightlines. New York: Institute for Theatre Technology, 1965- . Monthly.

This newsletter was known as *USITT Newsletter* until 1988.

Stereo Review. New York: Hachette, 1958- . Monthly.

This consumer publication reviews and compares new audio components, as well as records in the classical, pop, and rock fields.

Video Librarian. Bremerton, Wash.: Video Librarian, 1986- . Bimonthly except combined in July and August. E-mail: vidlib@ kndaco.telebyte.com

This trade publication contains editorials and news, reviewing nearly 200 videos for public, school, and university libraries.

Videolog. San Diego, Calif.: Trade Services Corporation, 1981- . Weekly.

A loose-leaf bulletin of news from the home video industry including reviews of new video releases.

Selected Video Recordings

Children's Video in Libraries: Highlights from the Association for Library Service to Children Preconference. Producer Shari Lewis. American Video Library Association/Library Video Network. 1989, videocassette, 48 min.

Copyright: The Internet, Multimedia and the Law. Producer/ distributor, Chip Taylor. Association for Information Media & Equipment (AIME). 1996, 2 videocassettes, 40 min.

Copyright Law: What Every School, College and Public Library Should Know; Copyright, New Issues. Writer/producer/director Andrew Martin. Association for Information Media & Equipment (AIME). 1994, videocassette, 39 min.

Fair Use Guidelines for Educational Multimedia. Writer/producer Robert B. Sorkin. Consortium of College and University Media Center/PBS Adult Learning Satellite Service. 1997, videocassette, 120 min.

Fast Forward: Libraries and the Video Revolution. Produced by the Library Video Network. 1988, videocassette, 18 min.

The Librarian's Video Primer: Establishing and Maintaining Your Video Collection. Produced by the Georgia Library Video Association. 1988, videocassette, 21 min.

Library Media Series. Produced by the Orange County (Calif.) Department of Education. 1987, videocassette, 5 tape set, 85 min.

Video, CD-ROM and the Web Motion Media and the Library of the Future. Executive producer, Sally Mason Robinson; producer, Debra Franco. American Video Library Association/Library Video Network. 1997, videocassette, 120 min.

Other Useful Reference Aids

A-V Online. 1964- . Irregular. http://www.krinfo.com/dialo/ Selective earlier coverage; 361,628 records as of January 1993.

Cassette Books. Washington, D.C.: Library of Congress, National Library Services for the Blind and Physically Handicapped. Annual.

"Guidelines for Audiovisual Services in Academic Libraries." Prepared by the ACRL Audiovisual Committee, Margaret Ann Johnson, Chair. *College & Research Library News* 9 (October 1998): 533-536.

Smith, Corinne H. "I Saw It on TV: A Guide to Broadcast Programming Sources." *College and University Media Review* 1, no. 1 (Summer 1994): 25-40. See also the electronic publication I Saw It on TV: A Guide to Broadcast and Cable Programming Sources. http://www.library.nwu.edu/media/resources/tvguide.html

The Video Annual 1992. Jean T. Kreamer, editor. Denver, Colo.: ABC-Clio, 1992.

Words on Cassette. New Providence, N.J.: R. R. Bowker. Annual.

SELECTIVE DISTRIBUTOR LIST BY ACTIVITIES AT ANNUAL AMERICAN LIBRARY ASSOCIATION CONVENTION: 1992-1997

Wholesalers and Distributors

Baker & Taylor Video
501 S. Gladiolus
Momence, IL 60954
(800) 435-5111, (815) 472-2444
Fax: (800) 775-3500
WWW:http://www.baker-taylor.com

Brodart Co.
500 Arch St.
Williamsport, PA 17705
(800) 233-8467
Fax: (800) 999-6799
WWW: http://www.brodart.com

Ingram Library Services, Inc.
One Ingram Blvd.
P.O. Box 3006
La Vergne, TN 37086-1989
(615) 793-5000

WWW: http://www.ingramentertainment.com

Greatest breadth of inventory in the industry; customized collection development programs, cataloging, and processing services.

Library Video Company
P.O. Box 110
Bala Cynwyd, PA 19004
(800) 843-3620
Fax: (610) 667-3425
E-mail: marybeth@libraryvideo.com

Educational videos and CD-ROMs, stocking over 7,000 titles for children and adults.

Professional Media Service Corp.
19122 S. Vermont Ave.
Gardena, CA 90248
(800) 223-7672, (310) 532-9024
Fax: (800) 253-8853

E-mail: promedia@class.org
WWW: http://www.promedia.com

Wholesalers of video and sound recordings; music, audiobooks, children's, and spoken recordings.

Single Source Distributors—Educational/Instructional

AIMS Media
9710 DeSoto Ave.
Chatsworth, CA 91311
(800) 367-2467, (818) 773-4300
Fax: (818) 341-6700
E-mail: Info@AIMS-Multimedia.com
WWW: http://aims-multimedia.com

ALA Video/Library Video Network
320 York Rd.
Towson, MD 21204
(410) 887-2082
Fax (410) 887-2091
E-mail: lvn@mail.bcpl.lib.md.us

Material for library staff training and building library collections.

Altschul Group
1560 Sherman Ave.
Suite 100k
Evanston, IL 60201
(800) 526-4663, (847) 328-6700
Fax: (847) 328-6706
WWW: http://www.agcmedia.com

Ambrosia Video Publishing Inc.
1290 Avenue of the Americas
Suite 2245
New York, NY 10104
(800) 526-4663
Fax: (212) 265-8008
E-mail: info@ambrosevideo.com
WWW:
http://www.ambrosevideo.com

Annenberg/CPB Math and Science Collection
P.O. Box 2345
South Burlington, VT 05407-2345
(800) 965-7373
Fax: (802) 864-9846
E-mail: mathsci@learner.org

Video, CD-ROM, print resources for math and science materials for educational reform, for pre-service and in-service teacher education, parent workshops, and for administrators.

Annenberg/CPB Multimedia College
P.O. Box 2345
South Burlington, VT 05407-2345
(800) LEARNER
Fax: (802) 864-9846
E-mail: info@learner.org
WWW: http://www.learner.org/
content/index.html

Educational audiovisual materials in areas such as foreign language, science, literature, psychology, mathematics, and geography. Available on video, videodisc, and CD-ROM.

Annenberg/CPB Project
901 E St. NW
Washington, DC 20004
(800) LEARNER

Barr Media Group
12801 Schabarum Ave.
Los Angeles, CA 91706-7878
(818) 338-7878
Fax: (818) 814-2672

Bullfrog Films
P.O. Box 149
Oley, PA 19547
(800) 543-3764
Fax: (610) 779-8226
E-mail: bullfrog@igc.apc.org
WWW: http://www.igc.apc.org/
bullfrog/index.html

Environmental video publisher
with over 500 titles. Public
performance rights for preschool
through university. Offers
collection of music and fine arts
videos from Rhombus Media
International.

California Newsreel
149 Ninth St.
San Francisco, CA 94103
(415) 621-6196
Fax: (415) 621-6522
E-mail: newsreel@ix.netcom.com
WWW: http://www.newsreel.org
African and Caribbean feature
films and documentaries.

Carousel Film and Video
260 Fifth Ave.
New York, NY 10001
(800) 683-1660
Fax: (212) 683-1662
E-mail: carousel@pipeline.com

Over 200 titles including network
documentaries, American Film
Institute productions, Academy
Award–nominated programs,
and independently produced
videos.

Chip Taylor Communications
15 Spollett Dr.
Derry, NH 03038
(800) 876-CHIP, (603) 434-9262
Fax: (603) 432-2723
URL: http://www.chiptaylor.com
Producer/distributor of videos and
multimedia.

**Films for the Humanities and
Sciences**
P.O. Box 2053
Princeton, NJ 08543-2053
(609) 275-1400
Fax: (609) 275-3767
WWW: http://www.films.com

Over 6,000 educational programs in
all subject areas K-12 and
college with public performance
rights. Available in video,
videodisc, and CD-ROM.

Films Inc.
5547 N. Ravenswood Ave.
Chicago, IL 60640
(800) 323-4222
WWW: http://www.publicmedia.
com/fientertainment

Hargrove Entertainment Inc.
P.O. Box 750338
Forest Hills, NY 11375-0338
(718) 657-0542
Fax: (718) 657-0542

Educational film, video, and
multimedia.

IVN Communications, Inc.
2246 Camino Ramon
San Ramon, CA 94583
(510) 866-1344, ext. 247
Fax: (510) 866-9262
WWW:
http://www.ivn.com/ftp/public
_html/ivncorp.html

Producer/distributor of Emmy Award–winning special interest videos covering such subjects as travel, history, business, nature, music, children's, documentary, etc.

Karol Video
P.O. Box 7600
350 N. Pennsylvania Ave.
Wilkes Barre, PA 18773
(717) 822-8899
Fax: (717) 822-8226

All age levels. Core curriculum, humanities, recreation, sports, hobbies, and leisure titles.

Kino International
333 W. 39th St.
New York, NY 10018
(212) 629-6880
Fax: (212) 174-0871
E-mail:kinoint@infohouse.com

Specializes in foreign language, classic, silent, and documentary films. Public performance rights available.

Landmark Media
3450 Slade Run Dr.
Falls Church, VA 22042
(800) 342-4336, (703) 241-2030
Fax: (703) 536-9540

Lucerne Media
37 Ground Pine Rd.
Morris Plains, NJ 07950
(800) 341-2293, (201) 538-1401
Fax: (201) 538-0855

MPI Home Video/MPI Media Group
16101 S. 108th Ave.
Orland Park, IL 60462
(708) 460-0555
Fax: (708) 460-0175

E-mail: bob@mpimedia.com
WWW: http://www.mpimedia.com

National Geographic Society
c/o Educational Services
P.O. Box 98019
Washington, DC 20090
(202) 857-7378, (800) 447-0647
(800) 368-2728
Fax: (301) 921-1575

Video discs, CD-ROM, videos, filmstrips, educational software.

NLCC Educational Media
P.O. Box 391960
Los Angeles, CA 90039-1527
(800) 722-9982
Fax: (213) 663-5606
E-mail: nlccemedia@aol.com
WWW: http://latino.sscnet.ucla.edu/community/nlcc

Videos of popular and rarely seen films about Latinos including dramas, documentaries, comedies, and performance.

PBS Video
1320 Braddock Place
Alexandria, VA 22314-1698
(800) 424-7963
Fax: (800) 344-3337
E-mail: www@pbs.org
WWW: http://www.pbs.org

Phoenix Films and Video
2349 Chaffee Dr.
St. Louis, MO 63146
(314) 569-0211, (800) 221-1274
Fax: (314) 569-2834
E-mail: heyjudedb@aol.com

Original live action film and video productions.

Pyramid Film and Video
P.O. Box 1048
Santa Monica, CA 90406-1048
(800) 421-2304, (310) 828-7557
Fax: (310) 453-9083
E-mail: info@pyramidmedia.
com
WWW: http://www.pyramidmedia.
com

Schlessinger Video Productions,
a division of Library Video Co.
521 Righters Ferry Road
P.O. Box 1110
Bala Cynwyd, PA 19004
(610) 667-0200
Fax: (610) 667-3425
E-mail: marybeth@libraryvideo.
com

Educational videos, specializing in
American history, biographies,
multicultural and Native
American studies, teen health
concerns, and holidays for
children. Original children's
programming.

Scholarly Resources Inc.
104 Greenhill Ave.
Wilmington, DE 19805
(800) 772-8937
Fax: (302) 654-3871
E-mail: market@scholarly.com

CD-ROM products and other
materials relating to Latin
American studies, women's
studies, genealogy, political
science, and history.

Time-Life Education
2000 Duke St.
Alexandria, VA 22314
(703) 836-7466
Fax: (703) 518-4124
WWW: http://www.timelife.com/

CD-ROM, computer software,
videos, and music products.

**University of California
Extension**
2000 Center St., 4th Floor
Berkeley, CA 94704
(510) 642-0460
Fax: (510) 643-9271
E-mail: cmil@uclink.berkeley.edu

Media distribution agency for
University of California. Award-
winning documentaries and CD-
ROM topics include
multiculturalism, psychology,
sociology, women's issues,
communications, history, health,
and art.

WGBH Educational Foundation
125 Western Ave.
Boston, MA 02134
(617) 492-2777, ext. 3840
Fax: (617) 787-4733
E-mail: theasahr@wgbh.org

Science Odyssey with Charles
Kuralt. Project resources such as
PBS series, trade books, videos,
posters, teacher's guides, Web
site, science theater, and
demonstrations.

Weston Woods Studios, Inc.
389 Newtown Tpke.
Weston, CT 06883
(203) 266-3355, (800) 243-5020
Fax: (203) 266-3818

Single Source Distributors—Independent/Alternative

A & E Home Video
c/o New Video Group
126 5th Ave., 15th Floor
New York, NY 10011
(212) 206-8600
Fax: (212) 206-9001
WWW http://www.aetv.com/index2.
    html

Best programming for television.
    Over 200 products; biography
    series; arts and entertainment
    TV.

Appalshop Films and Video
306 Madison St.
Whitesburg, KY 41858
(800) 545-7467, (606) 633-0108
Fax: (606) 633-1001
E-mail: Appalshop@aol.com
WWW: http://www.uky.edu/
    Projects/Appal

Baker & Taylor
2709 Water Ridge Pkwy.
Charlotte, NC 28217
(800) 775-1800
Fax: (704) 329-8989
WWW: http://www.btinfo.com

Baker & Taylor Entertainment
    Attn: Library Services
100 Business Center Drive
Pittsburgh, PA 15205
(800) 775-2600, ext. 2131
Fax: (412) 787-0368

3005 S. Parker Rd.
Suite 318
Aurora, CO 80014
(800) 775-3300
Fax: (303) 369-9578

Comprised of three operating units:
    Electronic Business and
    Information Services;
    Customized Library Services;
    and Distribution Services.
    Distributes books, video, audio,
software, and related services to
    retail stores and libraries
    worldwide. Entertainment
    division offices in Denver (west
    of the Mississippi River) and
    Pittsburgh (east of the
    Mississippi River).

Cinema Guild
1697 Broadway
Suite 506
New York, NY 10019
(212) 246-5522
Fax: (212) 246-5525
E-mail: thecinema@aol.com
WWW: http://www.cinemaguild.
    com

Educational, feature, and
    instructional media materials.

Direct Cinema Ltd.
P.O. Box 10003
Santa Monica, CA 90410-1003
(310) 396-4774, (800) 345-6748
Fax: (310) 396-3233
E-mail: directcinema@attmail.com

Over 600 titles including 48
    Academy Award nominees, 14
    Academy Award winners, and
    more than 60 ALA Selected
    Films for Young Adults.

EPH Productions
P.O. Box 1042
Ansonia Station
New York, NY 10023
(212) 799-9246
Fax: (212) 721-2346

Women's history videos, women's
    rights suffrage, and Afro-
    American women.

Facets Multimedia, Inc.
1517 W. Fullerton Ave.
Chicago, IL 60614
(800) 331-6197, (312) 281-9075

Fax: (312) 929-5437
E-mail: sales@facets.org
WWW: http://www.facets.org

Foreign, classic American,
documentary, fine arts,
independent, experimental, and
children's films on video and
laser disc.

Fanlight Productions
47 Halifax St.
Boston, MA 02130
(617) 524-0980, (800) 937-4113
Fax: (617) 524-8838
E-mail: fanlight@tiac.net
WWW: www.fanlight.com

Education videos on health care,
mental health, disability, and
family issues.

Filmakers Library
124 E. 40th St.
New York, NY 10016
(212) 808-4980
Fax: (212) 808-4983
E-mail: info@filmakers.com
WWW: http://www.filmakers.com/
index.html

Educational videos: anthropology,
psychology, African-American
studies, sociology, women's
studies, gay/lesbian studies,
disability issues, Native
American studies, etc.

First Run/Icarus Films
153 Waverly Place, 6th Floor
New York, NY 10014
(800) 876-1710
Fax: (212) 255-7923
E-mail: mail@frif.com
WWW http://www.echonyc.
com/~frif

Social, political, and historical
documentary and fiction videos
and films.

Flower Films
10341 San Pablo Ave.
El Cerrito, CA 94530
(510) 525-0942
Fax: (510) 525-1204
WWW: http://www.lib.berkeley.
edu/MRC/Flowerfilm.html

Frameline Distribution
346 9th St.
San Francisco, CA 94103-3809
(415) 703-8650
Fax: (415) 861-1404
E-mail: frameline@aol.com

Lesbian and gay independent films
and videos.

Midwest Tape Exchange
P.O. Box 5755
Toledo, OH 43613
(800) 875-2785
Fax: (419) 471-1029

New and used videotapes. Special
interest, children's, instructional
and hard-to-find videotapes.

Milestone Film and Video
275 W. 96th St.
Suite 28C
New York, NY 10025
(212) 865-7449
Fax: (212) 222-8952
E-mail: MileFilms@aol.com

Films of yesterday and today.
American and foreign feature
films, documentaries, and classic
animation.

**Multi-Cultural Books and
Videos, Inc.**
28880 Southfield Rd.
Suite 183
Lathrup Village, MI 48076
(810) 559-2676
Fax: (810) 559-2465
E-mail: multicul@wincom.net

Foreign language materials from
around the world.

Museum of Modern Art, Circulating Film and Video Library
11 W. 53rd St.
New York, NY 10019
(212) 708-9530
WWW: http://moma.org

National Film Board of Canada
1251 Avenue of the Americas
16th Floor
New York, NY 10020-1173
(212) 596-1770
Fax: (212) 596-1774
E-mail: Johnnfbc@aol.com
WWW: http://www.nfb.ca

Producer and distributor of award-winning films and videos including innovative animation and social issues documentaries.

Native American Public Broadcasting Consortium, Inc. (NAPBC)
P.O. Box 83111
Lincoln, NE 68501
(402) 472-3522
Fax: (402) 472-8675
E-mail: franka@efn.org
WWW: http://www.efn.org/~franka/video/VideoDistribution.html

New Day Films
22D Hollywood Ave.
Ho-ho-kus, NJ 07423
(201) 652-6590
Fax: (201) 652-1973
E-mail: curator@newday.com
WWW: http://www.newday.com

New Yorker Films
16 W. 61st St.
New York, NY 10023
(212) 247-6110
Fax: (212) 307-7855

William Graves Productions
1841 Broadway
Suite 1212
New York, NY 10023
(800) 874-8314
Fax: (212) 262-7628

Women Make Movies
462 Broadway, 5th Floor
New York, NY 10013
(212) 926-0606
Fax: (212) 965-2052.
E-mail: distdept@wmm.com

Women's films and videos, documentaries, and dramas.

University Non-print Rental Services

Indiana University
Instructional Support Services
Franklin Hall 0001
Bloomington, IN 47405-5901
(812) 855-8065
E-mail: teach@indiana.edu
Web: http://www.indiana.edu/~mediares/catalog.html

Over 10,000 videos, films, and other media are available for Indiana University faculty instructional use. Many of these titles are also available for rental to institutions of higher education, public and private schools.

Iowa State University

Instructional Technology Center
121 Pearson Hall
Ames, IA 50011-2203
(515) 294-1540, (800) 447-0060
Fax: (515) 294-8089
Web: http://www.itc.iastate.edu/
classroom/media/homepage.html

More than 7,000 film and video
titles are available for loan. Most
titles are available to off-campus
clients for a rental fee.

Kent State University

Audio Visual Services
Kent State University
Kent, Ohio 44240
(330) 672-3456, ext. 19, (800) 338-
5718
Fax: (330)672-3463
E-mail: Info@Media.Kent.Edu
Web: http://media.kent.edu/

More than 10,000 educational titles
in video, CD-ROM, and film
formats with a searchable
database on the Web.

Oklahoma State University

Audio Visual Center
121 Cordell, North O.S.U.
Stillwater, OK 74078
(405) 744-7212
Fax: (405) 744-8445
E-mail: rgpavc@okway.okstate.edu
(Director)
Web: http://www.av.okstate.edu/
libhome.htm

Houses over 4,000 video and film
programs, as well as the
negatives of several Oklahoma
historical films. In addition, it is
the site for the negatives of any
photographs taken by the OSU
photographers of campus scenes
or faculty staff of the OSU
community. Those archives are
also searchable.

Pennsylvania State University

Audio Visual Services
University Park, PA 16802
(800) 826-0132
Fax: (814) 863-2574
E-mail: AVSMedia@psulias.psu.
edu
Web: http://www.libraries.psu.
edu/AVS/INFO.html

A widely respected collection
of more than 16,500 films
and videotapes, those
recommendations of which are
based on opinions of faculty and
librarian/selectors from all
colleges, academic disciplines,
and campuses. This is the
largest academic non-print
collection among research
libraries.

University of Colorado at Boulder, Information

Technology Services, Video
Library
Boulder, CO 80309
(303) 492-1816
Fax: (303) 492-7017
E-mail: Barbara.Black@Colorado.
edu
Web: http://maxi.colorado.edu

More than 5,000 educational
videotapes and 16mm films
selected for teaching the
higher-education curriculum.
While serving the instructional
needs of the Boulder campus
faculty, the majority of these
programs are available for
rental to off-campus educational
users. Many titles are also
suitable for general audiences
and K-12 instruction.

University of Minnesota
Film and Video Rental Service
1313 Fifth St., S.E.
Suite 108
Minneapolis, MN 55414
(612) 627-4270,
  In-state (800) 542-0013,
  Out-of-state (800) 847-8251
Fax: (612) 627-4280
E-mail: film-vid@mail.cee.
  umn.edu
Web: http://www.cee.umn.edu/ufv/
  general.shtml

The library includes approximately
  10,000 titles in 4,000 subject
  areas.

University of Missouri
  Academic Support Center
505 E. Stewart Rd.
Columbia, MO 65211-2040
(573) 882-3601
E-mail: asc-media-lib@muccmail.
  missouri.edu
Web: http://www.missouri.edu/
  ~ascwww/medialib.html

A collection of 5,000 film and 4,500
  video programs (and a select
  group of laser discs) are
  available for short-term rental.

University of Washington
  Classroom Support Services
  Educational Media Collection
Box 353090
University of Washington
Seattle, WA 98195-3090
(206) 543-9900,
  (Reference) (206) 543-9907
Fax: (206) 685-7892
E-mail: classrm@u.washington.edu
  ldb@u.washington.edu
Web: http://www.washington.edu/
  classroom

Offers over 5,000 films and
  videotapes for classroom
  instruction from on-campus
  collection and access to off-
  campus media collections.

Utah State University, Audio
  Visual Services
Logan, UT 84322-3100
(801) 797-2658
E-mail: briast@cc.usu.edu
Web: http://www.usu.edu/~libavs/
  inform.htm

The AudioVisual Services catalog
  lists over 5,000 items. Materials
  may be accessed by title
  including series title, subject,
  and keyword.

Notes

1. *Nonbook Media: Collection Management and User Services,* ed. J. Ellison and P. Coty (Chicago: American Library Association, 1987).

2. Bill Gates, Nathan Myhrvold and Peter Rinearson, *The Road Ahead* (NewYork: Penguin Books, 1996), p. 21.

3. *Library Hotline* (August 15, 1994), pp. 2-4.

4. Russell Ash, *The Top 10 of Everything, 1997* (New York: Dorling Kindersley, 1996), p. 173

5. *Video Librarian.* http://www.videolibrarian.com

6. Sally Mason-Robinson, *Developing and Managing Video Collections: A How-to-Do-It Manual for Librarians* (New York: Neal-Schuman, 1996), pp. 20-32.

7. Ibid., pp. 34-39.

14

Outsourcing Acquisitions:
Methods and Models

GLENDA ALVIN

Outsourcing has earned a reputation for being cost efficient and has become an important as well as a necessary business strategy for reengineering the workplace. Some form of outsourcing has been utilized by libraries for several decades. Because they are not-for-profit institutions that rely on funding from other entities to survive, indeed exist, libraries have never been self-funding or self-sufficient. Whether they are public, academic, or special in mission, libraries have always had to collaborate and cooperate with their communities and funding sources. Over the past thirty years, as funding continues to precipitously decline, library administrators have sought new methods of enhancing service to their clientele while still maintaining quality collections. Since the main goal of any library is to provide resources to its users, the processing of those resources has been a focal point for outsourcing.

The federal government, as well as state governments and major corporations like General Motors, have engaged in privatization as a way of controlling rising costs. Privatization shifts the burden of payroll and other associated labor costs to businesses and organizations involved in profit making, thus posing a threat to labor unions, which always demand higher wages and better benefits. Some workers perceive it as a corporate business strategy wielded by Fortune 500 companies to trim the fat from their budget expenditures and provide stockholders with fatter dividends. Major corporations like General Motors want to outsource part of their operations to get rid of the demands of labor unions and to trim the work force of bodies that require not only salaries, but also benefits for disability, pension, sick, and annual leave. Perceived as a single-minded ploy of corporate greed, outsourcing has labor unions up in arms and even the Pope has denounced outsourcing because he thinks it causes unemployment.[1]

In the library world, administrators and librarians began using outsourcing for tasks that were related to general facilities management and did not require library skills, such as security, photocopy, and custodial work.[2] When automation came along, libraries outsourced their retrospective conversion of the card catalogs to companies that specialized in that type of work. Some non-library tasks could be done more quickly and cost-effectively by companies that specialized in the singular type of work involved than these same jobs could have been done when processed by the library staff who had neither the time nor expertise to engage in this type of work. The same observation held true for some library-related tasks, like binding and preservation, which require specialized training and are both expensive and time-consuming to maintain in-house.

Some librarians welcome outsourcing as a way to contain costs resulting from understaffing. Others perceive it as a threat to their careers and have become increasingly alarmed as they watch outsourcing expand into every type of library and library process. It has made an indelible mark on libraries in general and technical services professionals in particular, due to the fact that their jobs have been the most likely to be outsourced. However, as a management tool, outsourcing has often met with success, because library vendors and others have positioned themselves to supplement or totally replace functions traditionally facilitated by technical services librarians. It has also has met success as a method to contain library expenditures for personnel, processes, and services.

REASONS FOR OUTSOURCING

A library may elect to outsource a process or a function for a myriad of reasons. In the era of the shrinking dollar, not only have materials budgets shrunk, but also the size of the library staff. In order to reduce the payroll, library administrators have abolished positions or left them vacant after a staff member resigns or retires. The work left by the departed staff member's position is then divided among those who remain employed in the department, or a new person is hired with a job description that combines the work assignments once held by two different staff members. Occasionally, outsourcing has been used as a sort of punishment when the management and the library staff encounter on-going friction in their interpersonal relationships.[3]

In academic settings, financial aid departments are receiving fewer government dollars for supplying work-study students to academic departments. The library receives fewer student assistant hours to support simple clerical tasks such as filing shelflist cards, applying security strips on the spines or pages of books, adding plastic covers, or doing proprietorship stamping on new shipments of materials. The acquisitions librarian must evaluate the department's mission and goals in terms of what are the most important functions the staff and student assistants should perform. In other words, the essential functions of the acquisitions department have to be analyzed to assess the workload of the available staff to carry out the work and their abilities to get the job done in the most efficient manner.

Arnold Hirshon and Barbara Winters have determined two categories of reasons for outsourcing: strategic reasons and tactical reasons. In their opinion, strategic reasons for outsourcing facilitate "(a) enabling the library to refocus on its core operations; (b) having the ability to reengineer operations without having to redefine processes at a detailed level or undergo intensive staff retraining; (c) the ability to improve organizational flexibility; or (d) to create the opportunity to reassign the staff to more essential areas of the library." Cost considerations such as funding reductions, gaining access to job experience not found in-house such as preservation skills for archival and special collections, or bringing new impetus to a difficult or unproductive work situation are cited by Hirshon and Winters as tactical reasons for outsourcing.[4]

In the past, technical services departments have had something of a reputation for attracting staff members who favored habit, routine, and close attention to detail. These staff, it was believed, craved the stability and security of knowing what they would do each workday. In some quarters of the library world, technical services librarians and their staffs were stereotyped as people who did not want to interact with the public and who excelled at following procedures. Technical services departments are usually housed behind closed doors or on floors not accessible to the public, which adds to the perception of separateness.

Automation of library functions permanently changed the way acquisitions, serials, and cataloging departments performed their responsibilities. As acquisitions departments have striven toward an online environment and paperless transactions, there is no longer a need for library assistants to type five-part order forms for book orders and to file paper copies in "on order" and "orders received" files, because order processing and record maintenance can be done electronically. Nor is there a need for an accounting clerk to manually enter all transactions in ledger books and to maintain balances, because the automation system's fund accounting module processes payment data and generates management reports.

The more advanced and flexible automation systems reduced the amount of time on task for acquisitions librarians and library assistants, thus leaving them available for absorbing other functions they previously did not handle, such as serials, copy cataloging, processing government documents, order processing for audiovisual materials, and distributing library mail. In addition, acquisitions and other technical services staff have been cross-trained in public services areas like the circulation desk, the information desk, special collections, and government documents. One of the major motives for cross-training is insufficient staffing to maintain proper coverage of public service areas. When the acquisitions staff spends less time in the acquisitions department due to assisting other departments, that means they spend less time processing orders and handling newly assigned departmental responsibilities. As a way of balancing a juggling act of rotating work assignments, the acquisitions librarian may have to turn to outsourcing as a way to augment staffing shortages and maintain an effective workflow.

According to Joyce Ogburn, one vital reason for acquisitions librarians to outsource is to consolidate the services and materials they receive from one vendor. She observes that as vendors offer more services, there is a potential for libraries to realize greater gains in productivity by using a sole source for all of their vendor needs. Consolidating with one vendor not only centralizes customer support and quality assurance, it also provides access to "custom designed services, less overlap of responsibilities and integrated processing."[5]

Management and control of library staff also play a pivotal role in the decision to outsource processes, which in retrospect were once performed by in-house staff. In a widely read article in *Against the Grain,* Jack Montgomery writes that he "suspects outsourcing is a way of circumventing the difficult process of transforming an often resistant, entrenched, and tradition-bound workforce into a more economically cost effective work unit." Montgomery convincingly argues that vendors who are in the business of making money will not tolerate an unproductive staff. Libraries who have to contend apprehensively with civil service and union considerations are compelled to waste time and money attempting to reform library staffs that resent and resist having to adjust to a rapidly changing environment. He warns that if libraries are to continue to be viable institutions, they will have to conduct themselves more like businesses.[6]

This ideology points to a contemporary difference of opinion in library management. One sector of the library community embraces the philosophy that libraries are businesses because they have employees, manage finances, have facilities, are concerned with cost, market their services, and provide customer service.[7] Individuals who subscribe to this line of thought usually believe libraries should keep abreast of the latest business trends and corporate strategies like Total Quality Management (TQM), downsizing, and outsourcing. Another sector of the library community espouses the notion that libraries are educational institutions and repositories of culture with a mission to provide service as well as access and therefore should not be regarded in the same light as profit-making enterprises. At the 1996 Feather River Institute, Roy B. Conant, a vendor representative, told an audience: "the fact that libraries do business does not by itself support the assertion that libraries are businesses."[8] These attitudes are reflected in the ways different libraries have approached outsourcing. Some libraries have looked at the human component of outsourcing programs and made commitments to keep the lines of communication open and not to lay off staff. Others, especially libraries in corporate environments, have taken a more businesslike approach that focuses only on the bottom line and have outsourced entire library operations, leaving the librarians and their staff unexpectedly jobless.

Much of the published work agrees that the key reason for outsourcing is to concentrate on essential functions or what the literature calls core competencies. Many libraries have realized that after years of trying to be all things to all people, they can serve their community and patrons better if they focus their energies on a service-oriented agenda. By targeting the most significant functions that support their service mission, libraries can direct more energy and resources into reinforcing those processes. To date, most library reengineering ventures have started with the technical processing section, with the rationale being that it does not provide public service.

VENDOR SERVICES

The advent of library outsourcing of technical services processes has been made possible and practical by library vendors who have developed products and services that supplement or totally replace technical services functions. Over the past twenty years, library jobbers like Blackwell North America, Baker & Taylor Books, Midwest

Library Service, Yankee Book Peddler, and Coutts Library Services, to name a few, have positioned their companies to accept outsourcing responsibilities. They have deftly made the transition from book suppliers for firm and standing orders to service providers for a large and proliferating number of library-related functions traditionally within the purview of library technical services departments. Today's library vendor seeks to meet a variety of needs from simple physical processing tasks to assignments that are technologically sophisticated. They consider these functions "value-added services." Gary Shirk of Yankee Book Peddler explains:

> Supplying outsourced service is more than just a new market to exploit. Vendors view it as a strategic opportunity to strengthen their relationship with their customers. Librarians have expressed a legitimate need and the vendors would like to respond. Value-added services such as providing online access to vendor files, catalog records, and book processing are no longer peripheral services, they are essential service offerings.[9]

Vendors can conduct pre-order verification of bibliographic data by searching their own databases. They can search for duplicate orders by (a) checking the library's holdings via the Internet, (b) searching their computer's database of the library's previous orders, (c) loading the library database into the vendor's computer system, and (d) installing a feature in their software for desktop computers that automatically checks for duplicates. For example, BT LINK, a popular Baker & Taylor Books desktop ordering software, will check for duplicates in the ordering database as each ISBN is entered. If the library is in close proximity to the vendor or if the vendor is working on a major project for a library, they can also send their staffs to the library to do on-site checking of the library holdings. [10]

Jobbers can supply libraries with desktop electronic ordering software or accept electronic orders transmitted from the library's automation system through e-mail and EDI (Electronic Data Interchange). They can create electronic order records for the purpose of keeping track of the library fund accounting. This feature allows vendors the option of inputting library in-house fund accounting codes to process expenditures as well as process claims and construct management reports. Vendors possess the capability to furnish management reports on the library's activity, e.g., how many standing orders were shipped to the library during the fiscal year, or what the library's average firm order discount was during the previous year. They can also supply physical processing services

in the form of placing security strips in the books, applying ownership stamping, adding barcodes and spine labels, as well as delivering an assortment of binding selections.[11]

In the area of collection development, vendors are enthusiasti-
cally marketing contract acquisitions opportunities. With contract
acquisitions, the vendor and the library enter into an agreement
that the vendor will supply books based on an amount allocated by
the library and that the books must conform to a profile provided by
the library. The profile may identify subjects, reading level, audience, format, languages, and the price of books that the library believes will meet the needs of its patrons. Libraries interested in an
"Opening Day Collection" for new or expanded collections frequently
subscribe to this method of selection as a technique for guaranteeing
a certain number of books within a specified time frame.[12]

The most common type of contract acquisitions used by academic
libraries is the approval plan. The library allocates a portion of its
budget to a vendor who in turn supplies materials based on the library's profile. The books are shipped to the library for perusal as
to whether they meet the profile. If the decision is made that the
materials do not conform to the criteria set forth in the approval
plan profile, the library has the right to ship the books back to the
vendor and not be billed for the undesirable titles. Approval plans
provide the option of having the books shipped or having slips sent
which give a bibliographic description of the individual titles.[13]

In the area of cataloging, vendors can generate MARC records,
copy cataloging, original cataloging, and authority control, which
has given the approval plan a cousin—the purchase plan. With this
plan, approval plan books are cataloged and physically processed
at the point of shipment from the vendor. This makes them virtually ready to be put on the library shelves when they arrive, or
"shelf-ready." In most cases, allowing the vendor to process approval plan books means that the library no longer has the privilege of returning the books to the vendor if they do not match the
approval plan profile. Libraries that become involved in purchase
plans surrender a measure of quality control. They can, of course,
attempt to adjust the profile to narrow the number of books they
receive through the purchase plan that do not comply with the profile.[14]

The vendors' abilities to supply these services are due to an
occurrence that is seldom broached in library literature. Vendors
hire librarians to perform the cataloging and collection development, in addition to other jobs like sales and marketing. This allows the vendors to assure their customers that the outsourcing is

being conducted by qualified staff who have received the same training and have the same kind of American Library Association-accredited graduate degrees as in-house librarians. For these vendor-hired librarians, vendors offer travel, competitive salaries, and attractive benefits. They also offer job opportunities outside of public libraries, which often feature low salaries and high stress; academic libraries, which may bring demands for additional advanced degrees or tenure pressures; and special libraries, like law libraries, which often require a librarian to have a law degree, but do not offer a commensurate salary. In some cases, the availability of vendor-employed librarians has set up a somewhat awkward situation of having the in-house librarians compete with librarians in the private sector for jobs.

Book jobbers are not the only businesses that supply libraries with outsourcing services. At the 1994 Midwinter meeting of the American Library Association in Philadelphia, the Online Computer Library Center (OCLC) introduced a new product named "PromptCat." OCLC, primarily a bibliographic utility for catalog records, announced that it had formed a partnership with several leading vendors to supply catalog records for firm order and approval plan titles, and that it could attach a library's holding symbol to the record in its database. This meant PromptCat could expedite ordering, cataloging, spine labeling, and barcoding of books, in effect rendering them virtually shelf-ready at the point of shipment.

Libraries at Ohio State University (OSU), Michigan State University (MSU), and Louisiana State University (LSU), all Association of Research Libraries members, have implemented PromptCat, and each reports a high degree of satisfaction. Colleen Hyslop of MSU reported that the OCLC record matched the book and required minimal editing for their approval plan titles. The vendor informed OCLC which approval plan titles it intended to send to the library. OCLC then sent the catalog records on tape. MSU was able to send 90 percent of its approval titles received through PromptCat straight from the Acquisitions Department to the Labeling Department, and the majority of titles spent less than three weeks in the technical services department.[15] Mary M. Rider and Marsha Hamilton of OSU libraries implemented PromptCat with their approval vendor and discovered that it "streamlined the cataloging process by providing [cataloging] copy containing the unique OCLC number and holdings at a price generally below that possible using a local library staff."[16] By having the books arrive shelf-ready, OSU and MSU converted their approval plans into purchase plans.

Louisiana State University's library consolidated its firm and approval orders with one vendor. According to librarian Michael Somers, LSU's involvement with PromptCat resulted in books being placed on the library's "New Book Shelf" within two weeks of arriving at the library. [17]

The experiences of these three research libraries reveal that PromptCat has been an outsourcing success story in large research libraries. While some librarians have expressed alarm that technical services positions are diminishing because of outsourcing, some vendors take great pains to emphasize that outsourcing is a case of supply and demand from libraries. Acquisitions librarians, confronted with diminishing revenue and vanishing staff positions, started requesting vendor support in the form of book processing. In 1989, Douglas Duchin confidently defended vendors by asserting that the majority of outsourcing products and services offered by his employer, Blackwell North America, were requested by librarians and not devised by vendors wishing to encroach on library turf.[18] In a keynote address at the 1997 Charleston Conference, the president of Blackwell North America, Fred Philipp, stated that his company had become involved in outsourcing services in order to stay competitive.

OUTSOURCE PLANNING

After the library has made the decision to outsource part or all of its operations, then it is time embark on the planning phases of the process. The planning phases of outsourcing are not difficult or complicated to facilitate, but they can be time-consuming and somewhat labor-intensive. It is important to realize this at the outset in order to alleviate frustration from time constraints further along in the process. In preparation for outsourcing it might be a good idea to consult with librarians who have undergone a similar type of outsourcing program.[19] An outsourcing project may be assigned to a team, committee, or—depending upon the size of the library and/or the functions to be outsourced—the responsibility may be delegated to one person. After setting an adequate time frame for conducting the project, the second order of business is to closely examine every function in the department and evaluate which processes are the most vital or essential for the department to perform.[20] Some of the processes and issues that should be considered for outsourcing are:

how quickly books can be obtained,

how outsourcing might enhance the procedures for handling periodical subscriptions,

how procedures for finding out-of-print books can be simplified, and

what the time frame is both in-house and out for the physical processing of books, the ordering of continuations, and the order processing of audiovisual materials.[21]

Karen Wilson has recognized two important steps for implementing an outsourcing program: process analysis and cost analysis. During the process analysis phase, each function and the procedures which support that function should be weighed according to what will empower the department to run more cost efficiently yet effectively and still meet the goals and objectives of the outsourcing program. In addition to analyzing what functions should be outsourced, the department's current processes should be evaluated for improvements that could help keep them in-house. Processes that are kept in-house can be controlled more firmly by the technical services staff.[22]

One of the most touted benefits of outsourcing is cost savings. Therefore a cost study must document the actual savings the library will derive from the outsourcing project. One method used by many libraries measures the time-on-task for each process. This can be combined with the analysis of personnel costs, including salary and fringe benefits, of the specific staff members who perform the process. Hirshon and Winters find fault with the time-on-task method because of its inefficiency. In their opinion, this method does not allow for time spent on other job-related endeavors such as meetings or for leave time for sickness and vacation, nor does it take into consideration that people are apt to work more steadily when their performance and time management are being scrutinized. Instead of the time-on-task method, the authors recommend "total output measure," a strategy which examines the library's total budget for an operation, because it lends a "more useful" picture of the overall activity over a longer time span.[23]

Once the process analysis and cost analysis have been completed and drafted into a document detailing the outsourcing plan, it should be distributed to the staff for discussion and feedback. After all of the appropriate information has been compiled and feedback from the library community has been received, a final implementation plan for the outsourcing should be created. As a preliminary step, a Request for Information (RFI) may be sent to vendors to see what products or services they can supply to meet the library's needs. Vendors whose responses more appropriately fit the specific description set forth in the RFI should be sent a Request for Proposal (RFP).[24]

The RFP should clearly and concisely describe what type of outsourcing services and capabilities are being sought by the library. A Request for Proposal has two parts: the boilerplate and the functional specifics. The boilerplate serves as a precise narrative of the requirements of the proposal, while the functional specifics list the library's mandatory requirements for outsourcing.[25] The library should use an in-house staff member with proposal writing experience to write the RFP, or if funds are available from the library's budget or a grant, employ the professional services of a consultant with proposal writing experience.[26]

During either the RFI or RFP stage, vendors should be asked for references from libraries where they are currently conducting outsourcing services. These references should be surveyed for the evaluations and recommendations of the librarian managing the outsourcing program at their institutions. If time permits, the team, committee, or individual charged with implementing the outsourcing plan should arrange a site visit at the vendor's place of business and meet with personnel who handle the outsourcing for the company. Each vendor that responds to the RFP should be invited to make a formal presentation or to meet for pre-bid conferences to discuss its products and services.[27]

After the RFP has been received, the library may prefer one vendor to the other, but the contract may have to undergo a bidding process. Libraries are usually required to submit to the formal bidding process if the contract is over a specified amount. In most cases, bidding can be circumvented if the library can justify that it is contracting from a vendor that is the only company that can supply a unique product or service. To avoid the bidding process, the library usually has to present a case for purchasing the contract from a "sole source vendor."[28]

Once the outsourcing vendor has been selected and the contract has been negotiated, the library should immediately establish a working relationship with the company. The library should request a contact person who will represent the vendor and address any problems or issues that may arise from the implementation of the outsourcing plan. The library may be asked to identify someone from its staff who will be a contact person for the vendor. That person should be well informed about what the library hopes to accomplish with the outsourcing plan and about the vendor's contract.[29]

In many instances, the library does not have to bother with an RFI or RFP to find a vendor for outsourcing, because it has already established a working partnership with a firm or approval order vendor that has a proven track record from years of service. These libraries simply expand their services with that vendor to accommodate their outsourcing requirements. In the cases of the three ARL libraries discussed earlier in this chapter, MSU, OSU, and LSU, all employed Yankee Book Peddler, an approval plan vendor who had established a favorable service record with their libraries. The University of Akron followed this path when it made the decision to outsource its approval plan with Blackwell North America.[30]

Whether or not the vendor is new or familiar to the library, an agreement will have to be reached with the vendor concerning specifications, performance, and costs. At the outset of the outsourcing venture, the staff will have to monitor the vendor vigilantly to make certain that the administration of the agreement complies with the library's written expectations. When service has been established at a mutually satisfactory level of compliance, monitoring can be relaxed but still must be carried out.[31]

Noncompliance with an outsourcing agreement can mean extra time and work on the part of the library staff. For example, if a vendor is supposed to add security strips to the books and a shipment arrives without the strips, the process will have to be done in-house. This will necessitate the library having to purchase the security strips for just such an occasion and further time will be wasted calling the vendor to report the problem. In the case of PromptCat, if a book arrives with the wrong catalog record matched to it, the in-house staff has to correct the database by deleting the error record, identifying the correct record, and linking it to the book.[32]

Because the library has relinquished control over a process does not mean it is absolved of responsibility for the quality of the end product. Shelf-ready processing does not deliver shelf-ready books 100 percent of the time; therefore a smaller staff is needed in the technical services department for maintaining quality assurance. Keeping the communication lines open between the vendor and the library should always be a paramount priority for the library and the vendor; otherwise rancor, resentment, and frustration with lingering problems can sour the relationship. The outsourcing plan should allocate an adjustment period for resolving unanticipated impediments as well as refining procedures that may not have been well thought out during the planning phases.[33]

OUTSOURCING MODELS

Library planners who are contracting out services should consider "existing outsourcing models" to get ideas as to what is currently being done and whether they can be adapted for their library's outsourcing plan.[34] Outsourcing is a mushrooming trend in academic, special, and public libraries. There are several current examples of various levels of outsourcing programs in different types of libraries.

Academic Libraries: Florida Gulf Coast University Model

In the fall of 1997, Florida Gulf Coast University (FGCU) opened its doors as the state's tenth university, and its library featured a new outsourcing model. A library jobber, Academic Book Center, and OCLC signed a two-year contract to provide the library with a fully cataloged shelf-ready opening-day collection. They would continue to service the library with collection development, acquisitions, cataloging, authority control, physical processing, and funding accounting, which would in effect virtually outsource the library's technical services functions.[35]

OCLC offered Florida Gulf Coast University an array of outsourcing opportunities. Not only did it provide PromptCat to support shelf-readiness of books, but also OCLC Retrocon, which converts catalog cards to machine-readable format and TechPro, a product that aids libraries with "short- or long-term" offsite catalogs with physical processing projects. TechPro is useful for libraries that want to access cataloging expertise but lack the desire to add a professional cataloger to their staff. For example, a library might have a large video or record collection that needs to be classified, or it might need help converting its Dewey classification holdings to Library of Congress classification.[36]

Florida Gulf Coast University Library unveiled a redesigned role for a technical services professional. It advertised for a "Technical Services Team Leader" who would supervise both acquisitions and cataloging. The librarian who filled the position would oversee the approval plan and perform database management of the bibliographic records. This job description defined a role that combined acquisitions and cataloging experience, an emerging hybrid of two once distinct technical services positions. As outsourcing continues to expand, an increasing number of this type of job advertisement is appearing in employment sections of periodicals and library Web sites.[37]

Academic Libraries: The University of Alberta Model

By 1995, the University of Alberta Library, a major research institution in Canada, had suffered a critical 15 percent reduction in its
budget. The Chief Librarian, Ernie Ingles, and his staff worked together to devise a viable plan that would keep costs down but not
diminish the quality of the library's services and collection. From
the outset, it was made clear that retaining the current staff positions would be a high priority.

The library designated a Cataloging Outsourcing Advisory
Team, consisting of seven members, to devise a strategy that
would meet the library's goals of reducing costs while enhancing
service and freezing staffing levels.[38] The library decided to outsource as much of its technical services operations as possible.
This included acquisitions, cataloging, and physical processing of
library materials. The library became involved in extensive blanket order plans or what are called in Canada "Dealer Selection
Operations (DSOs)." The cataloging of library materials was outsourced to ISM Library Information Service, which devised a new
program, MARCAdvantage, to handle the library's business.

The University of Alberta Library reduced its technical services
operational expenditures with the help of the staff, who realized
the dire straits the library was in. It invested in retraining programs for the staff and was able to successfully convert an aston-
ishing forty positions into public service jobs. By constantly keeping
the staff informed about the progress of the outsourcing program,
making good on its commitment not to eliminate staff, and providing training to support employee retention, the University of Alberta
Library reaped staff support and cooperation.[39]

Public Libraries: Riverside County
Public Library System Model

The Riverside County Public Library System in California, consisting of twenty-five branches, was outsourced to a private vendor as
of July 1, 1997. The firm, Library Systems and Services (LSSI), is
based in Maryland. It is the first time in library history that a public library is being managed by a private vendor. The county's one-
year contract states that Riverside County retains ownership of the
system and maintains control over acquisitions. Another contract
condition provides that LSSI would render job offers to the library
system's employees that would allow them to keep their current
"salaries, seniority, and vacation levels." In turn, LSSI demanded

that the branches increase their open hours by 25 percent. The Follett Corporation, known for its college bookstore chains, owns 50 percent of LSSI.[40]

Public Libraries: The Hawaii Model

In June 1996, the Hawaii State Public Library System (HSPLS) announced that it had outsourced the entire book budget for its 49 branches to Baker & Taylor Books, a well-known and heavily used vendor for bookstores as well as school, public, and academic libraries. The company signed a five-year contract to perform acquisitions, collection development, cataloging, and physical processing for books, audio, video, and multimedia for the statewide library system. Since the books were supposed to arrive completely shelf-ready, the centralized technical services department was dissolved and the entire staff was reassigned to other positions in the library system. HSPLS also announced that the Information Access Company (IAC) would handle serials subscriptions. Regional branches had to reduce their periodical subscriptions to 100 titles and smaller branches were required to cut their paper subscriptions to 50 titles. Ameritech was designated as the automation vendor, replacing Data Research Associated (DRA).[41]

State Librarian Bart Kane issued a statement announcing that the total outsourcing of the technical services operation was the library's response to a 25 percent budget cut in the library system's budget mandated by the governor of Hawaii. In an HSPLS Web site message to the employees, Kane stated: "During a period of radical change, there is a natural tendency to maintain the status quo. Given the size of our budget cuts, the status quo would have meant shredding the book budget almost to nothing and closing some of the 49 public libraries (as many as 15 out of 49) and laying off employees. This prospect was intolerable to me."[42]

The basic stipulations of the HSPLS contract with Baker & Taylor were: (a) the jobber would supply 60,000 units of library materials for 1.2 million dollars to the public libraries of Hawaii during the first year of the contract, (b) that the charge for each book would be $20.94 regardless of its list price, and (c) no returns were allowed.[43]

From the beginning the contract was opposed by the Hawaii State Public Library System professional librarians and other employees. HSPLS librarians protested the privatization of collection development and aggressively advocated that the local librarians should have responsibility for collection development, because they were in constant contact with the collection and library patrons. Their skepticism and opposition to the total outsourcing of the technical services department were further exacerbated by a number of problems that arose at the outset of the implementation of the Baker & Taylor contract. The HSPLS librarians protested that some of the materials their branch libraries received were of poor quality and inappropriate content. They also documented that the library was receiving an excessive number of duplicates.[44]

The contract itself was revealed to have significant structural flaws. Standing orders were only allocated 3 percent of the budget, but librarian Sarah Preble noted in an October 19, 1996, presentation to the Hawaii State Public Library Association meeting that the administration's own budget data demonstrated that HSPLS allocated 14 percent to 31 percent of its budget to standing orders during the years between 1993 and 1995. She also faulted the contract for lacking a strong mechanism for evaluation and enforcement.[45]

In an open letter to the same conference, librarian Pat Matsumoto pointed out wording in the contract addendum pertaining to enforcement and evaluation of Baker & Taylor's performance: "The state acknowledges and agrees that the Performance Targets set forth in Exhibit B attached hereto and made a part hereof are target goals only and contract's failure to achieve any or all of them will not constitute an Event of Default." Matsumoto contended that the contract did not ensure that Baker & Taylor would deliver a balanced range of materials, because Baker & Taylor was not required to keep statistics for the subject fields delivered to the HSPLS libraries.[46] Noting that the planning and implementation of the outsourcing plan had taken place with very little staff participation, Matsumoto's letter introduced the fact that the staff had not been informed of the names of the people who wrote the RFP and the contract. She also inquired why Baker & Taylor was the only vendor to be interviewed by the staff when it was known that three vendors responded to the RFP.[47]

The administration of the outsourcing contract was hampered by shortsightedness. The library system continued to accept monographic gifts from the community after it had terminated the technical services department. The librarians had access to funds raised by their Friends of the Library organization and funds from a project with the Hawaii Electric Company to purchase books. In addition, the governor released $100,000 for the HSPLS librarians to spend on material selection. Since the catalogers were assigned to full-time public service responsibilities, nobody was designated to process new purchases or gifts and get them on the shelves for patron usage. The catalogers who volunteered to help with the problem were compelled to do so on the time available among their other reassigned duties. To address collection development, a Selection Advisory Committee was convened after the contract was signed and complaints were aired about the caliber of books received from Baker & Taylor.[48]

The HSPLS librarians and staff were supported by public library patrons who wrote letters to the local newspapers voicing their disagreement with the outsourcing contract. Critics emphasized that Baker & Taylor was a "mainland company" and that the library received a sparse number of books on Hawaii history and culture ("Hawaiiana").[49]

In its defense, Baker & Taylor offered a few points of clarification. The company explained that the outsourcing contract was signed on March 28, 1996, and the library's book budget had to be encumbered by the end of the fiscal year in June 1996 or it would lose the funds. This gave Baker & Taylor merely two months to order and deliver 60,000 shelf-ready units to HSPLS at a time when some of the branch profiles were incomplete or had not been sent to the company. The administration instructed the company to begin ordering without the profiles. CARL Corporation had gone to court to contest the manner in which Ameritech was selected to be the HSPLS automation vendor, and the change in automation systems had inhibited Baker & Taylor's ability to access the library's online system to check for duplicates until July 1996. The company insisted that shipments of unnecessary duplicates had stopped after December 1996. In a letter to the Hawaii Board of Education, which oversees the library system, Baker & Taylor presented an "action plan" that included sending a "Profile Update Team" to the HSPLS branches and announced that it had entered into a partnership with a Hawaii-based book company, which would supply HSPLS with Hawaiiana. Baker & Taylor strongly recommended that "HSPLS resurrect and enhance its internal communication process" and suggested "that the outsourcing program would greatly benefit from: (1) staff inclusion, and (2) consideration of branch library requirements and concerns."[50]

The HSPLS employees, along with their supporters and their union, mounted a well-organized and effective campaign to cancel the outsourcing contract. They testified about the negative aspects of the Baker & Taylor contract and the privatization of library jobs before the Hawaii Board of Education, which oversees the library system. They succeeded in getting the legislature to pass Senate

Bill 538, which required that the Board of Education "ensure formal involvement of the state's public service librarians in the selection of books and other materials." The bill was signed into effect by the governor on June 19, 1997, and made effective July 1, 1997. In addition, the Hawaii Government Employees Association, AF-SCME Local 152, AFL-CIO, filed a class action suit on behalf of the library employees against Bart Kane, the Hawaii Board of Education, and Baker & Taylor. In the civil suit the defendants declared that "government could not privatize nor contract our civil service jobs."[51]

Notified by the Board of Education that his job was hanging in the balance, State Librarian Bart Kane announced in a news release issued July 11, 1997, that he was terminating the outsourcing contract with Baker & Taylor. He cited nine areas of default and allowed the company just ten days to correct the alleged errors. Baker & Taylor subsequently admitted defaulting on providing 60,000 units to the library system for each year that the contract was in force, but said that the blame for the failure of the outsourcing contract should be shared by both parties.[52]

A review of the *ACQNET* postings on the subject and other documentation found on the HSPLS Web site reveals that the outsourcing effort led by State Librarian Bart Lane floundered for many reasons. However, three stand out among the others: (a) the state librarian's lack of communication with his staff, (b) decisions made in haste to get the outsourcing plan quickly under way, and (c) poor planning. Pat Matsumoto's "Open Letter" reflected a consensus of hostility and resentment among the library's staff, associated with not being included in the process at the beginning of the outsourcing program. There is clear indication that information was deliberately withheld from the librarians. Although there were competitive bids, the vendors appear to have been selected with very little information disseminated to the library branches, and the staff was seemingly at a loss as to why certain vendors were selected.

Instead of phasing in the outsourcing program and working with familiar vendors, the administration forced the staff to deal with both a new automation vendor and a new serials delivery system, and to relinquish control of their collection, all at the same time. The serials vendor became a source of aggravation for the patrons as well as the librarians, because of decreased versatility of computer access to journal articles. The effects of having to deal with too many changes within a relatively short time span, with insufficient planning and poor internal communication, spelled doom for the Hawaii outsourcing model.

The controversy over the Hawaii outsourcing model also ignited a firestorm among librarians concerned about the role the American Library Association should play when librarians' jobs are threatened by outsourcing or privatization. Some of the Hawaii librarians appealed to ALA to speak out against the privatizing of librarian jobs. The matter eventually reached the Association for Library Collections and Technical Services (ALCTS), which represents acquisitions, cataloging, and collection development librarians whose jobs are the most likely to be outsourced. ALCTS leadership contended the Hawaii outsourcing issue was a local management problem in which ALCTS should not get involved.[53]

Public Libraries: Chicago Model

The Chicago Public Library announced in an issue of *Library Journal* that it had signed a two-year acquisitions "service contract" worth seven million dollars with Ingram Library Service. The company will order, catalog, physically process, and link title records to Chicago's automation system, providing shelf-ready books. This model differs from the Hawaii outsourcing model because Chicago Public retains control over collection development. The collection development librarians can make selections from lists supplied by the vendor.[54]

CONCLUSION

Outsourcing is gradually changing the library profession on all fronts. Automation, serials, book cataloging, and vendor initiatives that lend themselves to outsourcing have all had a significant effect on the way technical services librarians are managing their departments. The new way of processing and managing demands adaptation to changing workloads and work assignments.

The approval plan and automation replace title-by-title ordering and batching orders by vendor or publisher, which frees acquisitions librarians from the time-consuming procedures associated with order processing and collection development work. Vendors' outsourcing capabilities and automation systems, which handle ordering, processing, fund accounting, and management reports, have had a startling effect on acquisition department responsibilities. In addition to monitoring approval plans for compliance, today's acquisition librarian needs to be aware of the basic rudiments concerning licensing agreements, resource sharing, and outsourcing planning. As professionals, acquisitions librarians must cultivate an awareness of new skills that are needed for technical services professionals. If their job changes, they must be ready and willing to adapt to meet the challenges presented by an electronic environment and changed organizational structures.

Acquisitions itself is no longer perceived as a full-time position in many libraries. Job advertisements usually reflect a combination of responsibilities, such as acquisitions/collection management librarian, acquisitions/preservation librarian, acquisitions/serials librarian, and acquisitions/circulation librarian. A new position, technical services librarian, which combines the job skills of acquisitions and cataloging, is increasingly being advertised in job markets. This appears to augur that acquisitions is losing ground as an autonomous technical services specialty. As libraries move toward the twenty-first century, outsourcing library functions and privatizing jobs will become more of a norm than an exception.

Notes

1. Brian Boland, "The Benefits of Outsourcing," *The Freeman,* January 1997, p. 39.

2. Gary Shirk, "Outsourcing Library Technical Services: The Bookseller's Perspective," *Library Acquisitions: Practice & Theory* 18, no. 4 (1994): 387. Sever Bordeianu and Claire Lise Bernaud, "Outsourcing in American Libraries: An Overview," *Against the Grain* 9 (1997): 16.

3. Kevin Miles, "Outsourcing in Private Law Libraries since the Baker & MacKenzie Action," *Bottom Line: Managing Library Finances* 9, no. 2 (1996): 10.

4. Arnold Hirshon and Barbara Winters, *Outsourcing Library Services: A How-to-Do-It-Manual* (New York: Neal Schuman, 1996): pp. 23-24.

5. Joyce Ogburn, "An Introduction to Outsourcing Library Acquisitions," *Library Acquisitions: Practice & Theory* 18, no. 4 (1994): 64.

6. Jack Montgomery, "Outsourced Acquisitions—Let's Meet the Challenge," *Against the Grain* 7, no. 2 (1995): 66-68.

7. William Fisher, "Libraries Are Businesses," *Library Acquisitions: Practice & Theory* 21, no. 2 (1997): 151-155.

8. Roy B. Conant, "Libraries Are Businesses: Not! A Citizen's Response," *Library Acquisitions: Practice & Theory* 21, no. 2 (1997): 158-159.

9. Shirk, "Outsourcing," p. 388.

10. Carmel C. Bush, Margo Sasse and Patricia Smith, "Survey of Book Jobbers; Capabilities for Outsourcing Acquisitions, Cataloging, and Collection Development," *Library Acquisitions: Practice & Theory* 18 no. 4 (1994): 400.

11. R. Charles Wittenberg, "Re-engineering and the Approval Plan: New Process or New Perspective?" *The Acquisitions Librarian* 16 (1997): 65-67; Bush, Sasse and Smith, "Survey," p. 400.

12. Bush, Sasse and Smith, "Survey," pp. 404-405.

13. Douglas Duchin, "Looks Like the Ball Is in Our Court—Library Support Services for Vendors," *Journal of Library Administration* 10, no. 1 (1989): 73; Bush, Sasse and Smith, "Survey," pp. 404-405.

14. Wittenberg, "Re-engineering," pp. 64-65; Bush, Sasse and Smith, "Survey," pp. 401-402.

15. Colleen F. Hyslop, "Using PromptCat to Eliminate Work: MSU's Experience," *Library Acquisitions: Practice & Theory* 19, no. 3 (1995): 359-361.

16. Mary M. Rider and Marsha Hamilton, "PromptCat Issues for Acquisitions Quality Review, Cost Analysis, and Workflow Implications," *Library Acquisitions: Practice & Theory* 20, no. 1 (1996): 21.

17. Michael Somers, "Causes and Effects: Shelf Ready Processing, PromptCat, and Louisiana State University," *Library Acquisitions: Practice & Theory* 21 (1997): 227.

18. Duchin, "Looks Like," pp. 71-72.

19. Lisa German, "In or Out—In-house Innovation and Outsourcing Technical Services for the 90's: A Report of an ALCTS Program," *Library Acquisitions: Practice & Theory* 20, no. 1 (1996): 21; Karen A. Wilson, "Planning and Implementing an Outsourcing Program," online. Internet. Available URL: http://www.ala.org/alcts/now/outsourcing4.html.

20. Wilson, "Planning," p. 1.

21. Jennifer Cargill, "When Purchasing Commercially Available Technical Services Makes Sense," *Technicalities* 4, no. 2 (1994): 7; Linda F. Crismond, "Outsourcing from the A/V Vendor's Viewpoint: The Dynamics of a New Relationship," *Library Acquisitions: Practice & Theory* 18, no. 4 (1994): 381.

22. Wilson, "Planning," p. 5; Hirshon and Winters, "Outsourcing," p. 23.

23. Hirshon and Winters, "Outsourcing," p. 32.

24. Wilson, "Planning," pp. 4–5.

25. Hirshon and Winters, "Outsourcing," p. 50.

26. Wilson, "Planning," pp. 1–2

27. Hirshon and Winters, "Outsourcing," p. 55; Wilson, "Planning," p. 3.

28. Hirshon and Winters, "Outsourcing," p. 51.

29. Wilson, "Planning," p. 5.

30. Julie Gammon, "Partnering with a Vendor for Increased Productivity in Technical Services or Bleeding Edge Technology," *Library*

Acquisitions: Practice & Theory 21 (1997): 229; Rider and Hamilton, "PromptCat," 10; Somers, "Causes and Effects," 225; Hyslop, "Using PromptCat," p. 360.

31. Wilson, "Planning," p. 5.

32. Somers, "Causes and Effects," p. 228.

33. Wilson, "Planning," p. 7.

34. Wilson, "Planning," p. 3.

35. Nita Dean, "OCLC, Academic Book Center, Solinet to Provide Automated Collection and Technical Services to New Florida University," online. Internet. 16 January 1997. Available URL: http://listserv.appstate.edu.acqnet/acqflash/287.

36. Ibid., pp. 1-2.

37. Cleta Alix, "Position Announcement, Florida Gulf Coast University, Faculty Librarian, Technical Services Team Leader," online. Internet. Available URL: http://listserv.appastate.edu/acqnet/acflash/131.

38. Murray S. Martin and Ernie Ingles, "Outsourcing in Alberta," *The Bottom Line: Managing Library Finances* 8, no. 2 (1995): 32.

39. Merrill Distad and Brian Hobbs, "The Client Ranks First in U. Alberta Library's Restructuring," *Library Acquisitions: Practice & Theory* 19, no. 4 (1995): 436-437; Martin and Ingles, "Outsourcing," pp. 33-34.

40. Jon Kartman, "Riverside County Outsources Library—Again," *American Libraries* (August 1997):19.

41. Paul H. Mark, "HSPLS Signs Three Contracts," online. Internet. 20 June 1996. Available URL: http://www.hcc.hawaii.edu/hspls. pr960620.html.

42. Barthlomew Kane, "Why Re-engineer," online. Internet. 9 November 1995. Available URL: http://www.hcc.hawaii.edu/hspls/why.html.

43. Eleanor Cook, "Summary of the Hawaii Public Library Outsourcing Contract with Baker & Taylor," *ACQNET* 7, no. 2 (1997): 1.

44. Stephanie Strickland, "Hawaii Librarian Appeals for ALA Support," *ACQNET* 7, no. 2 (1997): 3.

45. Sarah Preble, "HSPLS and Outsourcing," online. Internet. 19 October 1996. Available URL: http:www.hcc.hawaii.edu/hspls/preble.html.

46. Pat Matsumoto, "Press Conference on B&T Outsourcing Contract and Subsequent Statements: An Open Letter to Bart Kane," online. Internet. 3 October 1996. Available URL: http://www.hcc.hawaii.edu/ hspls /pmatsumoto.html.

47. Ibid.

48. Strickland, "Hawaii," p. 4; Cook, "Summary," p. 1.

49. Holly J. Huber, "Why Is a Mainland Company Choosing Library Books?" Letter, *Honolulu Star-Bulletin,* 12 September 1996, A15.

50. Kimberley Walker, "Baker & Taylor Responds to February 21 *Star Bulletin* Poll," *ACQNET* 7, no. 11 (1997): 1-2.

51. Pat Wallace, "Hawaii Outsourcing Update," *ACQNET* 7, no. 23 (1997): 1-3.

52. Pat Wallace, "Hawaii Contract with Baker & Taylor Terminated," *ACQNET* 7, no. 26 (1997): 1-2; George Herbert Elliott, "Hawaii Terminates Outsourcing Contract," *American Libraries* (August 1997): 18.

53. Sheila Intner, "Hawaii Outsourcing: Some Answers," *ACQNET* 7, no. 32 (1997): 1-2; Pat Wallace, "Response to Intner, Chamberlain, & Bloss," *ACQNET* 7, no. 33 (1997): 12.

54. Evan St. Lifer, "Chicago PL, Ingram in $7 Million Deal," *Library Journal* (March 1997): 15.

15

Basic Acquisitions Accounting and Business Practice

KAY GRANSKOG

An understanding of basic accounting theory and business practice on the part of acquisitions librarians is essential for the effective management of any acquisitions department. Yet, the business and accounting aspects of acquisitions work in libraries are often neglected in graduate library education. As a result, some librarians come to acquisitions work unprepared for the nuts-and-bolts of monitoring and expending a materials budget and working with vendors. This chapter provides a guide to acquisitions accounting and business practice by defining general accounting concepts and examining specific operations and records necessary for tracking expenditures for books, serials, and non-print library materials. It also examines the audit trail and the need for financial control of the acquisitions work flow. Other accounting concerns for libraries such as plant, salary, and equipment costs and expenditures are beyond the scope of this chapter.

Accounting operations, like size of materials budgets, vary widely among libraries. Depending on the accounting method used, libraries may have different year-end requirements. Many libraries have automated their accounting operations while others still use manual systems. The role of the acquisitions department in accounting operations also varies widely. Some acquisitions departments are authorized to order and issue payment for purchases. Others issue purchase orders and approve invoices while payment is initiated by the library's business office. For example, one library department may initiate purchases and approve invoices after ver-

---

This is a revision of chapters on the same topics written by Betsy Kruger and William Schenck for the first edition of this book.

ifying receipt, and another department may prepare vouchers which are forwarded to various accounting departments. Some libraries funnel all aspects of purchasing, starting with the issuance of purchase orders, through the central business office of a parent organization, and librarians have little autonomy in managing their fiscal affairs.

Despite these myriad differences, acquisitions accounting in *all* libraries is concerned with four basic questions: how much money is there to spend? (allocation); how much will a purchase probably cost? (encumbrance); how much is actually spent? (payment); and, how much money is left? (free balance). Good acquisitions accounting practices that carefully address these questions prevent overspending or underspending, aid in financial decision making and budget planning, and result in clear audit trails and good library-vendor relations.

THE IMPORTANCE OF FISCAL ACCOUNTABILITY

As nonprofit (or not-for-profit) organizations, libraries emphasize service rather than generating income. Nonprofit status does not, however, diminish or eliminate the necessity for fiscal accountability and responsible use of money. All libraries are obligated to obtain their money through legitimate means, to negotiate with publishers and vendors for the best price possible, to expend their money appropriately, and to document revenues and expenditures for the organizational entities that fund them. Public libraries are accountable to local governments, academic libraries to their parent institutions, and corporate libraries to their parent corporations. In turn, the funding body usually is accountable to state and federal governments. Any library that receives federal assistance or grants must account to the federal government directly for the expenditure of that money. Spending money appropriately means spending it for the purpose for which it was budgeted. Most libraries cannot use money allocated for books to replace a broken photocopying machine or pay an unexpectedly high utility bill. It is a primary responsibility of an acquisitions librarian to ensure that the library and those who fund the library receive the best return possible. This will not always mean accepting the lowest price. While conserving the materials budget is important, the effect of the purchase decision on other staff work flows should be considered.

Maintaining accurate accounting records makes it easier to monitor expenditures throughout the year, so that overspending and underspending are avoided. Overspending a materials budget is both sloppy financial management and illegal. Failing to keep track of outstanding purchase orders gives an inaccurate picture of the amount of money still available for purchasing materials and would no doubt result in a library being unable to meet its financial obligations to its vendors. Underspending budgeted funds is also risky. It may suggest to the funding entity that the library did not prepare its budget in an informed manner and may result in funding cuts the following fiscal year.

It is always important for a library to keep its own internal accounting records, even if all its purchasing is handled through the central purchasing and accounting departments of a parent organization. The primary purpose of an accounting system is to provide timely and accurate information on the status of the total allocation, encumbrances, and items received and paid for, then to provide appropriate documentation of those transactions. Even a simple ledger book for posting encumbrances and payments can help provide a clearer picture of current financial status than the less timely and often less specific reports of a large central accounting division.

Good accounting practices result in accurate financial data that form the basis for budgetary planning. A flexible accounting system can provide current and retrospective cost information that can aid in projecting future costs for various types of library materials and for materials in various subject areas. The first part of this chapter will describe and explain accounting practices that meet these needs.

Every library should be prepared for a financial audit—a systematic inspection of its financial records to confirm that accepted accounting principles are being used to track income and expenditures. Audits may be initiated by external regulatory agencies, by the central accounting office of a parent organization, or internally by the library itself to assure that the money it is responsible for is being spent appropriately. Good accounting practices include maintaining a clear audit trail, that is, a sequence of postings in an accounting system that are tied to original documents such as purchase orders, invoices, statements, and vouchers. An audit trail provides a clear picture of all financial transactions for a given purchase from the initial issuance of a purchase order through final payment. The latter part of this chapter will explore the audit process and how to prepare for it.

Finally, a library owes prompt and accurate payment to those vendors who, in good faith, ship materials promptly and in good condition prior to receiving payment. Vendors depend on a positive cash flow to maintain daily operations and may need to borrow money at high interest rates if customers do not pay their bills in a timely manner. Prompt and accurate payment makes for good library-vendor relations. The goodwill that accrues in such a relationship pays off in higher levels of service and a willingness on the part of the vendor to assist the library should special needs arise.

SOME BASIC CONCEPTS OF FUND ACCOUNTING

A library's operation fund is money used for day-to-day operations. The materials budget is derived from this fund, and money is specifically earmarked for the purchase of books, serials, and various non-print library materials.

While a very small library may maintain a single fund from which all materials are purchased, most libraries allocate money from the materials budget into a series of funds which may correspond to departments within the library, format of material, or subject. A public library may establish separate materials funds for the reference room, children's department, and branch libraries. If a library divides its materials budget by format, it may establish separate funds for monographs, serials, and non-print materials. Serial funds may be subdivided into periodical and continuation or standing order funds. While a small public library may have only one or two funds, a large academic or research library may establish several hundred funds based on a combination of subject and format considerations. Libraries that collect core materials through one or more approval plans (for example, publisher based, subject based, university press, or European blanket orders) may have separate approval plan funds in addition to subject area and format funds. Many libraries also establish a general fund from which replacements for lost or stolen monographs and serials are purchased.

An accounting system based on a collection of separate funds is known as a fund accounting system. Several accounts are maintained to track expenditures on each fund; these accounts include the allocation account, the encumbrance account, the payment account, and the free balance account. The accounts cumulate increases and decreases during the fiscal year. Bookkeeping involves careful analysis and recording of each transaction involving these accounts and requires access to financial information contained in purchase orders, invoices, statements, vouchers, credit memos, and all other fiscal documents related to a particular transaction.

Library accounting systems are based on the relationship between the money allocated in a particular fund and the expenditure of that money. This relationship is reflected in the classic bookkeeping equation:

$$\text{assets} = \text{liabilities} + \text{fund balance}$$

As the equal sign implies, the dollar amount of the assets must equal the sum of the dollar amounts of liabilities plus the fund balance for the equation to balance. Any change (additions or subtraction) in assets must be counterbalanced by an equivalent change in liabilities or the fund balance, or both.

In a library, the money allocated to a particular fund is an asset because it provides the future means of purchasing materials or reducing the amount owed to a vendor. Liabilities are claims to a library's assets, such as money earmarked, or encumbered, for a particular purchase or cash paid out to reconcile a debt. A fund balance is the difference between assets and liabilities. It represents free or unencumbered money still available to make future purchases of library materials.

For library materials funds, the bookkeeping equation is interpreted as follows:

$$\text{assets} = \text{liabilities} + \text{fund balance}$$
$$\text{fund allocation} = \text{encumbrances} + \text{payments} + \text{unencumbered balance}$$

Encumbrances are funds restricted for anticipated expenditures such as outstanding purchase orders. Even though a purchase order will not be paid until the library receives an invoice and the receipt of materials has been verified (except when prepayment is required), encumbrances are considered liabilities because the money has been committed and must be held in reserve until payment is made.

A fund's allocation account will probably remain fairly stable throughout the year. Most of the activity involving a fund will occur on the right (liability) side of the equation, resulting in increases and decreases in the encumbrance, payment, and unencumbered balance accounts where cost information from purchase orders, invoices, and other documents is entered.

Basic Acquisitions Accounting and Business Practice

Many libraries carry over encumbrances from one fiscal year to the next. For the sake of simplicity, let us assume that the Community Library combines outstanding encumbrances into one carry-over account that is used to pay for items ordered during the previous fiscal year. At the beginning of the new fiscal year, the current year fund will receive a new allocation. Before any funds have been encumbered or payments have been made, the fund allocation will equal the unencumbered balance:

fund allocation = encumbrances + payments + unencumbered
balance
= $0.00 + $0.00 + $15,000.00

Throughout the year, as encumbrances and payments are posted, the unencumbered balance will decrease proportionately, so that the amount in the allocation account always equals the sum of the three accounts on the right side of the equation:

fund allocation = encumbrances + payments + unencumbered
balance
= $3,000.00 + $8,000.00 + $4,000.00

If all the year's orders have been received and paid for by the last day of the fiscal year (again, an unlikely scenario in many libraries), the fund accounts would look like this:

fund allocation = encumbrances + payments + unencumbered
balance
= $0.00 + $15,000.00 + $0.00

A *T account* (shown in table 15-1) is a useful accounting form for visualizing the effects of various bookkeeping transactions which, whether performed manually or by a computer, affect a fund's accounts in the same manner. This form is shaped like the letter "T," with the name of the account noted above the horizontal line and increases or decreases to the account posted on the appropriate side of the vertical line.[1] T accounts correspond to the columns for recording increases and decreases on a ledger sheet in a manual bookkeeping system. In a computerized system, a T account may correspond to a group of similarly coded items on a disk or in a database. The accounts in the library bookkeeping equation can be illustrated by T accounts (table 15-1).

Kay Granskog

Table 15-1 Library Bookkeeping Equation Illustrated by T Accounts

Allocation		=	Encumbrances		+	Payments		+	Unencumbered Balance	
(dr)	(cr)		(dr)	(cr)		(dr)	(cr)		(dr)	(cr)

Balance

The abbreviations *dr* and *cr* stand for debit and credit. Debiting and crediting are methods of recording transactions in an equation. These terms can be confusing because of their association in popular speech. *Debit* connotes negative and subtraction; *credit* connotes positive and addition. These meanings of the terms must be disregarded in accounting practice; instead, substitute in one's mind the terms *left* and *right*. *Debit* is a traditional accounting term meaning simply to record on the left side; *credit* traditionally means to record on the right side.

Debits and credits affect assets and liabilities differently. Debits increase assets and decrease liabilities. Credits decrease assets and increase liabilities. They affect the accounts in a library materials fund as shown in table 15-2.

T accounts are referred to throughout this chapter to illustrate how typical transactions involved in purchasing library materials affect the asset and liability accounts described and how transactions are recorded either manually or by a computer so that the accounts balance. These transactions include allocating money to a fund, encumbering funds to cover the expected cost of a purchase, posting payments for an invoice, and adjusting for differences between the amount encumbered and the amount actually paid.

Table 15-2 Effects of Debits and Credits on Library Materials Accounts

	Fund Allocation	Encumbrances	Payments	Unencumbered Balance
Debit (entry on left)	Increase	Decrease	Decrease	Decrease
Credit (entry on right)	Decrease	Increase	Increase	Increase

FUND ALLOCATIONS:
HOW MUCH IS THERE TO SPEND?

Establishing various funds for materials purchases enables a library to distribute available money equitably among different library units or subject areas. Among the many factors that may form the basis for allocation decisions are the average cost of monographs and serials in a subject area (for example, science versus humanities journals); the makeup and size of the population served (for example, the number of children versus adults in the community, or the number of undergraduate, graduate, and faculty members in a particular academic discipline); historic patterns of spending; the growth of new research areas; and fluctuations in publishing patterns. Dividing the materials budget into various funds aids in monitoring expenditures and coordinating collection development. An acquisitions librarian's role in budget allocation varies from library to library, but this person most certainly will be called upon to provide actual cost figures and projections of future costs garnered from a knowledge of the publishing industry and familiarity with the library's arrangements with its various vendors.

At the beginning of the fiscal year, the amount allocated to each fund must be entered into the accounting system. Using T accounts, one can visualize the effect of this transaction. At the beginning of its fiscal year, the Community Library allocated $2,500 for its local history monographs fund (table 15-3). Encumbrances from the previous year have been rolled over into a centralized carry-over fund.

As noted earlier, debits increase assets and credits increase liabilities. Since the fund allocation (an asset account) has not been spent, the $2,500 is recorded as a debit and the balance of the account increases to $2,500. Any change in an account on the left side of the bookkeeping equation must be counterbalanced by an equivalent change to the account on the right side. The $2,500 debit to

Table 15-3 Allocating Money into a Fund

	Allocation		=	Encumbrances		+	Payments		+	Unencumbered Balance	
	(dr)	(cr)		(dr)	(cr)		(dr)	(cr)		(dr)	(cr)
Allocation	$2,500										$2,500
Balance	$2,500										$2,500

the allocation account is money available to be spent. Therefore, $2,500 is credited to the unencumbered balance account resulting in a balance of $2,500. In this double-entry transaction, a debit on the left is balanced by a credit on the right.

After the original allocation posting at the beginning of the fiscal year, most activity in a fund occurs on the left (debit) side of the ledger as funds are encumbered, invoices are paid, and adjustments are made. However, if the allocation is increased or decreased at any time during the fiscal year, this change will have to be counterbalanced by a credit or debit to the unencumbered balance. If the allocation is increased, the unencumbered balance also increases. If the allocation is decreased, the unencumbered balance also decreases.

ENCUMBERING FUNDS AND ISSUING PURCHASE ORDERS: HOW MUCH WILL IT PROBABLY COST?

The purchase of library materials poses some unique accounting problems that are not encountered with certain other expenses a library faces. Unlike predictable, regular expenses such as utility bills and payroll, the purchase of books and other library materials involves some uncertainty. Within the library's control, workflow considerations and personnel fluctuations, such as unexpected changes in equipment or staff members on unplanned medical leaves, can affect the flow of orders. Orders may not be sent to Acquisitions for processing on a regular basis or the quantity of orders sent may be too great for timely processing. Outside the library's control, the exact cost may be unknown at the time a purchase order is issued since discount, additional charges, and shipping fees are usually not known until the invoice arrives. The library also does not know when the vendor will actually deliver the item. The book may be out of stock or not yet published at the time it is ordered. If the book is out-of-print, the vendor may cancel the order altogether.

To keep track of how much money is tied up in outstanding orders, it is necessary to encumber funds to cover their estimated costs. The library would not know how much free (that is, available) money it had at any given moment if costs were only entered into the accounting system at the time payment was issued.

A purchase order, generated from the purchase order record, is usually the first document in an audit trail. It serves as a legal contract between a library and a vendor for the purchase of materials that will be paid for at a later date. With its issuance, the library financially obligates itself for the timely payment of delivered goods. By accepting a library's purchase order, the vendor is obligated to the timely delivery of the ordered items in good condition.

The purchase order record is also used internally as an encumbering document. It provides the basic information needed for initially entering the purchase into the library's accounting system. A well-designed purchase order record includes the following types of information:

1. reference information
   a. a purchase order number that ties an accounting entry to a specific purchased item
   b. the fund number/code or fund name, or both, to identify the specific library fund against which the cost of the item is to be charged
   c. the vendor name or vendor number/code, or both (either a standard address number or a number/code assigned by a library)
   d. date the material is ordered and received (The purchase order document sent to the vendor will not have a received date.)
2. financial information
   a. estimated and actual cost information (The estimated cost is the figure used for encumbering purposes and is what appears on the purchase order document. The actual cost can only be recorded once the library has received the material, verified that the material received was the material ordered, and approved the vendor's invoice, or if prepayment has been made.)
3. descriptive information
   a. author or title of the item, or both
   b. publisher's name and address
   c. edition
   d. date of publication
   e. ISBN/ISSN
   f. quantity ordered
4. information for the vendor
   a. library's name and address
   b. specific billing and shipping requirements of the library (Many libraries request that the vendor invoice in triplicate and invoice each shipment separately. Libraries may request multiple billing and shipping addresses.)

5. miscellaneous information for the library
   a. name of the person authorizing the expenditure
   b. specific location or cataloging instructions, or both
   c. free text fields for notes (not included on the purchase order document)

T accounts illustrate how an encumbrance transaction affects the accounts in a fund when a purchase order is issued against it. Suppose the Community Library wishes to order two books, each with a list price of $50. The library issues two $50 purchase orders against its local history monograph fund. The books are not available from the same vendor, so two purchase orders are issued (table 15-4).

Both purchase orders are recorded as encumbrances rather than as payments because the books have been ordered but not yet paid for. Further, they are recorded as a credit to the encumbrance account. Because an encumbrance decreases the amount of money available to be spent, the unencumbered balance must be decreased by $100 ($50 for each purchase order number). A quick arithmetical check confirms that the accounts balance:

Allocation balance	=	Encumbrances balance	+	Payments balance	+	Unencumbered balance
$2,500	=	$100	+	$0	+	$2,400

Monograph purchases are encumbered on a one-time basis. Funds are disencumbered once payment has been made. However, funds for periodicals must be maintained differently. Many libraries re-encumber each time the subscription is renewed. Computerized accounting systems can automatically re-encumber funds for the next year's serial payments. Once the books are closed at the end of a fiscal year, a special code (sometimes called a paytype), which was

Table 15-4 Encumbering a $50 Purchase Order

	Allocation		=	Encumbrances		+	Payments		+	Unencumbered Balance	
	(dr)	(cr)		(dr)	(cr)		(dr)	(cr)		(dr)	(cr)
Allocation	$2,500										$2,500
P.O. 299					$50			$50			
P.O. 300					$50			$50			
Balance	$2,500				$100						$2,400

input at the time the purchase order was first entered into the system, instructs the computer to re-encumber the prior year's expenditure for the new fiscal year. Other libraries choose to renew subscriptions annually without re-encumbering. Those who do not encumber monitor costs by projecting the dollar amount needed to pay renewals on a fund-by-fund basis rather than a title-by-title basis. The funds are specifically created for serial renewal charges. By carefully calculating the allocation for these funds, the need to encumber subscription titles can be eliminated by paying the renewal invoices as they arrive, thus expending the money. It must be noted that although these funds appear in the unencumbered balance account, in practice they are not considered available funds for other purposes.

Serial costs have risen dramatically during the past decade. Often the prior year's expenditure is not an accurate indicator of the amount of money that will be needed at the next renewal. The responsible acquisitions librarian will consider some or all of these factors when deciding either how much to encumber or allocate for periodical orders:

1. inflation rate
2. publisher price increases (due to changes in the size or scope of a journal, paper costs, or postage costs)
3. exchange rates (for items published in a different country)
4. subject matter of the journal (humanities titles may not have the same rate of inflation as a chemistry journal)
5. time of year paid (Some vendors offer a credit discount, or lower or waive the service charge if a portion of the projected renewal total is prepaid. Exchange rates may also differ depending on what rate is in effect at the point of payment.)

Paying for subscriptions annually (rather than multiple years) provides the best chance of projecting accurately. Every year periodicals will be added and canceled, but the majority of the active subscriptions can be used as data to calculate the rate of inflation on a library's subscriptions. When multiple subscription years are paid at the same time, the pool of data is reduced or at least skewed. Many librarians rely on the vendors to provide an inflation rate over all of the periodicals they service. While this is useful, the library's particular mix of subscriptions may be weighted differently than the overall vendor's file. The library may have a heavier concentration of science subscriptions than humanities or more domestic than foreign orders than the average provided by the vendor. It is helpful to know if there is a difference between the inflation rate quoted by the vendor and the results calculated on the library's own subscriptions. On the other hand, vendors sometimes offer better rates for multiyear subscriptions. It will be the responsibility of the acquisitions librarian to present the options and at least assist in deciding if lower overall cost or tighter control is more important to the library.

INVOICES, CREDIT MEMOS, STATEMENTS, AND VOUCHERS: HOW MUCH DID IT ACTUALLY COST?

Vendor and Publisher Invoices

An invoice is a document issued by a vendor or publisher that contains all the financial details of a purchase or transaction. Once an acquisitions department verifies that the material received was the material actually ordered, it can approve and pay the invoice or forward it, after approval, to the appropriate accounting department within the library or parent organization for payment.

It is well worth taking the time to become familiar with the invoice format of the library's larger vendors and publishers. Invoices can provide a wealth of information about both the vendor's business practices and the characteristics of the library account. Any arrangements made for discounts and handling and shipping fees should appear on the invoices. Inform the invoice processing staff of these arrangements so that invoices can be monitored to assure that the vendor is applying the correct discounts and fees.

Vendor invoices may provide the following types of information:

1. reference information
   a. library purchase order number and fund (It is useful to specify on the purchase order that this information should be included on the invoice. Large vendors and publishers with computerized billing systems can easily code the account so that purchase order numbers and funds are printed on the invoice.)
   b. invoice number and date
   c. customer name and number
   d. bill-to and ship-to information
2. vendor information
   a. vendor name, address, telephone and fax numbers, and e-mail address
   b. vendor's federal employee identification number (FEIN), which is assigned by the federal government and is

usually required before a library can issue a check to a vendor.
3. descriptive information
   a. author or title of the item, or both
   b. quantity invoiced
   c. information as to whether the item is coming on a standing order, approval plan, blanket order, or some other arrangement
   d. status reports indicating if an item not supplied is not yet published, out of stock, out-of-print, and so on
4. financial information
   a. list price (the publisher's stated price) and net price (the price charged to the library once discounts have been applied)
   b. the amount or percentage of discount
   c. postage, shipping, and handling charges
   d. total amount owed
   e. terms of payment (Invoices usually state the time limit on the vendor's receipt of payment before late charges begin accruing, for example, 30 days net.)
   f. conditions under which the vendor will accept a return and a returns address, when it differs from the payment address
   g. currency and remit-to requirements
5. shipping information
   a. how shipped (for example, UPS, parcel post)
   b. date shipped

An invoice is often the expending document from which actual cost information is taken and charged against the appropriate library fund. It is also usually the second document in the audit trail for a particular purchase. For these reasons, careful verification of the accuracy of the financial and other information on the invoice is essential.

Although procedures and requirements vary from library to library, invoice approval usually includes the following steps:

1. date stamping the invoice upon receipt of the shipment
2. checking the items listed on the invoice against the material received and the original order record to verify that the items received were actually the items ordered
3. resolving any discrepancies
4. noting the purchase order number and fund by each item listed and checking the net price

5. noting the vendor number (if used) on the invoice
6. approving by initialing and dating

Invoices approved in this manner are properly prepared for entering the payment transaction in either a manual or automated accounting system. The payment record can be tied to the purchase order number that was entered into the system at the time the order was placed and funds were encumbered. When payment is posted, the originally encumbered funds are disencumbered and any adjustments to the free balance that result from additional charges or discounts not known at the time of encumbering are made.

Using T accounts, one can visualize how payment transactions affect a fund's accounts. Suppose the Community Library receives an invoice for the $50 purchase it has encumbered for purchase order 299 against its local history monographs fund. The invoiced amount equals the amount originally encumbered, and the transaction is recorded as shown in table 15-5.

The $50 payment is posted as a credit or increase to the payment account and brings the balance of that account to $50. To balance the account, $50 must be debited to one of the other accounts on the right side of the equation. The payment does not affect the unencumbered balance since this balance was already reduced by the $50 encumbrance posted in the second line. Therefore, the $50 credit to the payment account is counterbalanced by a $50 debit to the encumbrance account. This posting, in effect, disencumbers the $50 originally reserved when the purchase order was issued, since this amount has now actually been paid to the vendor. A quick arithmetical check again confirms that the accounts balance:

Allocation balance	=	Encumbrances balance	+	Payments balance	+	Unencumbered balance
$2,500	=	$50	+	$50	+	$2,400

Table 15-5 Posting a $50 Payment Equal to the Original Encumbrance

	Allocation		=	Encumbrances		+	Payments		+	Unencumbered Balance	
	(dr)	(cr)		(dr)	(cr)		(dr)	(cr)		(dr)	(cr)
Allocation	$2,500										$2,500
P.O. 299					$50					$50	
P.O. 300					$50					$50	
Invoice 114				$50				$50			
Balance	$2,500				$50			$50			$2,400

More often than not, the amount encumbered for a purchase is not the exact amount the library actually pays the vendor. Most libraries encumber the amount of the list price since the discount passed on by the vendor (if any) is not always known at the time the purchase order is issued. At other times, an item may cost more than the original encumbrance. Posting payment in either of these situations affects the balances in all three liability accounts.

The Community Library received a 10 percent discount on the title ordered on purchase order 300 against its local history monograph fund, making the net price $45. The transaction is recorded as shown in table 15-6.

The $45 payment is credited to the payments account. Since the amount was $5 less than that originally encumbered, the $5 difference is credited to the unencumbered balance. The original $50 encumbrance is disencumbered since payment has now been made.

Shipping and Handling Charges

A library may have agreements with some of its vendors (and occasionally with publishers) whereby the vendor pays the cost of shipping. This occurs most commonly with approval plans and continuations. Unless an agreement has been made, the library pays for shipping and may also be asked to pay additional handling or service charges. Vendors make their money, in general, by keeping a portion of the discount they receive from the publisher for themselves. If the publisher does not discount a title to the vendor, which is frequently the case with non-trade presses, the vendor is apt to charge the library a handling fee. Periodical vendors almost always make their profit by assessing a service charge for each subscription they place for the library. These charges are negotiable

Table 15-6 Posting Payment for Less than the Amount Originally Encumbered

	Allocation	=	Encumbrances	+	Payments	+	Unencumbered Balance	
	(dr)	(cr)	(dr)	(cr)	(dr)	(cr)	(dr)	(cr)
Allocation	$2,500							$2,500
P.O. 299				$50			$50	
P.O. 300				$50			$50	
Invoice 114			$50			$50		
Invoice 28b			$50			$45		$5
Balance	$2,500			$0		$95		$2,405

based on the scope and size of the account with the vendor. The responsible acquisitions librarian will monitor charges carefully. However, the cost and time benefits of consolidating subscriptions and other orders with a vendor rather than ordering directly from each publisher are well worth the handling charges incurred. This is especially true when the number of subscriptions is large and the staff is small.

A library can process payment of shipping and handling charges in one of two ways: by paying them from one fund established specifically for this purpose or by charging back these costs to individual funds. In a manual accounting system the former is by far the simplest. In a good automated system, it should be possible to use either method easily. On list invoices, these charges can be prorated so that more expensive items are charged a higher percentage of the shipping fee and less expensive items are charged a lower amount. Less sophisticated systems will at least allow for figuring an allocation by dividing by the number of items on the invoice and charging equal amounts to the funds involved. Some vendors are able to itemize these charges for each item on an invoice or to incorporate the charges in the net price for each item.

Credit Memos and Cancellations

Vendors and publishers may issue credit due a customer in the form of a refund or a credit memo. The form this credit takes frequently depends on the amount of business the library does with the particular vendor. Because a credit memo can only be used to offset all or a portion of an outstanding invoice from the same vendor, a vendor will usually issue credit memos to its regular customers. If a library is requesting credit from a vendor or publisher it uses infrequently, it may want to request a refund rather than a credit memo to avoid having unused credit memos in its files for extended periods of time. However, publisher and vendor credit policies vary; some vendors will only issue credit memos. In this case, the library may have to place another order with the vendor so that the credit memo can be reconciled. Before using a credit memo the library should verify that it did indeed pay the original invoice on which the vendor is issuing credit. Unless a library's internal policies dictate otherwise, credit memos and refunds should always be applied to the fund from which the original payment was made.

T accounts again illustrate how a fund's accounts are affected when a refund is posted. As an example, the $50 book that the Community Library purchased on purchase order 299 on its local history monographs fund is found to be defective. Unfortunately, the library has already paid the invoice. To further complicate matters, the book has gone out of print, so a replacement cannot be sent. The vendor issues a refund.

The refund is posted as a debit to the local history monographs payment account and a credit to its unencumbered balance. The encumbrance account is not affected since the original $50 encumbrance was disencumbered when the invoice was paid (table 15-7).

Cancellations also affect a library's accounting system. A vendor may cancel an order because the item is out of stock indefinitely or out-of-print. Sometimes a library finds it necessary to cancel an order. In such cases, the original encumbrance should be disencumbered (increasing the balance in the encumbrance account) and the same amount should be credited to the unencumbered balance. Cancellations pose certain financial considerations. If the vendor or publisher ships the material before it receives the library's cancellation, the library is obligated to pay for the material unless the vendor agrees to accept a return. For this reason, it is wise to establish an internal procedure by which funds for canceled orders are not disencumbered until a safety period has expired. This safety period assures that enough money is available to pay for the unexpected piece.

Vendors' Statements

Most vendors and publishers regularly issue statements that detail any outstanding invoices and credit memos on a library's account. In many cases the library has already processed the payment, but

Table 15-7 Posting a Refund

	Allocation (dr)	Allocation (cr)	=	Encumbrances (dr)	Encumbrances (cr)	+	Payments (dr)	Payments (cr)	+	Unencumbered Balance (dr)	Unencumbered Balance (cr)
Allocation	$2,500										$2,500
P.O. 299					$50					$50	
P.O. 300					$50					$50	
Invoice 114				$50				$50			
Invoice 28b				$50				$45			$5
Refund 299							$50				$50
Balance	$2,500				$0			$45			$2,455

the vendor had not received it by the time the statement was generated. This happens more often when checks are issued by the central business office of a parent institution or by the state, rather than by the library itself.

Statements from large vendors with computerized accounting systems frequently reference all the information necessary for the library to track down whether or not it has already processed payment. Such statements include invoice or credit memo number and date, library purchase order number, author or title (or both) of the ordered materials, and the amount. Other statements are not nearly as descriptive; some may reference only the amount due and thus require quite a bit of hunting by the library staff to verify that the payment requested was already made.

A vendor may charge interest or late charges for any amounts received after the time period stated under terms of payment on its invoices. Libraries are obligated to pay late charges if they process an invoice after its due date. If a library initiates payment before the due date but the vendor receives it after that date, the vendor can still request payment of late charges. It is not unheard of for a library to receive a bill for late charges on payment past due by a few days. Most vendors and publishers expect payment within thirty days of receipt of material. It is useful in such situations to have the date of receipt stamped on each invoice.

Outstanding invoices listed on statements do not always reflect errors, failure to pay, or late payment on the part of the library. Vendors make errors, too. Outstanding charges on an invoice may actually be for items the library is withholding payment on because the items were missing from a shipment. Sometimes the charges are for items billed to the wrong library's account. If the library is current with its invoice processing and has a flexible accounting system, it will be able to determine with relative ease if the statement poses true discrepancies with the library's own records or if there has just not been time for payment to reach the vendor.

Vouchers

When checks to cover payment for library purchases must be issued by the central business office of a parent organization, the library must prepare a voucher to forward with the approved invoice for payment. A voucher is an internal accounting document that authorizes the central business office to disburse cash from the library's account to pay the invoice. Like all other documents in an audit trail, vouchers must be carefully prepared. The voucher should provide the following information:

1. name and address to which the check is to be issued
2. invoice number, date, and exact amount in U.S. dollars or appropriate foreign currency
3. description of the purchased items
4. authorized signature

Some libraries have been able to streamline this process by interfacing with the central accounting office of their parent organization.[2] This process requires much thought and coordination between the library, the accounting office, and the auditors.

TRACKING EXPENDITURES WITH MANAGEMENT REPORTS: HOW MUCH MONEY IS LEFT?

A flexible accounting system should be able to provide a current picture of fund activity. The detail and frequency of management reports produced by the accounting system depend on its sophistication. Computerized systems with indexing capabilities can produce a variety of reports on a frequent basis. Such reports are more time-consuming to produce with a manual system. All systems should be able to produce some sort of summary reports on at least a monthly basis that can provide answers to the following questions:

1. How much money is left to spend in a fund on a given date?
2. Is a fund over- or under-expended?
3. What items have been canceled?
4. What items have been encumbered and paid?
5. What is the total spent on a group of related funds? (funds grouped together by criteria meaningful to the library, for example, type of order, subject, adult, or children's funds)

Overspending and underspending can be avoided only if the fund manager can closely monitor encumbrances, payments, and the free balance.

The ability to produce reports that can answer two additional questions is helpful:

1. How much did this cost last year compared to this year? (used to project costs for serials or any items that are paid repeatedly)
2. Which invoices have been paid for a given vendor and in what amount? (used to reconcile vendor statements)

Tables 15-8 to 15-12 are sample management reports produced by the computerized accounting systems of a couple of large academic libraries. Table 15-8 is a printout of the outstanding orders, or encumbrances, on a monograph fund as of a specific date. The report provides the following information:

1. Purchase order numbers—assigned by the library
2. Vendor numbers—specific numbers assigned to vendors
3. Current obligation—the amount encumbered on the referenced purchase order number
4. Reobligation amount—does not apply to most monograph purchases (If the purchase order was for a serial purchase, this column would be used to indicate the next year's encumbrances.)
5. Paytype—a code that determines if the encumbrance is dropped once payment is made or if the encumbrance is to be re-encumbered for the following year's payment (This particular system uses the code "F" for one-time monograph encumbrances.)
6. Order date—date the library issued the purchase order
7. Date of last payment—not often used for monograph purchases since payment on a purchase order is usually only made once (For serials, this column would reflect the last date a payment was made.)
8. Date of last update—the last date a correction or change was made to the record
9. Author-title

The printout shown in table 15-9 is an example of how a different automated system reports encumbrances, payments, and cancellations for a specified period of time. The printout provides information necessary to construct an audit trail for each item. Not all items are at the same point in the audit process but the report makes it clear what transaction has occurred. This report shows the activity on a single fund for a specified period of time. The report includes the: (1) fund code and name, (2) date of the information, (3) previous free balance available in the fund, (4) previous appropriation, expenditure, and encumbrance, (5) list of current activity on the fund including the system-supplied voucher number, the purchase order number, the title, and change in the fund status, (6) current appropriation, expenditure, and encumbrance after accounting for the current activity on the fund, and (7) averages of some relevant totals. The report also breaks expenditure down by the subfunds assigned by this particular library. The report shows (A) a payment and the corresponding disencumbrance for an item, (B) a canceled item, and (C) a newly encumbered item.

Table 15-8 Outstanding Orders Report from an Automated Accounting System

Outstanding Orders—Replacement Fund

05-31-90

Purchase Order	Vendor Number	Current Obligation	Reobligation Amount	Pay Type	Order Date	Date of Last Payment	Date of Last Update	Author-Title
A913306	60525005	32.50	0.00	F	05/07/90			Baudelaire, Charles. Mirror of Art. AMS Press. 1955.
A044502	60525005	6.95	0.00	F	03/18/90			Baumbeck, Jonathan. Moderns and Contemporaries.
A945250	60525005	21.00	0.00	F	03/04/90			Bierce, Ambrose. Stories of Soldiers and Civilians.
A872370	08720002	5.50	0.00	F	02/19/90			Blake, William. Poems. Routledge & Kegan.
A945860	60525005	11.95	0.00	F	04/38/90			Bognad, Morris. The Manager's Style Book.
A044548	60525005	22.95	0.00	F	04/07/90			Bukowski, Charles. Women. Black Sparrow Press.
A945104	50962179	23.00	0.00	F	04/07/90			Carney, Thomas F. Content Analysis. Univ Manitoba Pr.
A944694	60525005	16.95	0.00	F	04/29/90			Cather, Willa. My Antonia. Houghton Mifflin.
A946168	08725004	2.95	0.00	F	02/19/90			Chopin, Kate. The Awakening. Avon.
A941401	60525005	24.95	0.00	F	02/19/90			Coleman, Arthur. Drama Criticism, Vol. 2.
A943349	60525005	8.95	0.00	F	03/04/90			Cuddon, J. R. A Dictionary of Literary Terms. Penguin.
A911527	60525005	12.95	0.00	F	05/07/90			Didion, Joan. Salvador. Simon and Schuster.
A872377	50962179	23.00	0.00	F	04/29/90			Dunn, Delmer. Public Officials and the Press.
A945257	30336982	12.95	0.00	F	03/24/90			Esslin, Martin. Samuel Beckett: Critical Essays.
A936396	99950000	22.00	0.00	F	02/26/90			Fonda, Jane. Jane Fonda's Workout Book.
A946113	10282004	12.00	0.00	F	10/31/90		02/19/90	Furtado, Celso. Diagnosis of the Brazilian Crisis.

A945272	21995800	12.00	0.00	F	01/23/90		Gallery, Rob. Men in Erotic Art: A Catalog.
A941764	10282004	22.00	0.00	F	02/17/90		Hagler, Louise. The Farm Vegetarian Cookbook.
A908864	50962179	18.95	0.00	F	03/19/90		Heath, Stephen. Cinematic Apparatus. St. Martins.
A924094	60525005	34.95	0.00	F	09/11/90		Hinchcliffe, Mary K. The Melancholy Marriage. Wiley.
A907374	10282004	37.95	0.00	F	05/24/90		Hurty, Walter C. Dynamics of Structure. Prentice-Hall.
A946124	10282004	8.95	0.00	F	04/29/90		Jaffe, Nora. The Evil Image. NAL.
A945278	42133000	8.95	0.00	F	04/25/90	04/07/90	Kaplan, E. Ann. Women in Film. U of I Press.
A944523	10282004	17.95	0.00	F	02/20/90		Keilor, Garrison. Lake Woebegon Days. Viking.
A944618	60525005	18.95	0.00	F	04/29/90		Lawrence, D. H. Lady Chatterley's Lover. Buccaneer.
A938427	08725004	14.95	0.00	F	01/23/90		Lee, Stan. Son of Origins of Marvel Comics. Fireside.
A928417	60525005	8.95	0.00	F	01/24/90		Lowe, David. Lost Chicago. Houghton Mifflin.
A938449	08725004	12.50	0.00	F	01/23/90		Martin, David. Wilderness of Mirrors. Harper & Row.
A041309	60525005	34.50	0.00	F	02/25/90		McGregor, Ronald. Exercises in Spoken Hindi. Cambridge.
A911571	60525005	6.95	0.00	F	02/26/90		Mendez, Pepe. Complete Course in Stained Glass.
A941756	10282004	24.95	0.00	F	02/21/90		Myers, Gustavus. History of the Great American Fortunes.
A946107	60525005	7.95	0.00	F	04/29/90		Newhall, Beaumont. The Daguerreotype in America.
A936427	10282004	20.00	0.00	F	01/13/90		Okakura, Kakuzo. The Book of Tea. Richard West.
A936430	10282004	22.80	0.00	F	01/10/90		Porter, Gene. Her Father's Daughter.
A936460	60525005	16.95	0.00	F	02/25/90		Ray, Benjamin. African Religions. Prentice Hall.
	Total	611.70					

Table 15-9 Fund Activity Report from an Automated Accounting System

intmo   Int'l Studies Mono   FUND ACTIVITY REPORT, 05/05/97

Previous Balance = $1,252.29 Current Activity = –$1,252.29		Appropriation $7,453.00	Expenditure $2,336.92	Encumbrance $6,368.37
PONUM	**TITLE**	A		
139921 8816050	X-Files		$25.40	–$29.90
139921 881594x	Neon Genesis Evangelion		$25.36	–$29.85
139921 8815926	Pretty soldier sailor Moon		$13.51	–$15.90
139921 8816049	Tenchi Muyo! in love		$11.85	–$13.95
139921 8816037	Tenchi Muyo TV		$11.00	–$12.95
139921 8816025	Neon Genesis Evangelion		$9.30	–$10.95
139921 8816013	You are under arrest		$10.15	–$11.95
139921 8815951	Grendizer		$9.30	–$10.95
139921 8815914	Laputa		$11.00	–$12.95
139921 8815963	Ah! My goddess		$11.85	–$13.95
139921 8816001	Nausicaa		$11.00	–$12.95
139921 8815999	C. M-C Box		$9.30	–$10.95
139921 8815938	G-Gundam		$27.19	–$32.00
139921 8815987	Dragonball		$35.55	–$41.85
139921 8815902	Ramma 1/2		$13.51	–$15.90
139921 8815975	Dragonball		$20.27	–$23.85

308

139929	8719433	Japan and the United States		$30.00	–$25.00
139937	8675211	Memory of the world at risk: archives d		$60.92	–$59.66
139941	8704739	Nonviolence speaks to power	**B**	CANCELED	–$5.00
139941	8800522	Subaltern studies		CANCELED	–$7.50
139941	8769217	The Manchus		CANCELED	–$30.00
478797	8800522	Subaltern studies		$0.00	$7.50
		SUBTOTAL =	$0.00 **C**	$346.46	–$420.46
CURRENT BAL =	–$1,178.29		$7,453.00	$2,683.38	$5,947.91

Year-to-date 84 payments made, averaging $31.94

18 payments listed above average $19.24

1 new encumbrance listed above total $7.50, and average $7.50 each

3 cancellations listed above total –$42.50, and average –$14.16 each

Expenditures by subfund:

REGULAR	$2,683.38	100%	MONO REPL	$0.00	0%
HOLD REQST	$0.00	0%	PERIODICAL	$0.00	0%
SERIALS	$0.00	0%	SETS	$0.00	0%
SER REPLMT	$0.00	0%			

Table 15-10 is a summary report of year-to-date activity on all monograph funds in a large academic library. This kind of report is extremely helpful to acquisitions and collection development librarians who need to carefully monitor the status of a variety of funds. The report details the following information: (1) fund number, (2) fund name, (3) original allocation amount, (4) year-to-date payments, (5) outstanding orders, (6) unencumbered balance, (7) percent of the original allocation that has been spent, and (8) percent of the allocation that is still available for making more purchases, that is, neither spent nor encumbered. The report illustrates a balanced bookkeeping equation: the sum of the year-to-date payments, outstanding orders, and unencumbered balance equals the fund allocation. The percent spent and percent available columns are useful for monitoring expenditures at different times throughout the fiscal year.

As mentioned earlier, library materials expenditures have less predictable patterns during the year than expenditures for personnel and utilities. For example, at the end of the first quarter of the fiscal year, payroll and utility allocations are usually one-fourth spent. This is not necessarily the case with library materials. Delays in publication, erratic purchasing and publishing patterns, and other factors can prevent a predictable expenditure of funds throughout the year. It may be necessary to attempt to increase or decrease expenditures on a particular fund to prevent overspending or underspending. The monograph funds summary report in table 15-9 provides some examples.

The report is dated the last day of the second quarter of the fiscal year—December 31st in this library. Unlike most materials funds, expenditures on approval plan funds and blanket order funds may be fairly predictable and even throughout the year since the library is receiving regular shipments of these materials. The publisher approval plan fund (1) is right on target at the end of the second quarter with one-half of its allocation spent and one-half of its allocation still available. (There are usually few if any individual encumbrances on an approval plan fund since shipments are automatic.) However, the European blanket order fund (2) is already three-fourths spent by the end of the second quarter. This fund should be monitored carefully over the next month or two, and the library should advise the vendor to reduce shipments or to stop them completely by a certain date to prevent overspending.

Underspent funds can also be detected. For example, the education fund (3) has spent only 8 percent of its allocation by the end of the second quarter. Only 10 percent of its funds are encumbered.

With 82 percent of the allocation still unspent and unencumbered, purchases must be greatly increased to prevent underspending and a cut in allocation the following year.

Although the political science fund (4) is only 27 percent spent, 62 percent of its allocation is already tied up in encumbrances. Only 11 percent of the allocation represents a free balance. New purchases must be greatly slowed for the remainder of the year to prevent possible overspending.

Table 15-11 illustrates another format for reporting summary spending. The figure shows one fund grouping in the report. This report was created early in the fiscal year. Ten percent of the agriculture funds are already encumbered or expended. This is normal for this point in the fiscal year. The fund line that lists "100 percent" spent requires a closer look. The fund is a carry-over fund. The high percentage is not a cause for concern because it simply reflects the outstanding balance from the year before. Each fund grouping will have the same information provided.

A report that is convenient but not absolutely essential is a report of invoices paid, sorted by vendor. Table 15-12 shows an example from a system at a large academic library. The report lists: (1) the vendor code, (2) the invoice number paid, (3) the amount paid, (4) the invoice date, (5) the date the invoice was paid, (6) the voucher number assigned by the system for audit purposes, and (7) the number of items paid on the invoice. When vendor statements arrive, this report helps the library staff to establish quickly whether payment has been made for a particular invoice or if additional attention needs to be given to a statement.

A NOTE ON APPROVAL PLAN ACCOUNTING

Approval plans can provide a means for simplifying accounting procedures for a significant portion of a library's materials budget. They can eliminate the need to encumber hundreds and even thousands of firm orders each year, to disencumber funds once payment is made, and to process countless invoices. Instead, a single-sheet invoice can be processed for each shipment and the amount simply deducted from the approval plan allocation. This makes the approval plan fund one of the easiest to monitor. Some libraries charge back approval plan purchases to individual subject funds. This may be done for political reasons to make sure every fund gets its share of the approval plan total or to allow the library to track more specifically the amount of money spent on various disciplines

Table 15-10 Monograph Funds Summary Report from Automated Accounting System

Monograph Funds Summary Report

12-31-90

Fund		Fund Title	Allocation	Year-to-date Payments	Outstanding Orders	Unencumbered Balance	% Spent	% Avail.
0001		Anthropology	2,516.00	612.98	1,280.41	622.61	24	25
0002		Architecture	5,203.00	1,275.42	2,422.85	1,504.73	25	29
0003		Art	7,810.00	781.29	858.81	6,169.90	10	79
0004		Biological Sciences	9,852.00	2,070.44	5,326.14	2,455.42	21	25
0005		Chemistry	10,391.00	3,040.66	5,180.71	2,169.63	29	21
0006		Chinese	1,743.00	512.58	890.40	340.02	29	20
0007		Commerce	16,734.00	4,083.70	9,817.64	2,832.66	24	17
0008	③	Education	4,500.00	360.25	459.10	3,680.65	8	82
0009		Engineering	28,038.00	5,690.98	17,019.12	5,327.90	20	19
0010		English	6,788.00	1,512.14	3,594.26	1,681.60	22	25
0011	②	European Blanket Order	36,000.00	25,821.45	.00	10,178.55	72	28
0012		French	2,215.00	412.72	1,407.28	395.00	19	18
0013		Geography	3,373.00	1,680.48	912.49	780.03	50	23
0014		Geology	3,433.00	768.43	1,821.17	843.40	22	25
0015		German	2,261.00	545.25	1,004.95	710.80	24	31
0016		History	11,686.00	2,826.85	5,784.29	3,074.86	24	26
0017		Italian	100.00	22.95	26.95	50.10	23	50

0018		Linguistics	2,075.00	103.75	1,556.24	415.01	5	20
0019		Mathematics	5,354.00	934.88	2,831.44	1,587.68	17	30
0020		Music	13,970.00	3,092.55	7,412.67	3,464.78	22	25
0021		Philosophy	1,977.00	394.95	964.88	617.17	20	31
0022		Physics	14,666.00	8,359.62	3,666.50	2,639.88	57	18
0023	④	Political Science	3,241.00	863.44	2,012.43	365.13	27	11
0024	①	Publisher Approval Plan	65,000.00	32,512.14	129.85	32,358.01	50	50
0025		Psychology	3,500.00	799.12	1,994.89	705.99	23	20
0026		Reference	7,460.00	1,612.45	4,416.85	1,430.70	22	19
0027		Religion	2,090.00	322.50	803.98	963.52	15	46
0028		Replacements	15,533.00	3,084.26	6,354.12	6,094.62	20	39
0029		Reserves	230.00	28.55	125.18	76.27	12	33
0030		Slavic	7,945.00	1,499.28	3,572.55	2,873.17	19	36
0031		Sociology	2,800.00	605.12	1,721.28	473.60	22	20
0032		Spanish	2,523.00	650.89	1,009.56	862.55	26	34
0033		Speech	495.00	128.55	205.49	160.96	26	33
0034		Theatre	566.00	180.18	299.45	86.37	32	15
0035		Women's Studies	3,648.00	568.84	1,429.95	1,649.21	15	45
		TOTALS	305,716.00	107,759.64	98,313.88	99,642.48	35	36

Table 15-11 Summary Report by a Group of Related Funds from Automated Accounting System

		Appropriation	Expenditure	Encumbrance	Cash Balance	Free Balance	% Avail.
FUNDS BY SUBJECT							
Materials Budget (Continued)							
SCIENCES							
AGRICULTURAL SCIENCES							
AGRICULTURE							
New Publications							
Agriculture Mono.		$15,734.00	$26.50	$4,627.66	$15,707.50	$11,079.84	30%
Agriculture New Ser		$0.00	$0.00	$0.00	$0.00	$0.00	**%
Agriculture Bl Ord.		$1,159.00	$151.12	$0.00	$1,007.88	$1,007.88	13%
New Publications	TOTAL	$16,893.00	$177.62	$4,627.66	$16,715.38	$12,087.72	28%
Reserves							
Agriculture Ser C/O		$102.39	$0.00	$102.39	$102.39	$0.00	100%
Agriculture Ser Ren		$62,513.00	$2,933.15	$0.00	$59,579.85	$59,579.85	5%
Reserves	TOTAL	$62,615.39	$2,933.15	$102.39	$59,682.24	$59,579.85	5%
AGRICULTURE	TOTAL	$79,508.39	$3,110.77	$4,730.05	$76,397.62	$71,667.57	10%

Table 15-12 Report of Invoices Paid by Vendor from an Automated Accounting System

Vendor : har   *** Subset of Invoices ***   Page 1

No.		Inv. No.	Amount	Inv. Date	Paid Date	Voucher	No. of Items
001	)	255999	$442.36	08-07-97	09-05-97	142207	6
002	)	249884	$863.24	06-16-97	07-30-97	141586	21
003	)	252038	$436.55	07-01-97	07-30-97	141585	7
004	)	249882	$1,342.95	06-16-97	07-14-97	141326	15
005	)	249883	$1,709.99	06-16-97	07-14-97	141325	23
006	)	245805	$867.92	05-06-97	07-02-97	140898	19
007	)	245804	$1,683.14	05-06-97	06-23-97	140797	24
008	)	244059	$651.34	04-22-97	06-11-97	140694	15
009	)	244058	$1,873.11	04-22-97	06-04-97	140631	31
010	)	244057	$1,266.08	04-22-97	06-04-97	140630	16
011	)	243551	$64.33	04-17-97	06-04-97	140621	1
012	)	242541	$1,280.43	04-09-97	05-12-97	140145	25
013	)	242540	$418.56	04-09-97	05-12-97	140144	10
014	)	241112	$1,756.40	03-25-97	04-30-97	139937	43

or areas. Unless this method is required by a central business office, it unnecessarily complicates what could be an efficient and streamlined approach to processing single payments for large shipments of materials. The approval plan vendor can always provide as a routine service detailed printouts by subject of approval plan expenditures.

ENDING THE FISCAL YEAR

The fiscal year is a period of twelve consecutive months selected by an organization as its accounting year. The fiscal year may or may not correspond to the calendar year. The fiscal year in many libraries runs from July 1st to June 30th, and often reflects the natural business year of the state legislature or other funding entity. The purpose of a fiscal year is to provide a means for measuring financial changes and tracking expenditure patterns from period to period. Data from several years can reveal trends not readily discernible from one year's data.

At the end of the fiscal year all fund accounts must be closed or their balance brought to zero. Unspent money is added to the fund balance and excess expenditures are deducted from the fund balance. Depending upon the accounting method being used, libraries can either carry encumbrances over from year to year, or they must clear all encumbrances at the end of the fiscal year. In the latter situation, all orders placed but not received from the end of the year may have to be canceled and any money left in the fund forfeited.

It is important for a library to understand the accounting method used by its parent organization or funding body and the specific year-end requirements it places on the library. A good internal accounting system permits a library to closely monitor its funds so that at year end the library is on target with its expenditures.

AUDITS AND FINANCIAL CONTROL

In the past, most libraries kept accession books. These books provided a record of each order, including author, title, publisher, price, dealer, and date of receipt. The accession book served as both the order file and as the accounting record. Today, accession books are usually only seen in archives, but the need to provide the types and quality of records described in this chapter has not changed.

All libraries are required to retain some records relating to the order, receipt, and payment of invoices for library materials. Specific requirements relating to the records saved and the length of retention vary depending on the legal requirements of each institution. Libraries that are part of a governmental unit need to determine what the appropriate regulations are for their governing agency. Regulations usually are based on legal or procedural requirements of the organization.

The standard method of reviewing compliance to these regulations is through an audit. "Auditing is the accumulation and evaluation of evidence about quantifiable information of an economic entity to determine and report on the degree of correspondence between the information and established criteria. Auditing should be done by a competent independent person."[3] This is the process that impartially reviews accounting procedures and documentation to be certain that funds are being used prudently and appropriately. It is a certainty that the library's compliance to these standards will be reviewed by an auditor at some point. Many acquisitions librarians face the prospect with some trepidation, and some who have been through the process write about it.[4]

Maintaining internal control of financial procedures *is* essential. Therefore, it is wise to be prepared for an audit by: (1) communicating with those who affect financial relationships in your own institution, (2) understanding the purpose of an audit, (3) knowing the current regulations by which the accounting system in use will be judged, and (4) understanding how the audit trail is created in the library's accounting system.

Communicating and Financial Relationships

Perhaps the single best first step to understanding and continuing an acceptable accounting system is to know the individuals engaged in financial activities with whom the acquisitions department will be working. These are the people who collectively know the regulations and local procedures under which the library must operate. Most would appreciate the chance to educate before a problem arises. Following is a list of the people or offices that may be able to offer assistance:

1. Library budget officer
2. Director of the library
3. Purchasing
4. Accounts payable
5. Financial management, including individuals responsible for developing the university's budget and for handling the university endowments
6. Auditors (internal as well as state auditors)
7. Agencies related to the parent organization that handle research funds and grants
8. Legal services[5]

Understanding the Purpose of an Audit

The goals of a financial audit are:

to verify the financial information given

to determine if it is fairly presented within the accepted accounting principles,

to make recommendations that could further enhance the efficiency and effectiveness of the financial operation.

Basic Acquisitions Accounting and Business Practice

The goal of an audit is *not* to disrupt, insist upon change for the sake of change, or to discover fraud, although if fraud is discovered during the review process the auditor will have a responsibility to report it. In most cases, the library will pass the audit with no difficulty.

Knowing the Current Procedures and Regulations

The acquisitions librarian should have a thorough understanding of the work flow in acquisitions. Most audit requirements are based in common logic. An impartial look at the way work is performed can often reveal inconsistencies or questionable practices. These practices should be questioned and, if needed, corrected when those performing the work are not under the scrutiny of the auditor. In addition, the librarian should verify the length of time documents must be retained to meet audit obligations.

Understanding the Audit Trail

The point at which an item is ordered is the beginning of the audit trail. An audit trail is a record of what happens to an order from its initiation through receipt and payment. The trail markers are the records that a library retains in order to document a purchase. As noted in the first half of this chapter, auditors will want to see evidence that the purchase was (1) requested with proper authorization, (2) received, (3) paid for appropriately. In the case of library materials, they should still be available for use.

An auditor not only examines existing financial records but also considers how information is kept and in what form. Because the ordering and receipt of books and periodicals differ in many ways from procedures the auditors are likely to be more familiar with, it is important to spend time with the auditors in advance of the actual audit to provide background and explanations of library procedures. A library that orders materials and spends money has an obligation to whomever provides the funding (be they private donors or government agencies) to demonstrate that the funds are spent carefully and wisely.

An audit trail is only useful if it can be followed. The best audit trails are those in which the amount of work involved in locating the various elements is minimized. Auditors—or others—should be able to locate easily a record of the order and the invoice from which it was paid. While organizing the various types of documents needed can be time-consuming, it may assist in problem solving later. Also, unfortunately, fraud does occasionally occur in libraries. Herbert Snyder and Julia Hersberger have written an extensive article detailing embezzlement in public libraries. In it they state, "One of the clearest findings from the research was that the libraries that experienced embezzlement had essentially no financial control."[6] A clear audit trail helps prevent this sort of abuse.

CONCLUSION

Monitoring and properly expending a materials budget and maintaining a responsible audit trail are central to acquisitions work. From the issuance of purchase orders to the timely payment of bills, careful acquisitions accounting practices result in ready and accurate answers to the basic questions they should address: What is the allocation? How much has been encumbered? What was actually spent? What is the free balance? A library should design an accounting system that can monitor the peculiarities of its own budget and meet the fiscal requirements and policies of its parent institution or funding body. A good accounting system is simple enough to be flexible, yet sophisticated enough to monitor properly current expenditures, provide data to reliably predict future spending, and perform well in an audit review.

Notes

1. For this and other definitions of business terms I have referred to but not quoted from Jay Shafritz and Daniel Oran, *The New American Dictionary of Business and Finance*, rev. and updated (New York: Mentor, 1990).

2. Kristine L. Murphy, "Interfacing with Central Accounts," *New Automation Technology for Acquisitions and Collection Development* (New York: Haworth Press, 1995), pp.175-189.

3. Alvin A. Arens and James K. Loebbecke, *Auditing: An Integrated Approach*, 6th ed. (Englewood Cliffs, N.J.: Prentice Hall, 1994), p. 1.

4. I appreciated four articles: Sharon Berger, "The First Audit," *Bottom Line* 5 (Summer 1991): 28-30; Carol Pitts Hawks, "The Audit Trail and Automated Acquisitions: Searching for Road Signs," *Library Acquisitions: Practice & Theory* 18 (Fall 1994): 333-339; Mary Faust, "The Acquisitions Audit in the Automated Environment," in *New Automation Technology for Acquisitions and Collection Development* (Binghamton, N.Y.: Haworth Press, 1995), pp. 191-207; Janet

McKinney, "Preparing for an Audit," *Against the Grain* 8 (April 1996): 77-78.

5. Carol Pitts Diedrichs, "Off to See the Wizard: Demystifying Your Financial Relationships," *Library Administration & Management* 10 (Spring 1996): 105-109.

6. Herbert Snyder and Julia Hersberger, "Public Libraries and Embezzlement: An Examination of Internal Control and Financial Misconduct," *Library Quarterly* 67 (January 1997): 1-23.

Bibliography

Alley, Brian and Jennifer Cargill. *Keeping Track of What You Spend: The Librarian's Guide to Simple Bookkeeping*. Phoenix: Oryx, 1982.

Davidson, Sidney, Clyde P. Stickney and Roman L. Weil. *Financial Accounting: An Introduction to Concepts, Methods and Uses*. 3rd ed. Chicago: Dryden, 1982.

Diedrichs, Carol Pitts. "Off to See the Wizard: Demystifying Your Financial Relationships." *Library Administration & Management* (Spring 1996): 105-109.

Hoffman, Herbert H. *Simple Library Bookkeeping*. Newport Beach: Headway, 1977.

Magrill, Rose Mary and Doralyn Hickey. *Acquisitions Management and Collection Development in Libraries*. Chicago: American Library Association, 1984.

McKinney, Janet. "Preparing for an Audit." *Against the Grain* (April 1996): 77-78.

Smith, G. Stevenson. *Accounting for Librarians and Other Not-for-Profit Managers*. Chicago: American Library Association, 1983.

Trumpeter, Margo C. and Richard S. Rounds. *Basic Budgeting Practices for Librarians*. Chicago: American Library Association, 1985.

16

Payment Ethics: Librarians as Consumers

CORRIE MARSH

Acquisitions librarians and staffs should be aware that the business arrangement involved in ordering, receiving, and purchasing of library materials constitutes a contract for goods and services. For the most part, this chapter will address the concerns of a library's acquisitions operations in dealing with specific types of problems and possible recourses when the need arises for consumer protection. However, it is also necessary for those involved in the acquisitions process to know the terms outlined in service contracts and to conduct the business of acquisitions using professional business negotiation techniques and ethics.

EXAMPLES OF SPECIFIC PAYMENT PROBLEMS

Whether the library is purchasing one or many books, maps, sound recordings, computer software, or an electronic database, it is contracting for service with a vendor or supplier.[1] The contractual arrangement may be in the form of a purchase order, letter, telephone call, or electronic transmission. Whatever the means of contact, it is important to communicate exactly what is desired and any special instructions or expectations. The service contract should specify length of service, price, quality and format of materials, special handling and shipping requirements, and payment schedules. Communication between both parties should be clear and specific in order to avoid payment problems and to avoid future misunderstandings.

RECEIPT OF DAMAGED
OR POOR-QUALITY MATERIALS

The quality of the product received has often been a source of contention. In the past decade, librarians and publishers have developed standards of quality for printed materials.[2] Acquisitions librarians should be aware of minimum standards and recognize any products received that do not meet them. Librarians should not hesitate to complain if there is a problem with the quality of paper, printing, or binding of books and journals. With expanding acquisition of microforms, audiovisuals, facsimiles, and electronic formats, libraries have experienced increased problems with the quality of materials. The production standards for these non-print formats are still in the development stages. Just as with printed materials, non-print items should be examined during the receipt verification process to assure that the product supplied meets the library's quality standards.

Libraries need to establish a returns policy with dealers so they can return materials that do not meet quality standards for durability and readability in library use. Several American Library Association committees, such as the Micropublishing Committee and Audio-Visual Committee, monitor problems with the quality of products. Further information concerning the standards for library materials may be obtained by contacting the National Information Standards Organization (NISO-Z39).

Methods of shipping and packaging materials can contribute to product damage. For example, a shipment from overseas may be sent in large or small crates and supplied by sea or air. Cargo shipped by sea will travel more slowly and be handled more roughly than air cargo, thus allowing for a greater possibility of damage. Packaging must be satisfactory to protect all materials, including individual items, in shipping.

Suppliers and publishers offer a variety of types of packaging. Methods of wrapping individual volumes include plastic vacuum-wrapped coverings, bubble wrap, or no protection at all. In this last case, items are shipped loosely in cartons and boxes, packaged in reinforced mailers, or packed in Styrofoam cushioning materials. Each method requires the careful attention of library staff when unpacking the materials. Tightly packing and taping a carton of individual volumes that is to be cut open with a knife will often result in damage to a volume packed too closely to the top. Plastic vacuum-wrapped volumes require time-consuming unwrapping and, unfortunately, the plastic offers no apparent protection. On the other hand, it is vital to request Mylar sleeves for the protection of shipping delicate or rare materials. Librarians must decide if their receiving areas can accommodate streams of Styrofoam "peanuts" and packing paper; adhering to local recycling practices may be a factor.

Shipping and mailing processes change. In the past few years, rush-handling services such as FedEx, Airborne, UPS, and RPS have become commonplace and affordable. It is advisable to check into local shipping contacts for special handling needs.

Librarians need to assess the best means of shipping and packaging and to analyze the variety of packaging techniques in order to identify those best suited to their library's receiving procedures. Both the library and supplier should agree to the methods of shipping and packaging materials in consideration of timely delivery and condition of the product. Where single-title or one-time contracts are entered into with a publisher or agent, packaging agreements may not be possible or cost-effective. If repeated use of a publisher or agent is planned, then agreements are needed.

FULFILLMENT SCHEDULES

Librarians involved in the acquisition of serials, continuation sets, and databases are familiar with contracting for length of service when they arrange for extended open orders and subscriptions. Many disputes have resulted from simple misunderstanding of order fulfillment time schedules. Librarians should communicate special requirements for timely service and allow for problems that may be beyond the control of the supplier. The reverse is also true: suppliers should promptly notify their customers of delays or special problems. Often vendors supply status reports to libraries.

Many acquisitions departments specify the time period for fulfillment of their purchase orders; commonly this is a 90-day cancellation period for domestic orders and a 180-day cancellation period for foreign orders. These pre-established periods allow libraries some control in their internal fund accounting for outstanding orders. Clarification of the order period to the supplier specifies the time in which the supplier must act. If the supplier is unable to fill the order within the granted time, the library may unencumber the funds and reorder elsewhere. In contracting for service with a dealer, it is advisable to document restrictions and set an automatic cancellation period if necessary, so that both the library and the supplier agree to feasible terms.

UNDERSTANDING ADDITIONAL CHARGES

Special service requirements such as rush service and shipping often incur extra handling charges that are passed on to the customer. Most suppliers offer a price guide to their standard extra charges for special handling and shipping. Charges for shipping and postage differ according to the method of supply. Many suppliers offer free postage for domestic shipments; the cost of foreign shipments varies greatly with shipping requirements. Direct foreign shipments are further complicated by customs regulations. Foreign purchases through a North American distributor usually are handled by the distributor for the library. While library materials are for educational use and do not incur U.S. customs charges, the shipments still require a customs broker to arrange for removal of the shipment from customs and to supply delivery to the library. The services of a customs broker are not free. A library should contact a customs broker in advance to determine charges and make sure the broker can meet the library's shipping requirements.

Often it is difficult to identify additional charges in an invoice. For many items shipped together, suppliers may include postage and handling fees in the cost of each item or combine the fees at the end of an invoice. In such cases the library has to calculate the separate charges. Compare each item's cost to that of the original order, and compare the total postage and handling charge in relation to the total item charges. Most domestic suppliers charge a standard postage percentage rate to an invoice total. The postage, handling, and service costs are usually outlined in the supplier's service contract. Librarians should be aware of additional costs and know how to identify them on each invoice.

The terms for additional charges should be understood before entering into a business arrangement. Individual libraries vary in the way they process extra charges: some are able to absorb the additional costs for postage or handling in the costs of materials, while others need to provide itemized details of cost charges to their accounting agencies.

In recent times, libraries have had to face the cost dilemmas of monetary conversion rates and pricing differentials, especially those involving overseas service arrangements. Regularly monitoring foreign exchange rates as a means of estimating encumbrances at the time of ordering as well as comparing the costs to actual invoices will enable the librarian to keep track of unusual fluctuations. Fluctuating values of the U.S. dollar have forced many publishers to pass on extra costs to their customers to compensate for price increases. However, U.S. libraries rarely receive a credit for

overpayment due to a sudden rise in dollar value. 'I ı.
imposing such extra costs without issuing equivalent cı
be debatable depending on the terms of the original order; it ıͼ
to check extra costs and communicate concerns to the supplier aͼ
soon as possible.

PAYMENT SCHEDULES

The payment process for materials is perhaps the most diverse of
all library procedures. In general, the library controls its own payment processing system, or it supplies documentation verifying receipt of items to a unit within its governing organization which
processes payments. In either case, the issue of expeditious payment is important to producers and suppliers. Libraries with the
ability to process payments and produce their own payment checks
have greater control over the paying activity than those who rely
on accounts payable departments outside the library. These departments can further complicate the payment process when item-by-
item invoice costs and elaborate voucher systems are required

The acquisitions staff must be thoroughly familiar with their organization's payment system, not only for assessing their department's processing of debits and ability to spend, but also for antic-
ipating the need to negotiate terms of payment with suppliers.
Typical business operations supply invoices requiring thirty-day
payment. Libraries need to be concerned with their organization's
capacity to meet this requirement; one of the quickest ways to up-
set the profitability of a small publisher or local bookstore is to fail
to meet their payment time schedules. Knowledge of the library's
accounts payable system will help determine if there is a problem
in meeting a supplier's payment schedule. If necessary, terms can
be renegotiated to guarantee a convenient and realistic system for
both the library and its suppliers.

If a supplier's terms for payment are not met, the library may
face the accrual of late charges as a penalty for its neglect in processing timely payment. The penalty is a justified action on the
part of the supplier, but fortunately it is rarely used. Libraries have
an extremely difficult time in processing additional invoices for
penalties and in justifying the additional costs to auditing agencies.
If a penalty is imposed, it is important to examine whether the
penalty is justified as a fair business practice and to investigate the
cause(s) in order to avoid future occurrences. The library must also
determine how to absorb the extra charge in its materials budget and must be prepared to justify the cost to administrators if

necessary. Many publishers and suppliers offer inducements toward faster payments in the form of volume discounts for payments received within specific time periods. If the library is able to process payments quickly, it can receive a substantial cost savings.

PREPAYMENT REQUIREMENTS

Many suppliers, especially serials subscription agents, require prepayment of orders or offer discounted prices for prepayment of orders. The library in turn must analyze (1) its ability to pay for products not yet received, (2) the suppliers' need and justification, and (3) the risks involved in prepayment ventures.

An excellent set of guidelines for prepayments is provided in the appendix to *Guide to Performance Evaluation of Library Materials Vendors.*[3] These guidelines are applicable to all types of libraries and dealers. They suggest various aspects to consider in ordering materials, such as order forms, claiming, returns, and payments. The special section about prepayment decisions explains the reasons why publishers may require prepayment, how the library can "investigate" the publisher, and precautions in processing prepayments. As with all other aspects of payments, restrictions imposed by the library's governing organization must be considered. Many organizations are simply unable to process prepayments due to state or local restrictions. In such cases the library may pursue other arrangements with the publisher or vendor or consider borrowing the publication from other libraries. If the library is able to prepay for materials, it should consider how it will process the order and payments simultaneously.

UNSOLICITED RECEIPTS WITH INVOICES

Libraries often receive unordered and unsolicited materials accompanied by invoices, which are discovered in the verification process. It is advisable to have a library policy for handling unordered materials and their invoices. The library is under *no obligation to pay for such materials*. Unsolicited receipts may be regarded as gifts according to U.S. Postal Service regulations:

a) the mailing of unordered merchandise or of communications prohibited by subsection (c) of this section constitutes an unfair method of competition and an unfair trade practice.

b) any merchandise mailed in violation of subsection (a) of this section, or within the exceptions contained therein, may be treated as a gift by the recipient, who shall have the right to retain, use, discard, or dispose of it in any manner he sees fit without any obligation whatsoever to the sender. All such merchandise shall have attached to it a clear and conspicuous statement informing the recipient that he may treat the merchandise as a gift to him and has the right to retain, use, discard, or dispose of it in any manner he sees fit without any obligation whatsoever to the sender.

c) no mailer of any merchandise mailed in violation of subsection (a) of this section, or within the exceptions contained therein, shall mail to any recipient of such merchandise a bill for such merchandise or any dunning communications.

d) for the purposes of this section, "unordered merchandise" means merchandise mailed without the prior expressed request or consent of the recipient.[4]

Further, it does not matter if the publications are foreign or domestic, since all material mailed to the United States falls under the jurisdiction of the U.S. Postal Service.[5]

The acceptance of unordered materials as gifts would appear to be a simple solution to the matter; in fact, the situation is very complicated. Problems may occur in several ways: telephone or written inquiries may be misunderstood as orders and result in shipped materials; foreign distributors may not be familiar with U.S. laws concerning unsolicited mail; and, more recently, publishers may have used "creative" marketing techniques to anticipate acquiring new customers.[6] In spite of legal protections, libraries cannot afford to avoid taking action in the event they receive unsolicited items. For example, a library may receive unsolicited materials from a supplier the library uses for other business, and the supplier may consider the invoiced item as an outstanding payment until the matter is settled.

The library should choose its actions in accordance with its own procedures. Acquisitions librarians should establish a policy of action and responsibility in order to clarify who will be responsible for handling unsolicited orders and what actions will be taken. Whether the library decides to accept the materials as a gift, pay for them, or mail them back, follow-up communication that educates the supplier is recommended.

CONSUMER PROTECTION

When payment problems occur and the library has made repeated attempts to solve them, its only recourse may be to pursue consumer protection. The library can contact local, state, or federal agencies for advice and assistance. In addition, various sections of regional library organizations and of the American Library Association serve as consumer advocates for libraries.

Federal Trade Regulations

Librarians as consumers should develop a practical knowledge of U.S. trade regulations. The *United States Code* provides explanations of the regulations required for sellers of merchandise. In addition to the postal regulations already cited, the following U.S. Code sections provide explanations of the regulations that may be consulted for clarification of various issues:

U.S.C., Title 15, Section 41-Consumer Credit Protection

Subchapter I-Consumer Credit Cost Disclosure

Section 1607-Administrative Enforcement

Part A, Section 1612-General Provisions

(These sections designate enforcing agencies and review procedures for enforcing regulations.)

Part B, Section 1638-Credit Transactions

(This section outlines forms and timing of transaction disclosure.)

Part C, Section 1661-Credit Advertising

(This section describes regulations about catalogs and advertisements.)

Part D, Section 1666-Correction of Billing Errors

(This section provides regulations concerning procedures for correcting billing errors.)[7]

While the acquisitions staff need not be legal authorities, they should be familiar in general with federal regulations in order to establish policies and procedures about payment problems.

Federal agencies are responsible for the enforcement of the regulations. Specifically, the Federal Trade Commission (FTC) and U.S. Postal Service are the primary agencies that a library may turn to for assistance as a consumer.

FEDERAL TRADE COMMISSION

The FTC is charged with maintaining free and fair competition. The Federal Trade Commission Act prohibits "unfair methods of competition" and "unfair or deceptive acts or practices." In addition, one of the main functions of the FTC is to provide consumer protection. Libraries requiring information about consumer protection or registering a complaint should contact their nearest FTC regional office.[8]

U.S. POSTAL SERVICE

The U.S. Postal Service is responsible for more than mail processing and delivery services for individuals and businesses within the United States. It also protects the mails and apprehends those who violate postal laws. Libraries in need of information or with complaints to register should contact their regional postal inspector.[9]

LOCAL AND STATE AGENCIES

Libraries that have problems with or questions about a supplier may contact their local Better Business Bureau or state consumer protection agencies for advice. They may also inquire about the supplier through these same agencies in the supplier's state of residence. If formal complaints or legal actions are deemed necessary, the library may pursue these actions through the state attorney general's office for clarification in regard to interstate trade. An understanding of one's state agencies can help when information is needed on how to obtain consumer protection.

Library Organizations

Local library consortia and state library organizations may be of assistance with consumer protection. Inquiries about a specific publisher or vendor may be forwarded to the Publisher/Vendor-Library Relations (PVLR) Committee. This is a committee of the Association for Library Collections and Technical Services (ALCTS). The charge of the committee is:

> To serve as the review and advisory committee on all matters of vendors of library materials-library relationships; to investigate these relationships; and to prepare recommendations and develop guidelines of acceptable performance for libraries and vendors for ordering and supplying of library materials.[10]

In the past the PVLR Committee has issued lists of publishers who have engaged in fraudulent practices. Librarians can monitor current consumer relations by keeping up-to-date with PVLR Committee activities. A library that wishes to file a complaint after all reasonable efforts have failed may send a letter detailing the problem and copy of all documentation to the Publisher/Vendor-Library Relations Committee at ALCTS, American Library Association, 50 E. Huron St., Chicago, IL 60611.

A MODEL FOR CONSUMER PROTECTION

The postal laws and U.S. Code of federal regulations provide protection from unfair trade and business practices. Most citizens, however, are familiar with the red tape involved in pursuing official government action. As a result, librarians have often relied on library consumer groups to intervene with suppliers when problems arise. Although positive action often results from these groups' activities on a library's behalf, consumer groups are usually not in a position to take legal recourse.

One model for consumer legal action is *Guides for the Law Book Industry*, developed by the FTC in cooperation with the American Association of Law Libraries (AALL). The development of the guidelines began in the late 1960s with an article that outlined eleven offensive practices in the law book industry and called for consumer action on the federal level if necessary.[11] In late 1969, the FTC announced it would conduct an investigation of the law book industry. In 1970, the American Bar Association (ABA) showed its support of these efforts by creating a Special Committee on Lawbook Publishing Practices to investigate problems and recommend means for protection. In a related action, the AALL created a Committee on Relations with Publishers and Dealers. The AALL also established standards for advertising new law publications.[12] In 1973, the FTC proposed guides that were meant to encourage voluntary compliance in fair trade practices and to "afford interested or affected parties an opportunity to present to the Commission their views, suggestions, objections or other information. . . ."[13] By August 8, 1975, the FTC established the *Guides for the Law Book Industry*.[14]

The definitions in the FTC's guides precisely describe all formats of legal publications, including nonprint materials, and establish the scope of the materials as those "designed primarily for use by members of the law profession and by law schools. . . ." The guides present a statement of the FTC's interpretation of the laws for fair practice between law book publishers and customers. The guides specify seventeen areas of fair trade; included are revisions, supplementation, titles of texts and treatises, subscription renewal notices, and billing practices.

With the establishment of the guides, law book customers may present their complaints directly to the FTC or may go through the ABA or state bar associations. The majority of law libraries have elected to channel problems through the AALL's Committee on Relations with Publishers and Dealers. Complaints are publicized in the committee's periodical publication, the *Publications Clearing House Bulletin*.

Recently law librarians have reassessed the effectiveness of the FTC's guides and have determined:

> The FTC *Guides for the Law Book Industry* have resulted in improved consumer protection and better relations with publishers. Now is not the time, however, to be satisfied with our accomplishments. It is instead the time for us to become such effective consumers that the law book industry will be proclaimed as a model in fair dealing and cooperation.[15]

Further analysis by law librarians suggests that the definition of the industry product, or law books, as materials is intended *only* for members of the legal profession and law schools. As publishers have recently broadened their markets to schools and consumers outside of the legal profession, it is unclear if these new materials fall beyond the scope of the guides.[16]

The success of law consumers in obtaining the FTC's guides was due to the support contributed by the strong lobby of the ABA and its members in Congress and the FTC itself—both of which are consumers of law publications. Many of the same issues dealt with in the guides for the law book industry exist in other areas of publishing: fair practice, advertising, and payment problems. The guidelines presented for bibliographic information and content revisions are also directly related to similar problems libraries have with the general publishing industry. Obviously, librarians are reexamining the scope of the law book guides; a broader application is needed. Perhaps the guides can serve as a model of consumer action for all libraries. As noted earlier, numerous organizations are addressing standards for quality and format (National Information Standards Organization, Book Industry Systems Advisory Committee, Serials Industry Systems Advisory Committee, and so on), and various consumer groups and government organizations exist to assist with business problems. Such groups should take note of the precedent set by the *Guides for the Law Book Industry*. If they can join together and document industry-wide problems, the FTC may act on a broader interpretation.

CONCLUSION

This chapter has outlined examples of specific payment problems faced by libraries and has suggested procedures for dealing with them using business techniques. If the library is confronted with a problem, it may utilize its own policies or turn to the wide variety of consumer protection services available on local and national levels. The following summary suggests professional ethics to be applied when dealing with payment problems:

Educate library staff, vendors, and suppliers about the business practices and policies of the library and its governing organization. Provide clear documentation that explains how to handle specific problems as they arise. Send a library fact sheet with orders to new vendors. It is also useful to educate the suppliers with whom the library does frequent business so that they are aware of the library's policies.

Provide friendly and courteous communication at all times with the library's business partners. There is no excuse for rudeness; often problems are solved through an agreeable exchange of information that allows differences to be negotiated.

Document all business transactions. An audit trail of orders and payments is a necessity in providing proof of actual transactions. Many suppliers require copies of purchase orders, payment checks, and all correspondence before they will settle a payment problem.

Take consumer action. Do not procrastinate when a problem arises. None of the resources for consumer protection can be of assistance if the library is not willing to right a wrong. As a general precaution, do not pay for materials until you are satisfied with delivery, price, and quality of service. The acquisitions operation represents the library as the consumer; for this reason, acquisitions has an obligation to negotiate and solve any violations in service contracts. Furthermore, if a problem is brought to the public's attention, other libraries may be spared a similar situation. Professional cooperation is important to the entire library community and may result in public recognition of unfair trade practices.

Notes

1. Rose Mary Magrill and Doralyn J. Hickey, *Acquisitions Management and Collection Development in Libraries* (Chicago: American Library Association, 1984), pp. 75-94; see also Stephen Ford, *The Acquisition of Library Materials* (Chicago: American Library Association, 1973).

2. American National Standards Institute, Z39 Committee, various materials standards in Z39 ANSI, 1430 Broadway, New York, NY 10018; see also various reports of the National Information Standards Organization (NISO-Z39, previously ANSI), U.S. Department of Commerce, National Bureau of Standards, Administration Building 101, Library E106, Washington, DC 20234, and the Book Industry Study Group, Inc., Book Industry Systems Advisory Committee (BISAC), and Serials Industry Systems Advisory Committees (SISAC), 160 Fifth Ave., New York, NY 10010.

3. Publisher-Vendor-Library Relations Committee (formerly Bookdealer-Library Relations Committee), American Library Association, *Guide to Performance Evaluation of Library Materials Vendors* (Chicago: American Library Association, 1977), appendix; see also *Guidelines for Handling Library Serial Orders* and *Guidelines for Handling Library Orders for Microforms* (Chicago: American Library Association, 1977).

4. 39 U.S. Code, sec. 3009.

5. 18 U.S. Code, sec. 1692.

6. Bookdealer-Library Relations Committee, American Library Association Midwinter Conference, January 1986, committee meeting discussion.

7. 15 U.S. Code, sec. 41; sec. 1607, 1612a, 1638b, 1661c and 1666d.

8. Office of the Federal Register, National Archives and Records Service, General Services Administration, *United States Government Manual 1997/1998* (Washington, D.C.:U.S. Government Printing Office, 1997), pp. 559-565.

9. Ibid., pp. 641-643.

10. American Library Association, *ALA Handbook of Organization 1989/1990* (Chicago: American Library Association, 1989), p. 44.

11. Raymond M. Taylor, "Lawbook Consumers Need Protection," *ABA Journal* 55 (1969): 553.

12. *Law Library Journal* 64 (1971): 440.

13. *Federal Register* 38, no. 39 (February 28, 1973): 5351-5354.

14. 16 CFR, Chap. 1, p. 256 (January 1998).

15. Reynold Kosek (Appendix 1 by Sue Welch), "Law Librarians as Consumer Advocates—Some Thoughts and Recommendations Based on the FTC Guides for the Lawbook Industry," *Publications Clearing House Bulletin* 9 (February 1986): 2.

16. Ibid.

17

Ethics in Aquisitions Management

BARBARA J. WINTERS

How should acquisitions managers think about ethics? To date acquisitions managers have tended to link ethics with vendor relationships: In September 1997 a word search on "ethics" in the online version of *Library Literature* retrieved 477 articles. Based on the use of "acquisitions" or "serials" elsewhere in the record, only 19 articles could be said to deal directly with ethics in acquisitions practice in the narrowest sense. Over half of these 19 articles (63 percent) dealt with library/vendor relationships. The rest dealt with isolated practices (such as discarding of library materials). None addressed ethical practice in a broader management sense.

This chapter discusses ethical concepts in four major areas of acquisitions management: planning/organizing, communication, supervision, and business relationships. The chapter will not deal with institutional integrity, although that is an interesting study in itself, but rather with individual integrity. The chapter will not discuss ethical theory; for that, the reader will find Woodward's "A Framework for Deciding Issues in Ethics" an informative summary with a good bibliography.[1] Rather, it will deal with practical ethical guidelines that can be used in decision-making processes. Finally, it will not deal with areas tangential to daily management of acquisitions operations, such as freedom of information issues. In addition, the American Library Association's (ALA) Association for Library Collections and Technical Services (ALCTS) has drafted an ethical statement that addresses collection development issues.[2] Others, most notably Ingetraut Dahlberg and Sheila Intner in numerous writings, have discussed another area tangential to acquisitions practice, the ethics involved with cataloging of materials.

For a general introduction to the discussion of ethics in broad areas of librarianship, the reader is referred to Robert Hauptman's *Ethical Challenges in Librarianship*, which, while not taking a real management approach to the topic, still contains a good overview of related issues as well as an extensive bibliography.[3] This work can be considered to be foundational, in that most articles dealing with ethics in librarianship cite it. The monograph edited by F. W. Lancaster is another good overview, one which deals more directly with issues related to management issues in libraries.[4]

The definition of "ethics" that we shall employ is Merriam-Webster's: "The discipline dealing with what is good and bad and with moral duty and obligation; a set of moral principles or values; the principles of conduct governing an individual or a group."[5] Setting one's own "moral principles" in a department that is characterized as one with "minimal self-determination of its objectives and control of its work"[6] requires ongoing thought and self-examination.

PLANNING AND ORGANIZING

What is the acquisitions manager's moral duty with regard to planning? We will use Petrick's definition of planning: "The intended, coordinated, emergent, and realized pattern of integrated, multidimensional decision processes and actions that provide organizational direction and prioritize objectives" and will keep in mind activities related to organizing as well as those related to planning per se.[7] It can be argued that haphazard planning, i.e., planning that does not take into account all major considerations related to human resources, organizational culture and behavior, budget, and quality operations, is unethical. It is easiest to see what ethical planning looks like by looking at an example of unethical planning, such as making a policy decision that compromises or trivializes the safety of staff, even if the decision is one that adheres to current legal safety standards.[8] Making sure the work environment is ergonomically sound is important, even though few laws currently govern ergonomics in the workplace.

Planning can also be said to be unethical if it involves spurious seeking of departmental input. Who has not had experience with having his or her opinion sought only as a technique for gaining support for a potentially unpopular decision? Acquisitions managers must remain open-minded, remembering that they can learn something from every single person who works for them and that they must have the integrity to do so.

Ethical planning provides a means for monitoring and keeping records; it guarantees that steps are taken so that any audit will receive a favorable result. Financial records are just one aspect of the library that is subject to audit. Compliance with rules and regulations of the parent organization can undergo an audit, as can operations in general. Therefore, the manager must plan with rules, regulations, and efficient operations in mind. For example, if managers work for a state institution that requires competitive procurement, they must be sure to include consideration of competitive procurement in budget planning.

Petrick further describes "culpably negligent planning" and organizing as that characterized by the absence of explicitly *intentional* planning or organizing, or planning or organizing that is inefficiently coordinated, rigidly unresponsive to emergent contingencies, or that provides unclear and unprioritized direction.[9] He goes on to recommend four steps that can be taken to facilitate responsible planning:

planning with awareness of the environment through environmental scanning;

planning formulation, analysis, and choice through "development of the vision of a desired future";

selected plan implementation to "coordinate organizational readiness to act through intentional enactment of policies [and] procedures"; and,

evaluation of the impacts and results of the plan.[10]

Planners and organizers must walk the fine line between making the best use of staff talents while remaining as impartial as possible to staff personalities and idiosyncrasies, especially during times when reengineering, downsizing, rightsizing, and outsourcing are being discussed. Petrick describes several techniques for "deceptive downsizing," such as raising the performance standards of a particular job to a level that may exceed the skills of the current employee with the eventual dismissal of that employee. While these types of techniques can be attractive to beleaguered managers, managers must consider the ethical implications involved, which as Petrick says can "erode organizational character" and—we might add—individual integrity, as well.[11]

Cargill talks about an audit method called a "friendly" or self-initiated audit. This kind of audit is employed in a situation where the department or library asks for design assistance and recommendations about internal controls *before* there is a problem. Extended to the arena of ethical planning, this could be a method managers use to place a guard on themselves against use of techniques such as deceptive downsizing or utilize during times when major organizational changes are being planned. Not only would the manager ask to be apprised of potential problems but also of possible breaches of ethical conduct. It is important that such an audit be performed during the planning stage.[12]

COMMUNICATION

Information is power. Ethical managers must be careful how they use their power. Salter describes the temptation to give too little information to those who need it or too much information to those who do not need it.[13] It is especially tempting in the acquisitions environment, which is again correctly characterized by Hewitt as "professionally isolated" within the organization, to share information (particularly private information about staff) to establish a more collegial feeling with peers.[14] However, managers must be sensitive to the fact that they may not only be violating ethical principles but even laws related to confidentiality in doing so. Has a staff member chosen to resign rather than to be fired? If so, did she reach a confidentiality agreement with Human Resources? It is incumbent upon the manager to keep such arrangements confidential, although they make for interesting chatter at break time.

A second ethical problem surfaces in this type of situation when the manager is asked to provide a reference for the former staff member. The temptation will be to get rid of a problem employee by passing him or her on to a colleague with at least a passable reference. Managers should reserve the right not to comment beyond giving employment dates or stating the details of the job description. At best the manager should write a reference that is neutral, stating dates of employment and type of work performed in the department: "During his employment at MidAtlantic University, Mr. Smith worked in the Acquisitions Department and gained experience with ordering and receiving library books and with invoicing procedures. This position requires attention to detail and knowledge of general library procedures." Any potential employer reading such a letter would understand that there may have been problems with the employee's work record.

Communication goes beyond just the acquisitions department. Hawks, in "Building and Managing an Acquisitions Program," describes the need to manage by policy and the need to communicate and negotiate policy decisions outside the department, particularly in times of crisis. Such negotiation needs to take place with appropriate administrators, collection managers, and cataloging managers.[15]

Looking at communication from a positive point of view, ethical managers must be certain always to make clear requests of staff members and even to explain the reasons for their requests when it is possible to do so.[16]

SUPERVISION

Personnel costs are usually the largest category of expenditure in any library budget, particularly in departments that provide staff-intensive services such as Acquisitions and Serials. Yet many acquisitions managers, because of the tyranny of urgency, can easily fail to incorporate ethical considerations into their supervisory methods and decisions on a day-to-day basis. Managers with integrity should have a human resources plan that reminds them what kind of work they need to get from each staff member and how they are going to go about getting it, so that off-the-cuff decisions rarely have to be made or, when made, will have a firm grounding in ethics. When drafting the plan, they should honestly question themselves about their assumptions. For example, what are their assumptions about employees with poor attitudes? Do they always assume these attitudes mean the absence of the work ethic, or are they more likely to assume that the problem is with the departmental system?[17]

Supervising with integrity includes a spectrum of activities, from ethical selection and development to employee appraisal and dismissal. Impartiality and objectivity are needed at each step of the process. Do all candidates who minimally meet qualifications receive equal consideration? Are there equitable development opportunities? Have the manager and the staff discussed what "equitable opportunities" for development means and reached consensus on the definition?

Employee appraisal is a major area for acting with integrity. Managers should design realistic performance standards and make them fit within the strictures of whatever automated systems they are using.[18] They should use words in written and oral evaluations that are constructive, not destructive. Discipline should never be arbitrary and capricious and, if and when it is necessary, it should take the same form (i.e., the same progressive steps) with all employees. Given their fiduciary responsibility to their parent organizations, managers should never look the other way for any employees. They enter an even more untenable ethical and legal quagmire if they look the other way for some employees but not for all. Managers should construct all records, especially personnel records, knowing that they could be open to public disclosure and should safeguard against any accusation of impropriety.

Salter reminds us that supervisors do not deal just with ethical issues but also with legal ones, such as civil rights, equal opportunity, equal treatment. He particularly reminds us that due process is a constitutional mandate.[19] It is also one of the major elements of the code of ethics of the American Library Association. Managers must be aware of how they "accuse" staff of missteps, and should rely on their Human Resources Department for whatever help is needed, even if that means seeking help with a "script" to use with the staff member, i.e., wording that should and should not be used.

BUSINESS RELATIONSHIPS

Acquisitions managers have a greater number and more variety of business relationships than most of their colleagues. They must work with business managers, accountants, and other financial officers in the parent organization. They must also maintain relationships with external vendors, possibly to a greater extent than even their directors. Finally, they have expenditure control of what is probably the largest portion of their library's discretionary budget, no matter how large or what type of library. The chapter on ethics in the first edition of *Understanding the Business of Library Acquisitions*, based on survey and focus-group-type research conducted and reported by Goehner, adequately covers the topic of ethics in vendor relationships, and the 12 articles mentioned in the introduction to this chapter complement and supplement Goehner's research so that we do not find it necessary in this chapter to replicate that work.[20] It is important, however, to mention one important development in the area of vendor/library relations that has come to fruition since the publication of all those articles and chapters:

In 1993, concurrent with the revision work that was being done on ALA's code of ethics, and believing that that code did not go far enough in addressing business relationships, the ALCTS Acquisitions Section drafted a statement of business practices to be used to govern these relationships. The guidelines, derived from the Principles and Standards of Purchasing Practice advocated by the National Association of Purchasing Management and the Code of Ethics of the National Association of Educational Buyers, follow in their entirety. Admittedly, these principles deal mostly with vendor relationships, but many of them can be generalized to apply to other types of business relationships.

An acquisitions librarian:

1. gives first consideration to the objectives and policies of his or her library.
2. strives to obtain the maximum ultimate value of each dollar of expenditure.
3. grants all competing vendors equal consideration insofar as the established policies of his or her library permit, and regards each transaction on its own merits.
4. subscribes to and works for honesty, truth, and fairness in buying and selling, and denounces all forms and manifestations of bribery.
5. declines personal gifts and gratuities.
6. uses only by consent original ideas and designs devised by one vendor for competitive purchasing purposes.
7. accords a prompt and courteous reception insofar as conditions permit to all who call on legitimate business missions.
8. fosters and promotes fair, ethical, and legal trade practices.
9. avoids sharp practice.[21]
10. strives consistently for knowledge of the publishing and bookselling industry.
11. strives to establish practical and efficient methods for the conduct of his or her office.
12. counsels and assists fellow acquisitions librarians in the performance of their duties, whenever occasion permits.[22]

It would be an interesting exercise to go back and apply these guidelines to one or more of Goehner's survey questions; for example, the first survey question related to social invitations, such as dinners, and whether they obligate a library or an acquisitions librarian to the vendor host. Certainly guidelines 2 and 4 speak to this situation. One could even argue that guideline number 3 applies, that is, if the librarian says yes to one invitation, he or she would be obligated to say yes to all invitations. This author has firsthand experience with evaluation of many responses to Requests for Proposal for library materials and can testify that there can indeed be at least a temptation to artificially evaluate one vendor higher than others if the evaluator has had pleasant social experiences with that vendor's representatives.

Vendors are our colleagues within our own professional organizations. Managers should remember to think about ethics from the vendor perspective as well as from that of their own institution. Goehner includes vendor questions in her survey. In addition, a good discussion of business ethics written mostly from the vendor perspective can be found in John Secor's "A Growing Crisis of Business Ethics: The Gathering Stormclouds."[23]

In thinking about relationships with other business partners, managers will have to consider additional factors not directly covered by these guidelines. For example, what should managers do when they come up against regulations that are too restrictive for the procurement of library materials? An object lesson in how to confront this type of situation presented itself to librarians who worked in publicly supported academic libraries in Virginia in the late 1980s. Those librarians were forced to implement the rules of competitive procurement for library materials. Rather than developing informal work-arounds to avoid ordering of specialized materials such as rare books and foreign publications via competitive procurement, they sought instead to have those types of materials legally exempted from the Virginia Public Procurement Act, and their negotiations were successful.

Other examples abound. Two are included here for the purposes of this discussion.[24] How many new acquisitions managers have been hired to "clean up" departments where there has been a recent history of nonpayment of invoices? They are faced with correcting the situation while trying to figure out the budget impact of catching up in one fiscal year for payments due in previous fiscal years. What are the ethical steps that managers in this situation should follow? Certainly, the steps will include notification of vendors and publishers that their money is coming, along with serious discussions with collection managers about budget impact and notification to financial officers in the parent organization. In order to address this type of situation, integrity intact, librarians should make sure they have real authority and internal administrative support before they develop a solution. They should negotiate whatever solution they develop with their administrators, possibly with associate directors and budget officers first, but finally with the library director, who has the fiduciary responsibility for the library, as well as responsibility to maintain uninterrupted service. Someday, acquisitions managers may be heads of technical services divisions, and, when they are, they must remember that associate directors with integrity should keep their department heads more accountable than their predecessor or predecessors in this particular acquisitions operation appeared to do!

Other managers may find that serious problems have developed in the financial offices of their parent organizations. What ethical principles govern the decision of whether and how to bring these problems to someone's attention? Having developed relationships and opportunities for cross-education with fiscal officers will be an advantage in these situations. Making sure that complete information has been gathered in a systematic fashion is critical, as is ensuring that every appropriate administrator in the library knows of the situation. Once probing questions are answered in the manager's own mind, guidelines 1 and 2 of the ALCTS statement may help him or her make the correct decision about pursuing the matter further.

CONCLUSION

It is not within the purview of this chapter to talk about techniques for making ethical choices; for a good discussion of such techniques the reader should see Richard Rubin's "Ethical Issues in Library Personnel Management."[25] While dealing with the ethics of supervision, Rubin describes a technique for making ethical choices that is generalizable to business situations, as well. For a sweeping discussion of application of ethical principles, the reader should see Joseph Petrick's *Management Ethics: Integrity at Work*, which includes an application section after each major chapter.[26]

What we have done is discuss general guidelines for helping managers distinguish between "what is good and bad" and practicing a sense of "moral duty and obligation" in major areas of acquisitions administration. Although management functions in acquisitions may be governed by varying interpretations of ethical principles, many "rules of thumb" can be held in common. Acquisitions managers should:

1. Know and incorporate into their management style and persona the ALA and ALCTS codes of ethics.
2. Plan and organize with integrity, taking into account major considerations related to human resources, organizational culture and behavior, budget, and quality operations.
3. "Audit" their decisions for possible breaches of ethical conduct or request such an audit from colleagues who are known for their integrity.
4. Think about ethical principles before sharing information orally or in writing.
5. Adhere to ethical and legal guidelines when supervising or planning for supervision.
6. Incorporate ethical principles into all business relationships.

We have discussed practical ethical guidelines that can be used in decision-making processes. The most important thing to remember is that a mere statement of ethical principles, or even a methodology for making ethical decisions, is not enough. Acquisitions librarians need not only know what our ethical standards are, but must be careful to *do* them.

Notes

1. Diana Woodward, "A Framework for Deciding Issues in Ethics," *Library Trends* 39 (Summer and Fall 1990): 8-17.

2. Association for Library Collections and Technical Services, *Guidelines for ALCTS Members to Supplement the American Library Association Code of Ethics* (Chicago: ALCTS, 1994), online, American Library Association, Internet, 14 July 1995, http://www.ala.org/alcts/publications/ethics.html. In the Organization/ALA Divisions/Association for Library Collections and Technical Services/ALCTS Ethics Statements. The ALA Code itself was under much discussion from the early 1990s until its eventual revision in 1995, and the reader is encouraged to become familiar with that code. It does not, however, go far enough to satisfy collection development librarians in its discussion of unbiased selection of library materials. ALA's ALCTS formed a task force to develop guidelines to assist acquisitions and collection development librarians in the interpretation and application of the ALA Code of Ethics as they relate to this area and to the area of business relationships. The guidelines for acquisitions managers are discussed at length in the chapter proper.

3. Robert Hauptman, *Ethical Challenges in Librarianship* (Phoenix: Oryx, 1988).

4. *Ethics and the Librarian,* ed. F. W. Lancaster (Urbana: University of Illinois, Graduate School of Library and Information Science, 1991).

5. *Merriam-Webster's Collegiate Dictionary* (online), 1997.

6. Joe A. Hewitt, "On the Nature of Acquisitions," *LRTS* 33 (April 1989): 105-122.

7. Joseph A. Petrick and John F. Quinn, *Management Ethics: Integrity at Work* (Thousand Oaks, Calif.: Sage, 1997), p. 129.

8. Ibid., p. 136.

9. Ibid., pp. 131, 168.

10. Ibid., p. 134.

11. Ibid., p. 143.

12. Jennifer S. Cargill, "Monitoring the Information Resources Budget: Acquisitions Accounting," in *Technical Services Today and Tomorrow* (Englewood, Colo.: Libraries Unlimited, 1990), pp. 50-62.

13. Jeffrey L. Salter, "The Right Thing: Ethics in Administration and Personnel," *LLA Bulletin* 58 (Summer 1995): 25-32.

14. Hewitt, "On the Nature," p. 107.

15. Carol Pitts Hawks, "Building and Managing an Acquisitions Program," *Library Acquisitions: Practice & Theory* 18 (1994): 297-308.

16. Petrick and Quinn, *Management Ethics,* p. 218.

17. Ibid., p. 283.

18. Ibid., p. 174.

19. Salter, "The Right Thing," p. 28.

20. Donna Goehner, "Vendor-Library Relations: The Ethics of Working with Vendors," in *Understanding the Business of Library Acquisitions*, ed. Karen A. Schmidt (Chicago: American Library Association, 1990), pp. 137-151.

21. *Sharp practice* is defined in the second edition of the Random House dictionary as "shrewd to the point of dishonesty."

22. Association for Library Collections and Technical Services, Acquisitions Section, *Statement on Principles and Standards of Acquisitions Practice* (Chicago: ALCTS, 1994), online, American Library Association, Internet, 14 July 1995, http://www.ala.org. In the Organization/ALA Divisions/Association for Library Collections and Technical Services/ ALCTS Ethics Statements.

23. John R. Secor, "A Growing Crisis of Business Ethics: The Gathering Stormclouds," *Serials Librarian* 13 (October-November 1987): 67-90.

24. Ideas or situations described in the test were taken from an ALCTS Acquisitions Section program entitled "Demystifying Your Financial Relationships," held June 29, 1994, in Miami Beach, Florida.

25. Richard Rubin, "Ethical Issues in Library Personnel Management," *Journal of Library Administration* 14 (1991): 1-16.

26. Petrick and Quinn, *Management Ethics.*

18

Acquisitions Personnel Management, Organization, and Staffing Issues

LISA GERMAN

Some see leadership as high drama and the sound of trumpets calling. But I see history as a book with many pages, and each day we fill a page with acts of hopefulness and meaning.

— George Bush, inaugural address, January 20, 1989

People ask the difference between a leader and a boss. . . . The leader works in the open, and the boss is covert. The leader leads, and the boss drives.

— Theodore Roosevelt, speech at Binghamton, October 24, 1910

There is no better feeling than the one that results from success-fully managing a group of people, be it large or small. When every-thing is working well, people are all working efficiently toward a common, stated, well-defined mission. Discussion of diverse opin-ions is valued, consensus is reached more often than not, and peo-ple respect one another. People work accurately and effectively through a work flow that is logical and efficient. Goals are well ar-ticulated. Necessary training programs are in place. Quality control mechanisms are in place that can spot potential difficulties. Communication among and between units or departments takes place routinely and as necessary. Staff know they perform an im-portant function for the library and understand their function in relationship to the whole.

How many times have we wished this was true? How can we facilitate this occurring in our libraries? What can we do as departmental managers to ensure this happens? If the only constant is change, how do we help people thrive in an ever-changing environment?

Barry suggests that there are five service conditions that customers use as criteria to judge service. All of these can be used in judging a well-run acquisitions department:

- Reliability—the ability to perform the promised service dependably and accurately
- Responsiveness—the ability to provide prompt service
- Assurance—the level of trust and confidence that the unit inspires
- Empathy—caring, individualized attention
- Tangibles—the appearance of the employees, their work area, and documentation.[1]

Acquisitions management is not just the efficient and accurate ordering, claiming, receipt, and payment of library materials. It is the effective management, coaching, leading, and training of the people who perform acquisitions functions. Most logically, it is this effective management of staff that will lead to effectively managed processes.

An acquisitions department is unlike most other departments in the library, except perhaps circulation. In acquisitions, there are generally few professional librarians and a larger support staff. In a very small library, there may be support staff doing most acquisitions clerical functions under the direction of the head librarian. In a mid-sized or large academic library, there are generally one or two acquisitions librarians, depending on the functions of the department. In some instances, there are more, especially if collection development, interlibrary loan, cataloging, or binding responsibilities fall within the acquisitions department. This high concentration of paraprofessional and clerical staff requires that the acquisitions librarian possess excellent managerial skills.

Many of these skills can be categorized in the following way:

- Know your environment
- The Golden Rule management theory
- Communicate, communicate, communicate
- Lead by example
- Management by gastronomy

KNOW YOUR ENVIRONMENT

Tom Peters and Nancy Austin state in *A Passion for Excellence* that there are only two ways to create and sustain long-term superior performance. The first is to take excellent care of your customers; the second is to constantly innovate.[2] In an acquisitions department, the customers are other library departments and the library users. Knowing their needs is critical for the effective management of the acquisitions department.

Every library has an organizational culture. Barker writes that the basic components are:

- What we do, make, produce
- The technology we use to do it
- How we communicate, cooperate, cope with change
- Our values: why we bother
- Our basic assumptions about ourselves[3]

Figure 18-1 applies these components to acquisitions.

Being aware of these needs and the time pressures that are often exerted on the customers of acquisitions is important to an acquisitions manager. For example, collection development librarians may not be able to turn in orders during the first few weeks of a semester because they may be involved with bibliographic instruction of new students. Hence, encumbrances may not be at desired levels and order staff may become aggravated because it upsets their work flow. However, if this is a pattern which occurs repeatedly, staffing adjustments can be made. Perhaps, for example, the order clerks can take vacations during the first few weeks of the semester, or acquisitions can find some way to facilitate the selectors' work at that time.

Hawks recommends that the acquisitions librarian visit other library units or departmental libraries to find out what services they want from acquisitions.[4] You might consider inviting yourself to departmental meetings. Ask questions about the service that is being received from acquisitions and solicit suggestions for areas of improvement. This can be important for both a librarian new to the library and a veteran. It is important to take the pulse of the customers of acquisitions every few years. It is one way of determining how your staff is performing. Are they spending time on tasks that are unimportant to other departments and not doing functions that are important? How does the work of acquisitions make the rest of the library more responsive? Make sure the in-

What we do, make, produce	The technology we use to do it	How we communicate, cooperate, cope with change	Our values: why we bother	Our basic assumptions about ourselves
orders	personal computers	reengineering	commitment to service	strive to procure the
claims	integrated systems	team management	fair business practices	best value for our
cancels	Internet	servant leadership	honesty in business dealings	institution's dollar
payments		e-mail		experts in publishing

Figure 18-1 Basic Components of Organizational Culture

formation learned is shared with all the acquisitions department staff members.

Innovation may mean listening to departmental library and customer needs and offering to provide new services in order to meet those needs. For example, if there is a staff shortage in cataloging which leads to a cataloging delay, perhaps a "fast cat" cataloging operation can be established in acquisitions.

Knowing the environment means also understanding things such as union or civil service contracts. Take time to read the contract and understand what it says. Take the following case:

> The serial renewal invoices had typically been paid after the due date. A method was established this year in order to avoid the potential thousands of dollars in late fees which would be assessed to the library. Zelda, the acquisitions invoice clerk, worked several hours overtime. Typically, overtime was not paid in the library; all overtime was taken in compensatory time. However, according to the union contract, employees have the option of either taking comp time or being paid overtime. Zelda chose to be paid overtime.

Had the supervisor not been aware of the commitments of the union contract, financial trouble could have resulted from Zelda's decision to be paid for her overtime work. It is important for the acquisitions librarian to talk through these decisions with the staff and to understand the ramifications of union contracts and other regulatory documents.

Take time to understand the people working in acquisitions and the relationships they have with each other. Often, it is the little things that matter rather than the big things. Some staff will remember each and every conversation you have with them and recite your words back to you. Others won't remember the conversation at all. Remembering people's sensitivities can be beneficial in the long run.

When dealing with a personnel issue, either positive or negative, it is important to know what support you will receive from upper library management. For example, if salary upgrades are not being processed due to budgetary woes, do not ask staff to take on responsibilities out of their classification. Similarly, it is necessary to have the support of upper library management when dealing with difficult personnel issues. If your library management is typically not supportive, then it is good to know that before you start to institute progressive discipline.

THE GOLDEN RULE MANAGEMENT THEORY

The Golden Rule states: Do unto others as you would have others do unto you. Similar to this Biblical admonition, the Golden Rule Management Theory says that you treat colleagues, library directors, and staff with the same courtesy with which you would like to be treated yourself. This is not a complex idea, but often it is more difficult than it seems. A friend once told me that there is a reason why there is only one Golden Rule: it is both universal and fundamental. It exists in one form or another in most cultures or religions.

The Golden Rule Management Theory is especially meaningful for the acquisitions librarian who has to deal with significant numbers of staff. It establishes a level of respect and communication among all levels of staff that is intrinsically important in motivating people, promoting excellence in the workplace, and promoting mutual regard for the missions and goals of the department. How can this rule be put into practice?

Use Active Listening Skills

It takes effort to listen. Keep engaged even when the speaker says things you disagree with or don't understand. Recognize that you can learn from staff members. React. I once had a supervisor who sat stony-faced when anyone voiced a complaint. The message that was sent was simple: "I don't hear you and I don't care." Be empathetic. That doesn't mean that you always have to agree. Restate the point. Show that you are listening. Let speakers finish a thought and resist the tendency to jump ahead or finish their sentences for them. People will find it easier to communicate with you if you are employing active listening skills.

Be Honest

Staff can spot a phony a mile away. They will respect honesty even if it is difficult. If you are reengineering, be honest with them. Let them know that their jobs are going to change. If you don't explain that time and time again, people may forget. That doesn't mean that you need to blurt out the first thing that crosses your mind.

Be Fair

It is impossible to care about everyone equally. There will be staff in the department whom you like and others whom you do not like. The important thing to remember is to treat everyone fairly. For example, if there is an office rule that you must notify a supervisor when you are ill, do not let someone disregard that rule. If staff are supposed to notify their supervisor if they need to make up time outside their scheduled hours, enforce that rule for everyone. When you walk into the department in the morning, say hello to everyone you pass on the way to get a cup of coffee. Many times I have heard, "she walks by me and doesn't say hello, but she says hello to her." People remember those slights even though it may be just an oversight.

Follow Through
It is very important with staff to follow through with your commitment. If you say you will do something, do it or go back to the person and let them know that you cannot do it. Not following through on what you say causes frustration. For example, if a staff member needs you to take an issue up the administrative ladder or to intervene with another departmental supervisor, do it or tell them why you won't do it.

Reward Good Work
Make sure that good work is rewarded. Let someone know if they have done a good job. Verbally tell them or consider writing a thank-you note. Thank-you notes, especially handwritten notes, are appreciated. If permitted in your organization, award superior performance increases to outstanding staff members.

COMMUNICATE, COMMUNICATE, COMMUNICATE

You often hear comments in organizations such as, "communication is lousy here" or "it seems to be a problem of poor communication." Organizations large and small have communication problems. Sometimes we think we are communicating well, but usually an event will occur that will bring the communication gap into the forefront. As managers of acquisitions departments, we communicate with vendors, selectors, users, the business office in the library and in the parent organization, and other librarians and staff throughout the library system. There are several things we can do to improve communication both within our departments and within the library.

Nothing can replace good communication each day. Let staff members know of new policies or procedures that will affect them. If you hear something nice about a staff member from another librarian, pass along the compliment. Nothing works like positive reinforcement. If a staff member has done a great job, say so! Stueart and Moran discuss the difficulties of upward communication. Staff may have trouble approaching supervisors due either to their own communication difficulties or the perceived rigidity of the manager.[5] Ways to combat this difficulty include being an active listener or engaging in social discussions.

Electronic mail is a good way to notify all staff of a particular policy or procedure, providing everyone has been trained how to use it. It ensures that you will both have a copy of what you communicated and that it was sent to all parties involved. It is the responsibility of the receiver to read it and ask any questions that might arise. Minutes of an office meeting can be distributed over e-mail quickly, cheaply, and more efficiently than if they are routed on paper. Announcements and policies can be easily distributed. If a particular policy is being abused, documentation exists that proves the policy has been communicated to all. For example:

> Jane and Amanda decided to make up time on Saturday. They did not check with their unit head, even though that was the departmental policy. The unit head came in on Saturday, found them working, and reiterated the stated policy. She then sent an e-mail message to the whole department reiterating that Saturday makeup time was a privilege, not a right, and she was sending out a message again for people who needed a reminder.

This sets the stage, in case it happens again, to revoke the privilege of Saturday makeup time if necessary.

Informal methods of communication are also important. Departmental parties can be a good way to bring together people who may not communicate daily. The benefits of social communication cannot be overlooked. People are more relaxed and the setting provides a good time to recognize folks who have worked particularly hard or have completed a difficult and lengthy assignment. Departmental newsletters, either electronic or on paper, are also a way to enhance departmental communication.

It is also important to communicate your department's successes both to the department and the outside world. I have a friend who talks about one of her first bosses with fondness. He is not the best scholar and probably not an outstanding librarian. He is, however, one of the best at motivating people. He constantly talks to his staff, rewards great work, and always sings their praises to other library staff members. He has inspired loyalty among his staff, and everyone works hard because they feel he appreciates it.

Establishing a staff Web page is a good way to communicate to people outside your own department. Acquisitions policies and procedures can be noted, along with contact people for questions and answers. It can also keep acquisitions staff focused on goals.

Communication beyond the acquisitions department is equally important. Devices you can employ in communicating with the selectors, customers, or departmental librarians include sharing vendor reports and profiles with selectors, having "brown bag" question and answer sessions or forums about acquisitions and fund accounting procedures. Offer to attend other department meetings to answer questions and also to ask questions yourself. Communication is a two-way street, and each day can provide a new opportunity for learning.

LEAD BY EXAMPLE

It is imperative that the manager set the tone in the workplace. Servant leadership is one philosophy that establishes a mechanism for embracing this concept. Advanced by Robert Greenleaf, a former executive with AT&T, the principle states that in order to lead, you must also serve. Being a servant to those you lead means that you listen to and respect those you supervise. Your leadership power comes from the skills you possess rather than from an administrative hierarchy. You recognize that you cannot do everything yourself, that you are dependent on those you manage, and that you all contribute to the success of your work. A good test of your capacity for servant leadership is to ask the question: "Would I want to be managed by me?"[6]

MANAGEMENT BY GASTRONOMY
AND OTHER HAPPY EVENTS

In many organizations, it is possible to reward people's hard work by offering superior performance increases. In some libraries this may be precluded by union or civil service regulations. If this is the case, it is still possible to consider other types of rewards. Thus is born the notion of Management by Gastronomy.

There are two underlying principles here. The first is that people like to be acknowledged for contributions. While money may be a great motivator, as noted before the recognition of accomplishments, both public and private, is very meaningful to all levels of staff and should be generously applied. The second principle is that eating together can help people transcend work problems. Staff parties, fruit and bagels at a staff meeting, and special treats occasionally combine these principles and can help create an atmosphere of collegiality. This is not meant to suggest that problems are solved, but it can set a tone of a working environment that leaves the group prone to open communication and problem solving. It is important to remember that there are other rewards in the workplace besides money, and food can be one of them.

PROBLEM SITUATIONS AND CONFLICT

In any department there are going to be conflict situations which will need to be resolved. In acquisitions, it could be a problem with a customer (departmental library or user), an interoffice squabble, or a problem that has arisen between the acquisitions librarian and an employee. These situations will occur even in the most content and efficient departments. Remember: all conflicts are not equal, sometimes conflict is good, and every conflict does not demand action. It is important to pick your battles. Some battles are more worthy of a fight than others. For example, if there is an employee in the department who is not working up to standard, has been in the department for forty years, and is retiring next year, is the problem worth pursuing? Probably not. On the other hand, if there is an employee who is on probation and not working up to standard, the situation should be addressed.

If the conflict is due to a performance problem, analyze the problem before discussing it with the employee. For example, if one staff member complains that another staff member's lack of productivity is affecting his or her work, look at the situation from both sides. Does a problem really exist, or is it a personality conflict between two people? Are departmental standards in place? If not, then the first discussion should be with the whole department about expectations. Set the expectations and discuss them to make sure that they are reasonable and attainable. Write them down and make sure everyone who needs one has a copy. Follow up to make sure that they are being met. Listen to the employee if she or he indicates that the standards are unreasonable. Perhaps the employee knows something that you don't know.

Sarah is the invoice coordinator. She keeps track of prepayment invoices, bills received without items, and problem invoices and statements. Her supervisor discovered that she was not following up to make sure that prepayment material had been received. All parties met with the department head to try to resolve this situation.

The problems were stated, and Sarah was given a schedule to follow. The department head explained the importance of Sarah's job and how critical it was to follow through to ensure that the library received materials that it had paid for. Notes of the meeting and the schedule for claiming and follow-up were distributed to all parties. Follow-up conversations have taken place to ensure that the employee is following the standards.

Sometimes these conversations take place, but the behavior does not improve. What do you do next? First, you need to give the employee enough time to change his or her behavior. If the behavior does not change, you need to inform the employee of the consequences. Sometimes this is a long-term process.

Janet had been working at the library for twelve years. She was a recovering cancer patient and had missed several weeks of work. Her schedule was somewhat erratic due to her illness. After she recovered from her illness, her schedule remained erratic. She often came in late and sometimes was late for her public service shift. Several people in the department had to pinch-hit checking in serials because Janet was not there. She rarely worked a forty-hour week and often was in time-without-pay status. She had been counseled several times by her supervisor about her schedule. Finally, after several discussions and no improvement, and despite her good intentions, Janet's manager wrote on her performance appraisal that her evaluation might be affected next year if her poor attendance and lateness continued. The following year, her lateness was marginally better, but she was still not working forty-hour work weeks. Her supervisor wrote in the evaluation that though she did a good job while she was in attendance, her rating would indeed lower if she didn't work full weeks and if her schedule did not stabilize. The manager also stressed how important it was that she worked a full week and that her poor attendance had an adverse effect on people within the department. They could not get their jobs done because they had to pinch-hit and do Janet's job. Janet seemed to understand this, and in the following year, her attendance improved dramatically. Her supervisor recognized this effort, gave her constant, reinforcing good feedback, and was able to write a strong performance appraisal in the following year.

This case illustrates that correcting a problem situation often takes years of discussion, positive reinforcement, statements of consequences, and more counseling. It can, as in the case above, result in a win/win situation for both the manager and the employee.

Situations will not always end on a positive note. In the case above, the employee did not understand the effect that her actions were having on other members of the department, whom she liked and considered to be friends. She also did not fully realize how important she was to the department. What happens when you have a very difficult employee who does not respond to positive reinforcement, counseling, etc.? You need to document the poor behavior, as well as your attempts at resolving the situation. Note the time and place of the meetings and who was in attendance. If the situation escalates, it is wise to invite another colleague to sit in on the discussions and, in fact, many union contracts require that you allow the employee to bring a union representative if he or she so desires. You must keep your supervisor and human relations staff abreast of the situation. Providing you have their support and you are following all civil service, union, and other organizational guidelines, you may proceed with disciplinary action. If you end up in a grievance situation, as long as you have tried all appropriate means to resolve the situation and have documented your work carefully, you can feel confident that you have done your best. Be prepared to spend many, many hours on this procedure. If, for some reason, you do not have the support of your supervisor, it is important to continue to try all the positive methods of modifying behavior. You may have to accept the fact that sometimes these methods do not work, but without upper management support, you have no other choice.

MANAGING CHANGE

Chances are good that you will be managing a department where the only constant is change. Library organizations, especially technical services areas, reorganize or reengineer to take advantage of new technologies and to better meet users' demands. Some of the impetus for change begins in the department, but most often, it is the library administration that initiates reengineering. Perhaps reengineering is needed in order to take advantage of new technologies, or is initiated due to an upcoming department head vacancy. In any case, it is always good to examine acquisitions policies and procedures repeatedly with a specific goal in mind. Clearly communicated reasons for change or goals from the outset are imperative for success. Below is an example of a path toward change:

The serials check-in staff had been using the new integrated system for one year. Reference librarians began noticing mistakes in check-in boxes. Combined issues were not being recorded properly, resulting in frustration among patrons and librarians. It became clear to the acquisitions librarian that quality control measures needed to be instituted. She called a meeting of the department and explained that patrons were having trouble understanding serials receipts, emphasizing the importance of accurate records now that they were available for the public to view. The acquisitions librarian noted in the meeting that 10 percent of everyone's work would be checked each day by her assistant. Mistakes would be returned to the person who made the error for correction, with 5 percent established as an acceptable error rate. After six months, everyone was expected to meet that standard. For the next year, accuracy rates would be tabulated for each employee, though they would not be used as an evaluation measure. They would be used the following year in the evaluation process.

In the example above, the goal was clearly articulated: improve the clarity of the serials check-in boxes. A strategy was developed to implement the goal, and the end was shared with everyone. Standards were adopted and a set amount of time was set for people to comply to the standard. At first, employees did not believe that they could check in serials with a 95 percent accuracy rate. However, after six months everyone was meeting the standard. All staff felt relieved that quality control measures had been adopted and were proud that they were able to do such good work. They understood the function they performed and the impact it had on patrons and other library staff. Reference staff as well as their supervisor gave the department staff positive feedback. This change was managed in a positive way, with positive results.

Follow these six steps, and managing people during a change process will be easier:

- Articulate desired goals at the outset
- Set up a strategy and share it
- Set acceptable standards
- Be accountable
- Give feedback
- Reward desired results

CONCLUSION

Management is not rocket science or brain surgery. It is not exact, and it is often not taught in a practical way in library school. Managing, coaching, and training people in a large acquisitions department can be both rewarding and fun. It is rewarding to watch a department move forward and know that you were instrumental in guiding the move. It is fun if you like helping people develop to their full potential. Mostly, management is common sense. Trust your own good instincts, listen to the little voice in your head, and heed its words.

Notes

1. Leonard L. Berry et al. "Improving Service Quality in America: Lessons Learned; Executive Commentary," *Academy of Management Executive* 8, no. 2 (1994): 32-52.

2. Tom Peters and Nancy Austin, *A Passion for Excellence* (New York: Random House, 1985), p.4.

3. Joseph Barker, "Triggering Constructive Change by Managing Organizational Culture in an Academic Library," *Library Acquisitions: Practice & Theory* 19 (1995): 10.

4. Carol Hawks, "Building and Managing an Acquisitions Program," *Library Acquisitions: Practice & Theory* 18 (1994): 297.

5. Robert Stueart and Barbara Moran, *Library Management* (Littleton, Colo.: Libraries Unlimited, 1987), p. 184.

6. Lorraine P. Holden, "The Team Manager as Visionary and Servant," *Manager's Magazine* 63, no. 11 (1988): 6-9.

References

Baldwin, David A. and R. Migneault. *Humanistic Management by Teamwork*. Englewood, Colo.: Libraries Unlimited, 1996.

Deeprose, Donna. *The Team Coach*. New York: Amacom, 1995.

Hegelsen, Sally. *The Female Advantage*. New York: Doubleday, 1990.

19

Licensing in Lieu of Acquiring

TRISHA L. DAVIS

In 1990, if anyone had asked library patrons to describe their vision of the library in the year 2000, many of them would have made the assumption that CD-ROM databases would be as common as videotapes. This relatively new technology had spawned products that were unquestionably exciting and glamorous compared to traditional print resources. The generation weaned on the television screens craved the quick retrieval, the colorful graphics, the at-your-fingertips menus and help screens. Patrons were thrilled to be relieved of the tedious burden of print index searching and the costs of dedicated online searching. Many were certain this new technology would mature into a viable standard for the Information Age. The Internet was beginning to show signs of functionality, but no one could have foreseen the power of the Web by the end of the decade. To patrons, the transition from print to electronic was a phenomenal success as libraries provided access to information that was simply not available in print.

Digital products have proven to be a mixed blessing to librarianship. What librarians could not or did not foresee was that their tremendous success and popularity with patrons would create burdens of an entirely new nature. In 1998, collection development is burdened with stretching shrinking budgets to cover the considerable costs of access. Reference staffs are burdened with trying to keep up with sophisticated databases that operate on complex and powerful search software that is neither simple to learn nor easy to teach. Automation staff are struggling to select, purchase, set up, maintain, and upgrade the many workstations and local area networks needed to support these products. The trend is shifting toward consortium-based acquisition, which may provide a better pricing model, but does not relieve the library of acquisition details and license obligations.

THE SHIFT TO LICENSED
ELECTRONIC PRODUCTS

As libraries moved from print to electronic resources, acquisitions functions moved from acquiring to licensing, from ownership to access, from copyright to contract law. Acquisition staff quickly recognized that the success of the new technologies grew from the fact that electronic products simply do not behave like traditional print resources. What librarians were not so quick to realize was that the database owners, producers, and distributors of these electronic resources also did not want to behave like the publishers of print resources. The profession was soon engulfed in lease rights rather than ownership, complex product definitions and pricing options, and finally licensing agreements and contracts to sign. Acquisitions librarians quickly learned that this new reality simply came with the territory.

Today, license agreements are almost unavoidable. They are so common that vendor catalogs often indicate what type of license is required, and Internet-based products include the license online. Because these electronic products are leased, not owned, the library only has the rights to use the database in specific ways. With traditional print, audiovisual, and even most computer software products, libraries purchase or acquire a copy of the item. As a rule, who uses it, where it is used, and how it is used are either not an issue, or an issue that is governed by local library policy and the Copyright Act of 1976 and related "fair-use" interpretations which adequately protect libraries' rights. The vast majority of electronic products, whether Internet, network-based, or stand-alone, require signed license agreements in which all access and use rights must be defined. The investigation, the negotiation, and the handling of these products and their licenses require working with new publishers, new vendors or different service representatives of established vendors, and in some cases the database owner or distributor. The rights to search, copy, and use the data are assigned in the license agreement. These are complex issues. The problems they raise are new to the library, and their solutions do not easily fit into our standard processes and procedures.

COMPLICATIONS IN THE SELECTION PROCESS

Considering the traditional steps in the acquisition process, the first step is to identify and select the item for purchase. These tasks are usually handled by a library user or a librarian with the help of advertisements, published reviews, and publishers' catalogs. The item to be acquired is normally described in standard bibliographic terms of number of pages, or volumes, or pieces. Information about the item's size, its format, even specific details about content are readily available from standard sources. This information is easily understood by library users, librarians, publishers, and distributors.

The acquisition or lease of a licensed electronic product involves unique challenges to these traditional acquisition functions. To begin with, only librarians trained in the specifics of database content, search software, microcomputers, network topology, Internet access, and World Wide Web site construction are equipped to handle the selection and acquisition process. To exacerbate the problems, the marketing information about electronic products that is provided in advertisements, catalogs, and even electronic messages cannot be standardized much beyond the database content. An understanding of access methods, required technology, and software is required. How the product will be accessed, distributed, and used in the library and through its distributed systems is mandatory to deciding whether the product is an appropriate purchase.

THE ACQUISITION PROCESS EXPANDED

After the initial product selection is identified, the standard acquisition verification of the product's bibliographic identity, pricing options, and availability is equally challenging. Again, due to lack of standards, the product's identity may vary by content and access options. A single database may be available from a half dozen providers, each with different search software, retrieval capabilities, and user functionality. These choices, with the related purchase, lease, and subscription options, all affect the price and availability. To investigate these details, acquisitions librarians must deal with either vendors or distributors that specialize in electronic products, or with their standard vendors and publishers who offer electronic products in addition to their usual inventory.

Dealing with standard acquisition sources is not necessarily the preferred choice. Often the sales and customer service staff of traditional library vendors do not have the expertise to answer specific product-related questions or to provide the additional information needed for a library's unique applications. Working directly with the electronic publishers can be problematic in that they require specific information on the library's application of their products. The librarian must be prepared to explain the library's requirements in a logical, detailed manner and work with the vendor to determine that the identity and price information are correct and complete.

The next step involves selecting a vendor/distributor and placing the order. The choice of where to place the order is actually fairly simple due to a limited number of options. Some products are only available from the database owner or a single distributor. Others are available from a handful of vendors that offer hundreds of electronic products. The simple act of placing the order can be complicated. While the standard library purchase order is normally accepted, the distributor may require a product-specific order form be submitted. In some cases, the library is asked to provide additional details about the product, the equipment to be used, and the permanent location of the product. At this point, a license agreement may have to be signed before the order even is accepted. Once the order is placed, the item(s) must be received and the invoice approved for payment. At this point, normal library operations will meet the need for those products delivered on physical media. Receiving the product is not difficult, unless the producer fails to adequately or properly identify the item. For access rights to external or Internet based products, however, there may not be any physical pieces to receive. Only the receipt of passwords and confirmation of access to the appropriate Internet provider addresses prove that the process is complete. Luckily, invoicing and payment are not problematic issues unless delayed by license negotiations.

How does the acquisitions librarian make this expanded work flow effective? How does the library assure that it has acquired the correct product at the best price? Someone on the staff must become expert in the technology required to access the database. Someone must be able to communicate in very specific terms the library's needs. Someone must learn to deal with the highly specialized publishers and distributors of electronic databases who are not experienced in working with librarians or the library environment. This "someone," often the acquisitions librarian, must also deal continuously with the added burden of license agreements.

THE CHALLENGE OF LICENSE AGREEMENTS

License agreements have become a fact of life in the electronic publishing world. Yet nothing about them is standard or predictable. While most librarians understand the need for license agreements, libraries often are puzzled as to how to handle them because each one is unique. There are four major challenges associated with handling license agreements:

- Determining their existence;
- Understanding their content;
- Deciding what must be negotiated; and
- Identifying who should negotiate and sign them.

When ordering machine-loaded bibliographic and full-text databases, the library must assume that a signed license agreement is a basic requirement for purchase. The ease of manipulating and copying a mainframe- or microcomputer-loaded database provides an excellent opportunity for abuse of the copyright. Even with restricted access to Internet databases it is possible to download and copy large portions of the data. For the library, the purchase or lease of these databases is quite expensive in terms of the product rights, access rights, and the equipment needed for access. Thus, the accurate preparation and thorough negotiation of the license agreement to meet the library's needs are of benefit to both parties, the information provider as well as the library.

First, the acquisitions librarian must ascertain which products require a license agreement. With a careful analysis of the agreement, the librarian can determine when and how that agreement will affect the acquisition process. It is always advisable to ask about the existence of a license agreement before ordering. Some publishers are happy to send a copy of the license immediately to allow the licensee to review the contract and determine if the intended use is allowed. Catalogs for electronic products often include a note about license agreements in the product descriptions. Some electronic products require a signed license agreement, in the guise of an order form, for the product or service. Even if the library orders the item using the standard purchase order form, the distributor may require a signed order form before filling the request. For other products, the library's standard purchase order is acceptable because a passive license agreement is part of the shrink-wrapped product.[1]

Unfortunately, some distributors do not mention the existence of an agreement in their advertising or catalog. The contract is simply sent after the order is placed. In some cases, the first shipment of the product may have been received and the invoice paid before the library realizes that there is a license agreement to be signed. It is not uncommon to receive a shrink-wrapped passive license with the product and a separate agreement to be signed for the multiuser network application of the same item. In recent years, many online products require all users to register with a screen-based license before accessing the product. Passive licenses, such as shrink-wraps or click-ons, normally cover single-user, single-machine, single IP address applications only. Any signed license agreements override the passive or generic ones.

Once the license agreement is located, the content must be carefully analyzed. License agreements are a form of a legal contract and are written in legalese. Unless the librarian is trained as an attorney, it will take two or three detailed readings of the license agreement to ferret out the important rights and restrictions. Each contract is different; even those issued by the same distributor often have widely variant clauses. To add to this challenge, most sales and customer service representatives cannot offer much help with interpreting these license agreements. Often a phone call to the provider requires speaking with a third or fourth party to confirm a definition of a term or a phrase in question. This person, in turn, seldom has any experience in the library environment and may have difficulty understanding the library's questions.

ANALYSIS OF LICENSED RIGHTS

The next task is to decide the terms to be negotiated. These fall into two broad categories: the rights and restrictions that govern how the library and its patrons use the product, and the warranties and labilities each party agrees to. If the library is a public institution, the contract also must be modified to comply with local and state laws.

The most important issues for negotiation evolve around (1) the definition and number of users, (2) method of access, and (3) use capabilities and restriction, including purposes for use. In many cases, the definition of the user is not important. As long as the library is willing to pay the fees for open access or agrees to limit use to a specified number of simultaneous users or IP addresses, the licensor is satisfied. Some licensors, however, wish to carefully define who may use their product and under what circumstances. They lay out explicit language to describe the user in terms of their particular affiliation with the academic institution or corporate body. Such clauses must be carefully studied and negotiated.

The restriction on method of access can be complex in today's world of local- and wide-area networks. Licensors have been very creative in their definition of approved access, with definitions based on variables such as the site of the server, the location of the user, or the method of accessing the network. Some vendors are willing to allow any means of access to a local area network; others are quite restrictive. The contracts that are most problematic restrict use to one limited site or through a single password. Sometimes these limited definitions of access entirely prohibit the product's use on the library's network or by all library users. To control use by requiring such specific means of access is unrealistic.

It is much easier for libraries to understand restriction on use capabilities. Most librarians will readily acknowledge that the user should not copy the database, download or print entire files, or modify the search software. Yet, each contract may stipulate varying use capabilities and restrictions which must be clearly understood and acknowledged. It is not logical that one product will allow up to fifty print copies of search results while another product limits the patron to a single copy. By signing the contract, the library commits to communicating these restrictions to all staff and patrons.

Most license agreements include extensive clauses concerning warranties and liabilities, printed in capital letters or boldface so they cannot be missed. The bottom line is that most licensors will not warranty either the content of the database or the performance of the search software. In fact, distributors normally acknowledge that there may be errors, inconsistencies, and omissions in the data. They want to make it perfectly clear that the licensor is in no way liable for any loss or damages due to the use of its database. Most librarians will agree to all of this as these same issues existed with print products, and libraries have learned not to worry about them. What should be questioned, however, is language that limits any warranty of guaranteed access hours or performance of the database medium, i.e., the CD-ROM or the tape. The contract may state that loss of access due to the Internet is out of their control, but they should warrant the availability of the database on their server. For media-based products, replacements for lost or damaged items may be available for only a limited time period or at considerable additional cost. Given the nature and delicacy of these media, such terms are, for the most part, unreasonable. There are many other troublesome issues hidden in these contracts, under headings such as Force Majeure, Termination of License, Indemnification, Severability, and Governing Law. There may be stipulations concerning the type of hardware used, the method of returning outdated tapes and disks, and the terms of invoicing and payment. All such issues must be identified and considered by the staff involved in acquiring, operating, and using the product.

CONTRACT REVISIONS AND NEGOTIATION

Each library needs to identify the person(s) responsible for negotiating and signing the license on behalf of the institution. Acquisitions librarians are often the most effective negotiators because they are familiar with the product, the intended use, and the database owner or distributor. Many contract deletions or amendments can be negotiated between the librarian and the database licensor, especially those regarding license terms, use capabilities and restrictions, warranties, and liabilities. These negotiations often focus on the sections describing the local network or system capabilities, defining the location of the library users, and stipulating the extent of local security measures. Once negotiated, the final contract can be referred to the attorneys to work out the specific contract language and to the appropriate administrators for signature. Most database producers and distributors understand the complexities of this process. Yet for every one that works smoothly and cooperatively with the library, there are those who fail to understand these negotiations and the amount of time they take. Often, the salesperson will hound the librarian to speed up the process, send notices inquiring as to the status of the agreement, and worse, threaten to hold up shipments or cancel the subscription.

Once terms are negotiated, someone with administrative authority and, hopefully, legal expertise, must certify that the terms of the agreement are acceptable and sign the license, or, must continue to negotiate for alternative terms. There is no question that license agreements should be reviewed. However, many librarians do not have readily accessible legal resource people, so that the duty falls to the library director or other senior-level authorities who may not be too eager to deal with it.

LOCAL IMPLEMENTATION

The final challenge for libraries is to monitor the fair use of electronic databases. This is not an entirely new frontier. Most librarians are intimately familiar with the Copyright Act of 1976 and the fair-use interpretations on copying. These license agreements move far beyond the traditional fair use boundaries into larger questions of who, when, where, and how. If the library has agreed to specific limitations concerning use, they are obligated to communicate these limitations to all parties involved and ensure that they understand and abide by them. The extent of liability depends entirely on the intent of the agreement and the attitude of the parties involved. In the act of opening an Internet site, accepting a passive license, or signing a contractual agreement, the library must acknowledge that it may be legally liable to the terms.

How can the library assure fair use rights? The best approach is to begin at the point of acquisition. The selectors and end-users of the product must understand the use limitations before the decision to purchase is finalized. The appropriate automation staff must be consulted to assure that the desired method of access is secure, adequate to meet local needs, and legal. Reference and circulation staff must understand how they may be required to monitor both the type of user and the usage. And, most important, methods must be established to notify the user of all use capabilities and limitations. If these requirements can be met, the license can be negotiated, signed, and the product acquired.

READING THE FINE PRINT: A FRAMEWORK FOR THE NEW AGE

Each library will shift into leases and licenses at its own speed and in its own manner. Although no standards exist, answers to the following questions normally are found in the license agreement. Libraries may use these questions as a starting point for analyzing and evaluating the content of an agreement. In answering these questions, the library will identify the people on its staff who must be involved in the process and which policies and procedures must be revised. In time, the process will become more normalized, but not in the near future.

DEFINITIONS

It is important to identify all the issues that need to be addressed when negotiating a licensing agreement. Following are a list of questions and issues that are fundamental to establishing a successful license. Acquisitions librarians and other librarians who find themselves in a position to stipulate specific items of agreement need to look at these several areas thoughtfully, confer widely, and read carefully.

Parties to the Agreement

- Exactly who is signing this agreement?
- Who owns the database content?
- Who owns the search/retrieval software?
- Who produced the product?
- Who distributes or provides access to the product?
- Is the license an agreement between only two parties: licensee and the licensor?
- Does the license refer to rights of any third parties?
- Does the license ask us to be responsible for the actions of any third party?

Ownership Rights

- Are we actually acquiring a product that is ours to keep forever?
- Do we own the physical medium?
- Do we own the rights to the content?
- Do we have ownership rights to the operating and search software?
- Do we have the right to transfer or sell this product?

Lease Rights

- Exactly what are we leasing?
- Do we have any permanent rights?
- Do these rights disappear when the lease or subscription is ceased?
- Is there mention of discs, manuals, or other products being returned?
- Are passwords updated on a regular basis?
- Do log-on routines change regularly?
- If this is a subscription, may we keep and use the product when the subscription ends?

Users

- Who are my primary user groups?
- Does the license specifically address these groups?
- Does the license include all possible definitions of users?
- Will this product be used by users from more than one location or institution?
- Will there be multiple simultaneous users?

- How many simultaneous users will we allow?
- How will users access the product?
- Does the method of access define or limit the user in any way?
- From where will these users access the product?
- Does location of the user define or limit access in any way?

Access

- How do we plan to use this product?
- Does the contract stipulate the type of equipment or system required?
- Will this product be used on a network?
- Does our definition of network agree with the license?
- Is remote access allowed?
- Is access limited to certain IP addresses?
- Is location of users a factor?

The Database

- Are there any limitations on searching?
- Are there any limitations on printing copies of the database?
- Does it allow electronic copies? In what forms?
- Are we allowed to transmit the search results electronically to others via the Internet?
- Are there any limitations on downloading from the database?
- Is a specific level of access guaranteed?
- Are the hours of availability specified?

Search Results

- Does the license mention any limitation on use?
- Does the license limit use to certain purposes?
- Will this product be used by patrons for other than educational purposes?
- Can search results be shared with others?
- Can search results be shared via interlibrary loan?

The Software

- Is there any need to copy the database?
- Do we want to make a backup copy of any data?
- Do we need to convert to another medium?
- Does the license either require or forbid the use of other software?

Product Maintenance

- Is the license or warranty voided if the proper equipment is not used?
- Does the contract define work station appearance or signage?
- Are we required to upgrade software in order to keep our license valid?
- Must we return software, discs, or instructional products at any point in time?
- Is there a specified method for returning products?

Access control

- Are the security requirements reasonable?
- Are there user registration requirements?
- Must we provide usage reports?
- Does the contract specify audit rights?
- Is there any mention of assuring copyright notices and logos are printed on all copies?

Hidden Costs and Penalties

- Are there penalties or fees for late returns?
- Are there charges for replacement discs?
- Are we responsible for sales or property taxes, tariffs, or import fees?
- Are we charged interest on late payments?
- Does the agreement address attorney's fees and court costs?

Contract Term and Termination

- Are all sections of the agreement and its attachments available for review and signature?
- Does the license state that all contractual modification must be initialed by both parties?
- Does the term of the agreement match the term of the subscription?
- Can this agreement be automatically renewed?
- Does the vendor hold cancellation rights to the license?
- What are our cancellation rights and requirements?
- May we terminate for cause? How is that handled?
- Does the "Act of God" clause seem reasonable?
- What happens if the vendor files for bankruptcy?

Warranty, Liability, and Indemnity Clauses

- Does the agreement provide any warranty or guarantee for the database or software or manuals, or access and availability?
- Are we willing to live with a limited warranty statement?
- Do we have any option to return the product for a refund?
- Is the vendor asking us to indemnify them or hold them harmless to other parties?
- Does the license allow the vendor to change the product?

Miscellaneous Provisions

- Is the vendor allowed to assign this contract to another party? Are we?
- Does the governing law section conflict with our jurisdiction?
- Is there a confidentiality clause?

Note

1. "Shrink-wrap" refers to the practice by some software producers of building license acceptance into the opening of the wrapping on the product. If a user opens the package, he or she accepts the terms of the license by default.

Bibliography

PUBLISHED RESOURCES

Bosch, Stephen, Patricia Promis and Chris Sugnet. *Guide to Selecting and Acquiring CD-ROMs, Software, and Other Electronic Publications.* Chicago: American Library Association, 1994.

Buchanan, Nancy L. "Navigating the Electronic River: Electronic Product Licensing and Contracts." *Serials Librarian* 30, no. 3/4 (1997):171-182.

Davis, Trisha L. "Acquisition of CD-ROM Databases for Local Area Networks." *Journal of Academic Librarianship* 19, no. 2 (1993): 68-71.

———. "The Evolution of Selection Activities for Electronic Resources." *Library Trends* 45, no. 3 (1997): 391-403.

———. "License Agreements in Lieu of Copyright: Are We Signing Away Our Rights?" *Library Acquisitions: Practice & Theory* 21, no. 1 (1997): 19-27.

Hersey, Karen. "Coping with Copyright and Beyond: New Challenges As the Library Goes Digital." In *Copyright, Public Policy, and the Scholarly Community.* Washington, D.C.: Association of Research Libraries, 1995, pp. 23-32.

Schmidt, Karen, Carol Pitts Diedrichs, Joyce Ogburn and Christian Boissannas. "Perspectives on Acquisitions." *Journal of Academic Librarianship* 24, no. 1 (1998): 73-82.

ELECTRONIC RESOURCES

Association of Research Libraries. "Licensing Electronic Resources: Strategic and Practical Considerations for Signing Electronic Information Delivery Agreements."
http://arl.cni.org/scomm/licensing/licbooklet.html

California State University Libraries. "CSU Principles for Acquisition of Electronic Information Resources."
http://www.lib.calpoly.edu/csuecc/principles.html

Principles for Licensing Electronic Resources. AALL, ALA, AAHSL, ARL, MLA, SLA draft.
http://arl.cni.org/scomm/licensing/principles.html

Stanford University Libraries. "Copyright & Fair Use."
http://fairuse.standford.edu

University of California Libraries, Collection Development Committee. "Principles for Acquiring and Licensing Information in Digital Formats."
http://sunsite.berkeley.edu/Info/principles.html

University of Texas System. "Software and Database License Agreement Checklist."
http://www.utsystem.edu/ogc/intellectualproperty/cprtindx.htm

Yale University. "Licensing Digital Information: A Resource for Librarians."
http://www.library.yale.edu/~llicense/index.shtml

Contributors

Glenda Alvin is currently the Head of Acquisitions for Tennessee State University Libraries in Nashville and has previously held positions at the College of New Jersey and the University of Central Arkansas. She has worked in acquisitions and collection management for 16 years and has published several articles. She is a member of the Black Caucus of the American Library Association and presented papers for the 1994 and 1997 national conferences.

Gary J. Brown is Director of Library Services Latin America for Blackwell's. He has spent over 15 years in the information industry, serving as Midwest Regional Manager with Faxon, marketing representative with Addison-Wesley and the Scholarly Book Center, and editor with Scott, Foresman. Brown has a formation in Spanish literature from the University of Madrid, New York University, and the University of Wisconsin, and has taught at the University of Connecticut and Northwestern University.

Karen E. Cargille is Head of the Acquisitions Department at Geisel Library at the University of California, San Diego, where she has worked for over twenty years. Before coming to the Acquisitions Department in 1991 she was Head of the Science and Engineering Library at UCSD. She has written and spoken on various acquisitions-related topics at both ALA and at the Feather River Institute and is currently serving as co-editor of "The Balance Point," a regular column in *Serials Review*. She is an active member of NASIG and the Association for Library Collections and Technical Services.

Steven Carrico is the Head of Gifts and Exchanges in the Acquisitions Section of the Resource Services Department and the collection manager for library science materials at the University of Florida Library. He has written an article for

Serials Review demonstrating the value of exchange programs in academic libraries, and an annotated bibliography on exchange programs in academic and special libraries. He is active in ALA's New Members Round Table and currently is the editor of its newsletter, *Footnotes,* and a member of the editing team that is revising the ARL SPEC Kit, "The Gifts and Exchange Function in ARL Libraries."

Carol Pitts Diedrichs is Assistant Director for Technical Services at The Ohio State University Libraries. Previously, she was the Head of Monograph Acquisitions at the University of Houston Libraries. She is active in ALA and NASIG, serving most recently as a chair of the ALCTS Acquisitions Section and as a Member at Large on the NASIG Executive Board. In addition, she has served as editor in chief of the journal *Library Acquisitions: Practice & Theory* since 1990. She is a frequent speaker and writer on the management and automation of libraries with particular emphasis on technical services. In 1991 she received the Esther J. Piercy Award from the American Library Association's Association of Library Collections and Technical Services.

Lisa German is Head of Acquisitions at the University of Illinois Library at Urbana-Champaign. Previously, she was Head of Acquisitions at Wright State University in Dayton, Ohio. She is active in ALA and serves on committees in the Association for Library Collections and Technical Services and the Association for College and Research Libraries.

Kay Granskog is the Head of Acquisitions and Current Processing at Michigan State University Libraries, where she has worked for 13 years. Prior to this appointment, she was the Head of Monograph Acquisitions at MSU Libraries. She is a member of ALCTS and served a number of years on the Publisher-Vendor-Library Relations Committee. Granskog was involved in the pilot project that became OCLC PromptCat. She has contributed articles to library acquisitions and technical services journals.

Joan Grant is Director of Collection Services at New York University's Bobst Library, where she has worked since 1980. She is active in the Association for Library Collections and Technical Services and currently serves on the Executive Committee of the Collection Management and Development Section. She has written, taught, and given presentations and workshops on a number of collection management issues including collection evaluation, approval plans, and cooperative collection development.

Charles Harmon has been Director of Acquisitions and Development for Neal Schuman Publishers, Inc., since 1995. Prior to that he served as Director of the American Library Association's Headquarters Library and Information Center for five years. His other library experience includes positions in school and public libraries. He is the co-author of *Protecting the Right to Read: A How-to-Do-It Manual* (Neal-Schuman, 1995) and has served as editor of *The Bottom Line: Managing Library Finances* (MCB University Press, Great Britain) since 1994.

Thomas D. Kilton is Modern Languages and Linguistics Librarian and Professor of Library Administration at the University of Illinois Library at Urbana-Champaign. He has written extensively on library collections and the procurement of materials from Europe, with a recent emphasis on Eastern Germany since German unification. Under sponsorship of the ALA Bookfellows Program (1992) and the Humboldt University (1995), he has lectured on North American librarianship at five Eastern German universities. He is past president (1995-1996) of the Western European Specialists Section of the Association of College and Research Libraries (ACRL), a division of the American Library Association.

Margaret Landesman is the Head of Collection Development at Marriott Library, University of Utah in Salt Lake City, where she was previously the Monographs Order and Gifts and Exchanges Head and later the Acquisitions Librarian. Her interest in out-of-print and rare books led her to spend a sabbatical year in London in 1984-1985 working for the firm of Pickering and Chatot, which in turn led to her writing in this field. In recent years, electronic formats and coordinating their acquisition for Marriott, the Utah Academic Library Consortium, and Pioneer, Utah's Online Electronic library, have come to consume much of the time which should be devoted to these topics and led to her receiving the Utah Library Association's Librarian of the Year Award in 1996.

Y. Peter Liu is Associate Librarian, Library Systems Support Department, University of Delaware. Previously he served as Media and Microcomputer Librarian at the University of Illinois at Urbana-Champaign, where he worked for 11 years. He is active in the Audio-visual Round Table of the American Library Association and Multimedia Round Table of the International Federation of Library Associations and Institutions. Liu has regularly written and given presentations on academic media and system librarianship.

Mary L. McLaren is Processing Services Team Leader at the M. I. King Library at the University of Kentucky in Lexington, where she has worked for the past ten years. Within the library's recently established team environment, she also serves as Monograph Processing Team Leader and Acquisitions Librarian. Committed to exploring and implementing the use of new technologies within processing services, she initiated the use of the OCLC PromptCat Phase II service into the library's workflow. She has been a contributing column editor for *Against the Grain* and is a regular participant at the Charleston Conference.

Corrie Marsh is the Senior Field Sales Representative for Gale Research, Inc. Prior to joining Gale, she worked for Ovid Technologies, UMI, and NOTIS systems. Marsh has also worked as collections and acquisitions librarian in several academic libraries, including George Washington University, Brown University, Georgetown Law School, Old Dominion University, and Louisiana State University. She is active in ALA and has served on several committees including ALCTS' Publisher-Vendor-Library Relations, American Association of Publishers Joint Committee, and Best of LRTS. Marsh has written for professional publications and served on editorial boards as a reviewer, and as a consultant to several libraries and publishers.

James R. Mouw is Head of Serials at the University of Chicago and has previously held positions at the University of Illinois at Chicago and Gardner-Webb College in North Carolina. He is also adjunct professor at Dominican University School of Library and Information Science (formerly Rosary College) where he teaches the class on serials, and is active in the North American Serials Interest Group (NASIG) where he is serving his second term as a member of the board. An active member of ALCTS, he is presently a member of the Acquisitions Section Executive Committee and is chair of the Publisher-Vendor-Library Relations Committee. Mouw is a regular contributor to library journals, focusing on issues related to the acquisition of serial titles. He serves on the editorial boards of *Serials Review* and

Newsletter on Serial Pricing Issues. In 1998 he will launch a new column in *Serials Review* which will focus on issues related to serial standards.

Karen A. Schmidt is Director of Collections and Assessment and Professor of Library Administration at the University of Illinois at Urbana-Champaign, where she has worked for 16 years. Previously she was Head of Library Acquisitions there. Schmidt has written extensively on acquisitions, collections, and library history, and is the editor of the first edition of this book. She is active in ALA and has served on committees in ALCTS, ACRL, and LITA. She holds a Ph.D. in library and information science from the University of Illinois, where she also teaches.

Patricia Glass Schuman is President of Neal-Schuman Publishers in New York, which she co-founded in 1976. She held positions at the Brooklyn Public Library, Brandeis High School, and New York Technical College and has served as Senior Acquisitions Editor for the R. R. Bowker Book Division and Associate Editor of *School Library Journal.* As ALA President in 1991-1992, she launched ALA's first nationwide media campaign to focus public attention on threats to the public's Right to Know—including library funding cuts, censorship, and less access to government information. Schuman is a founder of ALA's Social Responsibilities Round Table, and the ALA Feminist Task Force, and has served as chair of the Legislation Committee and Endowment Fund-raising Committee. She spearheaded the drive to endow the ALA Scholarship Fund. Schuman is author/editor of seven books and more than 75 articles and has received a number of awards for her contributions to the field of publishing and librarianship.

Scott Alan Smith is regional sales manager for Blackwell's Book Services (formerly B. H. Blackwell, Ltd., and Blackwell North American, Inc.). He represents the company to academic and research libraries in 11 states, from the Pacific Northwest to the upper Great Plains. A past member of the Book Industry Systems Advisory Committee (BISAC), Smith has also been a speaker at the College of Charleston Conference and the Feather River Institute. He lives in Portland, Oregon.

Barbara A. Winters is the Director for Central Services at the Wright State University Libraries in Dayton, Ohio. She has worked in libraries for 24 years and has 17 years of experience in technical and automated services operations. In 1987, while serving as Head of Acquisitions at Virginia Commonwealth University in Richmond, Virginia, she was an active planner and participant in the process to implement competitive procurement among the publicly supported college and university libraries in the Commonwealth of Virginia. Winters is an active member of the American Library Association and its standing Committee on Professional Ethics, as well as ALA's Association for Library Collections and Technical Services (ALCTS). Winters' concern for a meaningful and practical statement of ethics for acquisitions managers resulted in her chairing the ALCTS Acquisitions Section's Task Force on Ethics and that task force's subsequent publication of its *Statement on Principles and Standards of Acquisitions Practice*. Winters was a member of the editorial board of *Library Acquisitions: Practice & Theory* from 1991 to 1996. In 1993, she received the ALA/ALCTS Esther J. Piercy Award for continuing contributions and leadership in the field of library technical services.

Index

and collection development, 206
foreign acquisitions, 100
future trends, 220-221
Internal Revenue Service, 209-210
organization and management, 205-206
out-of-print material, 200
processing of, 207
and public relations, 206, 219
resources on, 222-223
serials, 165
Golden Rule Management Theory, 351-352
Gorman, G.E. and J.J. Mills, *Guide to Current National Bibliographies in the Third World*, 104
Government agencies, 329
Government depository programs, 164
Grey literature, 108, 127
Gross margin, 70-72
Guide to Current National Bibliographies in the Third World (Gorman and Mills), 104
Guide to Performance Evaluation of Library Materials Vendors, American Library Association, 91, 326
Guide to Reference Books (Balay), 104
Guides for the Law Book Industry, 330-332

H

Hardware, 3, 7, 29
Harrassowitz, Otto (German vendor), 111, 113, 114-115, 133
Hawaii State Public Library System outsourcing model, 276-280
Higher Education Funding Council's (HEFC) project in England, 33, 44
Hispanic Society of America, 126
Hong Kong, 132-135
Hsin Hua (New China Bookstore), 134
HTML format, 33, 37

I

IDEAL of Academic Press on World Wide Web, 41-42
ILAB. *See* International League of Antiquarian Booksellers
Industry Statistics Report, Association of American Publishers, 38

Information Age, 224
Information revolution, 228
Information technology, 1, 228
Ingram, 62
Integrated Library Systems, 193
Intel MMX (multimedia extension chips), 227
Intellectual property issues, 199
debate over, 12
and electronic products, 30, 234
"fair use" interpretations, 28, 234, 361, 367-368
and librarians, 26
See also Photocopying
Interlibrary loan, 9, 26, 347
increases in, 12, 27
international, 107, 127
non-print materials, 238
out-of-print materials, 180, 198, 238
See also Libraries
Internal Revenue Service, 209-210
International Digital Electronic Access Library. *See* IDEAL of Academic Press on World Wide Web
International interlibrary loan, 107
International League of Antiquarian Booksellers (ILAB), 189, 194
Internet, 234
ACQNET (discussion group), 78, 279
Backserv and BackMed, 217-218
discussion groups, 78, 106, 200, 203, 240
gifts and exchanges, 221
and licensing, 361, 362, 363
and monitoring, 30
"netiquette," 240-241
non-print materials, 238, 239-241, 242
out-of-print material, 191-192
SERIALST (discussion group), 78
Taiwan and Hong Kong, 133
See also Electronic products; Online catalogs; World Wide Web
Invisible market. *See* Libraries
Invoice approval, 298-299
Invoice payment process, 4
Iran, 138
Iraq, 138
ISSN, 159-160, 167